BLACK WHITE OTHER

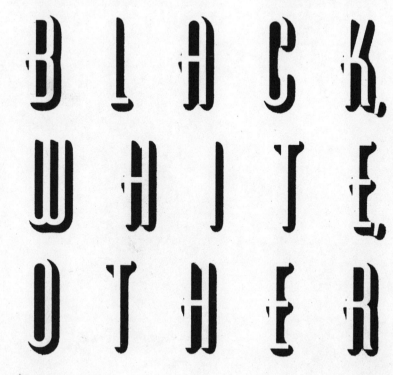

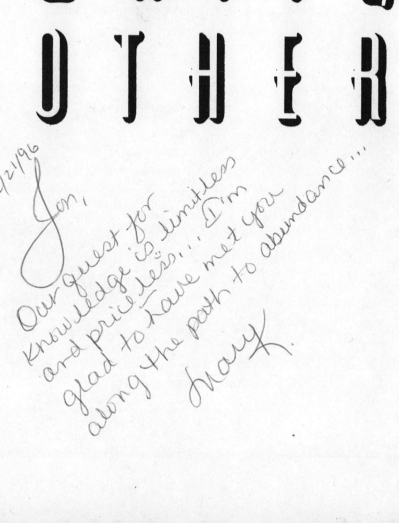

12/21/96

Jen,

Our quest for knowledge is limitless and priceless... I'm glad to have met you along the path to abundance...

Mary

BLACK, WHITE, OTHER

Biracial Americans Talk About Race and Identity

LISE FUNDERBURG

William Morrow and Company, Inc.
New York

The author gratefully offers her appreciation for the following photographs:

Jeffrey Scales   photographed by Jeffrey Scales
Sallyann Hobson   photographed by Brett S. Cantrell
Neisha Wright   photographed by Vincent F. Wright
Jacqueline Djanikian   photographed by Aileen Culligan
Seth Price, Kimani Fowlin, Eliza Dammond,
Adebowale Adegbile, Marpessa Outlaw,
Deborah Gregory   photographed by Joyce George

It is the policy of William Morrow and Company, Inc., and its imprints and affiliates, recognizing the importance of preserving what has been written, to print the books we publish on acid-free paper, and we exert our best efforts to that end.

Library of Congress Cataloging-in-Publication Data

Funderburg, Lise.
    Black, white, other : biracial Americans talk about race and identity / Lise
Funderburg.
      p.   cm.
    Includes index.
    ISBN 0-688-11824-0
    1. Children of interracial marriage—United States—Case studies.
    2. Interracial marriage—United States.   I. Title.
HQ777.9.F86   1994
306.84'6—dc20   93-39296
                                                       CIP

Printed in the United States of America

First Edition

1   2   3   4   5   6   7   8   9   10

To my parents,
Marjorie Lievense Funderburg
and
George Newton Funderburg

Contents

Introduction

*Once you see yourself truthfully depicted, you have a sense of
your right to be in the world.*
—novelist Paule Marshall, *in a 1992 National
Public Radio interview*

The year that Emmett Till—a fourteen-year-old black teenager
from Chicago—was lynched in Greenwood, Mississippi, for (supposedly) whistling at a white woman, my black father married my
white mother. It was 1955.

Only my father's mother and older brother drove up from
Georgia for the simple wedding, held in the side chapel of Philadelphia's First Unitarian Church. My mother's parents, in Chicago,
didn't come at all. There was some talk about her father still recovering from an operation—then again, he wasn't exactly thrilled
when he heard my mother was about to marry a black man. "I want
to crawl inside a hole," he had said.

My mother's father lived for only four more years. Before he
died he came to like my father. They shared the same work ethic,
and it seemed clear to Grandfather that his new son-in-law was
going to provide for my mother, my two older sisters, and me.

9

Rumor has it that although my maternal grandmother never said anything outright against my father, in the beginning she was overheard telling friends that he was German. (With the same delicate counterfeit, she neglected to mention to fellow members of her Methodist congregation that my mother had converted to Unitarianism.)

As children, my sister and I felt none of their discomfort. Our grandfather was gone before my first birthday, and our grandmother, who lived to be one hundred, never said or did anything to suggest that we didn't completely belong. On our father's side, too, there was never a suggestion that our membership in the family was marginal. *That* message we got elsewhere.

For as long as Blacks and Whites have chosen to settle down and marry in this country, they have confronted the question: *But what about the children?* More often than not, this is posed in warning rather than out of curiosity. Underneath lies a widely held assumption that the racial divide between white and black is vast and unbridgeable. And so while two independent adults may be considered free to deal with the folly of their choice, they are appealed to on behalf of the undeserving offspring who will supposedly suffer the results. Children of interracial unions are born into a racial netherworld, the conventional wisdom continues, destined to be confused, maladjusted, "tragic mulattoes," the perpetual victims of a racially polarized society.

For all Americans, not just the biracial ones, nothing about life or identity is so clear-cut or guaranteed—and certainly nothing that has to do with the issue of race. Such sweeping generalizations reflect the laziness of a society that, if given the choice, will often oversimplify rather than appreciate complexities and coexisting realities. I set out to write this book partly because I had never seen that question—*What about the children?*—asked of the children themselves. At least I hadn't seen it asked without the assumption that there was some inevitable tragedy to be revealed.

Of course, I also chose this subject because it was about me. To talk with so many other biracial people gave me a chance to look at myself, to reconsider my own ideas and questions about who I am and where I fit. I was hungry to know how others had negotiated the tightrope between black and white—and whether or why some felt there never was any tightrope in the first place. I didn't believe we all fit the tragic mulatto mold, but would other biracial people agree? What, if anything, would I actually share with people who also had one black and one white parent? How profound would the differences be between those of us, like my sisters and I, who "look" white and those of us who "look" black (or somewhere in between, frequently mistaken for Puerto Rican or Greek or Sicilian or Pakistani or . . .)? What would we have in common?

Each question pointed to the ways all of us—from every race and culture—look at race. On what axis, I wondered, does a person's sense of his/her racial self turn? Were my hair to have been as curly as my father's, were my skin tone to appear in real life the way it often (curiously) does in photographs, would the world react to me differently? Would my life have taken a different road? How much of my person and my sense of race have to do with my appearance, with the particular combination of black and white that I am, my skin color, my hair texture, my blue eyes? How much of it has to do with the people my parents are, where they come from, who their parents were, the locations of our generations on the time line of American history, the coincidence and impact of myriad choices they and I have made? And how much comes from outside, from history and society and other forces that we may not even realize are at play?

Yet another motive for this book was a desire to recognize the significant increase in the numbers of mixed-race people in this country. I knew our ranks were swelling; I'd noticed us all my life and could practically see the expansion.

To find real numbers that would corroborate my observation was another matter altogether. What numbers *are* available only hint at how many of us are out there. Some population experts and multiracial support networks estimate that there are currently at least one million mixed-race people in this country (of all mixes, not just black and white). The National Center for Health Statistics (NCHS) tabulates births by race and reports that birthrates of children with one black and one white parent have been climbing. In 1991, 52,232 such births were recorded, compared to 26,968 in 1981, and 8,758 in 1968, the year the Center began keeping track. The NCHS grand total for these births, from 1968 to 1991, is

616,850. (The NCHS itself acknowledges that their numbers are probably undercounts because the father's race is unspecified in a significant number of births each year—620,000 in 1990.) Beyond the year of birth, no demographic group tracks the total number of black-white biracial people in America.

Why not? One reason may be that although racial identities are classified and considered for myriad reasons in this country, dividing people along *this* line is widely considered insignificant—just as the U.S. census does not include identity categories for left-handed people with brown eyes. No one disputes that the characteristics exist, but they are not considered definitive. The closest that most questionnaires and forms come is "other"—an open-ended throwing-up-of-the-hands by social scientists and bureaucrats. Adding to the sense that biracial identities are illegitimate is the fact that most people with one white and one black parent, when given the opportunity to label themselves, have historically chosen (or been forced to choose) one or the other parent's identity, and that most likely has been and continues to be "black."

Despite growing numbers, public images of mixed-race people—who have been part of the American landscape since the first Africans reached America's shores—remain scarce. To become a part of the media landscape, to be recognized in images that are used to promote and illustrate, is to be conferred a certain legitimacy. In my interviews, I asked each person to name all the biracial people they'd seen in film, literature, entertainment, or the news. These lists, invariably, were short. A handful of people knew the term *tragic mulatto*, which was applied to the doomed protagonists of such novels as Nella Larsen's *Quicksand* and *Passing;* Walter White's *The Autobiography of an Ex-Coloured Man;* Harriet Beecher Stowe's *Uncle Tom's Cabin;* William Wells Brown's *Clotelle;* and to the film leads in *Showboat, Pinky,* and in both versions of the four-handkerchief tear-jerker, *Imitation of Life* (based on Fanny Hurst's 1933 novel).

More people, especially those under thirty, cited actresses Lisa Bonet, Halle Berry, and Jasmine Guy and musician Lenny Kravitz. Often, though, these names were listed with the same assurance as singers Vanessa Williams and Lena Horne, who both have two black-identifying parents. Other mistaken assumptions cropped up frequently. "Malcolm X?" one person tentatively offered.

The confusion is understandable, exemplified by the lack of accurate, specific, nonderogatory language for this experience and background. *Webster's Ninth New Collegiate Dictionary* (Springfield, Mass.: Merriam-Webster, 1988, p. 778) defines *mulatto* both as someone who is "the first generation offspring of a Negro and a white," and as "a person of mixed Caucasian and Negro ancestry." Although use of the word has been noted as early as 1593, according to *Webster's,* the group was generally thought of as a subset of Blacks—at times afforded slightly more rights and privileges than people with pure African ancestry, but never given equal footing with Whites.

Confusion surrounding race stems from the illogic used to define it. Slavery laws and social practices set a precedent—which survives to this day among many Whites and Blacks—of regarding anyone with a trace of African blood as black. Some states codified it as the one-drop rule or *code noir* (black code). In others the classification was mathematical, climbing back the branches of the family tree in fractions—one sixteenth, one thirty-second—to one's great-great- or great-great-great-grandparents. Less formally, in many instances, race was simply in the eye of the beholder. The "eyeball test," as it became known, took into account hair texture, eye color, and shape of nose, ears, lips, body, and skull. Testers could be school administrators, bus drivers, policemen, employers, strangers—anyone who felt obliged to separate white from black. When my mother and father went to city hall for a marriage license, the clerk took a quick look at my father and checked off Caucasian. My father corrected him.

In some instances, the knowledge (or mere rumor) of African ancestry has been equally determinative, even without corroborating physical "evidence."

A paradox of the one-drop rule is that it is never a two-way street. The theory that any amount of "black blood" makes a person black has no corollary within other racial groups, especially not Whites. One can be black and have "white blood" (even to the point of having a white parent, as many people in this book do), but one cannot be white *and* have "black blood."

People who do choose to live as white knowing that they have black ancestors are considered to be "passing." Mixed-race people have passed (or "crossed over") for different reasons over time. When segregation and Jim Crow laws were still on the books, many kept secret their black roots in order to take advantage of economic opportunities. Some would leave their black community in the morning, go to work as a white person, and then come home each night. Others, like my grandfather, passed for their tours in the military, not always intentionally, but because they didn't correct the cursory judgment a recruiter had made.

Some passed to escape the genuine risks and hardships of being black. To pass entirely into a white world required the severing of community and family ties, and often the most practical way to do this was to move far from home. Families would sometimes cooperate, mourning the passing relative as if he or she had died. Tolerance of passing eventually disappeared, replaced by black pride and calls for unity: passing became synonymous with cowardice.

For many biracial people, an awareness of this history continues to inform their racial self-concepts. No one in this book, for example, passes. They may live and work primarily with white people, and some may not talk much about being part-black, but most speak with great pride about their black heritage (in fact, more often than they do of their white heritage).

A biracial woman who strongly identifies as black, but on the basis of her appearance is most often assumed to be white and Jewish, explained. "It mystifies people," she said. " 'How can you call yourself black? You don't look black!' [But] in the black community it's just accepted. Ever since slavery and before slavery there were mulattoes and light-skinned people who were black."

Her point speaks to the incredible power the one-drop rule had and continues to wield. Historically, only the black community has taken in the offspring of miscegenation (although not always gladly, depending on the circumstances of the parents' relationship or the advantages bestowed on the child because of its white heritage). The notable absence in this book of biracial people who identify solely as white in itself reflects the persistence of the one-drop rule—participating in this book would have jeopardized their white status.

Some biracial people who identify as black acknowledge the societal pressures at hand. As one woman said, "In this country, saying you're black is making a political statement: My father is black, I'm black. American society is very concerned with definitions, very concerned. This is a culture that doesn't do well with ambiguity."

Consequently, when biracial people choose to embrace both racial heritages, they meet with confusion and criticism from both camps. When white-appearing biracial people tell white people of their black heritage, sometimes the white person will say, reassuringly, "I never would have known if you hadn't told me." Other times the same phrase suggests absolute disbelief.

One biracial man says, "A lot of Blacks get upset if they ask you exactly what you are and you come back and say, 'Biracial.' One response is, 'What? Are you too good to identify with Blacks?' I say, 'It's not that I'm too good at all, but I'm composed of two different races and I choose to value each of those.' It's not as though I'm going to write off my mother's race for the convenience of pleasing somebody else's view of what I should or should not be doing. I don't have time for that."

Still others—especially those younger than twenty-five—are forging a self-concept that is deliberately biracial. "I see myself as a butterfly," one woman said. "I belong to the world." Another gladly accepts whatever label is bestowed on her—black, white, or mixed—provided it is cast without aspersion. The vantage point many biracial people feel they have been born into—"always seeing two sides of the coin," as one woman described it—has served, for some, to devalue the coin itself.

For the purposes of this book, racial identity is defined not by pseudoscientific measurements or by appearance, but by how people choose to define themselves. The people who appear in the pages that follow met a simple—and completely subjective—racial criterion. They needed only to have one biological parent who identified as black and one who identified as white.

As the book shows, this seemingly specific definition still allows for a wide range of parent origins and differences. At least two people in the book have one black parent who chose to pass as white. Some of the parents, particularly those from other countries (Canada, Jamaica, Nigeria, Ireland, Kenya, Denmark, Iceland), only confronted notions of themselves as black or white when they came to the United States, and in many cases, seem to accept the labels with tolerant bewilderment.

In his book *Who Is Black?* (University Park: The Pennsylvania State University Press, 1991, p.29), sociologist F. James Davis notes that some sociologists and anthropologists have estimated that 75 to 90 percent of black Americans have white ancestors and possibly 1 percent of white Americans—millions of people—have black ancestors (presumably without knowing it, of course). My own definition of racial identity here is as artificial as every other that has come before. But as flawed as *every* definition of race probably is, the emotions and consequences of those definitions are very real.

My sisters and I, like some biracial people, had home lives relatively uncomplicated by the subject of our race. We were loved by our parents and relatives, never challenged by them on our racial allegiances or entitlements. Outside the family, we have found both black and white people with whom we exchange love and respect, people who may be interested in this odd inheritance, but not threatened or offended by it. Still, many people *have* felt threatened or offended by our parents' relationship, by our mixed heritage, by the fact that we look white but take pride in being half-black. The camouflage of our skin is disturbing to them, irreconcilable. We are fortunate that the offended have never used violence to express themselves, but their reactions to us have been unsettling and at times, quite painful.

Emmett Till's mother, Mamie Mobley, returned to school and became a teacher after Emmett was killed. She once said in an interview that her son's death taught her that education was the only hope for us all. "Learn until your head swells," she advised. I hope this book will give all who read it a chance to learn something about each other and themselves.

A Note to Readers

This book is based on interviews with sixty-five people conducted between January 1992 and January 1993. The interviews included in the book have been edited for clarity and continuity. In some cases, comments are in answer to specific questions I had asked.

Interviews typically lasted between two and three hours. In some cases, at either my request or theirs, I met with people a second or third time. The structure of each interview was always essentially the same: I asked people to tell me about their lives, especially as related to the development of their ideas about race and their own racial identity. Understandably, people covered ground at different speeds, some dwelling on stories from school days, others on tales of family, work, or relationships, for example.

The structure of the book and its chapter themes grew out of those stories. Each chapter begins with a selection of brief comments and anecdotes. A short introduction to the theme at hand follows, followed by three to seven oral histories. Three people's stories appear as lengthier "self-portraits." These are placed between chapters.

Aside from providing context for readers in each introduction, I have done my best to get out of the way, to leave each person who tells her or his story to bear witness directly to the reader.

17

To find people for this book, I asked for names from friends, acquaintances, and strangers. I placed newspaper advertisements and—with much help from kindhearted souls—posted flyers on street corners, in health clubs, offices, schools, libraries, churches, and social-service organizations. My search for interviewees found its way to computer-mail systems, company bulletins, and the newsletters of multiracial support groups. I traveled to the Pacific Northwest; the San Francisco Bay area; Atlanta, Georgia, and its suburbs; Alabama; South Carolina; and points along the eastern seaboard from Washington, D.C., to Boston, Massachusetts.

Although I did not aim to produce a statistically reliable sample from my pool of interviewees, I tried to cast a wide net, to correct for the limitations of my own affiliations and for the sway of greater social patterns and trends. Initially, for example, there were disproportionate numbers of women who responded to ads or were referred to me, and many more people under twenty-five than over.

At the heart of this book is an exploration of the diverse ways that people experience a seemingly uniform heritage. Problematically, the very terms used to discuss this subject are the ones often being disputed. Along those lines, it is essential to point out that my use of *biracial* refers only to the common experience of having parents with two distinct racial identities, specifically, where one is black and one is white. The term is used for efficiency rather than to express partiality. I use *interracial* to refer to a relationship between two monoracial persons or groups. *Monoracial* refers to the self-determined dominant identity of a person or group. *Caucasian* and *White* are used interchangeably, as are *African-American* and *Black*.

The racial labels others use I have left unchanged. Some people refer to their parents as a biracial or multiracial couple. Some refer to themselves as interracial, multiracial, biracial, or mixed-race people, and then use the same terms to refer to those for whom the mixture occurred many generations ago.

At least one person pointed out he was using terms (such as *mulatto, black, white*) only for the sake of our discussion, terms that he does not use in day-to-day conversation. He won't use them, he said, because he does not believe in such a thing as race.

I am large, I contain multitudes.
   —*Walt Whitman*

PART ONE

DAILY LIFE

CHAPTER I

Parents and Family

One time I got the flour out, and when my dad came home, I had covered myself in flour, from head to toe. My dad asked me what I was doing, and I told him, "I'm gonna be one color."

And he said, "Why are you going to be white?"

I said, "Because we don't have any black powder." And he looked at me, and he just kind of shook his head, and I asked him, I said, "Dad, what am I?" And he told me that I was a beautiful little girl.

"No, Dad, that doesn't work. What am I really?"

"What do you want to hear? What do you want to be?"

"I don't know what I want to be. I just don't understand why I have to be anything; I don't understand what's going on."

Finally he told me, "Well, you're black and you've got really nice hair. Does that sound good?"

"Well, I guess so."

And he said, "Okay, that one will work for a couple of years. Go with it."—Sandra Shupe, p. 188

My grandmother raised me. She grew up not far out of slavery and experienced a lot of prejudice. She always told us to be

23

careful of whites and don't trust white people. She would talk about poor white trash, and I remember asking her, "Was my mama poor white trash?" And she told me, "Yes."—Omatteé Carrasco, p. 82

When I was three years old, I was really sick. My father had ordered some medicine from the pharmacy, and since my mother and I were walking in that direction, we picked it up. My father didn't know we had, so he walks in and the woman behind the counter says, "I'm sorry, Mr. Zarembka, but your maid and your son have already come by for it." I was a little more upset about the son part than her thinking my mother was a maid.—Joy Zarembka, p. 324

My father never said anything about being African-American, never tried to show what that was to him. I believe he dislikes African-Americans. European-Americans, too. He hates white people because they're white people and he can't be one of them, and he hates black people because they're black people and he is one of them. Sometimes I'll go visit him and I'll try to figure out whether he wants me to be white today or black today. So I'll say, "I'm black," and he says, "No you're not; you're blah-blah-blah."

"Okay, I'm white."

"No you're not; you're my baby."

What race I should be just depends on the day, on the mood, on how much he had to drink.—Mark Durrow, p. 359

When I was thirteen, I went to the grocery store with my dad in a predominantly black neighborhood, and we went up to the checkout stand and my dad picked up Jet *magazine, because he always got that. And the woman at the counter said, "Excuse me sir, that's not a* TV Guide." *And he looked at her and said, "I know what it is. Thank you." And I just died. The look on his face, "Do you think I'm stupid? I know what this magazine is." I will never forget that. I just died when he said that, you know? It was so funny, and she was so embarrassed because she thought, well, what would a white guy be doing with a black magazine?*

I thought it was great. I thought it was great! Because he's very up front, and it was like, "Don't give me any shit. I'm not an idiot."—Jacqueline Djanikian, p. 309

My mother's sister, she's black, and she used to say to me, "You're going to have to decide what you are, if you're going to be black or white." I remember all these Christmas things with her, like if I wanted to get a black Baby That Away, or a white Baby That Away. She would call up to ask, and I would say, "Okay, I want the black one." And then I would call up, "No, no, I want the white one." My parents were just too intelligent that way. They got me this Sasha doll from London that you couldn't tell if it's black or white. They really picked everything, so she has kind of my color skin and brownish hair and she could be Italian or Greek or black, who knows?—Nya Patrinos, p. 134

It takes two people to create a biracial child: a mother and a father. Like all parents, they may be largely responsible for shaping how their children see themselves and the world. What parents teach about race comes, in part, from their own experience of race.

Few interracial couples escape all the land mines that are historically placed in their paths: from being disowned by both sides of the family to the occasional stare or muttered comment on the street. While some couples would respond to such treatment with bitterness or might even retreat from each other, others remain steadfast in their commitment to one another and to the family they have created together.

It wasn't until 1967, in the U.S. Supreme Court's *Loving* v. *Virginia* decision, that remaining antimiscegenation laws (still on the books in seventeen states at the time) were overruled. Richard and Mildred Loving were the appellants in the case. In 1958 the newlywed Lovings were arrested in their Virginia hometown for being married to each other. She was black, he was white. Rather than face incarceration, they moved back in with their respective parents, then moved together to Washington, D.C., where they lived for several years. The Virginia judge's ruling also ordered that they never visit Virginia together. Miserable in their exile, they asked for help from Robert Kennedy, then attorney general of the United States. Kennedy directed them to the American Civil Liberties Union, where two lawyers took on their case. Nine years later, the Lovings and their lawyers changed the law of the land.

Laws against miscegenation existed in America as early as 1661. By and large, they targeted only groups that were not allowed to marry Whites, sometimes reflecting regional concerns. (Laws in Arizona prohibited Whites from marriages with Negroes, Mongolians, Indians, Malay, or Hindu people; Oregon prohibited Whites from marrying anyone more than one-half Indian or one-quarter Negro, one-quarter Chinese, or one-quarter Kanaka [Hawaiian].) In some states, including Maryland and Louisiana, legislators also wrote in provisions against Indians and Blacks marrying, probably to prevent the formation of a coalition between the two oppressed groups.

Laws and the threat of social censure never successfully precluded interracial relationships and the conception of biracial children. Still, since the *Loving* decision, black-white marriages have increased dramatically: According to the census, they jumped 378 percent from 1970 to 1992 (from 65,000 to 246,000).

If such families almost certainly invite some level of criticism and rejection, why have people continued to cross racial lines? Are interracial couples visionaries, living out a utopian ideal? Are they retaliating against or perpetuating an earlier American miscegenation: the slave master's rape of the slave? While the preponderance of racial mixing in early U.S. history was between white men and black women, today, according to the census, 85 percent of black-white interracial marriages reverse that configuration. Does this gender shift speak to alliances of power and powerlessness or something else altogether? Somewhere in the answers to why these couples come together lie clues to what information they will give their children about race.

This chapter presents more oral histories than the other chapters. For many people, their first (and longest-lasting) impressions of race come from parents and family; for biracial children, the very existence and nature of their parents' relationship often provides a paradigm for understanding or valuing race. The parents' relationship might communicate that love transcends racial barriers, and serve as evidence that people can bridge what have been considered immutable gaps in color, culture, and experience. On the other hand, parents may behave in ways that cement divisions and distinctions, and not always intentionally. "I used to wonder if my mother really liked black people that much," one woman said about her white parent.

Many black-white couples think they and their children are all part of the same experience: that they are equal participants in their multiracial family. They expect that their children will experience the world as they do, and that the views they hold, their children can hold, too. Mindy Thompson Fullilove is a psychiatrist who has studied racial-identity formation in biracial people (and is herself biracial). She explains what she found to be the more accurate dynamic between parents and children:

> *The parents' perspective on this problem is really different from the kids' perspective. That's what's most striking. The parents, at best, think they've done something wonderful in putting together a family that defies racial convention. For them it's an issue of love conquering all or an affirmation of what they wish for themselves over and above the conventions of society. For the parents it's this consciously chosen thing to live in this way; but the kids didn't choose, they just have to grow up in the midst of it. That's a really important distinction, because the parents tend to think it's the same for the kids as it is for them. And it's truly not.*
>
> *Now that doesn't mean the kids and parents don't agree about what it is, but the perspective is profoundly different: A white person and a black person come together to create a family, but the family, the kids, are biracial. And they've got to make some sense out of this. Those are completely different tasks. And to the extent that most parents never get that—they just think of this wonderful thing that they've done for their kids, and it's all multiracial and wonderful and a wave of the future. They really don't get that it's a different thing for the kids. Whatever it is. And that it—what the kids are doing—is changing over time. So it's different for the people who are a generation ahead of me than it is for my kids. It's not the same set of tasks.*

Some of the following stories suggest that whatever parents' intentions may have been, what their children have learned may not be what their parents intended to teach.

❧

Rosa Emilia Warder
Age: 34
Residence: Oakland, California
Occupation: Foundation writer and development coordinator;
Children's book author

Rosa Emilia Warder grew up in San Francisco's upper western addition neighborhood, which was, at the time, racially and ethnically mixed. Her parents were three times removed from the mainstream: an interracial couple, artists, and political radicals. Rosa was a red-diaper baby, the only child of two Communists who met through their political activities.

Even Warder's name was a political statement. Rosa *honored Rosa Parks, who launched the Montgomery, Alabama, bus boycott of 1955.* Emilia *was a feminized tribute to Emiliano Zapata, a Socialist Mexican revolutionary. Repercussions of her parents' political affiliations came early on. In the early 1960s, when Warder saw that a little girl her age resembled a poster of Africans she had seen on the Communist party nursery walls, she told the girl that she was African. "I thought she was beautiful," Warder says. "That was not something she wanted to hear in 1962, so she decked me."*

Because Warder had fair skin and long braids, some black children taunted her, once calling her a "honkey nigger" as they tied her hair to a railing. For the most part, white children simply ignored her. Warder's parents taught her to recognize both sides from a positive vantage point. "I identify as African-American and European-American," she says. "I've never thought of myself specifically as white or black. As a kid I remember wanting to be one or the other during different periods. Now I assume that people see me as black or African-American or whatever—people of color—

*whatever their phrase of the moment is. That doesn't really affect what I
know, and it's not something I really spend any time thinking about."*

My mother is the European-American member of the
family. She grew up in Bend, Oregon, which is still a very homogeneous white community. She grew up in a fairly wealthy cattle-
ranching family and left home when she was twenty to go to study
art at Reed College. Then she worked her way to California, where
she met my father.

My father grew up in Abilene, Kansas, where he was in one of
two black families. His parents died by the time he was thirteen.
He grew up with aunts and uncles after that point, and then joined
the navy. He was a jazz musician during World War II, and he
worked his way to California; my parents met in the early fifties, at
a jazz club where he was playing. My mother was an artist. She was
doing sketches of musicians and he was playing. In terms of how
their families reacted, my father's family—being just his sister and
the aunts and the uncles that were still alive—were really pretty
accepting of Nancy, my mother, and their marriage.

My mother's family, on the other hand, was totally not accepting and disowned her when she did get married. That was an
interesting contradiction, because there are a lot of illegitimate
children in my mother's very upper-crust family who were kind of
ignored, and so it was just part of that whole history of denial and
strange goings-on. So I actually have never met anyone from my
mother's half of the family. My mother has a younger sister who's
still alive who I've never met, she has a younger brother who I've
never met, who are all somewhere in Oregon. Every time I'm up
there, I think I might walk right past them on the street and I
would never know.

My mother's still alive. Growing up she was red-haired, blue
eyes, looks very Irish, although she's not, she's actually Scottish
and English. Now she's totally snow-haired, but she's seventy-two
years old. She looked basically very red-haired, pale-skinned, kind
of an English-looking woman. My father was fairly chocolate-
skinned, darker-skinned.

My parents stayed married until my father died in 1980. It was
not a terrific marriage, necessarily. My father was ill pretty much
the last twenty-five years of his life. He had diabetes and every

complication that went with it, from cataracts and glaucoma to circulatory problems, eventually prostate problems and then strokes. So it was not an easy marriage at all, just from the health standpoint, and then with the dynamics of him not being able to work a lot of the time as well. He taught music, which was good; it kept his mind alive, but was not particularly financially rewarding, and he wasn't able to travel anymore on the road with bands because of his dietary needs and insulin needs. So it was more of a care-giver relationship the last twenty years or so.

A lot of the biracial families I know are divorced. I mean, a huge percentage. It's hard for me to say exactly what percentage, but I know as a kid, of my contemporaries who were biracial, my family was the only family that was intact, and I really think the main reason was that my mother wouldn't leave my father because he was so ill.

When I was a kid, my parents would take turns getting arrested for sit-ins in San Francisco. Downtown San Francisco is tremendously different from the way it was then, and my mother used to do things like follow black people downtown to see where they were working so that she would be able to say to others, "There's a possibility you can get a job there." Race was something that was discussed. A lot of what my parents would say to me was around struggle. It was a reaffirmation for me that the way things are doesn't mean you're anything less than anyone else; that you can be whatever you want to be; that we're fighting so things will be better for you than they are for other black people. I don't know if it's turned out that way, but that was the idea.

I heard speeches by Malcolm X, and I remember a time when my parents felt that Martin Luther King was not as important as Malcolm X because he was the one who was really doing the most militant work.

My mother was angry at times about being told that she was sort of an honorary black person. That really used to piss her off, because she did not want to have her whiteness discounted. She just wanted to be a white person who wasn't being an idiot. I remember those kinds of conversations coming up, but between the two of them I don't really remember any conflict around that. I was always told that I was African-American and European-American, and those were the actual terms they used—which I guess was unusual at the time—because they were so entrenched in the political rhetoric.

I was always a mixed child. I never heard the word *biracial* until I was much older. Pretty much, "mixed" was used, or the whole range of everything I was, and I didn't only know I was white and black. I knew I was Jamaican, French, Scottish, English, Modoc Indian—I knew all the pieces, the whole picture. And being in San Francisco, I went to very international places. Part of nursery school was in Chinatown; I still know certain Christmas carols in Chinese. I went to Jewish community center camps and the after-school programs. I danced in a very white European ballet company, played music more with the black and Latin kids when I was a teenager, so I had a chance to be everywhere, and that seemed real, the way it should be.

I think the biggest contributors to my racial identity would be my parents. Because they were both artists, they were so interested in culture, and both came from such different cultures, I had an almost visceral experience of what that was. I remember sitting on my mom's lap at symphony concerts for kids in San Francisco, and hearing her talk about how she learned to play this when she was a child, the dance, going to art galleries. She still is a working artist. I knew where that part of my culture came from; I knew what parts of Europe it came from. She was a fanatic reader, so she would pass things—still passes things—on to me, and the same thing with my father. The music was a part of our lives: There were always music classes going on in the house, there was K-JAZ playing all the time in the car, and then the civil rights stuff they did often had me in child-care clusters with books and materials and posters on the walls that were very revolutionary-minded.

I was seven or eight when I started to realize that people were different cultures and colors, and there were injustices based on what you look like. I remember watching the sixties riots on television and talking about them with my parents. My mother kept a file on old magazines: *Jet*, newspapers, magazines—stuff that was printed in the late sixties that has all the original articles about the civil rights movement from pretty early on. Ten years ago she gave me the file, and I instantly knew what it was.

If nothing else, having this background probably makes me a less bigoted, racist person in a society where it's damn hard not to be racist. I just did not have that option of saying, "Well, I'm not going to associate with you," because I'd cut off half of my life. That's probably the number one benefit.

Emma Baker

Age: 62

Residence: South Carolina

Occupation: Retired teacher

Emma Baker (a pseudonym) is the oldest person who appears in this book. Because of her family's lifelong silence about the cir-cumstances of her birth, she asked at first that her name and picture not be used. But after much deliberating (and some coax-ing), she decided to provide a picture of herself. "What happened, happened," she told me. Until our interview, she says the only person she'd ever spoken to extensively about her racial identity was a curious
niece to whom she is particularly close. The niece once asked—when the two of them were alone—why her aunt's siblings all had such darker skin than her aunt did.

Baker has never identified as anything other than black, although she is old enough to have lived through the terms Negro *and* Colored. *"I do not like the word* black," *she says, "because there are so many different colors of black, if you will, starting from the color of the true black Africans, all the way up to just about white.*

"I prefer 'Afro-American.' Some of our leaders are going to 'people of color,' and that's a lot to say. To say 'black' is shorter, but Afro-American or just American, is fine."

A family friend said that my mother worked for this white family in a nearby town. My mother stayed in their house; it was maybe ten miles from where her mother lived. She had no trans-portation during those times to get back and forth and the pay was very little, so they probably had some shanty stuck back some-where for her to sleep.

This family friend said that the man for whom she worked is or was my father. I guess, my mother being black, she couldn't say no, because she worked for the family. I don't think it was a matter of how she felt towards him. If it's true, I think it was a matter of—from what I've read of this happening, and I've read many books about this same kind of thing—where the master would go to the cabin where the black woman was. It was not a matter in some instances of how she felt about him, emotionally, it was just that she was trained to do that. She was black and he was white and she was supposed to do what he said.

At home, when I brought up the subject as to who my father was and where he was, it was a no-no. It was just like a dirty word, so from an early age I knew not to say anything more about my father. My other sisters, who were half-sisters of course, were darker than I. There was one who was lighter but not as light as I am.

This [family] friend, who was about twelve years older than I, told me when I was a teenager that this man was my father, or at least this is what she heard the older people say. During that time, the houses were little that Blacks lived in, and some parents would talk, not in front of their children, but the children would be maybe in the next room, listening, and they kind of knew what was going on.

When I became an adult, I used to shop at a supermarket, and this same family friend who told me who my father was—yet I didn't know if that was true—said it was rumored that he had a brother that worked in this store. This man was always polite to me. He cut meat, and when I went in there, being a Black, I was not treated like the other Blacks. He didn't give me anything because it was not his store, but he was more courteous, he cut better pieces of meat for me and that sort of thing.

From the way he behaved towards me, a young black lady, it just made me think that perhaps he was my uncle. Nothing was ever said, but he was always courteous, and it was not that he was trying to make out with me, not that kind of thing. Even the other people who worked in the store, they all acted the same way this man did, so maybe he told them who I was. But they treated me differently, and I always wondered why—I thought that maybe what this young lady had told me was the truth.

The word *father* I could never use. Kids would come to school and have on a dress—this still kind of grabs me, and I'm sixty-two years old—they would have on a little dress and I would say, "Oh, that's pretty." And they would say, "My daddy bought it." Like I said, those two words, *father* and *daddy*, were words that I didn't have in my vocabulary.

I was poked fun or picked at in school by some, and others who were my friends did not talk. There were some, though—you always, always had this—those who were darker would pick, would jeer. I was called names: "half-white bitch," "half-white monkey." And there were other names, let's see . . . "your mother crossed the fence" and that sort of thing. I never fought, I was not a fighter, and I wouldn't go back home and tell. I didn't say anything. I didn't want to hurt my mother. In my world, you're not quite white and you're not quite black.

Sonia Trowers
Age: 23
Residence: Philadelphia, Pennsylvania
Occupation: Law student

Sonia Trowers's mother, a nurse, is from British Columbia, and her father, a microbiologist, is from Jamaica. They recently celebrated their twenty-fifth wedding anniversary. Trowers and her younger sister grew up in New Rochelle, New York, where their parents still reside.

Of all the people I interviewed, Trowers's complexion would fall at the browner end of the spectrum. "As opposed to other biracial children," she says, "you can't necessarily look at me and tell. I'm not one of those people constantly being asked, 'What are you?'"

Trowers's father telephoned me the day after his daughter responded to my advertisement in her university newspaper. He wanted to check me out, to see if I was legitimate. What else had I written? Who was my publisher? Why had I decided to write this book? His parental concern satisfied, he launched into stories about his two daughters, about their

achievements and their earlier experiences with color. When Sonia was
eight, he said, the two of them went to do some errands. A stranger
approached and asked her what she was. "I'm a CanJam," her father
remembered her saying proudly.

When we met for the interview, I asked her why she had responded to
my ad. She said that whenever she sees television programs on biracial peo-
ple, the portrayal of them is always negative. In fact, she said, she thought
the particular people who were featured "would be screwed-up regardless of
what color their parents were." Those people, in her opinion, make it easier
for others to argue against interracial marriage and dating. She saw my
book as a forum where she could show that there are normal biracial people
in the world, who don't think "this is a big deal."

When my mom finished nursing school, she traveled all
throughout Europe and then came to New York and happened to
find a job for six months. My dad had just finished getting his
second degree, and they both were working at the same hospital.
They met, fell in love. But she already had a job she was supposed
to start in Canada, and so they decided she would come back
afterward and they would get married. So that's how they got
together.

I think they got married around twenty-nine—that's kind of
old for those days—and had me about four years later.

In terms of their families, the funny thing about that is my
Jamaican grandmother has the typical West Indian prejudice as far
as it comes to African-Americans. So for my grandmother, thank
God, my dad was saved. God forbid he should have married some
black American woman. For her, this was seventh heaven.

My mother's family is very, very religious. They were Bap-
tists. Or was it Methodist? We're Presbyterian. They were very,
very religious in the true sense. Not just, "Oh, we go to church
every Sunday." And so they never had any problems with the
marriage. I mean, my mom is the most naive thing in the whole
entire world. She grew up on a farm in Canada. She really has no
clue what's going on in the real world, and that's how her family is,
too. They just really truly view everyone as God's creations. My
mom said they never voiced any negative feelings; their only concerns were whether she was going to be able to deal with how *other*
people were going to react to her.

The majority of that may stem from the fact that they're not specifically from this country, but also that religious thing is a one-in-a-million find. In New Rochelle, the church we went to was Presbyterian, and some neighbors of ours also go there, people that live a few houses down from us. They would always sit in the same row and were always very nice to us. Then we come to find out their daughter started dating this biracial guy. Her parents were *totally* against it. She wanted to go to college; they told her if she didn't break up with this guy, they weren't going to pay for her to go to school. He was biracial, very light-skinned, but they automatically classified him as black. That's when I stopped going to that church. I thought that was the most hypocritical thing in the world, that I could be sitting next to these people, worshiping with them, but obviously, when it really came down to it, they really thought they were a whole lot better than me. At that point, I just told my mother, "I'm not going there anymore." That whole thing really turned me off big-time. I can't even speak to those people anymore. I'd much rather have people in my face, telling me "I think I'm better than you."

My sister and I went to Catholic grammar school, and we were the only people of color in the whole entire first through eighth grade. I guess that's when things started to get a little bit weird. I started to realize I was different from everyone else, and I remember at that time my dad would always explain and I always knew that I was mixed. I never really had any problem with that. I knew who I was. But at that young age, I do remember going to school, and everyone had straight hair and I didn't have straight hair. Things like that seemed really important at the time. To me, at that young age, having a white mother was something that made me a little bit better. I was a little bit closer to what everybody else was.

The weirdest thing is I was always very popular. I never really had racial problems with other people. I might have had racial problems within myself, seeing as I was the only black person, and maybe once in a while people called me Oreo, but no one ever really made offensive comments.

Around eighth or ninth grade, when boys started to become an issue, that's when I started having problems. All the people I was friends with were white, and I would go to these parties and when people were playing stuff like spin the bottle, I started feeling a little bit uncomfortable. I just knew that these white guys in this group I associated with wouldn't have any interest in me. Not that I was really interested in them being interested in me, but I started feeling not so comfortable with the people I associated with, as far as social settings went. Before that, no problem. As soon as dating and going to dances came up, that's when I started having problems.

Before, when we would go to parties, I was always the center of attention. But then I started to feel like I had to pull to get people in conversations with me. Once it had come [to the point] that people really did start getting asked out, by then I had decided to transfer to public school because I had wanted to be in a more mixed segment of society.

My dad has always been totally against public school. "Public school is the biggest evil!" He's not Catholic, but he liked the idea of nuns being around and controlling you and me not being around any guys. That was a huge fight. My mother went to public school and believes if you can get an education for free—we happened to live in an area with a really good public school system—why not?

That caused a very big rift in our family for a few months because I was just adamant on wanting to transfer. It finally came down to my father saying, "Look, I'm not going to make you do something you really don't want to do. If you really don't want to go back, I'm not going to force you, but I'm totally against this, and I just want you to know that if you do it I'll be really pissed off. But I'm not going to hold you back."

So I did it. I really couldn't make clear to my dad why I wanted to transfer because his idea of public school was that I was going to be around all these bums and all these low-life people, and I wasn't going to care about school and I would do drugs and I would this, that, and the other. "Oh, if you're surrounded by the bad element, you're going to come into the bad element." And the unfortunate thing is, being that my dad is from Jamaica, I really do believe he has a certain amount of, I wouldn't say hostility, but definitely, maybe, less respect for American Blacks than for people who are from the West Indies. So he was afraid of me being around those type of people and what kind of effect that they were going to have on me. He also meant low-life Whites, low-life people in general, but it just so happened that the area we lived in, the majority of the low-life people did happen to be black.

I was a really serious tennis player, so I said, "Oh, they're in a bigger division, I'll have better competition, I'll have a better chance of making it to the states. Oh, I want to continue to take Latin, I want to take independent Greek," I want to do all these things that weren't available to me at the private school. So I based it on that. But I think he knew deep down inside that I was lying; I think he always knew.

I never really had to do anything to convince my mother because she was never all that up on the idea of paying for me to go to school, especially when I was in high school. She thought it was good for grammar school because you could build basic study skills and get more attention. But she figured once you get to junior high and high school, if you haven't got it by then, you're not going to get it. My mother also is a lot more down-to-earth than my dad is. My dad's not really an elitist, but money is important to him and having a professional career is important to him, and he does value people with good educations. Whereas stuff like that never really made a difference to my mother. My mother thought I would be a better person being exposed to different segments of society, whereas my dad was always a little bit afraid of what the effect was going to be on me.

My high school years were the best, most unconfusing years of my life. I made so many great friends that I'm still friends with now; I hung out with this group of fifteen kids, and half of them were black and half of them were white and we were all friends and we all liked the same music and liked to do the same things. It was weird because when I left the Catholic school, I was under the assumption that you had to go this way or that way. So I didn't really expect to go to public school and have a lot of white friends, but that's exactly how it worked out. Most of the white people I hung out with were Jewish. There's some determining factor in that; I don't know exactly what it is. I don't know if it's that Jewish people sometimes also might see themselves as a persecuted race or whatever, but all the good friends I've had who've been white have been Jewish.

*   *   *

It's weird. I don't know if this makes sense: I always consider myself mixed, but I also consider myself black because the way I was brought up was that that's how people were going to view me. And I think it worked perfectly for me, probably because of the way that I look. Just because I was always going to be accepted by the black community, you know? There were iffy situations where I could or could not be accepted by the white community, and so I always had the comfort of knowing that I fit into the black community. But I always did identify myself as mixed. If someone asked me, I would always say, "I'm mixed. My father's black, my mother's white." But I definitely felt comfort that I knew there was somewhere I definitely fit in.

I guess I had always had this naive attitude about race, how it didn't really matter. And going down south for college was a whole new experience I had never expected, like going into a store and all of a sudden all the clerks are following you around, and people finding out that I was mixed and just thinking it was the oddest thing in the world. They couldn't believe that wasn't still illegal. I really do believe that up until that point, in my head, everything was fine with how I'd grown up, but I guess that was naive because I was living in a very small world. I expected that everyplace else was the same as where I grew up and there weren't all these problems.

Also, it was the first time I was around black people who talked really negatively about Whites. I didn't believe that there were really prejudiced people out there or people that would look at me weird because I was mixed or hold it against my parents because they had made this crazy decision. I had my first really negative feeling towards Whites in general when I went down south.

When I first got to college and would talk about race issues, people would look at me like I was crazy. They would be like, "You have been living in this little glass box; where the hell have you been?" So I really started to have problems, because I can really honestly say that for a while there, I really started to become very antiwhite because of the experiences I had. Had I had all these experiences when I was younger, then I would have expected and been prepared to deal with it. But for a while I was very antiwhite and had problems with that because I always felt very guilty. But then I would think my mother is the exception to the rule. She's different than the majority of the people there. I really had problems with that; I really felt guilty about it.

When this whole Clarence Thomas thing was happening, a friend of mine who lived here in Philadelphia invited me over to dinner. His mom, she's a dentist and teaches at Temple, started going on about what a horrible person she thought Clarence Thomas was. And then she said, "Can you believe that he gets in bed with a white woman every night? To me that just says it all." And I was kind of sitting there snickering.

Sometimes when I'm in situations with younger people, I'd say, "Oh, that's pretty funny, my mother's white," because I like to see them squirm. But in that situation I thought it would be a little bit too uncomfortable—I had to stay there for the rest of the night—so I figured I just wouldn't say anything about it. It really doesn't bother me when people say stuff like that, but sometimes I think it's funny to make them think about what they're saying and to make them realize everything's just not black or white. There are exceptions—there are generalizations that can't be made—and I don't think people realize that.

I have these friends who were part of the Five Percenter Movement. It's a black movement similar to Islam, but they consider it not to be religious. And they consider they're the five percent that are on the right track and the other ninety-five percent of us are people who are totally lost. We don't realize that the white man's the devil, and the only way we're going to help ourselves is to kill off all the people who aren't of color—then everything will be okay. And these people were almost brainwashed. And I have this one friend who I had gone to high school with, and then I came back home and he had this new name and all these crazy ideals. I sat down with him and I said, "You really believe all these people are the devil? You really believe they hate us and are totally hostile?"

"Yes, yes, I believe that."

But he was someone who had been over to my house a few times, and I put it to him: "You met my mother. You really believe that my mother is really sitting there hating you and hating me and wanting us to drop dead and doing everything she can to keep us down?" He never really said, "Oh you're right, I agree with you," but I could see that maybe made the wheels start turning in his head that you can't just put things in such a generalized manner.

Same thing with mixed people. So many people say to me when they find out I'm mixed, "My God, you're so normal to be mixed! Everyone that I know who's mixed is so confused and you're the most normal person!"

I'm like, "How can you generalize?" You just can't do that; it's impossible.

I'm very outspoken and very independent, and I think my parents didn't have to be as concerned as maybe other people were because they always knew from day one who the hell I was.

But when things would happen, I would tell them both. My mother couldn't believe it, she'd be shocked; my dad would laugh and think it was funny. They were always receptive to hearing it. I don't think they would ever specifically ask me, but I think that's because whenever funny things or different things came up, I was always open with them, so they knew that if I was having a problem, I would address it to them.

Danielle Williams

Age: 22

Residence: San Francisco, California

Occupation: Junior paralegal

Danielle Williams says that not a day goes by without her being reminded of her biracial identity. As a result, it is a topic of paramount importance to her.

Regrettably, she says, her father's general irresponsibility toward her and her older sister has helped form her view of all black men, something she has struggled to break free from in the last few years. Her mother's supportiveness and sensitivity throughout Williams's childhood has just recently started to fall short of her needs. As Williams expands her racial identity, exploring how much black and biracial fit in her life, she feels alone, except for the comfort she gains from confiding in her sister Simone.

My parents met when they were still in high school. They had mutual friends, and they'd hang out at the same diner in New Haven. I don't really know much more about their courtship, so to speak, but they were married in August '66, and my mother's family—she's white Irish-Catholic, and my father's black—completely disowned her. She was married at eighteen. My father was nineteen, I believe. She moved out of her house, lived with her in-laws. My father was in the army at the time, and then he was sent to Germany. She lived with his parents and worked a couple of jobs to save up money. Finally she moved to Germany to be with him. They lived there for a year on the army base, and that's where my older sister was born.

My maternal grandmother was very concerned with offspring and how the children would feel and how they would identify and how people would treat them. Those were valid concerns, but I think they masked her own personal fears and her own dislikes of the situation—which was kind of strange because my mother's always told me that she grew up in a very racially mixed area, a lot of black families around.

My mother's first playmates were black children. My grandparents had lots of acquaintances and friends who were black people, but it was just sort of that idea, like, "They're nice to have as friends, but let's kind of keep it at arm's length," which is weird, because by the time I came around and started understanding and learning [about my grandparents], I'm surprised that's the way they were. I guess they changed, having two granddaughters who were racially mixed, and a black son-in-law. I guess they just were forced to, and they just had to change.

So here's my mother, eighteen years old, living in Germany, barely speaking German, just picking it up as she's there, and having this child with this black person. I don't think my father's family was too hip on the idea either, but they're much more accepting. They let my mother live with them, and they really took her in and taught her a lot. My maternal grandparents had done everything for my mother and her sister: They didn't have to make a bed, they didn't have to lift a finger, so my mother was not only thrust into leaving her home, leaving her family, but she didn't know how to do anything. My father's family really nurtured her and taught her how to cook and take care of things.

After Germany, my parents came back and lived in West Haven, Connecticut. Things quickly declined between them. They were separated, they went back and forth and in an attempt to get back together they had me, which was planned, I'm happy to know. By the time I was three, my parents were divorced, and the relationship between my mother and father was nonexistent. They couldn't speak to each other or be in the same company.

As a small child, I was conscious of race when I walked down the street and people didn't think my mother was my real biological mother. When I was around five or six at a baby-sitter's house, this black child was making fun of me and calling me a "high-yellow baby." I wasn't going to tolerate that, and I whipped around and pulled up my sleeve and I was like, "What are you talking about? Don't you know that I'm white?" My mother was the center of my universe when I was little, as for most children, and my father was not around, and my mother's white. Not only personally but visually I wanted to emulate her in every way possible. So it was at a very young age that I knew that I was different.

Having friends in grammar school was not easy, especially black friends, because they accepted me but there was always that difference. And then with white friends there was always that difference. I thought, "Well, who's going to understand me?" I thought, "Maybe black students will, because I don't look white," and my hair was a little Afro, I had little patchy skin, and I looked either mixed or a lot of people thought I was Puerto Rican. But there was always that distance between my black friends in grade school and myself, just sort of like, "Yeah, we like you, but you're not really like us; your mom's white."

Because I was raised by a white person and because most of the people I was surrounded by were white, that became my culture. I had proper English; I didn't talk the way a lot of inner-city young black children I went to school with did, and my clothes were probably different, too. All these differences were there, no matter how much I tried to find this connection, to say, "Look, maybe I'm half-white, but people look at me and don't think that. There's gotta be some sort of connection here. We're discriminated against—whether people think I'm Spanish or mixed or black—we're both discriminated against because of what we look like. So there's got to be a connection."

Around second grade, we had this thing in school where we were supposed to stand up and talk about ourselves and talk about our family's culture, religion, ethnicity—what we were. I stood up and said that I was Irish-Catholic, and my teacher, in front of the entire classroom, said I didn't know what I was talking about and I needed to sit down and go home and ask my mother. I couldn't believe it. She was a white woman, and she all but laughed at me when I was a *child*! I was *eight years old*! And she was like, "No, you're not." And I was like, *"No! I am!"*

Had my parents been together it would have been more complicated because my father's family are Baptist. But it was just my mother, and I was going to catechism classes and I was Catholic and I was Irish and this teacher was like, "No."

That's okay, because my mother came to school the next day and told her off. She went and talked to the principal and talked to the teacher, and in front of the entire classroom—although it might have been to the side—the teacher apologized to me.

I told my mother about it because my mother always treated my sister and I as though we were people, not children, and we could say what we wanted to. She grew up with that idea that children should be seen and not heard, and that was not her belief. So my sister and I were very vocal and shared lots of things within our family, the three of us, so I marched right home and told her what happened.

I don't know exactly which grade it was; I don't recall much from my childhood, and I think that's because things were unhappy. I just block it out. My sister has an excellent memory; she can remember everything, from when we were babies, but my mother told me the "high-yellow baby" story. My baby-sitter saw it, told my mother, and they were dying in laughter, so the story's been related to me.

After my parents split, we had visitation rights. Everything had to be done through the courts because my parents could not communicate and my father was completely irresponsible.

Child support had to be done through the courts. It had to be taken directly out of his paycheck. He just showed no responsibility or concern for his children. And he didn't have to because we didn't live with him, and he could just brush us off. In my eyes, I don't see how that would be easy, but it seemed easy for him. So we had visitation rights once a month for the day—not overnight—every third Sunday of the month. A lot of times I wouldn't go and that upset him, but I didn't care. He'd come to pick us up, and I'd decide that this day I wasn't going to go.

When we did visit with him, we didn't do anything. He never planned anything for us to do. It was always on Sundays, so there were always football games on TV, so he'd do things like have his friends over to watch football. He was supposed to come pick us up at ten o'clock. He was always late, always late bringing us home. We were supposed to be home by five-thirty, 'cause we had to go to school the next day, but everything was always late, completely unorganized, nothing planned. He has three siblings, and sometimes we'd go over to my cousin's house and see them and my grandparents, but he never took us to a park, never took us to a movie, never threw a Frisbee.

He'd pick us up and he'd be like, "Oh, have you girls had breakfast?" Well, of course we had breakfast; we were children. Children wake up at like seven o'clock in the morning, and they're ready to start their day. Here we'd been waiting for three and four hours for him to show up. My mother had friends and a serious boyfriend at the time, and she'd go and do things with them. This was her one day off, she was a single parent, so she wanted to take advantage of it. She would have a baby-sitter come for that interim between when she left and he was supposed to show. Sometimes he'd just never show up, never call. Needless to say, I did not like my father. For a young child I was very astute and perceptive. My sister, not that she wasn't those things, but her emotional side was brought out more, and she always wanted my parents to be married. She wanted that union and that family, because the whole nuclear family was really important to her. Not that it wasn't important to me, but we just dealt with it in very different ways. So she was always trying to keep that tie and wanted to be close to my father. All my life, my father has taken out his anger and his frustration with his failure of relationship with my mother on my sister and I, and he would manipulate us. My sister was drawn into it, and I wasn't.

All of this that I'm saying is really important in terms of how it's molded my view, not only of men but particularly of black men, which in my later years and now has had a tremendous impact on my relationships with black males and how I view them.

Anyway, things were not good, and a lot of times he would try to position my sister and I against my mother, that kind of thing. When I was twelve, a really bad incident happened. My sister and my father were having an argument, and I was getting upset; they were yelling and I was getting really nervous—my father's a very big man. He never hit my sister and I, but he was very intimidating, he's like six feet and a big guy, so my sister's like, "Danielle, get your stuff. We're leaving."

Fortunately, my maternal grandparents lived all of three, four blocks from my father. So we're screaming and crying, running through the house, trying to grab our stuff. I was a figure skater at the time, so I had my skates and all this stuff to carry, and we run out of the house and we start leaving and he's screaming, *"Come back here!"* He gets in the car with his wife, who by the way, used to be my mother's best friend; that was one of the reasons they broke apart. My father had this uncontrollable infidelity disease. So he gets in the car, we're running, he's driving down the street, we're about two blocks now from my grandparents' house, and he's like, "Come on, let's work this out, get in the car, I'm your father." Actually, he wasn't so much like, "Let's work this out." Basically he was like, "I'm your father, listen to me and get in the car and just stop this ridiculousness." And we were like, "No. We're not."

He gets out of the car, throws my sister against the car, starts screaming at her, and, to this day, I still feel guilty about it, but I ran. I wet my pants, I was so afraid. Luckily, there was someone home at my grandparents' house, my aunt.

Finally, Simone got away from him, somehow, and she ran and caught up. My father came to my grandparents' house, had this screaming fight with my aunt, and she was like, "Look, just get out of here. You're making these girls really upset and you have no place here." It was at that point that I decided, Fuck this, I'm not going to waste my time with this person. My parents went back to court, and visitation rights were legally terminated. My sister also agreed that she did not want to see him anymore, and we had some sort of a restraining order on him, and he was not allowed to come within a certain distance of my sister and I. My mother told us that if he ever came by our school, that we should call the police, and that remained in place until we were eighteen.

He never even tried to pursue anything. If he loved us so much, he could have kept sending birthday cards, kept sending us letters, but that never happened. I don't believe there was any contact all those years. I'm sure he called up, harassed my mother, tried to stir things up again. Those years are kind of blurry, but yeah, there was no contact, and then I just sort of put it out of my head as much as I could, and I decided that I didn't have a father and that was the way it was. And at the time my mother was involved with this man, this white man. They were together for three years, and he lived with us for one; he didn't really become a surrogate father, but he was just a friend. We thought he was okay, very okay. My mother wouldn't be with anyone who didn't like her children or if we didn't like them.

My mother never disappointed me. Neither did my paternal grandfather, Henry Wilder Williams. He was great. He kept in touch. He and my mother had a very good relationship. He knew that my father was messed up, and he always felt bad. He'd say to her, "Suzanne, I don't know what's wrong with my boy." He had a little homemade business—this little red pickup truck and a garden—and he'd drive around selling his vegetables, so he'd come by and visit us. It wasn't very often, but we were able to keep in touch with him. That's the only positive association I have, because my paternal grandmother was very attached to my father and defended him at any length. He was her son and he could do no wrong, but my paternal grandfather saw beyond that.

All through my college years at Smith there were racial problems. My senior year was very disturbing. A black freshman was harassed by women in her house, who took this black baby doll, cut off her head, and hung it over this woman's bed. They followed her in the bathrooms—horrifying things one would not expect from the polite, Miss Proper Smith Woman. The administration and the com-

munity refused to believe it was anyone within the Smith
community. Well, it was. Through these incidents and through our
Thursday night black dinner and black TV night, I started becoming more into my blackness and more into my black friends, more
into learning about black culture, black leaders, black literature,
and I started feeling really good about who I was, but at the same
time it brought distance between my white friends and between
my mother and I.

When we had racial problems at school, I'd talk to her about
it. Of course she was supportive, in the way that she could be, but
she just couldn't understand because she's white. Part of me understands that. I *do* understand that, and I'm not angry because she
can't understand, but it's difficult. I guess part of it makes me
angry because I can't talk to her about it. She doesn't walk down
the street and experience what I experience, and that's just a fact.
It was very difficult in my senior year, because I was becoming
close with these black women, and identifying that within myself.

I sort of have this new term: I would say that I am a "black-
slash-biracial" woman. And a lot of times you might hear me say,
"Well, look, I'm a black woman, this-this-this-this," but then if
someone says, "What are you?" I'll say, "Oh, I'm biracial." And
that might sound confusing to some people. It's confusing to me.

I am *two* things, you know? And then people say, "Well,
you're not. You're biracial." But people don't make it into one
thing. It's not a legally noticed race. That's why I like the word
mulatto. Because mulatto means only black and white. When you
say biracial, it's a mixture of any two, and for me, being mulatto is
so special that I want an official word, just as white people have
white and black people have black, and Japanese and whatever.
When I say "mulatto" or whatever, I want people to say, "I know
what that is." Growing up, people didn't know what mulatto
meant. I had to explain it.

But now I really feel more like a black woman, some days, and
other days I feel like a biracial woman, and that difference comes
when I come in contact with black people who won't accept me for
being a black/biracial person. To them, I'm not black enough.
Take the Rodney King trials. When I talk to some of the black
people I work with about it, if they want to say, "All white folk
this, white folk that," I see them kind of look at me first. They

don't want to step on my toes, and then they feel a little distance from me.

But I feel okay when they say that sort of thing because I say it myself. And in some ways, I don't trust white people. I'm not going to assume that someone's guilty before proven innocent, so to speak, but I have to keep my distance. Then at the same time, I have to keep my distance from black people, not as much as I feel right now a distance from white people, but a distance because I can't associate with black people who hate white people or who are separatists. I would definitely say that at this point in my life I am the marginalized tragic mulatto.

That might sound really dramatic and poetic, but I don't have a community that I can call my own and that understands both sides. For that, I'm grateful that I have my sister. I wish I knew more biracial people who felt like I do. I have a very close friend who's biracial—but he identifies as black—and it's wonderful because he's the first black male that I've *ever* in my life been close to. There was a time when I was afraid to go out with black guys because my father had set this image. When I was a kid riding around in cars with him, he'd do that catcalling to women and just reinforce the stereotypical image of black men—that they're always sexually aggressive and offensive, treating women like objects, which I'm sure white men did, too, at the time.

Sometimes I wish I was one or the other, but being biracial has made me a stronger person and has kind of given me my own special gold card because I can understand black culture and white culture. I can talk to white people and talk so they'll understand me, and I can talk with my brothers and sisters, and they'll understand me, too, to a certain extent on both sides. And so it's a very special thing and a place to be, but it's a very lonely place, too.

I'm starting to feel more distance from my mom because I'm feeling more into being black. And I wish I had my father. My father's so wrapped up in being angry at the world and angry at my mother, and angry at me because I figured his shit out, because I knew that he was a liar. I know that he's a manipulator. And I know that he's selfish.

I tried to be in contact with him when I was a junior in college. I was in Spain for the first half of the year, and I wrote him a letter. I decided, I want to have a relationship with my father. It didn't work. He responded, but once I tried it I realized that I wanted a father and I wanted a friend, and he and I, we're never going to be friends. And I don't want him to know anything about me.

Simone J. Williams
Age: 25
Residence: Boston, Massachusetts
Occupation: Day-care teacher

Simone Williams is Danielle's (p.41) older sister. She says they used to have very different outlooks on life, but that has begun to change. "The older we get, the more we come to a middle base where we can basically relate. She was like: white guys, rock and roll, ripped jeans, T-shirts. I was more of the outdoors person; she's more of the pocketbook-jewelry person. I was mostly into black guys, and I knew my father the most. She really didn't know her father."

Most people who know their fathers try to date people who are similar to their fathers, which is my syndrome. My sister does not have it because she was not affected by it, and I think her mind is much broader and open compared to mine. But then you go through life, you go through experiences, and you become influenced and things change you, and if a man is as black as coal I will not touch him because of these experiences I have had. If he is light-skinned, maybe a couple of shades darker than me, fine. It sounds narrow-minded and I know it is, but it comes from trying to have a relationship or friendship with my father and having it always end up in lies and being disgusted by it.

I was such a daddy's little girl. I can remember when my parents were still together, when Danielle was a little baby, and they were at a party and they had an argument and I had a choice. My mother came to me upset and she said, "Simone, I'm leaving. I'm going home with your sister. Are you coming with me, or are you staying with your father?" And I said, "I'm staying with

Daddy," and I thought it was the greatest thing. I had a great time at this party; he took me to his sister's house, so I got to see my cousin, got to play Barbies, and I just thought Daddy was the best person in the world because he took me out.

I was really young, gosh, younger than four or five, but I do remember it like yesterday. It's crazy, but there are those little moments that I really savored, and so when he did go away, I blamed my mother. I told her I hated her; I was very, very disturbed by this. I think out of the two of us children I suffered the most emotionally because I *knew* him and Danielle didn't really have much attachment to him, and all she really knew was her mother, so nothing was really being taken away from her, and the person she loved, her mother, was being hurt.

So I used to feel like it was Mommy and Danielle over here, and Simone over here, because my buddy was gone. Where's Dad, you know? Then when I got to fourteen, I realized he was a jerk and I took away his visitation rights. I told my mother, "Please go to court, call your lawyer. I'm sick of this. I don't want to see him anymore. If I have to go to court with you, I will." It didn't come to that, but she was astonished that a fourteen-year-old had come to her and said these things.

The day before my seventeenth birthday and the day before my eighteenth birthday, both days I ran into my father. I saw him when I was almost seventeen, and I was surprised, shocked, happy, scared—all these feelings—and I just stood there and he said, "Hello, Simone." And I said, "Hi, Dad." And he goes, "How are you?" I said, "Fine." And then I don't remember what it was—I think because it was a negative—but he said something that hurt me and I ended up walking away from him. And he disappointed me. It's been how many years from fourteen to seventeen, and you're going to say something negative to me? What kind of a person are you? Day before my eighteenth birthday, I see him again, and I thought, "A year later, I do not forget, okay?" I'm walking on the sidewalk, he's driving in a car, and he's screaming out the window, "Hey, Simone! Hey, Simone!" And I see that it's him. Well, I don't want to be bothered with him, so I ignore him, so he gets louder and people are starting to watch. So I say to a guy who's standing there, "Excuse me sir, this man is bothering me. Can you please call the cops or something?"

Seth Price
Age: 28
Residence: New York, New York
Occupation: Restaurateur

During the time Seth Price lived with his father, from ages six to eighteen, he believes he was influenced more by his father's identity as a painter—more concerned with art than material comfort—than his identity as a black man. Price, although almost exclusively exposed to his black relatives, arrived at a distinctly nonracial identity. "I feel different than just about most of the people I meet," he says. "I don't feel like I'm black; I don't feel like I'm white. I just sort of feel an affinity to lots of people, like, 'Ah, I sort of know that.' "

I was born in Manhattan; my mom was white. She's English and Irish and French mixed. She lived on Ninety-sixth Street on the West Side, and she's the daughter of an alcoholic and a not physically blind, but mentally blind mother. And my dad was black from Jamaica, Queens. I don't really remember where we lived for the first three or four years.

They met in the High School for Art and Design. They were seventeen, and they never got married. Their parents didn't want them to be together at all, on either side. My mother's parents kicked her out of the house when she decided to keep me, and her sisters basically decided not to talk to her. She ended up living with friends and stayed with an aunt while she had me.

My mother's parents have passed away, and I never met them, but from what my [paternal] stepgrandmother tells me, they were both having a really hard time with it and giving my mother no support. They didn't like Blacks. And her father was a semiviolent alcoholic. He never beat my mother, but he would rant and rave and would break things. He used to go on about every other race than his own, even to the point of being prejudiced against his wife because she wasn't Irish.

And my father's father—he's a very stubborn and a sort of violent man—wasn't giving anyone any support either.

The story gets sort of muddy for me at this point, but when I was two or three, my stepgrandmother on my father's side ended up adopting me. She decided she would take care of me and it would be best for my mother to sort of disappear. And that's what happened.

On my father's side of the family, there was an openness but also a nontrusting of Whites. They would have friends, but what was unsaid was that when the chips came down, white friends wouldn't be standing there, so they were never equals. My grandmother, my grandfather's first wife, would say things like, "They're the ones you always work for and you just have to keep that in mind." She made comments about my mother, but in the sense of mothers talking about their sons' girlfriends or wives. Sometimes you'd hear the words, "He always picks white people," but then it wouldn't go any further than that. Like if he would have picked a black woman, it would have turned out just dandy. And my stepgrandmother had white friends she played bingo with. If she drank, which she did when I was younger, she would come home and say things like, "They're so two-faced." I didn't understand the context of it, but there was some bitterness. I always got this sense of disappointment.

So my stepgrandmother had me while my dad was in school—he'd turned down a basketball scholarship to go to art school, which his dad wasn't very happy with. He went to Pratt, in New York, and then Mills College, in California. When he graduated, they decided it was time for me to go live with him. I was six. They took me on a vacation to visit my father in California and then told me I was staying. And he was a hippie kid, I guess, doing lots of drugs, experimenting with religions, and trying to decide what he was going to do with his life. I'm sure he wasn't more than twenty-three. We were Buddhists for a while, and we were some Korean religion and also the Church of Scientology. Hinduism was interesting, and there was the Muslim religion for a while. We went through a lot of stages. But throughout all of this, he was always responsible. I never saw him out of control. Always, in my experience, if he said he was going to show up somewhere, he showed up.

*   *   *

I don't know exactly why I mostly date Latin and white women. I think maybe they look like my mother; I always wanted to be with my mother. When I was younger, I had always wanted to find her, and I would ask my father basically once a year or once every six months, where was she? And he would always say he didn't know; he thought she was in New York. And I would go, "Well, do you have the phone number?"

On my seventeenth birthday he bought me a drink in a nice restaurant and told me that he had found my mother. He had put an ad in *The Village Voice* with her maiden name and his phone number, and she had called. So she flew out to the West Coast and we met.

Six months after that I decided I was moving to New York to see her. I stayed with her for about six months and then got a place on my own. For me it was a completion. Definitely. Because I had felt incomplete not having a mother.

Kimani Fowlin
Age: 24
Residence: Fort Lee, New Jersey
Occupation: Ballet company administrator and dancer/choreographer

Kimani Fowlin graduated from Sarah Lawrence College in 1990. She keeps a framed photograph of the day on her desk at work. In the picture, she stands flanked by her parents. Fowlin wears a black graduation robe, accented by a strip of Kente cloth. Father, on one side, beams. Mother and daughter, both bronze-skinned, wear their hair in cascades of dreadlocks.

My father is Jamaican and my mother is Jewish. They met in the sixties. At that time my mother was a barmaid, or a bartender as they call it now, in Greenwich Village, and a friend of hers introduced them.

My mother gave him a hard time at first. She was a rebel; she had always been a rebel. She basically left him in a bar and just said, "I'm going out with this other person." But he came back the next day to continually pursue her, and he just stayed with her, and finally she realized that "this man is such a gentleman, what am I doing?" Came to her senses. And they got together and got married and didn't tell her parents. Before she married Dad, she had a baby out of wedlock with a black man. That was in the late fifties, and there was big confusion about that. Her parents told her to get an abortion.

She was all freaked out at the time because she knew she wanted to have the baby. So she moved in with the father, who was an alcoholic and somewhat abusive. She called her parents, and they said, "The only way we'll take you back is if you put the baby up for adoption." She had no choice, she felt, and she did that. I guess that was a good thing because she was seventeen or eighteen and in no position to raise a child.

Gina, the baby, came looking for my mom about eight years ago and found her. It's like we're this huge happy family now. It's been hard for Mom and Gina, but it's been a good experience finding out that I had a sister I never knew until the day I was going to meet her. It was a complete shock. I said, "Mom are there any other surprises? Please let me know *now*."

My grandmother and my grandfather and basically my mom's side of the family are very conservative people—white middle-class Jews. It's nothing intense and serious; maybe older relatives are more into the religion, but my grandmother's loosely based. But it was always hard for Grandma and Grandpa. When my mother was younger they sent her away to a home because they didn't know how to handle her. She was hyper and something that they never expected. And my mom had ideas and views about things that conflicted with the views that my grandmother and grandfather had and expected her to have. So she was radical and a rebel for this family.

After my parents got married, they didn't let her parents know. But one time she brought Grandma over, and Grandma saw his things in the house and questioned it. So that's when my mother told her that they eloped. And Grandma's really an amazing woman to come from her kind of background and to do a full three-sixty, to grow and learn to love and accept us as her family. She's one who analyzes and is a constant growing person, which is very special . . . someone who didn't stop and die in their beliefs. I'm thankful for that, but it's still hard. Grandma and I still to this day confront each other with race issues, and it's so hard. It's complex because I can respect her but I'm angry with her for why there have to be issues to begin with. Why don't you like my hair? Because it's so foreign to you?

As far as my father's family goes, when they got married, it was in the late sixties, that his family started coming over from Jamaica. Basically they're all here now. His mother and father had both died by the early seventies, so I didn't get a chance to know them very well. We're closer, I think, to my mom's side of the family, but there's this deep love and yearning for us to get together with my father's side. I don't know. We're kind of lazy in terms of getting the family together, but they're all here in the New York City area. And they're very proper Jamaicans, that middle-class-sort-of-bourgeoisie Jamaicans, assimilated to white American standards. The straighter your hair is, the better it is. Corporate. Very proper. Very much into school, getting a good education, the basic standards, and you don't deviate from that. I *want* to get closer to my Jamaican roots because I feel that I've been denied that out of the family not really being close. But every time I do see them I express that need that I really want to know about my history. We've been to Jamaica many times but never to Dad's birthplace or where the family lives, and I'm just interested in getting closer to that part of *me*.

As long as I can remember, I've always felt that way. I kind of feel like I'm not really here with my mother's side of the family. I'm kind of in the middle. And I want to feel closer to Dad's side of the family so I can know that part better.

Ever since I was very young, Mom has been problack. It's a weird situation; she hates being white. She hasn't become black—she can't. Her skin color seems kind of dark, but it's because she uses Sudden Tan, which she does for two reasons: because she had melanoma, she has cancer, and she cannot be exposed to sunlight, so it protects her skin; but also it gives her color. Her color is very white, with freckles. And she detests her color and the fact that she's white. She does not like the white race.

So basically, she was the black influence. My dad was the more white one in the family. Very interesting. But she's a very angry person and just hates the injustices of what Whites have done to Blacks constantly and still do and just hates being a part of that race because of that. She finds beauty in the black race in every aspect, like physically: the big nose, the big lips. It's a kind of warped situation, though, it really is confusing, but I guess I can understand. I wish I had videotapes so I could show you how we communicate and how within a public situation—let's say we're with a group of black people—Mom will take on this black persona. She fools people all the time. To me, she doesn't look black, but she's got the attitude. And I would get very upset at that: "Mom, just be who you are." I used to get very angry and want her to be who she is. Then, I realized that I made comments that my mom would make which were very superficial, very judgmental, very unfair to make: about interracial couples, about white people, about black people.

For example, in this bar there was this white bartender, and I made a comment to a friend to the effect that she was "*very* white," which is something that my mom would say. And this friend was also a friend of that bartender's, and it hurt her. And then I started thinking about the things I had been saying and I felt that it wasn't fair, that it was what Whites do to Blacks all the time, and I was just doing it in reverse. I'm working things out in that way not to judge people on a racial basis. Mom continues to do that, but I want to be separate from her. A lot of people put us together, including my sister, and I'm like, "No please, I'm my own person. Mom is the way she is."

I don't like the way my mom is with people because it's not what she is. It's one thing if you *are* black and you switch in and out of a black vernacular or whatever you'd want to call it. Mom isn't, and so it just would get on my nerves when she would do that, because it's not really her. And it wouldn't be like she would switch back into herself. She would keep that black talk and confuse people. It's just false pretenses, and I don't like that. When I'm talking to friends, we go back and forth. It's not something we stay in all the time.

Now my dad, he's white in his beliefs and morals. I hate to be so general and say "white," but what was taught to him in Jamaica was "the lighter, the better." So I guess in his search for a woman, and also what he likes in a woman, that says something about who he is. It's funny how he's very comfortable around my grand-mother, and my mom's like, "Oh, let's leave those two old white folks alone." It's very funny.

When I'm around Jewish people, I love to shock them and say, "Yes, I'm Jewish." And at times I get this overwhelming feeling of how lucky I am to come from such diverse cultures. I can really say that *this* is me and *this* is me. But because I really haven't delved deeply into each one, I'm not really a part of it, and that's where I think I'm losing. I wish I had grabbed onto one—actually I wish I'd grabbed onto both—but I took the superficial aspects of both. I think that's partly because of my mom and my dad. I get angry at them a lot for that because I wish they had directed me. What I've come to on my own, I guess, is being a black feminist. Basically right now that's what I'm really hooked into—black women and making our own and existing on our own, and just understanding our own hardships separate from men. Very much what I've studied and learned has been male-oriented, and now I'm becoming more women-oriented. It's been refreshing. It's like I have a voice, too.

In terms of what my parents told me, Mom and society helped that, in saying that my younger brother and I are black. Our skin is brown, but we are seen as black. Most people don't think I'm biracial. They can't tell. So Mom was very honest and very like, "This is what society is about. Don't be sucked in. Be strong. You're a black woman. You'll be seen as a black woman." Around black people I just usually say I'm black. If I'm with people who are white, I like to say I'm biracial to show them that there's more than what they see: "You're white? You look black!" I want it to be apparent that I'm this *and* this.

But eventually I don't have anything to hide from anyone. I do tell black people the truth, or it can come out; it doesn't matter to me. I'm very much into psychology and feeling the vibes and seeing when is the right time. Usually right off the bat with white people I let them know, "Hey, I'm also half of you," so I can have the liberty to make comments and things they think I shouldn't say but I can.

In college I knew this white man who was into the superficial aspects of black women and black culture. It really grossed me out.

Unfortunately, I was attracted to him, and then he used me. Then he started to grow dreads—yuck!—tacky-looking things because his hair was just pin-straight, and he did one of these teased numbers and it just looked horrible.

So he's growing these tacky-looking dreads, and I was really angry at him for all that he had done to all these different black women. Just a phony, superficial wannabe. And then this other guy who was a punk white guy started to grow dreads, too, and I was angry because it means more than just the style and "Wow, it's cool; we can grow it too!" It's a more spiritual thing that these people really shouldn't be wearing. They can do what they want, but that's just my own personal feelings.

So I confronted them, and they said, "Yeah, but how can you say anything? Your mother's white, and *she* has dreads." And I was like, "Well, that's a different story, and that's none of your business." I guess they had a point, but I didn't look at her as being white. I do but I don't. It's really confusing.

CHAPTER II

Self-Portrait

Sallyann Hobson
Age: 42
Residence: Silver Spring, Maryland
Occupation: Medical illustrator

After she married a black man, Sally Hobson's Italian-American mother was disowned by her family. The estranged relatives lived in the same town in northern New Jersey, where they still live, forty years later. Hobson grew up going to school and seeing those relatives on the street, although many refused to make eye contact with her. Despite such fractured relations on that side of the family, her mother has demonstrated a loyalty to her husband and to the family  *they created together that has influenced Hobson profoundly. I found Hobson via a contact at the Interracial Family Circle, a multiracial support network in the Washington, D.C., area.*

My parents met originally through a mutual friend at a birthday party. My mother has also told me stories of living at home as a young girl, sixteen years old, and my father doing mason work

60

and carpentry for her family. My father was twelve years older than my mother.

I think there was some attraction from the very beginning. And when my father asked my mother out, my mother knew right then that this was something her family would not be pleased about, and she began seeing him clandestinely. There was a dual thing here—not only the race issue but also her age.

This was in Orange, New Jersey, which brings up something else: the racial makeup of the town and the way things were. We're talking about 1948, 1946, years when in the town or Orange, New Jersey, Blacks lived in the town and Whites lived in the town, primarily Italians, which my mother's family was. The Italians pretty much ran the town—they were the mayors and city officials—and the Blacks who lived there had *no* political say.

So this relationship was not going to be well received in those days, not at all. At one point, apparently, my mother's family found out that my father was seeing my mother, and they sent her to California with a one-way ticket to live with her aunt, to stay there until she got her head together. By this time she was a little older. I guess she had been sneaking around seeing my father successfully for about two years or so. And my mother has to this day a letter that my father sent her that said, "If you don't come back I will come and get you. I love you and I want to marry you."

So my mother snuck away from the trailer where she was staying with her aunt, got on the train, and came back cross-country. Her brothers found out she had left California, and so in Penn Station in Newark, she sees her brothers, who have come to the train station because they found out what train she was on. On one side are her brothers; on the other side is my father. She waved to my father to go away, and she went home with her brothers. They hit the ceiling about her coming back. How could she do this! That night, when they went to church, my father came to the house and picked her up, and she never went back again. He brought her to his mother's house, and they got married. This was 1949. They stayed together until he passed away in 1981.

Apparently, once she married my father, her brothers were infuriated, and for the most part she is dead to this day to many members of her family. This has been a very sad thing, not only in my mother's life but in mine and my family's. My brothers and sister have different feelings about this. I won't speak for them. I will only speak for my own feelings about it and what I have worked through in my own coming of age and maturity about this. My mother still, at this point in time, has contact with her mother and her sister, my grandmother and my aunt, who are living in the same home with her brother. My grandmother and my aunt call my mother almost daily, but she is not allowed to call them, and when I say not allowed, then we get into the unspoken rules of the game, how it's played. The rules we have all followed in my family whether we knew it or not and which I, for the first time about two or three years ago, began to break.

I can count the number of times I've seen my grandmother on my right hand and probably have fingers left over. The times I remember were when we were out shopping and we would just bump into her, and my grandmother never denied us. Now my mother's brother, who was a city official, if he saw her walking down the street, he would not speak to her. He would not acknowledge her existence. Certainly not as his own sister. But her mother would greet her and hug and kiss her publicly, but not any further than that. I can remember those hugs because they were crushers. This woman wanted to see us, but could not own the reality of it, I guess, for a lot of reasons. Again, I can't go into their heads; I can only share what my experience with it was.

Anyway, this went on for a long time. Occasionally we would meet in that way, and then there was some clandestine visiting. My mother's sister would come and visit, but she would have to sneak over. She couldn't let the other family members know she was coming. She would bring her son, who we went to school with— and everybody in school knew he was my cousin. It's so incredibly ridiculous. But this is how we lived.

As a child I'd say, "This doesn't seem right, something about this isn't right, but, okay, this is how it is." And you grow up like this and you take it in stride and you just say this is how it is, and if I want to see Aunt Rose, then this is how we're going to see Aunt Rose. And I notice that every time she comes over she's making sure nobody sees her come in, and she makes some comment about how, "Uncle Frank would be upset if he knew I was here." So there's a little element of excitement and a little element of intrigue there, like we're getting away with something here. We're getting over on Uncle Frank who is "the bad guy."

For a long time I thought that was the way it was, for years and years and years, until about three years ago. It was Mother's Day. We had taken my mother out to dinner and afterward, as my mother and I sat in her kitchen, the phone rang. It was my grandmother. She said, "Happy Mother's Day. Would you like to come over?" I was thrilled. I get to see my grandmother who was by this time, eighty-some years old. This woman now is ninety-two. And so I said, "Not only is it Mother's Day, but I get to see Grandma Bridget. Wonderful!"

So we drop everything, grab our coats, get in the car. My mother had to really think about where her mother lived, because that's how many times she'd been over there. Zip. It's in the next town, it's fifteen minutes away, and she had to find her way to her mother's house. So we got there, and by this time it was evening; it was starting to get dark. I left my mother off in front of the house, and she went in. I went to park the car, and when I came down the street, I saw my Aunt Rose with the door cracked open, and she's looking up and down the street. I came in and I was so excited. I said, "Hi Aunt Rose, how are you?" And she said, "Keep your voice down!" And I said, "Keep my voice down?" I'm thirty-nine years old and she told me to keep my voice down? She said, "Yes. My niece lives upstairs, and I don't want her to know my business," and then we go into the house.

So here are two women, my grandmother and my aunt, frantic. These are two very nervous ladies, and they're running around, "Would you like some cookies? Would you like some lemonade?" And my grandmother is saying, "I want to show you my room," and all the things she's been knitting and all the things she's been crocheting. On the living-room wall is a picture of her mother and father, my great-grandparents, and my great-grandfather looks like my brother Joe, and I'm just soaking all this up in a matter of seconds. I'm almost overwhelmed with this, and we're sitting down and I could see how nervous they were—it wasn't going past me this time. It was right there, and I knew what was happening. I guess we were there about fifteen minutes or so, and they said, "Well, we're sorry you have to go so soon." They were so nervous

and so afraid that Uncle Frank would come back. And so they let
us know it was time to go.

My mother started to cry and I started to cry and my grandmother started to cry, and as we walked out and they said their
good-byes, it was very difficult for me. I felt very bad. I felt vio-
lated at that point. I felt that something was wrong, that this was
not the way it should be, and that I wasn't going to allow myself to
be treated like this.

I shared this with my mother in the car. We're both crying
still, and I said, "This is not right. I know Grandma loves us, but
this is not right." For me, that started the process of a great deal of
really looking at what was going on with me in a lot of areas of my
life. Now I did not have a lot of those experiences; my sister just
had one recently, with my aunt, the same Aunt Rose, who was
recently hospitalized. My mother and my sister went to visit her in
the hospital, and she just about freaked out. She wouldn't eat. She
was so nervous and afraid that someone would show up, a family
member or a friend, and then she'd be in this very uncomfortable
situation. It was just a mess.

We did try to reach out after that experience on Mother's Day.
I've talked to my brother Eddie about it. I'm the oldest, I have a
sister Barbara, my brother Edward, and my brother Joseph is the
youngest. Edward and I are close, and I talk to him about this. We
did try to reach out to my Uncle Frank. We actually called him, and
I have that conversation on tape. We reached him at work, my
mother spoke to him, and he said, "I'm old and sick and there's no
reason to start problems in the family, and things are just the way
they are." My mother said she would like to see if we can get closer
to the family and have things the way they were, and I remember
him specifically saying, "Oh, no, it's been too long now, and there's
no reason to start this stuff up." He said, "I'm sorry, but that's just
how it is."

If you're doing something you believe is right, why would you
be sorry? That question came up for me. He was just very matter-
of-fact and businesslike as you please, and my mother was saying,
"I'm your *sister*, you're my *brother*. This is crazy stuff here." And he
just held on stubbornly: "This is how it is. I can't move from this
position after forty-some years." So she's not talked to him, except
for that, in forty-three years. I have talked to my mother a great

deal about making such a big decision, and she *never* has said she regretted it. I've asked her about this, and she says, "No, no, no, this is what I wanted." But I somehow can't believe she didn't say at one time, "Hey. It could have been different." At least *once* in her life. She's a human being.

But she was in a position where there was no turning back. If there's one thing I can say I've learned from my mother, it is total commitment. Because this woman was committed to her relationship with this man, she was committed to her family. What was her alternative? Her family and her community had completely turned their backs on her.

She said, "I loved your father, I married him and I loved you kids and this was my life." She has told people in my presence that "my children are my life now." Of course, there's some good stuff about that and some not-so-good stuff about that.

My mother is one of eight children, and she's on the lower end. She just recently had a brother who died, and there was an article in the local paper about him and about four generations of my mother's family, and they completely left her out of it. She cuts these things out, and she saves them and she tells me about them. It's really difficult for most people to keep from saying, "Hey! Why don't you hate these people's guts? How is it that you can even talk about them after the way they've treated you?" So in my family there was also this forgiveness, this is still my family, no matter who or what—we're talking about unconditional love, as far as I'm concerned. My mother didn't walk around with a sign saying, "This is unconditional love, guys. Check it out." It wasn't like that; it was very subtle.

Again, there is good about that and there is not so good. I used to worry that she was in serious denial. That this woman was in incredible pain and just shut it all off somehow. But that's not the case anymore. The older I get, the more I realize my mother's strength and her ability to survive, her coping mechanisms. Sometimes they're somewhat more effective than other times, but that's what it's all about.

When I was about ten years old, I remember my mother got this phone call and started to cry. She could hardly tell us what had happened, which was that her father had died and her family didn't call and tell her. I really didn't appreciate the significance of that until much later. I was upset that this man was dead, but I never saw him before in my life. It wasn't like a living, breathing person whose lap I'd sat in. He was just a name to me, unreal in many ways. For the most part, that was my experience with that whole side of the family.

Now my father's side is quite the opposite. From the very beginning, my father's mother completely accepted my mother.

I find that interesting, especially when I consider many black women's attitudes toward white women these days. Young black women, especially. To have a white woman dating or married to a black man is—believe me—bad news. And they will let you know in no uncertain terms. I hear it because as far as they're concerned I'm in the same boat, so they talk freely about how many black movie stars marry white women and how horrible it is, and their attitudes about that. Those who know me look at me like, "Are you going to say something?"

What I do depends on who I'm talking to and who's in the room. If I feel it's worthwhile to make a comment then I do, but if I feel that opening my mouth to say anything will be casting my pearls before swine, then I won't do nothin' about it. I'll keep my mouth shut. Because some people, you can't talk to.

My dad's family, who also lived in Orange, were different. His mother and his sister lived in the same house, and they accepted her as a woman and as my father's wife, and also as this young woman who didn't know very much about cooking, especially about cooking for a black man. So they showed her a lot. My grandmother Sally and my Aunt Mary were like my mom's surrogate mothers since she really did not have her own mother now. And she became very close to them, and they became close to her.

There were also friends and some family members who would come up to visit from North Carolina, where my father was from. He came up to New Jersey from his hometown when he was about sixteen years old, worked as a cook and did other odd jobs, and I guess he started doing carpentry work and had his own business. For a time, when my mother and father first got married, my mother would help with his business, which was convenient for my father, because here was this white woman who was able to be receptionist and liaison with these clients, and my father would then go out and do the work. People thought that my father worked for my mother. So there must have been some advantage there, too, in those days, for him, with that situation. My father did the best he could with what he had. He was a black man living in 1949, trying to feed a family. By this time I was born. My sister came eighteen months later, then five years later my brother, and five years again, my other brother.

My parents had an effective relationship in many ways, and in some ways not. Overall, my father was the head of the household, without mistake. There was no denying that, and my mother did what my father said for the most part. She was primarily interested in raising her family and doing for her husband. This woman gave up a lot of stuff. She gave and gave and gave.

We lived in a predominantly black neighborhood. Poor people just trying to make it. My mother was the only white woman for blocks. She worked for a while, then hurt her back. My father said, "Stay home," and she did, she stayed home with us. But my father worked throughout, whatever jobs he could get, doing mostly carpentry work, and toward the end he was doing fairly well. He was doing general contracting, and he would hire other men to go out and do mason work and bricklaying. He was working on a house when he had a heart attack, and he died at home in bed.

My father was a terrible tease. He enjoyed life, he enjoyed people, he teased us mercilessly, and I miss him very much now, still. My mother does, too. She talked about him today. It was a really dramatic and terrible loss when he died, for my mother especially, because this was the man she left her whole life for. I don't know if I could do that. I really don't know if I could do that. To say, "I'll never see my family again?"

Even though we grew up in a primarily black neighborhood, I did not notice that my mother was white. I guess I knew she looked different, but it wasn't a thing for me. I didn't see my mother as a white woman. That's really true.

I went to a public grammar school that was right across the street from where we lived. There were white kids that went at the time. And then I went to junior high school, where my cousin Bob, who's the same class as me, started to go, too. That was a new thing for me. My mother let me know, "Well, your cousin's going to this school." And so there was some excitement, and I was very anxious to tell people that he was my cousin. Some of the girls I went to school with, I would tell them that my cousin went to school there, and he's in such-and-such a class.

"Well, what does he look like?"

"Well, he's got blue eyes and he's got blond hair," and they were like, "Whoa!" And I'd say, "Yeah." So they all wanted to meet him and talk to him and everything. He and I got along fine. He was always a real studious kid and quiet, and he never was flashy in any way. But he never pretended he wasn't my cousin, either. If there was a problem, I was not aware of it. If there was a problem for *him*, I was not aware of it. And there may have been, because he doesn't keep in touch. I sent a Christmas card just last Christmas, and I've not heard from him.

He talked to my mother recently—he's still living in the area. They say one thing, but the actions aren't the same as what they say. He tells my mother, "This is ridiculous how Uncle Frank acts," yet, he doesn't try to find out where I am to give me a call and say, "Thanks for the Christmas card," or send me one. I guess maybe that's the way it is.

What that Mother's Day trip to my grandmother's did was to open the door wide for me to come to completion with my feelings about this, to grieve this loss in my life and to become complete with it. And I have done that for the most part. In a process like this, it's years. I had begun before that day, but just scratched the surface. And then when that happened, I really started in earnest, talking about it and grieving it. Because it was a lot of sadness that I had *no* idea was there. It was more sad than I really imagined. It was real sad—a lot of crying, just like death, grieving for a long time. And not going around telling everybody that this is the reason why I was sad, either, but knowing that this was the work I had to do.

I wrote a letter to my uncle soon after that experience, but I never heard anything from him. In it I talked a lot about false shame and me owning all this false shame. And my mother bought it, too; she bought it all. She owned it and she communicated to us,

I'm sure unintentionally, but in very subtle ways, that she had accepted this. She never said, "Forget it," and she never said, "I've done some terrible thing here." It just seemed somehow to be accepted because she did not reject them. In my mind it was difficult to understand how she could still talk to these folks and say, "This is my brother and my sister and my mother and father," when she, as far as they're concerned, is literally dead. She's dead! And some of her family wishes she was, I'm sure. It's hard to imagine someone like that and then to imagine that they're members of your own family, the same gene pool and everything. *Wait a minute!* It's scary to me now to think about it.

Then we decided to try and reach out to Frank. My brother went to my uncle's church and talks to the deacon and tells him the story. So the deacon goes to my uncle, and my uncle cussed him out. In church! He told him that if he brought this up again he would leave the church. My uncle's high up in the church, so this is how strongly he feels about this. This is a committed bunch, I'm telling you, unshakable on both sides.

I understand he's got cancer. See, you can't carry around this crap. None of *us* have ever been drug addicts, none of us have ever been in jail, we've never gotten in any trouble. We've always been good citizens and good students, names in the paper every now and then. They know we're not scum. But to deny all that—I just don't believe you can walk around with all that and have it not show up. And he's got cancer.

Where I eventually came to is that they're where they are and my grieving is over. I've done a great deal of work over the last few years with this and feel complete with it. Every now and then it comes up, but rarely. Now the next one will be when my grandmother dies, God forbid, but the woman is ninety-two. She's going to go sometime. Then I will go to the funeral.

The last thing was my Uncle Mike's death, and my mother was very upset. My brother was like, "I'm not going to the funeral." I played around with it and decided that I would go if it was at the end of the week, but that I would not go out of my way to take time off from work. If my mother died, everything would drop and I'd be gone. I wouldn't even ask for time, I'd just say, "See ya."

Sure enough, his funeral was a Wednesday. My brother was not intending to go to this funeral, but knowing that my mother did want to pay some respects, he called the funeral home—Italian funeral home in our hometown—and told them the situation. They set up a private viewing for my mother. So my sister went with my mother and viewed my uncle's body *before* the rest of the family did. She signed the book and everything, so they *know* she was there. It's laughable. To see these people dance around this issue and pretend; it's like they don't acknowledge reality. It's silly.

Four months later, I interviewed Hobson again. She had called to say something important had just happened that I needed to know.

My grandmother died on Saturday evening. They did not call my mother right away to let her know this, and she went up to the nursing home the next day to visit, my sister and my mother did. They walked into an empty room and with an empty bed. My sister said, "Oh my goodness, what has happened?"

They go to the nurse's station and the nurse starts crying, and so then they go and get the head nurse and the head nurse in the hallway tells my mother that her mother is dead. And so my sister at first was pretty upset, and she goes into my mother's brother's home, where my grandmother had been living with him and my mother's other sister. It's a home she is not allowed to go to, that if she does go she's sneaking over there and has gone over there maybe three times in the years since I've been born. They go over there, and the cousins and relatives are in the living room, and someone said, "We just tried to call you."

My sister let that go. They were pretty upset, and the grief's set in by this time. They decided that they would have the wake Monday and Tuesday, and then Wednesday would be the funeral.

I drove up on Tuesday night and went straight to the funeral home. I had talked to my mother and sister on Monday, and they told me it was pretty rough but that there were a lot of relatives they hadn't met before and that they had been received well. So this was the best possible scenario. I mean, I had gone over this many times in my mind—what would happen if my grandmother died, would I go to the funeral or wouldn't I?—and I had decided years ago that I would. My brother Joey said he would not go.

I got to the wake on Tuesday, and I really didn't know what to expect, except my brother Eddie had told me he'd had a good experience and was glad that he went. He said that he was having mixed emotions about whether he should go or not, it had been so many years. He said a couple of prayers outside the funeral home and decided to go in. Well, when he gets in there people were hugging him, kissing him. People he had never met, never seen before. They'd never seen him, didn't even know he existed. There were some who said nothing to him, who were obviously not at all impressed he was there in any way, shape, or form, but they didn't say anything negative to him.

The same thing had happened with my mother earlier that same night. And she was just overwhelmed with the response of these family members who hadn't spoken to her in forty years.

So I drive up and I get there and I walk into the funeral home. It really was strange because there were people over in the corner talking about one of my cousins who I knew, and it was like walking into a room full of strangers and being related to all of them and not knowing hardly any of them.

It was very strange. I would say there were a good maybe sixty, seventy people there, and I probably knew three. And I hadn't seen *them* in years. Of the rest, I was probably related to fifty. I recognized my cousin Bob, who I'd gone to school with, him and my Aunt Rose. I recognized her and my Uncle Frank, but the rest I did not know.

When I walked in, I started to walk up the stairs, and there was one woman was standing in the door and she looked at me and she said, "You're Sallyann," and I said yes and she opened her arms and said, "I am your cousin Marina." She hugged me and kissed me and said, "I'm so sorry that it's taken me so long to say that to you," and then she introduced me to her twin sister, and she started to introduce me to all these other people, and then I said, "I've got to find my mother."

My mother was still crying, she was still very upset but yet overjoyed. She was sitting in the front row with the rest of the

family, which was just, it was all too much, and then she said,
"This is my sister," who I'd never met before in my life, my
mother's sister and her husband.

My mother's sister Mary is the oldest one now in the family,
and she is the mother of the twins. The only siblings left are
Bridget, Mary, Frank, Rose—I think that's all of them. Out of
eight. So it just was like that, and I hear people talking behind me
asking who my mother was, saying, "Well, they say she's a sister,
but I've never seen her before," those conversations happening
and I'm wanting so much to turn around and say, "Yeah, well, I can
tell you a story about how come!" but I didn't and nothing like that
happened.

Then the cousins started bringing out pictures of my great-
grandparents, pictures I've never seen before. They started pour-
ing out all this information about our family and who said what and
what they used to do and how they used to behave, things I had
always wondered about and never knew. And then one came to us
and said, "We want your mother to ride in the family car tomorrow.
Do you have any problem with that?" I said no, and then I just lost
it. I started to cry. I really was overwhelmed by what was happening. It was almost too much, all in one night.

I'm still trying to recover. And there was more. We went to the
funeral and we stood up when they asked for family members to
view the body for the last time. We stood up when they asked for
the grandchildren. We filed by and there Uncle Frank was, sitting
over in the corner, and I reached over on my way past him and I
took his hand and I thanked him for taking care of my grandmother, and he didn't say anything to me except "Okay," and he
squeezed my hand. That was all he had ever said to any of us; he's
not said anything to my mother, to my knowledge, he's still not
said anything to us, but he did do that.

I heard later that when they were trying to get the arrange-
ments together and who should they contact, he kept skipping over
my mother, but then the other sisters said, "Well, wait a minute,
we notice that you're doing this and it's going to stop." This is what
I heard later on. But just before we got in the cars to go to the
cemetery, one of the cousins, Marina, came to me and said, "You
have to understand about Uncle Frank. He was a young man when

all this happened, he was a kid"—apparently a teenager when my mother and father got married—"and that he's just keeping a promise."

Then we got into the car, and I did not have an opportunity to really talk to her about this, but it all makes sense to me. I understand that my mother's father was very much against it then, along with at least two of her brothers, including Frank. But he was very young and may have been just following along with what the older men in the family felt. And who knows what he told his father on his father's deathbed? Who knows what promises he made to these men and that he has kept all these years? Who knows? I have not specifically gotten an answer to this and I may never, but I have a feeling that maybe this man is holding on to beliefs that may not have even been his own.

This is, for me, the essence of racism. This is something that is taught, not something you're born with. This is something that you are taught, you're allowed to latch on to, you adapt it into your own personality and character, and just as you have held on to it, you can also let it go. I don't know what my grandmother might have said to him before she died. Perhaps she said, "I want this crap to stop, and it's going to mean a lot to me before I die to see the family together." Maybe she said that and maybe that's why he has let some of this go. I don't know because I may never get the opportunity to really talk to him. I wish that would happen, but I'm not going to run after this man.

In any case, he is trying very hard to maybe find a way to release himself from this. I don't know; that's the sense I get. But like I said, family members were walking up to me, looking in my face and saying, "Are you Ann's daughter?" They were shocked! Especially the younger ones. They were very, very cordial and very pleasant and they walked up to us. We couldn't come to them; we didn't know who they were. They welcomed us and told us what their names were and where they lived. Some of them gave me their phone number and address. I went home [to New Jersey] last weekend, and Marina and Diana, the twins, and their parents invited us to dinner and we went there for the day. We got down there about maybe one-thirty or so, and we were there until after nine o'clock at night. They cooked a huge Italian meal and pulled out their best silverware, the whole bit. It was beautiful. And the twins were at one time professional singers, they even serenaded us; they couldn't do any more.

At dinner, they were talking about how their grandfather and their father came over from Italy through Ellis Island. I almost lost it because I thought, "Here's my family: one half came over from Italy, like millions and millions of others, on ships and through Ellis Island, immigrants with tags hanging off of them; and the other side came under the ship in chains. That is exactly what my family makeup is, and it was just very difficult for me to keep it together at points, when they talked about their families and what their relatives did and things like that.

It's very hard for me still to reconcile that, to say that this is okay with me. The only reason half of my family came over in chains was because of their skin color and because people had power over them. Instead of being treated like human beings, they were like animals, and it makes me angry. And how I am the embodiment of both people: One half of me society has mistreated in a big way, and the other half of me is that oppressor. This is nothing new. I had thought about this many times, only it didn't hit me with such power because I didn't have the pictures and the names, the faces to go with it. It's one thing to imagine that maybe your relatives came over; it's another thing to hear somebody say, "Yup, this is exactly what happened." It's really quite another thing.

So what am I going to make of this? Do I intend to drag this anger and pain and sadness around with me, or do I intend to complete with it, be done with it, and move on to everything that I can be and be Sally, as much Sally as I possibly can be and the best human being I possibly can be? That's my goal, that's been my goal all along with this. Otherwise, why bother? Toward the end of the evening I was really losing it. I tried to explain to them, maybe it's just all this driving back and forth and the emotional exercise, and they understood that.

After dinner it was also interesting to hear them—not only interesting but difficult—to hear them share the problems they had living in the community where more and more Blacks moved in, how the Blacks were disrespectful to them, next-door neighbors were giving them problems. It was difficult, even though I'm aware that there are many militant Blacks who, just because you are white, will hate you. That's the other side of the coin.

They were saying that we weren't the only ones that had been mistreated, that was part of it, but I also know that they don't really have an understanding of what prejudice is. They said, "We're not prejudiced," and then they said, "Uncle Frank is not prejudiced." *They said this to my mother!* They said, "Frank is not prejudiced, Ann, but he just has a problem with you."

Well, they just don't understand. They're making an attempt, but they have an education process to go through, and perhaps, with enough time and if we can keep the communication lines open, then they may become educated about this issue, but right now it's obvious to me just from that comment that they're not. And that's okay, I'm willing to accept them where they are right now. As long as they do not mistreat me or my mother in any way.

At least my brother and sister and I are being cautiously optimistic. Joe is not. He flat out told me on the phone, he said, "I don't want anything to do with any of them, and if they contact me I will tell them what my feelings are."

And I said, "Well, Joe, you've had many opportunities to do that, and you have not taken them. I understand where you are and I accept you where you are." But I want him to understand that he needs to resolve this at some point in his life.

It's possible that this is his resolution; I strongly doubt it. I don't think Joe has done the work that needs to be done to come to resolve with this. I can almost guarantee you of that. At the Loving Conference [a recent daylong event sponsored by the Interracial Family Circle and where Hobson was a guest panelist], when I commented that my mother's family turned their backs on my mother, I looked over at Joe. His face twisted up and he was crying. The anger and hurt and pain of this is so close to the surface for Joe I can't tell you—and he has not expressed any of it to anyone, so there's no way in the world you're going to tell me that Joe has done the work he needs to do to come to resolve with this. He has not. Where he is now is in serious denial, but, like I said, I accept him, he has every right to be angry, so do we all. Some of us have worked through that anger: myself, one of them, and perhaps Eddie is another.

I had thought about this for a long time, how would it be when

Grandma died, and this was probably the best-case scenario, the one I thought least likely to happen. But it did happen. I walked in there not holding my head in any way rather than who I was, not ashamed in any way. I walked in there thinking hey, if it's going to be business as usual, then I'm down for that; if it's going to be something other, that's wonderful. So at this point right now, if not one of them ever calls me again, I'm okay. I'm really okay. Because I had to do that other work, see, this is what I'm saying, and it's very, very important to do the work. So that I can be okay no matter what they do. Now, I'm willing to be open. Like my brother said, it's on them now.

I'm not going to run around trying to be a family member. If they want to invite me to family functions, I'll make every attempt and effort to come. But if they don't, then I can be okay with that, too; my whole life long I've been responding in a particular way—it's not going to feel uncomfortable or hurtful if none of them ever call me again. I'm not sitting by the phone. With these two cousins, especially, it's been the opposite. They have called, I don't know how many times; they're waiting to come down here. It's almost too much too soon; I need to take this very slowly. I can't all of a sudden be Super Cousin because you saw me for the first time.

After dinner that evening my mother's sister, Mary, who's seventy-four years old, took me into the kitchen and flat out apologized. She said, "I am very sorry for the way the family has behaved toward you. I want the past to be the past, and I look forward to a relationship with you in the future." That is exactly what she said to me. I told her I would share my feelings with her at some point, to really tell her what I went through in my life. And I told her about Joe. I said, "My brother does not feel that way, and you need to know that before you start calling him."

And as Joe said to me, "Now that Grandma died everything's supposed to be hunky-dory." Well, it's not hunky-dory, believe me, it's not. But I am willing to be open about it, and I can let my anger go long enough to express my feelings and to express my desires for the future. I want a relationship with my mother's family. I want very much to understand my roots and to at least get some idea who my ancestors were. And that's doable. I don't want to be over their house every weekend or them at mine—I just want a normal family relationship, if that is possible. But I need to feel free to express my feelings about the past. If they say, "We don't want to talk about that," then we got a problem.

It has really been something, and I'm sure that more will continue to unfold on some level. I look forward to it, but I would like to take it slow, that's all.

CHAPTER III

Neighborhood

I have no idea—even as a psychiatrist, as bright as I am— looking back, why I never fit. But I never did, and the only time I remember being happy is when we lived in a mixed neighborhood and I had mixed friends. And when I say mixed, I mean different cultures as well as race. I've never, ever been happy in an all- white setting.—Saundra Robinson, p.161

Strange as it may seem, where I was born in South Carolina was not just a black community; there were Whites that surrounded us. But they were separate. You were supposed to know your place. We were like friends, but different; they made you feel differ- ent. Even though you might have lived next door, you were still separated by customs, by what the law was. It was something the older Blacks and the older Whites had come up with, and you just knew. I laugh at it now, but I remember that if you went to the neighborhood grocery store, if they gave you change, they would drop it in your hand rather than letting their hand touch yours. It's kind of silly, isn't it? But they would either do that or put it down on the counter. They didn't touch, but yet those same people had Blacks working in their home and taking care of their children and making biscuits for them with those black hands. It wasn't gonna hurt them to touch my hand, but I could have gone in their house and made biscuits for them if I could have made good biscuits, and they would have eaten them.—Emma Baker, p.32

Where I live now, in Oakland, sometimes I wonder when I'm walking down the street and I pass a black person, do they know that I'm part black and [do they] feel comfortable with that? I often notice that when you're passing a person on the street, black people will be more open to you, looking at you, smiling, and saying, "Hi, how's it going?" And you don't know them. I haven't really noticed that so much when I pass white people on the street, and I don't know if that is because black people recognize that I'm part black and feel a connection to that, or white people just are doing what they're doing, or it just happens to be the time of day and the person's mood. I do feel connected in a way to this neighborhood because I am part black, but then again I feel, not really scared, but a little bit hesitant because I am part white, and somebody might resent that.

Having grown up sheltered in Berkeley, I think that when I do eventually end up living somewhere else I'm going to probably be faced with a lot of new situations. My sister had a white boyfriend, and they went to visit his family in New York once. They were staying in his mom's house and everything was fine; they were having a nice visit. Then this neighbor met my sister and thought for a while and came to the mother and said, "You know, there's something strange about her." It must have been something about her features, and they ended up being kicked out of the house, because the mother didn't realize that Caitlin was part black. I have a feeling that's something that I might be faced with, but I haven't really traveled anywhere yet.—Kyria Ramey, p.201

In the environments I grew up with, because people thought I was white, nobody shielded any of their attitudes from me. So I see through the representations a lot of white people make about who they are and what they believe in. I watched that stuff the whole time I was growing up because they didn't know that I was there; they thought I was somebody else.—Jeana Woolley, p.250

When I asked people to tell me about their lives and about their developing sense of a racial self, they often responded by talking about where they had lived and who surrounded them there.

In reading this chapter, it is most important to understand that many people saw their neighborhoods as their first introduction to the world at large. That new neighborhood might have been as small as an apartment complex or a two-block strip of street, as large as an entire town or city. But as soon as they were old enough to step outside of home, they found themselves in a new, more complex world.

For many, neighborhood was where their emerging self-images were first tested. Their parents might never have spoken of race or of difference, but a little white girl down the street may have asked, "Why is your skin dirty all the time?" or a black girl may have asked, "Why do you have such light eyes?" As children, many biracial people were picked on for being different from their neighbors, left behind, threatened, or beat up. Others were held in high esteem, celebrated for their "exotic" looks, for being physically or experientially different from their peers.

While most people I interviewed grew up in predominantly black or predominantly white neighborhoods, some lived in mixed communities. (Racial segregation marks a significant portion of American residential life. According to *American Demographics* magazine, a study by the Knight-Ridder newspaper chain analyzed figures from the 1990 U.S. census and showed that approximately 30 percent of black Americans and 65 percent of white Americans live in racial isolation.)

There are many types of mixed communities. One is the changing neighborhood, usually developing or decaying. Another is the neighborhood integrated by intention. Examples of the latter, where the inhabitants truly accept and enjoy the diversity in their community, seem few and far between. They are fragile, easily affected by real estate trends, changing school resources, and the establishment or disintegration of employment opportunities. A few of these mixed neighborhoods were mentioned by the people in this book—although some say the diversity they knew in their childhood has long since disappeared, its delicate ecology disrupted perhaps by something as small as the departure of one or two families.

At first glance, what could be better for a biracial child than to grow up in such a neighborhood? But more than one person who had grown up in a mixed environment felt bittersweet disappointment once they began to travel or relocated to other types of communities. They realized that the communities they came from—which were relatively untroubled on issues of race—were not the norm, that not everyone felt so easy living among people from other racial groups. In fact, their integrated neighborhoods led them into thinking that race alone did not determine community—a belief which successive experiences repeatedly contradicted.

Many biracial people's most important experience of a neighborhood was to take leave of it. Only after relocating did some of the people interviewed realize what they had been missing (or what they had once had). The new neighborhoods often differed not only racially but also socioeconomically. The move from an all-black community to an all-white one might also mean the move from a middle-class neighborhood to a poor one. The new community's acceptance or rejection of the newcomer could weigh as heavily on matters of class as on race, but how to distinguish which played a bigger role?

Omatteé Carrasco
Age: 31
Residence: Hayward, California
Occupation: Airline ground staff

Omatteé Carrasco and her older sister were raised by their paternal grandparents (whom they called Mama and Papa) in several neighborhoods, which were all in and around Oakland, California. Carrasco's parents had divorced, her mother had moved away, and her paternal grandmother won custody through the courts.

When the family integrated a nearby suburb, neighbors harassed them. A happy home life turned into a troubled adolescence when her grandmother became violent. At one point, in a fury, she tried to shoot Carrasco's sister. Her husband stepped between them and the bullet went through his leg. This was the last straw for Omatteé, who ran away soon after. She was fourteen.

"It was funny," she remembers, "because I'm making this big runaway scene, and my grandfather's behind me in the car staying a block behind. But I knew he was there. He wanted me to go, too, because he would try to make her stop abusing us and she wouldn't. The police would come, and I'm tore up from head to toe, telling them, "I fell down the stairs; my dog did it," things like that. So he wasn't going to stop me from leaving."

Carrasco stayed with her father for the next two years, but felt like an unpaid housekeeper and child-sitter for his new family. Next, she went out on her own, sleeping on park benches at first, staying with friends and in flophouses. She worked in a bubble-gum factory for a while and had her first child, a son, at sixteen. She found an alternative high school that would accommodate her need to work a full-time job and got her diploma there. In 1984 she and her son's father married, and have since had three more children.

When I was thirteen months old, my older sister and I went to live with my father's parents in Oakland. My grandparents were basically middle-class black. Not upper-middle-class, not professional, but my grandfather was a truck driver and union truck drivers were making outstanding money in those days. He raised us well. They provided for us really well. We actually moved to Hayward, just outside of Oakland, but we didn't last long—they ran us out of Hayward.

I think I was five, but I had the late birthday so I wasn't in kindergarten right away. But my sister was in school, and I remember the neighbors would spray-paint our house with obscenities, and they threw eggs on my grandfather's Cadillac.

Back then, Hayward was all white, very segregated. We were the only Blacks living there that I had any knowledge of. I recently met a woman who had attempted to live there back in the late sixties and had the same experiences. They burned crosses. They still do but not like they were doing back then. And my interpretation of white people was they spat on me and they threw rocks. We couldn't play in our own backyard; they would throw things over our fence. They scared my grandmother to death. I believe that she would have stuck it out, because my grandmother was a strong black woman—five foot nothing and full of fire—but my grandfather worked nights and we would be there alone in the house, and he was going to lose his job if he had to keep coming home from work because they'd thrown big rocks through our living-room window.

We lived there less than a year—maybe six, seven months. What really made us move was an incident that happened with my sister on her way home from school. Some older white man grabbed her and told her that she was a little nigger bitch. She should have been home and Mama, that's what I called my grandmother, went down to the corner to find out why she wasn't home yet and found this white man holding her and shaking her and calling her names. That's when we left. Just like that. We moved back to Oakland, but higher up the hill, where it was basically all-black—some Portuguese and Puerto Rican, but no white.

We didn't play with any of the neighborhood kids in Oakland

because my grandmother was strict and really, really sheltered us. To a large extent, I don't understand, but to an extent, I do, because as soon as she did start allowing us to go and play at the playground after school, how many times did she have to come down there and pull kids off of us who had pulled handfuls of our hair out? One girl almost peeled the skin off my sister's chest. This one female was telling my sister that "your mother's poor white trash," and my sister said, "Well, your mother's a black bitch," and they went at it. I was raised that if my sister goes at it with anyone, then I'm going to have to go at it, too, and every time we got involved with kids, that's what would happen.

The kids just knew there was something different, something wrong with us. My sister is closer to your complexion. Black kids back then didn't have long hair. They had very short, nappy, nappy hair. And the first thing they would do is try to rip our hair out, because it was long. So they knew that there had to be something, and their parents probably told them that somebody's white and that's how they got that hair or that's why my sister was so light. But I could not have told them that my mother was white because I didn't know. I used to stop them and say, "No, my mom is black and here comes my mama right now," because I thought Mama and Papa were my mom and dad.

When I was young, the only contact I had with my father was when I saw him in courtroom battles. He was trying to get custody of us back from my grandmother, but he never won. He tried, and he tried and tried and tried. And I believe what made him stop trying was dragging us through it—and Mama made it dirty. She made it really dirty.

Mama couldn't stand the fact that my mother and my sister's mother was white, and that my father had then gone and married *another* white woman and had *more* little mixed-up kids. She could not stand it. I'm saying that this was not *tolerated*—not where I grew up, not by my experience of life, not from my family experiences, not from my community, school, nowhere. It was unacceptable.

My father used to tell us, "I wanted you to have the best of both worlds." I never understood that concept. I was grown before I understood what he was trying to say to me. As a child I never understood that because there was a time I was angry about why can't I just be black or why can't I just be white? Why do I have to be mixed up? I used to go to school, and when they said, "Choose your race," I would choose everything or I refused to choose any, and it got me expelled from school.

The woman told me if I did not check the box to say I was black I was going to be suspended, and she had to suspend me, too. But I just wouldn't check it. I was going through a peaceful protest type thing within my own self because I didn't fit in any-where. I really didn't. My adolescent years, early seventies, you had your black student union, you had the Latino student union, the Asians had their caucus, everybody had something, and no one wanted me. The black student union people told me straight out, "You are not black enough." I was ridiculed as a child for the way I spoke. Black people would come and tell me, "You talk like a white girl. You think you're white." Because of the way I speak? I went to the same schools they went to. It's grammar. It's English. I don't be hanging on the streets, you know what I'm saying? And my grandparents taught me properly. Proper English was always enforced in the home.

Even though I did get a lot of rejection from Blacks, they were also the only people that accepted me. This started way back, when masters were getting with slaves, and who took care of those little mulatto children? The black community did. I am accepted a lot more in the black community than I was growing up, but am I accepted totally? No. And that became really clear when my sister and my dad and I were extras in a movie [*Made in America*] that was shot in Oakland recently. It starred Whoopi Goldberg and was about an interracial child. It was so exciting to be involved in it all, but I could not believe one thing that happened; I heard stuff that I hadn't heard since I was a kid.

One female was getting so angry because it appeared that my sister and I were getting better scenes than she was getting, and I don't know if she intended for us to hear the comments she was making or she thought we couldn't hear and so felt free to talk. She was making comments like, "Well, I guess they want them out there because of their hair or their skin."

I'm like, "I'm still just an extra, just like you," but I will say that I did get closer in and it might have had to do with those things. My sister and I were wondering, "Do you think they want us a little more visible because they're going to be addressing this issue of this child being interracial?'' See, when you look at me, you can just think, "Oh, well, she's black," but if you really look, you'll start thinking, "Hm, she's not all black." And I think they might have pulled us a little closer in to get that, to show that there are multiethnic people in the neighborhood or walking down the street.

So we had done a scene in which we're shopping for books in a bookstore, and Whoopi Goldberg and her daughter are talking. It was one of the scenes I liked the most. I got to be close to her, I got to spend a lot of time with her, see the kind of person that she is. The female that's talking about my sister and I in a negative manner is also in this scene. She's on the other side of the row of books. When we finished shooting that night, the director told everyone, "Remember exactly what you have on. You must come back tomorrow in exactly the same thing. Ladies, don't forget the same colored socks, don't forget your rings that you have on, and come back with the same hair. Okay?" I can picture this female, she has beautiful hair, good length, at least as long as mine, but it was coarse, there's texture to her hair, thick and curly.

Do you know how she came back the next day? Totally permed and processed. In fact, she was in there, swinging her hair around, talking about how her hair was "straighter than straight." I'm dying! *I'm dying!* I'm like, "Did you hear him when he told us to come back the same?" I mean, her hair was gorgeous, like how Janet Jackson wears her hair, really straight and curled under—I think they call it the wrap, something like that. Gorgeous, sleek, black, shiny, nothing wrong with it. But that's not what she looked like yesterday when she looked like a black woman that has black hair. Now she looked like a black woman with processed hair. The director called us into the set, he took one look at her, and sent us all right back out.

He wouldn't shoot the scene. He even got her to try and make her hair go back to the way it was yesterday, and she lied and told him she could. The rest of us are back in the extras' holding room, and she's up there with a curling iron. I'm like, "You know as well as I do that is not going to make your hair go back to what it was before you permed it."

We didn't get to redo the scene. I'm hoping that they had

enough from the two days before, because otherwise that scene might not be in the movie at all. It was so important to her to show my sister and I that her hair could be as straight as ours and we knew that. My sister and I knew that. "This reminds me of high school," I said. "This is how they acted when we were kids growing up: the petty jealousy trips."

I never envied anybody. I never have. I have admired people, but when I really admire someone, there's a reason. But I've never just envied people, and I've often felt that I was being envied for no reason. Black women can do a lot more with their hair than they could even five years ago. The last two years, they've made incredible advances, black women going around having hair down to here if they want hair down to here, you know? I felt a relief from that. I don't get looked at and sneered at and jeered at as much as I did when I was younger.

Neisha Wright

Age: 28

Residence: Glen Cove, New York

Occupation: Gymnastics coach and student teacher

Neisha Wright's mother and father met in a Greenwich Village nightclub. Neisha's mother, who is white, was pregnant with her first son, Toby, at that time, but was no longer with the baby's father (also white). Wright's father assumed paternity of Toby while he was still in utero; his sense of being Toby's father even extended to later custody battles with Neisha's mother over all the children they were raising.

The young family bought a house in the Long Island suburbs, in a white neighborhood. They were not received well, and in 1965, Ebony *magazine ran an eight-page feature article about their house being firebombed by local teens.*

When we met at her apartment, Wright showed me her pictures from elementary school. She pointed out that in her third-grade class photograph, the year before she moved with her mother to New Mexico, all the children's faces are white, except for one—hers. In the next year's photo-graph, all the faces are brown, except for three white children standing to one side. "Look how well I fit in," she said, pointing to the second picture. "I'm as brown as everyone else."

I was born in East Meadow, Long Island, December 1963. Not very far away from here. Lived there till third grade. It was a fairly average, normal existence, except for things that happened like the firebombing that was written about in *Ebony*. I don't remember that particular incident—I was too young—but I remember getting taunted on the way to school. I remember people outside our house and just vague, different memories of living there.

From East Meadow I remember the cross burning on our lawn. This was the late sixties, and it was kids. Kids fueled by their parents' racism. Their parents knew enough to keep it inside the house when they said, "All those fucking niggers, the nigger-lover woman down the street, I hate them, I'd like to do this." And the kids would go, "Oh, yeah, let's do that." They didn't think up these things by themselves; they heard it from their parents. I got beat up a lot. My father didn't know about it. I got pushed around a lot, and my older brother's thing was, "Let's not worry Mom and Dad. Let's not tell them."

I remember being teased and pushed around by older boys. And my big brother, Toby, was my hero. He always came to my rescue. The memories are pretty vague. Occasionally, I have floods of memories, things I know I remember but I've blocked out for years and years and years.

I don't remember thinking life was completely unpleasant, ever, throughout my whole childhood into adulthood. I remember thinking, well, this unpleasant episode really sucks, but never that life itself was terrible and unfair and unpleasant. Kids in the neighborhood were like a Doberman pinscher. Sometimes they were your best friend, and if they got mad, the racial slurs were flying. Some were consistently my friends, some were consistently my enemies, and I liked that because I knew where I stood.

I remember hearing the word *nigger* for the first time when I was about six years old. I'm sure I had heard it before, but it was the first time I knew what it meant. My father had left by then, and a bunch of kids were taunting my older brother and me, saying, "It's about time we drove that nigger father of yours out of town," and "Your father's nothing but a nigger."

And I went to my father when he came to visit and I said, "What does that mean? Why are they saying this about you? I don't understand. Did you do something bad?" I really don't remember what his response was, beside the fact that he hugged me.

The hug was like, despair is what it felt like. Like, tired of fighting kind of hug. And this was too much. Having to explain this to his daughter was too much. And he was feeling my pain and his own pain. My parents went through it from day one. You know, the phone rang constantly. We changed our phone number I don't know how many times, but that's not what broke them up.

What broke them up was that they were different people. My mother became a hippie, and my father was trying desperately to assimilate—desperately—into white mainstream culture. My father was trying not to hide from his ethnicness, but make it invisible by being bigger than his race. Does that make any sense? He was trying to get ahead for who he was.

They split up, and my mother got custody when I was in the third grade. We moved to Albuquerque, New Mexico, where I went to fourth grade. There were Latins, Mexicans mostly, Indians, a few black kids, a few white kids, and me. I wasn't teased anymore. People didn't call me names anymore. People assumed I was Mexican or something else, and it was okay because everybody else was brown, too. It wasn't an oddity. People didn't stare at me. In New York, I got a lot more of that than anything in New York: I got a lot of stares.

After fourth grade I got tossed around a bit—my whole sense of time is kind of messed up until high school. My father, although he had agreed to the custody conditions—or maybe he didn't and he just lost in court—had a hissy fit and came and kidnapped us. We were kidnapped back and forth quite a few times. The first time was after the end of fourth grade. He came to visit us for the summer and took us with him. He took all of us because my older brother Toby was his adopted son and he had raised him. Also, my mother was so firm in the fact that "all my children are brothers and sisters, it doesn't matter who their father is, they come from my body," that he would have traumatized us even more by separating us. I think he recognized that—or it might have just been a fluke. I don't know that he was conscious of the trauma he was causing, or I don't think he would have done it. It was a horrible thing. It was horrible.

I ended up doing most of fifth grade in Jamaica, Queens, where my grandmother lived. I lived with my grandmother and my two brothers. And my father was there sometimes, but my father was trying to dodge the subpoena person. So he was like a shadow. He'd be there all of a sudden, and then he'd be gone. So my grandmother was really raising me for that year. I always felt really close, really connected to my grandmother, but except for her, even on that side of the family, I was devoid of black culture.

My grandmother taught me how to cook chitlins and pigs' feet. My grandmother tried to teach me how to Double Dutch and just do things and speak in ways that were identifiable as black, which my father doesn't do. When I started to pick up the "jive" that year, my father got very upset with me and told me I sounded uneducated and like I was a street kid.

I think my father was raised by his father to believe that assimilating into the white culture was the only way to make it. Obviously, my father and his brother both married white women; that's got to tell you something about the way they were raised. My grandmother, on the other hand, seemed extremely black-identified. She was the only person who gave me any sense of my black culture at all. My father gave me this sort of worldly kind of thing, if anything at all, in my childhood. But I definitely felt totally alienated and isolated from black culture when I was growing up.

Brad Simpson
Age: 31
Residence: San Francisco, California
Occupation: Medical center administrative assistant

Brad Simpson describes his father as "asphalt black" and from Chicago, Illinois; his mother is white and from Bend, Oregon. Simpson, the oldest of three sons, spent time in both states. Until he was nine, when his parents separated, the family lived with his paternal grandparents in a predominantly black Chicago neighborhood. From there, he went to Oregon with his mother and brothers. Simpson lived there until he graduated from college—except for a year he spent studying in France. He then went into the Peace Corps, spending three years in Zaire. Before settling in San Francisco, he returned to Oregon to work as an agent for the U.S. Immigration and Naturalization Service.

In Chicago, there were a lot of racial and cultural cues, like African art around the house and things that were instilled to be important to us. But at that point my dad's family were still trying to break me into being this Jehovah's Witness. Jehovah's Witnesses aren't supposed to salute the flag, and at that time, people were saluting the flag and going through the Pledge of Allegiance before class, and sometimes I would do it, sometimes I wouldn't. I was really wishy-washy. So they just knew that something was up with this person—we gotta break him—so they were always beating that on me more than any other thing. That was more from my father; he was more hard-core. He'd been broken by it, and he wanted to see me subjected to the same.

When I was eight or nine, Dad was caught having an extramarital affair, and Mother couldn't stand it. She'd had enough of his abuse—I guess he was an alcoholic then, too—and she grabbed the kids and said, "I'm going back to the West Coast." She split with us, and that was the last time he and I saw each other for twelve years.

Once we left Chicago and moved out to Salem, the energy changed a lot. Part of it was that I was extremely angry. I was blaming myself for my parents' split-up, and so I was a hell-raiser, totally. I went in and trashed a couple schools and got suspended and then thrown out. Trashed the restroom area, just raging, breaking whatever you get your hands on and sabotaging. I put the dispenser of napkins up on the door, soaking wet, so the next person that walks through gets it on their head. I was angry, I was always fighting. But I was going through the pecking order. You know, you get to a new school, new kid on the block.

You show up and it's like, "Oh, who's this?" And they're just going to try to get under your skin on any level they can find. It's not just racial, you know. Kids got to find their pecking order just to see what you can take and what you can't take. And so that whole first year I just fought, and I'm not much of a fighter, besides verbally.

I can remember being scarred definitely when we moved. When the other kids discovered that the word *nigger* freaked me out—at that time, in the middle to early sixties—when they finally found that right little hole to put that knife, I was always constantly fighting. Fighting, fighting, fighting. They called me nigger, I'd have to fight. And once that starts with kids it does not stop until you finally accept "It doesn't mean anything to me." Then you move on to the next level.

The racial mix of the school was very, very white. Salem, Oregon? Homogeneous zone. In those communities they are oppressed extremely, to the point that they're so brainwashed it's like, don't make waves. I know, because I was born in Portland. After I came back from the Peace Corps, I spent two years in Portland again, and I went to school in Eugene. I lived in that area most of my life. I *know* how those people think.

Why is it in every one of those communities—Portland, Eugene, or Salem—if you can find any kind of diverse population, they always live in the most broken-down areas? They go to the shittiest schools. What kind of person can you produce after they get out of twelve years of shitty schooling and they can't even speak fucking English correctly? Whose fault is that? Theirs?

My own school wasn't like that. It was a public school, but don't forget that's my mother's side of the family and they lived in the white neighborhood. We lived with them because we didn't have any place to go. My mother was struggling—by then she had finished her school for nursing—just trying to raise three boys and trying to pull out of the nightmare any way she could, and so she went to the family for support. There were years where we were staying with our grandparents through the summers and those kinds of things, just to make ends meet.

Eventually we moved to Bend, Oregon. Even more intensely redneck. But I guess for me my saving grace was I was the total athlete. I was on the track team, and I found my acceptable niche in that intensely redneck area. If you're an athlete or you sing or you dance, as a minority, oh, things are fine, you work right in. My last name's Simpson, they used to call me O. J. all the time, because during then O. J. was rushing for all the yards, and I played on the football team. I walk down the streets now and people still call me O. J. to this day. It's like, oh, get over that shit. Give me a break!

But yeah, especially through high school I can recollect having dreams that I was white, totally lily white. Not daydreams; night dreams, when you're out. There's a couple—where I'd be walking through a store and I'd be fitting in with everybody, I'd be acceptable, and things-would-be-fine kind of dreams. That went on for the longest time, and I never really reconciled that until I moved to the Bay Area, with a large black community here that's allowed to express itself and be out. It's sad because I recognize now that I took so much abuse, and I used to laugh along with some of those derogatory comments. I worked on a construction crew up there, trying to make money for school or summer, and you're working with a lot of rednecks and, "Oh, why don't you nigger-rig this? Oh! Sorry!" Everybody would freeze. And I'd laugh, just laugh it off. *Now* I'd put that person in their place immediately for using that kind of term, and then we'd move on.

For the longest time, I thought I was white, but then every now and then there would be awkward social situations at work, like "nigger-rig," or just blatant. We're playing kickball, just the kids, and the ball goes over a fence. I go over to get it, and the person in this yard has the ball in his hands, and he won't give it to me. I'm like, "Hey, we're trying to play kickball, cough it up. What's up? Do you want to come play?"

"Oh, I want to get me some of that dark meat."

At that point I was in junior high, very easily intimidated by somebody who was an adult. He threw the ball down and started running after me, and I ran off terrified. He jumped over the fence and he was screaming and hollering, "Whoo! We're going to have some dark meat on the grill tonight!" And I remember that as vivid as if it happened yesterday. He had to be at least twenty-five. Big barrel-chested white guy. It's sad, because I don't forget that.

I talked about this with my brothers. We all were going through the same kind of frustrations, and that was my only support network at that time. We'd get together and we'd just joke about the racism, and that would be a therapist kind of outlet for us. I think it really saved us from getting in much more serious problems, besides having that athletic outlet that kept me good and tired. If I didn't, no telling what kind of shit I would have gotten into. But high school wasn't an unhappy time. I was the jock, you know, I had a lot of things at my access, plus I had a lot of things going for me photographywise. I was head photographer my junior and senior year. Both of my cups were full on extracurricular and work. I was happy, I was dating, but at that same time I knew I could not ever settle down and live in that area. I could not stand to deal with that kind of intense racism. There was not anything there that I could identify with and be comfortable with in terms of really being able to identify with people who can understand what you're going through. So I knew I had to finish school and get the fuck out of there.

Then I went to the University of Oregon in Eugene for two years. At U of O there was no real diversity. It was sad; it's so fucking sad. As much as I tried to remain blind to it at a certain point, I would literally go walking down the main thoroughfare of campus, and *every* person of color, with the exception of Asians, was there on athletic scholarship. Every single one. It was really sad.

That's no representation of what's happening out here in our society, you know? Even if you go to Eugene, there's a large Latino population. Where the hell are they? Why aren't they in there on scholarship so other people can get an example of what's happening? It's not well rounded. When you go to the admissions office of any school, that's the real crunch of who we accept and who we don't accept and how you get in and how culturally biased are our tests, and what are our requirements and what are ways to meet those requirements, and if you don't meet those requirements, how can you work up so you can meet those requirements? It's exploitation clear and above. If I would have had a little bit more education then, I would have raised total hell on that campus when I should have been raising hell, when it had much more cutting edge to it. Now it's sad. It's got the business school and I see three fourths of the student body walking by in suit and tie, and you ask them about fiery issues and it's like, "Oh, no, I don't want to break out of the status quo because I need this certain grade so I can get a job with XYZ company."

After two years I went to France. At the time I was majoring in international studies, and I started to speak French. I was like, I'm young, I don't have anything tying me down, why am I learning this crazy language, no one here speaks it. Let's go to France and check it out.

Going there changed some of my views about the world. The French have a bubble it takes a good three, four months to break through. Once you get inside you have a friend for that entire time you're there—and that did happen—but it takes a lot longer. They've got a large immigrant population that comes up from Morocco, Algeria, Tunisia, just to do strictly gut work for three to six months a year and then go back home. And so it was with the offspring of those people that I pretty much found a haven with. I didn't *only* hang out with them, because I did have my French contacts, but in a certain sense it did give me a different identification. The most classic example that really brought it to me—and I think this was the first time I ever, as an adult, cried over a racial issue—was trying to get into a club. Me, a couple other Americans who were white, and a couple of my Moroccan friends try to get in, and it's all full, according to the bouncer. We decide we're not leaving.

"What do you mean it's full?"

Oh, well, they changed their idea. "Well, we just don't have any more tickets. You have to have a ticket to get in." Lo and behold, somebody else comes up, a French person, and they buy a ticket and they get in.

And so we're like, "What's up with that? Well, we can still buy a ticket, right?"

"Oh, no, no, no, no, no."

They seemed to be wishy-washy on it, and so, as an experiment, we just let a couple of the [white] Americans go, and I tucked in behind them. The Americans buy a couple of tickets, bouncer lets them through. He comes to me: "You're not getting in."

I was like, "What's up with that? I'm American like them." I got my passport—which you carry all the time in France—boom! Oh, I'm an American.

"You can go in."

I didn't go in. I was like, "Why can't these guys go in?"

"They're Moroccan. They're dirty people." That's what he said. Then I lost it. I started breaking down. I almost grabbed that person and was going to throttle him right there. He was going to lose his life or pry my hands off his neck. And it all broke down. We started throwing rocks at the place, and there was anger floating around, and it was obvious what was going on.

There's the same shit here in this country. Look who does the gardening. If you ever look at the Latino population when it comes into clash, or mixing in with this culture, what happens? The Latino population gets pushed over into certain pockets, and that's where they go to school and take care of business. It's still the same shit.

After France I went back to Eugene. I wanted to finish my last two years of international studies. By then I tried to develop more of a world view and get outside of our context of borders and the United States and into what's happening around the world and equate that to what's happening here.

My friendships at school didn't really change. I mean, the available pool there, everyone's a student, so that whole dynamic never really changed. On top of that, I was still on the track team, so I still had a lot of minority, quote-unquote, people-of-color friends. How I was accepted by guys on the team depended. I was a distance runner, let's not forget that, and most people of color who are ethnic minorities, especially on a track team, have this cultural bias where they don't think that they can be distance runners. So already I was off in the white-boy crowd. If you want to talk three miles on the track or ten thousand meters—six miles—it's strictly pretty much an all white-boy thing unless you're from Africa. Then for some reason it changes. So on that level I was rejected just because I didn't work out with those guys. Also I wasn't from LA, like a lot of the black students were. I don't go through the same kinds of things. They knew, they could see that.

Now I view myself as straddling the bridges. On one side my family's white, the other side is black, and it's funny because for me to even say those words—just what I told you, my family breakdown—was very, very difficult for me, especially in junior high. Now it's just like, it just comes out and it's very natural, it's very flowing. I'm a mixture of both.

I like to have the ability to go into either of the two extremes, the white side or the black side, go in and be with the boys watching the football game and go in and "Hey, homey, what's going on!" and immediately identify pure black and just be in that atmosphere and get that support, because that's important. But then on the other side, I still like to be able to have my white contacts and live my life in that area, too. That's what I've been brought up in and that's nice, too.

The white example would be basketball. I play with people who I met through a friend I made in the Peace Corps. I'm the only minority in the whole building, with the exception of the person who opens the door, the director of the gym, but our group is all white boys.

On paperwork I'll say I'm black, because they only give you "white" or "black" or they give you "other," but at that point in time, there's a certain amount of benefit you can get [from "black"]. If you put "white," you're in there with everybody else and their damn granny, and I know when I walk through the door, I know they're not *thinking* that. So I put black on everything, even though when they see me it's like, "There's obviously some mixture there, but you're not asphalt black, either." So you try to use it. It can work to advantage with the current system that we have.

Valur Edvardsson
Age: 25
Residence: Atlanta, Georgia
Occupation: Telemarketing team manager

Valur Edvardsson's letter was one of only five responses to the many ads I'd placed in several southern newspapers. He wrote that he'd been born and raised in Iceland and that when he came to the U.S., he'd had "to learn how to be black."

Because he often gets quizzical looks when he mentions his birthplace, he brought along an oversize picture book of Iceland to our interview, in case I wanted to know what it looked like.

Edvardsson's mother became pregnant with him when she was seventeen. She was in Denmark, continuing her schooling as he says many Icelandics do (Denmark once governed Iceland), and she met his father. An American, he was in architecture school there after a tour in Germany for the U.S. Army. Edvardsson says his father was determined to stay in school despite the pregnancy. His mother concluded that a future together looked bleak and went back home to Iceland. At eighteen she gave birth to Valur, her first son.

When I think back on my mother being eighteen, having me, I thought that was so old. Now I look at girls that are eighteen, and I'm like, they're having kids? So I think back, my mother was just young and crazy.

So she went back to Iceland and she was pregnant with me, and my father stayed in Denmark and continued school. Of course, everybody in Iceland is white. There might have been one or two Blacks in all of Iceland, and the population probably at that point was about 175,000 people, and there was a U.S. military base there, in Keflavík, so about the only Blacks that were there were on the base. Everybody else was just Icelandic and living their Icelandic life, and so she went back home. It's just the past few years she was talking about how, at first, her family was kind of upset that she was with a black guy, and then she had me and everybody was happy that she had her kid.

About six months later she met a military guy, this white guy, Barry, who was really young at the time, maybe twenty or something. He had just joined the navy and they shipped him off to Iceland, and every weekend the navy guys would go out to town and mingle with the women. So I guess she met him at a club or someplace, and they fell madly in love and got married a few months later. And so they're doing their own little thing in Iceland, and back in Denmark my father meets another white woman and he has my sister.

My stepfather [Barry] was with my mother since I was six months old, and when I was a little kid, we moved to California for a couple years, to Thousand Oaks, which was right next to L.A. When I was a third grader there, I started having little trips that I'm different from my brothers and sisters. That's when I started to think about it. It wasn't a major deal at all. It wasn't nothing that was on my mind every day or every night or whatever.

And then my mother, when we were in California, she came out with this picture: "This is your real father."

I was like, "No."

"This is your real father, and I met him in Denmark, blah-blah-blah." I distinctly remember that. I was surprised and I was sort of crying, just bawling my eyeballs out, and I think back now and I have no idea why I was crying because it wasn't like she was saying, "He left me." She wasn't saying anything like that. She was just like, "This is him and look at him and I met him here." I don't know if I was crying because my image of what the family was now was not what it was—I don't know if I could have had deep thoughts like that when I was little, but I remember crying.

On our way back to Iceland, my real father happened to be in D.C., so my mom said, "Barry and the white kids, go to Iceland and we'll meet you up there and we're going to let Valur meet his father." So I met my father. I first met him when I was ten years old. I was like, "Oh yes, this is my real dad." I got this big pride thing: "He's like me!" And I started identifying with the color that I had. That was a big thing, the color. After about a month of being in D.C., we went back to Iceland.

But in Iceland, I really started thinking and started having my little quirks of, "You're not my father," when my stepfather pissed me off and was scolding on me. Then I can remember my brother having the trips, "Well, you're the black one," and that's when everything started coming out of the woodwork as far as me being different. And it still wasn't a problem in the sense that I didn't feel bad at all or ashamed or missing something, until I started turning fourteen.

One day my brother said, "That's because you're black," or something. He was three years younger than me, we're both little kids, and you know kids are vicious at that age. Plus I used to always beat up on him anyways, so he deserved to say that to me.

But he said that to me, and that really upset me. That was the only thing I can remember that was kind of off-kilter as far as the color thing, because everybody up there's white. I mean, the whole family was white, everybody was white, but I was just one of the bunch—it was no big deal. Plus I grew up speaking Icelandic. And there's no dialect changes in Icelandic at all; there's no southern, northern, there's no prejudice, nobody's shunning you for that, there's no history books saying this or that, there's no TV, nothing, you're just another person—with a tan.

The only thing in Iceland, though, is that there's no Blacks up there, or anybody of color, so that when they see you, they just have a good stare at you. There's no prejudice, there is none at all because they haven't had the history to build up the prejudice of why they're better or whatever. I think when Icelandics go to Europe or to the United States, they see Blacks as maybe exotic or different, not as something that's less than or worse or crazy. But an American White might think that in the back of their head, no matter how unprejudiced they are.

I can remember one time being at a movie theater with my uncle. We were just watching the movie and some kid in the back goes, "Sjadu svertingjan!," which means, "Look at that black guy down there!" I turn around, it was just another mixed kid like me. I was real little, maybe in first grade, and I said to my uncle, "Look at him, he looks just like me." And it was just really strange that he said that out of the blue. He was with his little buddies or something; he might have been probably ten or twelve or something.

That just sticks out in my mind as another thing that made me start thinking about how I was different.

At fourteen my stepfather was stationed in Norfolk, Virginia, so we were going to live in Virginia Beach. I started really thinking about, "Oh, I can't wait till we move to the United States, black women, black women," that's all I was thinking about.

And then—this is when my mind starts reeling on the differences—I can remember coming off the airport in Norfolk, Virginia, and the first thing that hit me was the heat. I was like, "Oh my God, it's so hot," because in Iceland, it's like fall in New York or something all the time. And here were all these bugs, and in Iceland there's flies and a few spiders and stuff, a couple of earthworms, that's about all the insects we have up there. I can remember everything was just a big foreign experience all of a sudden, because when I was in the United States before, I was a little kid and all my thoughts were just playing. I wasn't into the culture as I was this time, because now I was much older.

Driving from the airport to the hotel, I'm sitting in the front seat with my mother, she's in the middle, my stepfather is driving. We stop at a light and these black guys, the construction workers, are on the side of the road, and one guy nods his head. Then we go to another light and another guy does the same thing, and I'm like, "Hey man, all these guys are saying hi to me!"

A few months later I met a black guy, and he told me, "You're in the United States now. And when you're in school, you got to do what the black people do, this little nod that means 'Hi.' "

And so this is when I started to learn how to be black, because I was basically white, according to my peers. In fact, my hair was all long, it was down to my shoulders, and a lot of people thought I was a girl. So I had my hair that style and went to ninth grade and just black people everywhere, that's all I remember, just black people and I just gotta be like them, and my friend, this guy who befriended me, this black guy who lived in our neighborhood in the military housing, he was telling me everything about black people, "You gotta do this and gotta do that, and don't say this and do this and do that."

I remember specifically the nodding of the head, shaking

hands, and being strong and not taking stuff. I remember thinking, This is like a big club. It's like you're part of the black club now, and you're different from everybody else, you're not with the white club anymore. Well, no. The white people didn't seem like a club, they just seemed like there's people everywhere, and the black people were a club that you had to join and you had to do certain things to be part of that club, and if not, you would be chastised or joked—which was a term I learned.

For the next two years, I had to learn how to be black because I was discovering white people would not interface with me. Now all of a sudden the white girls in school—not that all of a sudden I wanted white girls or something—the white girls and the white guys, they were just on their own, they were just different people now, and I was all of a sudden placed into the black club. And I thought that was really strange, coming from Iceland where everybody would just talk to everybody else.

Okay, I'm learning how to be black and all the black ways. Had a black girlfriend, and that was really different and neat and all exciting just because it was different. Of course, all my girlfriends were black all of a sudden, because there was no interfacing with white people except for casual stuff in the classrooms. No real friends or anything.

I felt like I'd lost a whole set of humans that I would interface with, a whole set of people I could share ideas with and talk to. I thought it was a shame. And then I really felt bad, too, that now I'm forced to be in this thing with all these other people, and I have to act like this, and if I don't act like this, they'll joke you, and they did—they were vicious back then. "Oh, why do you talk so white?" "Why you gotta do that?" "Why you live with a whole white family?" "Don't you feel different living with them white people?" You know, all that stuff, and I had to learn how to talk like that, too. I'm serious; I had to learn how to talk like that. When I do talk that way, I feel like I'm on a charade. I feel like an actor, like I'm acting black, because I have to be part of the black club. I'm being real honest here, and I feel good that I can talk. If you were black or white I'd have to hold back on some of the things that I'm saying.

But I'm sixteen now, and this is where it really gets good. My real father, Edward, he's done school, had another kid with a

Danish woman, went to England, met another white lady, moved to Miami, and had two kids. In 1980 Miami was one of the fastest-growing cities of the United States, and by this time he's a full-fledged architect, going to start his own business.

I'm this rebellious teenager now, going to do what I want to do and go where I want to go. I'm supposed to go visit my father the summer before eleventh grade. Me and my mother are arguing constantly, and I'm like, "I'm just going to live down there with him," and she's like, "Fine."

So I moved down there, and all of a sudden I'm this almost-grown person invading on this family. When I moved to Miami, it seemed to me like black people in Miami are *black* black. Black, black, black, black. And I mean colorwise and culturallywise and everythingwise. I guess they haven't had a chance to really integrate, as we know in the South or in the North. Of course, there are some light-skinned Blacks down there, and then you've got your Whites, the Jewish Whites, and then you have *all* these Hispanics that look like me. I'm like, Huh! I'm in *my* land now.

And it was so funny: I went there and all of a sudden—this was really strange—I wasn't a part of the black crowd anymore, at all. They wouldn't associate with me, in the sense that I wasn't a peer of theirs. I was just some spic now, I was some mixed Hispanic, whatever—nobody knew what I was. So my peers now were all Hispanics, and I knew people that looked just like me, all light-skinned and curly hair and all varying features, a spectrum between white and black. These became my friends, and I was with them and everything was cool with these people because none of them, in all their varying shades of colors, had any qualms about who you were. You were just somebody that was not black or you weren't white, and I fit most comfortable with humans when I was living in Miami because of that peer stuff.

Even when the Latinos found out I wasn't Hispanic, it was no big deal. I was mixed, and the thing is in Miami, the father might be a dark-skinned Puerto Rican and the mother might be your complexion, and it just doesn't matter. Everybody's just a big soup bowl of people, and I was part of that. At that point I started yearning for someone that was mixed. I wanted to have some-body—I was into the girl thing, of course—I wanted to have my girlfriend or my wife be mixed so I could talk about all the little trips I've had and everything. But what was I supposed to say? "What are you? What are you? Are you mixed?"

People would ask me that, and people would come up to me speaking Spanish because I used to work at Burger King down there. And I'm like, "I don't speak any Spanish." In fact I was the only person in the whole place that didn't speak Spanish. I did learn some Spanish: *"El hamburguesa con queso?"* The hamburger with cheese. I had to learn all that stuff, and, of course, I learned some of the cusswords.

Then my father decided, "Okay, well, time for you to go back to Virginia, because your mother raised you and she deserves to see you graduate from high school." So I went back, and now I'm back in Virginia and all these black people claim they're so black. I'm like, "You're not black; you don't understand what black is. Black people are *black* people. They're not light-skinned with curly hair and everything."

I remember talking to people like this: "If you looked in Miami, you would know what black people are. If you were down there, they'd just think you were another Puerto Rican or spic." I don't say that because I'm prejudiced, it's just a word. But it kind of pissed me off that they had this big pride trip, you know? I mean, Blacks as light as you saying, "I'm so black and bump the white people and blah-blah-blah." And I'm like, "You don't even know what black is." After living in Miami, I had this big attitude that I knew now, suddenly, the races.

CHAPTER IV

School

In school, everyone would say, "What are you?" I was called Zebra and Oreo. I also got things like "African bootyscratcher" because of my mother being from Africa. In social studies, someone brought in a zebra skin, and one kid was like, "Oh look, it's Joy."—Joy Zarembka, p.324

I was new at school, and no one spoke to me at first. But the black kids saw me not hanging out with the white kids and not trying to behave as though I was a white girl. And they paid attention to different things that happened in the classroom. For example, when we did our reports in American History, I did mine on how Abraham Lincoln was a racist. That went over really well with the teacher. But those little things got around, and by the twelfth grade a couple people talked to me in passing, and then it grew from there, so by the time I graduated from high school I had some friends.—Zenobia Kujichagulia, p.278

My high school English teacher asked me to come up to her desk just before class was over, and she asked me if I had a job. I told her, "No, I don't have a job."

And she said, "Well, I've got a job for you if you'd like to have it. If you would like to work for me, I can get you on early session, and you can be out by noon and you can make some money."

I said, "But doing what?"

And she kept talking about all the benefits, and I said, "But doing what?"

And she said, "Cleaning my house."

"Cleaning your house?" My instinct was anger, but I thought I'd better talk to my mother, so I backed off.

I went home, and my folks hit the ceiling. The next day the teacher asked me if I'd made a decision, and I said, "My parents said I can't work for you. I can't clean anybody's house. My father works every day so I don't have to clean anybody's house, and my mother doesn't either." Then my white friend Carol Russo jumped right up and said, "Why didn't you offer this job to me?" And the teacher was very, very embarrassed, and I was very, very angry.—Larene LaSonde, p.334

At some point, my parents decided they weren't going to trust the Detroit public schools with my education, and they sent me to private school. So I went out to Grosse Pointe, Michigan, which is probably one of the lily-whitest suburbs in the world. My first year there, in sixth grade, I was the only black male.

The clothes that I wore and the way I talked was not the way that the other kids dressed or spoke, and in order to feel as though I belonged, I started to change my speech, my dress. When I found out that Brooks Brothers was where most of the kids' parents did their shopping, I begged my mother to please take me and buy me this shit so I could not feel as though I didn't belong.

In eighth grade, something happened, I don't remember what, but I felt like I was being persecuted for being in the middle of all these white people. I started a list of everybody who was in the KKK at the school, and I used to carry this list around with me. I designed their robes, and I would add to the list, mostly teachers that I felt didn't respect me. That lasted for a couple of months. I don't know why I was so angry.—Michael Mayson, p.229

High school was my worst problem. From black women I would get, "She thinks she's too white, she needs to start acting her own color." I would get no association whatsoever if I would try to be friendly. White people didn't give me a hard time, didn't say much of anything. Basically, nobody stopped to take the time to get to know me, and I was real quiet.—Danette Fuller, p.364

The history books my father gave me when I was a kid didn't do anything for me. So I learned who George Washington Carver was—it didn't mean anything to me. Until I was in college. And [then] it was more than just learning about the black culture. I lived in the foreign exchange dorm. So I learned about black culture, all different kinds of black: Caribbean, Jamaican, Haitian, Latins, Asians. Iran. Iraq. Mediterranean cultures.

When I got into college was when I had my first really good friends who were black. I finally felt like I was learning about who I was ethnically. I mean, I knew who I was as a person, personally, as a woman, sexually, but not as an ethnic person.

It's hard to express what I learned; it's hard to discuss in a matter of hours or minutes or even days. I don't know, just the things you learn about black culture. The things you know. The music, the movements, the intimacy, the things that come along with being black that I was ostracized from growing up—I still don't know how to Double Dutch. Shit like that, I can't do it.—Neisha Wright, p.87

School is fraught with opportunities to explore and experience race. Children have struck out from the circumscribed world of their neighborhoods, beyond the reach of their parents' and neighbors' arms and into a wider sphere. What people learn in school only begins with the lesson plan. Schools are often miniature universes, self-contained societies that last a semester, a year, four years. The notion that their primary influence on people is academic is often false. Especially in the elementary years, playground struggles, first crushes, cliques, and popularity contests can have equal or greater impact.

Some of this instruction may be institutional, but much of it is informal and social. In high schools and colleges, people often encounter steadfast racial divisions: De facto segregation of social clubs, fraternities, and sororities; secret societies; race-based dorm assignments; and separate orientations for students of color all communicate the normalcy of race-based isolationism.

Even the most ostensibly benign choices can have repercussions for biracial people. Where one sits in the classroom, in the cafeteria, on the school bus; where one stands on the playground, in the class photograph; which major one chooses or what grades one gets can indicate to other students and even teachers incontrovertible racial allegiance or identity. Once that allegiance has been presumed, all sorts of attendant baggage is dumped alongside it.

Teachers, vested with the authority of the school, may encourage or stigmatize the biracial student based on those presumptions or on the student's complexion and features. More than one person noted significant changes in teachers' treatment of them after meeting the white parent.

Biracial people are also virtually invisible in the curriculum. The absence of material that represents or includes people with backgrounds like theirs is so prevalent that many biracial people have never thought to consider the possibility of inclusion. Again and again, the message is that there are two options: black or white.

◦⟨∞⟩◦

René-Marlene Rambo
Age: 41
Residence: Oakland, California
Occupation: Vice president of legal affairs and administration for a
radio broadcast company

From third grade through sixth, René-Marlene Rambo's elementary school and neighborhood in South Central Los Angeles shared the same racial mix. She and her younger brother were alone amongst Japanese- and Chinese-Americans, most of whom would not or were not allowed to associate with her.

Rambo identifies strongly as black and always has. Ninety-five percent of her friends, she says, "are black profession-als," although her younger brother, who lives in Hawaii, has a more mixed group of friends. "I could never live there," she says. "It's not black enough for me. I would die." Her father is black, from Rambo, Texas, and her mother, since passed away, was white, from Detroit, Michigan.

I spent the first eight years of my life in an all-black neighborhood and went to an all-black elementary school in Los Angeles. Primarily black. There actually were maybe about a third Asian there. I didn't realize that then.

The teachers there, the *black* teachers, really gave me favored treatment. I used to always get in trouble for talking, but there clearly was that, "You're light and you have straight hair." I could do something and not get yelled at the same. I knew that I was held in higher esteem than other kids. That was a combination between my looks and that I was good in school. I just knew. Lots of kids who were light really had an uppity air, and so for me it was real important to show that I was part of the crowd. You'll see that theme in my life: "Hey, I'm just one in the game."

Then my family moved to this all-Japanese-and-Chinese

neighborhood. Probably the most racist environment my parents could have put us in. When I was in my other elementary school, almost all black, I was one of the most popular kids. Then, at nine years old, I get thrust at the bottom of the heap. The school's all Japanese and Chinese, primarily Japanese, a few Chinese, a couple of Whites, a couple of Jewish kids. In the sixth-grade class, maybe three Blacks. The couple of Blacks they had there weren't real academics. But my first experience was fourth grade. We were doing the academic placement tests, and I was always very good in math, and I finished. And the teacher yelled, "René, what are you doing?"

I said, "I'm finished."

She says to me, "You can't be finished," because nobody else in the whole class was finished. "Bring me your paper!"

So I brought her my paper and she scored it and I had ninety-seven percent. And that was the first experience, because she assumed I was going to be dumb. One of the things I have to say about the Japanese children: There was lots of emphasis placed on education, and so, because I was the top in the school in math, they were forced to accept me more. They didn't *like* me necessarily, but I was more palatable.

There were two fourth grades and two fifth grades, and I was always tracked in the lower of the two classes, even though I probably tested higher in almost everything than most of my peers.

And I couldn't go over to their houses to play, so I pretty much walked home alone. The thing for me is that my mom and my dad were really great in allowing me to stay friends with my best friend, Leslie, who I had moved away from. By the time I was nine we were very bonded—I mean, Brownie troop, all my friends were black, we went to the Unitarian church, so if there was *any* place that there was mixed families, it was there. The Unitarian church had Hanukkah and Christmas, so my brother and I got exposed to both, and as I went into high school, I was very pro-integration. That really was my thing.

But anyway, I went to this all-Japanese-and-Chinese elementary school. I did okay. Probably could have done better, but they had low expectations of me. But it was really hard on my brother. My brother had really severe asthma, and had missed a lot of kindergarten and the first grade. He started this school in the second grade. He was already a typical little boy, but he was a nonreader. And he was subjected to probably some of the worst racism that you could ever experience. I only know a little bit about it, but when my brother was in the seventh grade he had a bleeding ulcer. That's how severe it turned out. And I found out maybe four or five years ago that his second-grade teacher used to take him into the coatroom and shake him and say, "You little dumb nigger. You little dumb nigger." Every teacher said something was wrong with him. The principal told my mother that he was retarded and would never graduate from high school—my brother, who graduated [in 1974] from UC Santa Barbara.

As far as making friends went, there was one Chinese girl, Dorothy Wong. We were kind of friends, a little bit. I could go to her house. The Chinese were more tolerant than the Japanese. But I guess there was never anybody I would call.

I realize now that these Japanese were the children of parents who had been incarcerated during World War II, and I didn't know that at that time. So these children had some connection to that, and they were very kiss-assy to the teachers. It was good for me educationally, because there was a much higher level of expectation at the Japanese school than there had been at the black school—I had to do a term paper in the fourth grade—but these kids went to Japanese school after regular school, so they didn't play out on the streets. The difference was very dramatic because I was used to playing on the streets after school. Now I would walk home by myself. That's when my compulsive eating started. I got into the habit of buying a candy bar and going home and watching television and eating crackers.

I was real independent, and I didn't feel as intensely the loss of not having friends, or if I did, I'm not cognizant of it, because I still had close friends from before. There were two kids across the street: the Takadas, Donna and Eddie. Donna was a little bit younger than me, and we used to play together. But I remember being at her house one day, and her mom came home and her mom hit the ceiling. So I wasn't really accepted in the house.

I knew what it was: They were prejudiced and they didn't like black people and I wasn't accepted. I didn't fit in. The junior high school I went to was very mixed: about a third Jewish, about a third

Asian, and a third black. I really didn't fit because clearly I wasn't
Japanese; I wasn't as fast as the Jewish kids—they could date at
twelve—I didn't fit in with them; and I was too academic-
bookwormish to hang with the typical black kids. So I was really
kind of in never-never land. But junior high wasn't that bad. It was
an excellent junior high, academically. I viewed myself as black, so
whatever friends I met in junior high were all black.

One of the most racist things that ever had happened to me
was done by a black junior high school teacher. I was on the college
preparatory track in junior high school, and I had her for English,
which was never one of my better classes. I [liked] math, because
English was too arbitrary. Math, it was right or it was wrong, no
discussion. And no matter how hard I worked, no matter how hard
I did, I always was getting B's on whatever I turned in to her, even
when I *knew* it was better quality. Anyway, I had her for my sixth
period. The day before report cards came out, she had told me
what grade I was getting. Now, I had algebra, I had Spanish, and
I had advanced science before English, and when my report card
got to her it had straight A's on it.

I will never forget this: I was sitting in the last seat on the right
hand side, doing whatever, and I heard her say, "René, whose
report card is this?"

I said, "It's mine."

She changed my grade to an A. It was like I couldn't be smart
because I was black. And she was a black teacher!

I never talked to my parents about those kinds of things. I
never asked them questions. I don't think they knew how to deal
with it. It took until I was twenty for my mother to understand that
I identified black. That was very hard for her. She looked at it as
these were her *kids*, and so we were Jewish and we were black, and
she didn't understand the fact that I viewed myself as black. It was
very hard for her to understand that.

So high school was pretty black. I had black boyfriends, I
mean, that's all I hung out with. My brother started at that high
school, but then busing started and he went to Hamilton, which
was primarily Jewish, and my brother became a hippie. I mean he
was *out there*. And I was still doing good in school; you know,
cheerleader, class president, all of that kind of stuff. So we were
very different in that kind of regard.

But they never stop tracking you. When I was in high
school, I was a California State Scholar, yet the counselor encouraged me to go to a state college as opposed to a UC [campus of
the University of California]. They shouldn't have tracked me
there. So I'm very cognizant of being treated different. I had it
a lot at Harvard.

I graduated from law school in 1977 and then worked for ten
years doing labor management, negotiating labor contracts. I decided I wanted to be a city manager and that there were two ways
to be one: I could work for the city of Oakland, and work in seven
different departments for the next eight years, or I could go back to
school. So I packed up my butt, locked up my house, and I went
back to school full-time at thirty-eight, for a master's in public
administration at the Harvard Kennedy School of Government.

I started the program in August of '88, came back in September to rent my house—the person who was going to take it fell
through at the last minute—and my mom, who had been in remis-
sion from breast cancer, took sick. I lost my mom that October. So
I ended up not going back in the fall. They kept telling us my mom
was going to get better. She didn't, and she died a week before my
parents' forty-first wedding anniversary.

The director of the Harvard program said, "Go ahead and
come in the middle of the year. You know everybody from the first
class, and then you'll get to know two groups of people."

I had already quit my job, and I only had enough money saved
for a year, so I said, "Well, you know, that's not bad. I'll go to
Boston, start the program in February, work that summer, graduate
the next January." So here I start this program, and everybody, of
course, remembers me; I'm really outgoing and friendly so everybody thinks I'm cool, but what I didn't know is that going back to
school full-time after being out eleven years is an adjustment. It
was also too soon after my mother's death. And I was going from a
three-bedroom, two-bath home that I owned into a tiny three-
bedroom apartment with two white girls, one twenty-two years old,
and the other thirty-one. And I had the smallest room, so it was just
too much. And with six classes, it was an exciting environment, but
it was too much.

But I'll tell you my first experience at Harvard. Came to
school, everybody's all happy to see me. The admissions dean said,

"You need to get your ID card." She said, "Here, I'll give you a note." She gave me a note and sent me over to the main campus and told me to get my ID card. Now they had issued me an ID card in September, but of course it had been sent back.

When I get there, the little clerk, he didn't know what to do. I said, "Here's the note." He said fine, and he goes to ask his boss, this white boy, what he should do.

His boss says, "No problem. She has the card from the registrar, all you need to do is issue her a new ID card and change the last number from 000 to 001."

Fine. So he comes back, and the clerk says, "This is what you have to do."

He's sitting there typing the card when the white boy sees me. *"Wait! WAIT!"* And I mean literally, he leapt across the desk. "Uh, uh, uh, uh, uh, what are you doing?"

I said, "I'm getting my registration card."

"Have you registered?"

I said, "I don't know where I am in the process, the registrar sent me over here."

"Oh, you can't have your card. No, no. These registrars, they have it all mixed up. We can't give you the card."

And I knew, I knew what it was. And that was like three-thirty on Friday. "When will I get my card?"

"Monday."

And I said, "Well, school starts Monday, and they have given me my card so I could get into the gym and—"

"No, no. You can't have it. Stop doing the card!" Made the guy stop. Now he had just authorized him two seconds ago before he saw me, so I knew what it was. And it wasn't a battle I was getting ready to fight; I didn't feel like acting a fool. So I said, "Fine." I knew I wouldn't have my card Monday; I knew he wouldn't get it there, that there was no way he was going to be able to get it there.

So he went back and I said to the little clerk, the little guy, I said, "He must be really hard to work with."

He says, "No, no. But you know, we get people off the streets all the time who are pretending they go here."

As if somebody black can't go there.

Nomathombi Martini
Age: 19
Residence: Berkeley, California
Occupation: College student

When Nomathombi Martini responded to my ad in the Oakland Tribune, *he enclosed a copy of a term paper he'd written on race relations during his freshman year at UC Berkeley (Cal) for an African-American studies class. He described the different environments he'd lived in and wrote that he has always felt "caught in the cross fire of racial attitudes."*

Although Martini knows his father, who is African-American, and sees him occasionally, he has never lived with him. "I don't know what my father's story is. I really don't have the patience to sit down and talk to him. He's full of disappointments, and I love him but I don't really trust him or believe in his word. But it's not a black thing, it's a father thing. He's off in his own world, and I'm off in my own world."

From day one my mom didn't claim my father; she didn't want to have that much to do with him. He was pretty much, not really a playboy, but he was in the movement to free love and all this other stuff. He had multiple girlfriends, and so my mom just couldn't deal with it and she left the country when I was one year old. Went to Guatemala, where she met my little brother's father, and we stayed down there for two years. When we came back we moved, my mother and I, to Berkeley, and then we moved to Oakland, where my brother was born.

I didn't quite realize the difference in color until we moved from the house in west Oakland to north Oakland. The neighborhood was all black. I went to a mixed child-care center—my mom made sure of that—but my school became more a black school. It was about that time where I was the constant victim of harassment and abuse by the neighborhood kids for being half-white. My nickname was White Boy, they used to call me White Boy Noma.

Obviously I'm not white, I'm black, but they used to call me White Boy just to pesterize me. They stole my Big Wheels, they broke into our house, the neighborhood kids did.

Also, they would talk about my mom. They'd make sexual gestures to my mom, and they would have no respect in front of me to my mom. It seemed like they were trying to run her out of the neighborhood. My mom still feels like she's very alienated, because everybody has their little family functions and barbecues and people talk to people and she's always left out. She stayed because it's cheap housing. She's physically disabled; she's on welfare; she can't afford housing anywhere else. It's a good area, not so much crime compared to other neighborhoods in Oakland, and she's a rebel. And I wouldn't really want to be raised all my life in the suburbs and not realize that this is where my brothers and sisters are. I consider myself black and white, but this is where my other side of me is, in the black neighborhood.

I also got a lot of criticism about speaking proper speech. I don't speak street talk and I never did. When I try I sound really weird. I do pronounce words wrong because of Oakland, like *wif*, *birfday*, *bafroom* and things like that. But I don't speak street talk, and I don't really understand it. I'm more proper. They would say, "Why do you talk so proper?" "Why do you talk like you're white?"

And I explain, "I was raised by my white mom."

"Oh, that's it."

The Oakland school system did fail me. That's why I eventually did leave to go to boarding school. I had a slight reading disability due to the Oakland school system. They neglected me in my lower classes. My mom said it was racist; I didn't believe it was racist; I just believe that a lot of kids didn't get the attention other kids did, but it just so happened that a lot of white kids passed and a lot of black kids didn't.

When I continued on I had a hard time. I bonded with a friend in the neighborhood who I called my cousin. He was my protector, my big brother, because I had nobody. We'd go kick it, and we ended up being the biggest thieves in the world. We used to run around stealing anything we could get our little hands on, riding bikes and doing fun things that kids like doing.

I really don't know why he befriended me. He was a troublemaker, he was in the in crowd, everybody knew him. Maybe because I was a good follower at the time. Whenever he wanted to go do something, I would go with him. Eventually he went to jail. He comes out and then goes to jail again, throughout my youth. Then I get popped with him. I get busted for something I did. I've been stealing for about three years and finally get busted at thirteen.

My mom's the one that turned me in. To stop me. It was, I think, one of the toughest things she had to do, because she had to go to the police station with me and because I would have been home free. She brought me into the police station and said, "He did this," and they arrested me, read me my rights, took my picture and my hand prints, and it scared the crap out of me. It really scared me straight. I never did anything like that again. Now I have intentions of being a cop when I graduate.

That same year, I received a scholarship to go to Woodside Priory in Portola Valley. There was only one other black kid there—he was mixed, very light complexion—and he denounced his race. I only stayed there for about three quarters of a semester before situations started where people would call me nigger and tell racial jokes around me. At first I'd laugh along with them, because I didn't know how to take it. I was like, "Okay, well, whatever." Then when they called me nigger—I could see the hate in their faces and that they were trying to hurt me—I started building up anger. Eventually I got in a fight with one Palestinian kid who would not get off my back.

The dean of discipline said, "Well, this is not a place for you. We can't have you here." Anytime something turned up missing, the students blamed it on me. The teachers were great, very supportive, but they understood the situation. They knew that it was going to be hard for me to grow, and so they got me out of there. The dean of discipline worked at Hanna Boys Center, a boarding school, and he said, "I know a better place to send you than Oakland school districts." Just during that semester, one kid got shot in the hallways of Oakland Tech—the school I was supposed to be going to—another kid got into a fight on the bus and was followed home and stabbed to death, and the janitor was also stabbed to death. My mom was like, "No way, you're not going to this school. Obviously the school system's already failed you; you have a reading disability."

excellent dialogue of internal conflict

I left Woodside and went to my boarding school, Hanna Boys Center, which is in Sonoma Valley, an hour north of San Francisco. It's in the wine country; it's a retirement town. There's about five Blacks in the whole town, but the attitude of the town was a lot better than what I just came from, which was very upper class: Kids at Woodside were coming to school with BMWs, Mercedes-Benzes. These were all kids who are on the track to go to Stanford and Harvard, places I wouldn't even imagine myself going to.

So I get transferred up to Hanna, and the school is a rehabilitation kind of institution. It's not like a regular boarding school. It's an individual one-on-one training and a chance for students to take a time out of life and understand who they are and what they're about and where are they going, and that's basically what I learned from it and basically what it has done for me. While being there I established myself.

I had a big problem, coming from a black neighborhood and being called white, and coming from a boarding school that's all white and being called black. That's the nice way of putting it. I was very mixed up. I didn't know who I was, which side to pick.

Up to this point, I had thought I was black. I didn't understand why people in the neighborhood were calling me white. I looked black, I was hanging around with black people, people looked at me and saw black, that's what I thought. If you knew me and where I lived and who my mom was, which a lot of the neighborhood children did, then you knew I was half-white, and then I was a victim of their racist attitude. But when people didn't know me, they thought I was black. I mean, okay, well, I thought I was black, I mean, I'm black. Yeah, I have a white mom, but I had a black father, the black genes dominated, I'm black. I mean, I'm mixed, and that's the way I looked at it.

And then when I went to Woodside, I looked at it like, "Well, I'm most definitely black here."

Hanna Boys Center has a hundred and twenty staff and eighty-four boys. You only get to see your parents one time a month, and you never need to leave campus. It's like a world within a world. Kids come in there with racist attitudes once in a while from different neighborhoods, but most of them are streetwise, most of them have problems at home and don't have time to worry about stupid things like race. So you all bond, you have your family, you

Proud of both sides

have your group there. You also have your enemies, but it's such a closed environment that you have to get along within the program to succeed and stay there. It was hard at times. There's no fences, no gates or anything like that, no dogs or security people keeping you there; you could leave anytime. But it was something that I learned to like, I learned to appreciate, and I learned to grow. I didn't always like it, but I appreciated it.

I figured out that I was mixed, that I was going to be as proud of my white as I was of my black side. This is where I started figuring out that I'm going to be happy of my accomplishments as well as my failures.

I started moving very good in the program, and things started working out for me. I was a freshman, and I moved to the group home, which is a house unlike any other dorm. You're allowed to go off campus, sign out and go off for the night. I started to see what this valley was like. It was a white valley. Then I went to the local high school my sophomore year, and it was really cool.

I still lived at the Hanna Boys Center, but I went to the public school. So I was around girls all of a sudden. They thought it was cool that I was black, to a point where sometimes it seemed really fake. "Why don't you grow dreads? You'd look really cool!" And they expected me to be a good athlete, to be dumb in school, and to be very funny.

I was those things and more, but I didn't do it because of them; I did it because of me. Before I started getting into athletics, I wanted to prove them wrong because the other black student at the high school was selling dope. He was the average stereotype of a black person to them, and this is a community who only perceives what black people are through the news, where whenever you turn on a TV, there's a Black robbing somebody, black crime, black on black, black on white. I wanted to prove to them that I am about a lot more than that, because they were looking at me as a person, which was great, but still, beyond that, I am black, and I wanted to establish myself as something different.

So I set goals for myself. Okay, well, what can I do to impress these people or let them know that I'm not about all this other stuff? First thing I did was get involved in the student body government. The end of my first year I was there, I was elected student body vice president, the first black member ever to do that at the school. And I thought it was a great accomplishment, considering that these students didn't even know me before that year; I just come into their school—these are kids who grew up together from knee-high, they all know each other, and I'm the outsider, coming into their high school—and all of a sudden I'm saying, "I'm here. Please accept me." And they did.

They voted me in after they had time to get to know me. I was stuck in all the bonehead remedial classes when I got there, which really pissed me off, and then after that first year I got myself in the honors courses and I surprised a lot of people: I was involved in student body government, I played football, and I had a part-time job.

That kept my mind off a lot of other things, and it kept me away from my boarding school, which I really didn't want to go back to. It was very restrictive and very protective for liability reasons. Whenever we left in somebody's car, we had to have their license number, the insurance policy, phone numbers of the parents, and then we had to check out what time we were leaving, what time we were planning to be back, where we were going. I had to ask a week ahead of time to stay out past nine-thirty.

There were two Blacks in the school when I first came, three the next year, and when I graduated there was five altogether, out of twelve hundred. The majority of students were white. This town revolved around wine, so there was a very big population of Mexicans who have their own problems, like *West Side Story*. All the Whites didn't like the Mexicans, and the Mexicans didn't like the Whites, and the Blacks were in the middle and nobody bothered us. We were such a small minority, we weren't a threat to anybody. It's not like we huddled around in our own group, but we were always there for each other, and we understood personal things that other people didn't understand. We had the common bond of being black.

I was introduced to white girls, which was fine. At first there was nobody else to see. It wasn't because of that, but I just got to the point where, my mom's white, so what? There's no color lines. I'll see any girl as long as she's pretty and she has a nice attitude. It didn't bother the young people in the valley, but it did bother the older generation. I would walk down the street with a girl and people would stop their cars just to look at us walking hand in hand. I fell in puppy love with this girl my junior year: We kissed one time and that was it. She told her mom, and her mom said, "You can't date him." Her mom literally told me after that, in person, "What would the neighbors think?"

And I had this strange moralistic idea that, okay, I'm glad her mom wasn't hypocritical about not saying it to my face. Yet I never had to face this before, and I went off on a racial tangent. Every time I had something in history class about Blacks and Whites, I always had something to say about race, and it just annoyed the hell out of my classmates, who understood to a point, but thought I went too far. My senior year I became very militant in class, and anything that wasn't right I blamed it on race.

At this point of time, I'm identifying as myself, but I guess I am identifying black as well because I do have this vendetta, I have this anger in me that I have to blurt out stuff in class about South Africa this, the government is doing this, or that black neighborhoods are not getting money.

People were getting tired of hearing it. Maybe it was to the point where I was carrying the torch for them, where they didn't have to. I look back now and say that, but then I was just pissed off and I was going to say whatever was on my mind.

When I first went up there, I felt safer in the streets of Oakland because I don't like the country. I heard rumors about people being strung up by trees and telephone poles, and I thought I was going to be lynched. Eventually, I felt safe in that community, like nobody's going to mess with me here—I can say what I want, do whatever I want.

But then I go to Cal and I get introduced to a new, different side of my generation of black students, black women: educated girls, girls that are not on the street. These are girls that I've been looking for all this time, girls who speak street language and everything and are down with the latest trends and everything, but they're also past the mental barriers of racist concepts, at least within their own black race.

The black community at Cal is really cool because regardless of who you are, as long as you're black, you fit in the black community somewhere, they'll accept you. I felt like an outcast of the black community this whole time, and now that I'm at Cal, I fit in all of a sudden. These are educated Blacks. They understand that situations are situations, people are people, but yet above all I am black, and they look at me as black. They know I claim white as well, and they understand that, and it's fine with them. They understand that my mom's white and I can't neglect her side.

But one thing that threw the black community, or my black community at Cal, was that I'm in a white fraternity. They call it a white fraternity because there's no Blacks in it. I call it a Greek fraternity. But to other people, it's a white fraternity just because it's not Alpha Phi Alpha or the Kappas or something like that—which are in the black Greek system.

I chose mine because, for one thing, the black fraternities don't have a house to live in. I need some place where I could live my four years through college. I'm used to living in boarding schools, but I don't want to live in the dorms—I'm used to being around a family of guys. And I'm used to being around all different kind of guys; my boarding school was not just black.

The biggest thing is that I didn't want to segregate myself against other races, because in the black fraternities there's only black, and that's fine, but then I'm neglecting the other side of my family. I'm yearning for two sides. I'm split. I don't think I'd be any better in a black fraternity than I am right now in the white fraternity. I understand that if I go down to some places in the South, not all my [fraternity] brothers will accept me. They'll accept me for being a brother, because I've been through the same initiation ritual and the same secret stuff that they have, and yet, I'm still black and they will not call me a brother. I understand that, but I'm not down in the South, I'm in this community up here, and this is the community that's getting me by, these are the people who I feel care about me and who I care about.

The people in the black fraternities and the black sororities that I know, they don't associate with my house because my house is a white fraternity. They don't have parties with my house, but I go to their parties and they accept me. That's fine. I don't wear my letters all the time, but I'm not afraid to.

Another thing that pisses me off about color, is like, you have the black engineering company, the black student group, the black this, the black that, the black choir. If you came out with the white choir, the white student group, the white civil engineering company, people would cry bloody murder. And I just don't find the logic in that, I don't at all.

In school we were talking about the Rodney King thing and Malcolm X's theory of being separate and Marcus Garvey and having two nations, and everybody's like, "Yeah, Blacks should just have their own communities, their own everything. Whites should have their own." And I'm listening to this. I'm so scared that could ever happen, because I don't want to deny either side. And then the professor said, "Well, what about people like Noma and the other mixed students, what kind of position would they be in?"

I'm just like, "I wouldn't want to pick a side. I really wouldn't, I wouldn't want to be in that position to pick a side between my mother and my father, between these friends and those friends, because there's, there's dicks on both sides, there's no perfect side, there's none at all. I haven't experienced a perfect side yet, and I can do with both of them or I'm going to do without both of them."

Lisa Feldstein
Age: 28
Residence: San Francisco, California
Occupation: Third-year law student

Lisa Feldstein had attended her last class of law school on the day we met. The school was Boalt, at UC Berkeley, the same law school René Rambo attended, on the same Cal campus where Nomathombi Martini is an undergraduate. Feldstein and her younger sister grew up in New York City's Spanish Harlem; her mother is black, and her father is white, from an Orthodox Jewish family. Her parents' marriage was not completely welcomed by the families. "My mother's parents were very concerned, but they felt like they'd be there and they'd be supportive and they'd stand by her. My father's mother was dead. His father said, 'You're an adult, you make

your own decisions,' and his two brothers stopped speaking to him. One sat shiva for him [a religious mourning ritual]; he was dead, he didn't exist anymore. The one that decided he was dead was upset that my mother was black; the other brother was more upset that she wasn't Jewish."

Feldstein says she responded to my ad in the Bay Guardian *out of a curiosity sparked by attending a few meetings of Cal Berkeley's Students of Interracial Descent, one of the largest multiracial college groups in the country. "It was the first time that I'd really had any significant contact with groups of people who'd grown up in circumstances like my own," she remembers. The novelty wore off quickly, though, in part because she was one of only two older students. "Everybody else was an undergrad, and they were mostly from Berkeley. I felt that I was in such a different place in my life than they were, so I stopped going."*

When I was born we lived in the Bronx, and when I was a month old we moved to Franklin Plaza, which is middle-income housing in New York, in Spanish Harlem, on a Hundred and sixth between First and Second. Growing up there was really uncomfortable for a couple of reasons: One was that people were always asking me if it was true that my father was white. The other reason was my mother was the social worker at the local elementary school—so she was the enforcer, the one who called your parents if you were truant. So they didn't like her very much, and I was her daughter.

Another reason was that I came into first grade reading on a fourth- or fifth-grade level, and I had math skills and I could function. So I got a lot of special attention, partly because my mom worked there, and partly because I just came in with better skills, 'cause I got taught all that at home by both my parents. And I couldn't jump Double Dutch. That was a big deal. I was really small, and the kids would pick on me.

When I was in the first grade, I don't know why, but I made this book all about pigment, and my mom still has it. It's a finger-painted book, and it was full of all sorts of ideas. I must have asked why people were different colors. Or maybe I just came across this word and asked what it meant. The book is things like, "Pigment is what makes people different colors." I would draw something and say, "Maybe this has pigment. Maybe it doesn't."

In the fifth and sixth grade I went to Professional Children's

School, and in the fifth grade there was one black kid in my class and he was in the sixth grade, and he was really surprised when I showed up, because there hadn't been any other black kids. When I was a sixth grader, there were two black kids who were fifth graders, and I was actually friends with both of them. I didn't want to leave there, but my parents made me go to Hunter because the Professional Children's School's high school was terrible. I got into Hunter, and I was very unhappy. It's a public school, but you take an exam to get in; you take the test in the sixth grade and you start in the seventh. My memory is that my parents told me I had to take the test, and if I didn't want to go I didn't have to. When I got in they said I had to go, that they didn't know what they were going to do if I hadn't gotten in.

In my seventh-grade class there were four black students, including me, and I was the only one who got in on scores. With everybody else, they had an affirmative-action policy where they were under court order to bring in kids from neighborhoods that were underrepresented, and those were mostly minority neighborhoods. I know those kids got under a certain score and had to go to summer school, and supposedly this one six-week program was supposed to bring them up to speed on the six years that they had missed or whatever.

The reality was that I was the only black student left in my class at the end of seventh grade. There were others in the school as a whole, but in my grade, we started with four and I was the only one who survived. I thought it was so cruel. The school talked about having this great affirmative-action program, and I thought it was just vicious. I hated their arrogance. The whole attitude at Hunter is, "You're the smartest kids in New York City and you're better than everyone else and you don't need to talk to anyone else and we're not going to teach you typing because we're not training you to be secretaries." I tried desperately to get thrown out for three years. I got into fights, I failed classes, I did anything I could to get thrown out because I thought my parents would let me go back to Professional Children's School. I couldn't get thrown out.

In retrospect, Hunter was definitely a very good education. I learned a lot. It's a pretty weird place, though. I run into people who went to Hunter, and there's something about them that's all the same. It's weird because you start in the seventh grade and then no one new comes in except the next year's seventh graders. People leave, but there's no new blood, so it's a very isolating environment. I ended up not graduating from there. I transferred out, and I graduated from City as School, a public alternative school. I went and figured out how to apply for a transfer, and when I'd done all of that—and my parents at that point were afraid that I would drop out—I said, "I really want to go to this school without walls, and I want to work at South Street Seaport for English credit. I hate school."

And they were like, "Oh, okay." So my mom finally let me go, and I liked that much better, but I was only there for one semester. One advantage of going to Hunter was that everything appeared on my transcript as a semester ahead, so I only needed one term of credits to graduate.

It wasn't until I started college that race became an issue. The first thing that really struck me, the first week of school [at Hampshire College], was when I was standing with some people I'd just met and this black woman came over to me and introduced herself to me and ignored these white people I was with. She said, "I make a point of meeting all of the black students on campus." I thought she was incredibly rude. She worked there as an administrator of some sort, maybe minority recruitment or something. But I was really offended; I thought she was incredibly rude.

There were relatively few black students at Hampshire, and they tended to stick together. They made it real clear I had a choice: I could hang out with them, or I could hang out with these other people I was hanging out with, so I stayed hanging out with the friends I'd made. I can't remember exactly how they made it clear—part of it was their behavior; they would definitely stick together, and they would do the same kind of singling me out from a group and inviting just me to something if I was with other students who were white.

I had an argument with one of them about identity, and I said I thought it was really silly that they would go to a school that had all of these things to offer and then only talk to people who looked like them. She got really angry and said I was wrong and we had to stick together. After that none of them would talk to me except one woman I'd gone to high school with.

So I went to Hampshire for a year and a half, and then I went to India for half the year, and that was, in theory, connected to what I was doing at Hampshire. I never actually did any of the academic work I was supposed to do with it, but that was why I went, and shortly before I left for India I got engaged to a white man from Canada. When I came back we got married in August of '84. I was twenty and he was nineteen, and we hadn't wanted actually to get married yet; we just wanted to live in the same city and we couldn't—we got married because he was a Canadian citizen. We got married and we lived in Boston and that was hard, that was really difficult. I remember once when we were walking on Boylston Street a black man spit on us.

Colin and I separated after two years. I was going to UMass at night, and then it was starting to take forever to get my bachelor's, so my last year there, I quit my job and I went back to school full-time.

I started to have all these run-ins with the black students there; that was like the next time anything significant happened. I checked out the black student organization. I was kind of curious to see what it was like, because when I was in India I started to become more curious about black culture, and I found out that my father had suggested to my mother that I should go to her alma mater, Talladega, for undergrad, that it was time I learned something about my black roots. And my mother said, "You should have thought of that eighteen years ago. It's a little late; it would be culture shock. She couldn't survive a black campus in the South. She wouldn't know what to do."

But I was at UMass, and I walked into the black student office and the first thing you saw was this poster, this guy with a machine gun, and it says, "By Any Means Necessary." I was like, "I don't think I'm necessarily politically aligned with these people." We would argue all the time. They thought that I had too many white friends and I needed to make a decision, and the decision needed to be that I was black-identified. And I didn't see why I needed to make that decision. They were like, "If you don't, then by default you're white-identified."

And I was like, "No, I don't think so. I don't really think of it either way. I'm just who I am." I ended up being the black student who graduated with the highest GPA that year, so they had to give me their academic award. That was sort of uncomfortable for everybody. I had to go to the awards dinner, and I was on really bad terms with most of these people—there were a couple I had sort of an uneasy truce with and a couple people who we enjoyed arguing with each other, but we weren't friendly—and I was dating this man at the time who was like a Nazi's wet dream. He was tall and blond and muscular, and he *really* was out of place at this awards dinner. He was actually less ill at ease than I was because I thought it looked like I was making a statement and I wasn't.

And when I was shopping for law schools, that was a really difficult decision for me. I wanted to leave Boston—I knew that—and one of the places that I applied was Howard. I was thinking that maybe I wanted to pursue a career in civil rights law; at this point, I had done my undergraduate degree in American Studies with a focus on urban issues, and what I had specifically become interested in was housing issues, which mostly affected minority neighborhoods. I started writing all of these papers on housing issues in Harlem, but it was all entirely academic to me; it was like none of this had anything to do with me. I was really fascinated by these issues, but it seemed like even though I'd grown up in Spanish Harlem, I grew up in an interracial family that was middle-class and educated, and these people I was reading about weren't the people I'd grown up with.

So I looked at Howard because they have such a good reputation in civil rights law, and I thought that would be useful, and I talked to the recruiter and he said that based on my GPA and my LSAT scores that they would give me like ten thousand a year, and their tuition was only six thousand.

So then I had this real dilemma. Part of it was that Howard's got a great reputation in one area and nothing else, and if I couldn't get a job in civil rights, I'd have a hard time getting a job. So I was concerned that if I was going to spend three years in law school, I wanted to be able to work after it, and I was really nervous. I asked the recruiter if I would fit in there.

He said, "No, you won't. The general belief at Howard is that there are two kinds of black students. You have black inner-city kids, and you have kids from the rural South. I want you because I'm trying to prove that there are other kinds of black students and that they run the gamut. And no, you're not going to fit into either of those groups."

interaction Black - White

I appreciated his honesty, but I turned down the scholarship. I decided I didn't need three years of that. It was clear that if the recruiter who wanted me would tell me I wasn't going to have a good time there, then I didn't want to go. So I got into Boalt and decided to go there. I also wanted to live in San Francisco because my dad grew up here and I thought that would be kind of cool. So I moved out here and got an apartment in the Haight and started at Boalt, and I've never been in as racially a charged atmosphere as the Berkeley campus. It's really frightening.

Berkeley doesn't have a white majority anymore, and the faculty hasn't caught up with that yet, so the students are feeling like they don't have role models. There aren't, really. For instance, I think .02 percent of the faculty is black women or something like that; there are tiny, tiny numbers of people of color teaching. Especially in the law school—because you're learning a set of rules that are based on a structure that's very white establishment—a lot of the students of color feel very, very alienated there, and it's very, very charged. I went to the minority student orientation a week before the regular orientation, mostly because they were doing skills training, like how to brief a case, and I thought it would be a good head start.

By the end of the week I thought it was sort of a bad idea, because one of the things it did was it created these very tight cliques, and when the white students arrived the next week, you already had these friendships that looked like they'd been there for years. These people had just met, but it meant that it was very hard to create any kind of interracial friendship. The other problem was that it meant regular orientation was largely a waste of time for the students of color.

I was sort of sorry I'd gone after all, but I went, and during the week there was a panel discussion on student life at Boalt—there was a black student, a Latino student, and an Asian student and a Native American student—and they were talking about all the wonderful things Boalt had to offer students of color. I finally said, "Well, all of this is fine, but the school's three-quarters white and you haven't mentioned that at all. How do you interact with the white students?"

And no one would say anything. Finally, the black student said, "Things around here can get pretty tense; you'd best stick

Stick with your own kind (handwritten margin note)

with your own kind." I was floored. I didn't really know what to think. I talked to this woman who ended up being one of my closest friends at Boalt—she's Latina and her husband is white—and she was feeling this same way, like, "What does that mean? Who are *my kind*? Where do I fit in?"

And then the next week the same black student and a friend of his who's also black came up to me and said, "You never hang out in the Law Students of African Descent Lounge."

And I said, "I'm not sure I feel particularly welcome there."

He said, "Let me give you the combination." All of the offices have locks so that homeless people don't sleep in them. He said, "Give me something to write it down on."

I said, "I'll remember."

He said, "No, I don't want any white people to hear."

And so I was like, "Well, I don't want it."

"Oh, I'm just joking."

"I don't think it's funny. My father's white. I'm not black."

And he's like, "Oh, sorry," and kind of walked away.

There are two other students in my class who have one black parent and one white parent, and they were very black-identified, but they also got recruited very heavily by these same two guys who were like, "You belong with us. Why don't you come with us?" And I didn't want to be recruited. Again, I wasn't willing to make this decision that these were the only people I was going to talk to for three years, which is what they really wanted you to decide. It was okay to talk to the Latino students, you know, and the Native American students; if you *had* to you could talk to the Asian students, but you should avoid white students unless they prove themselves. And it's been really, really uncomfortable for me there. It's always been very stressful. I'm not black enough, and I don't particularly want to be what they consider black enough. Most of the black students won't talk to me. Some of them just walk by me, they won't say hi, they won't look me in the eye. Sometimes I'll go into the lounge if there are students there who I'm friendly with, and some of them are friendly no matter what. There are a couple who will be friendly if there aren't other black students around.

avoid the whites (handwritten margin note)

I've tried hanging out in the lounge a couple of times, and it's just really uncomfortable. For them it's this retreat and they can *polarization extreme?* (handwritten)

complain about all the things that bother them, but I feel like they create so much of the tension themselves. I know so many white students who feel completely alienated; they didn't come to Berkeley expecting to have to jump through hoops to be allowed to talk to someone who was black. I think having things like a black student organization is important, and I understand the support mechanism that a lot of people need, especially if they have always functioned in a predominantly black environment. That's really important, but it seems like it's taken to extremes.

There was an enormous amount of outrage last year when one of the students printed up these shirts that said "NWJ," like NWA [Niggaz With Attitude, a rap group], but it was "Niggaz with JDs: Your Worst Nightmare." It was supposed to be funny, and I thought it was kind of funny, and the black student organization was like, "You don't air our dirty laundry in public." Like, "How dare you do something like that without clearing it with us first." And this guy did it by himself, it was his little fund-raising project, and they were furious with him, and so now nobody talks to him either because he did something that didn't pass the junta.

I had seen Boalt as an opportunity to be in an environment with a lot of black students who were coming from more of a similar background, who maybe had the same educational levels that I did and some more worldly experiences that I hadn't found when I was going to, say, UMass-Boston, where they tended to be mostly poor inner-city kids who had gone to Boston public schools.

And it wasn't like that at all. If anything, it was worse. Maybe some of them fear that they won't be seen as black enough because they're functioning within this white power structure, I don't know. The students who tended to be more accepting of me were this guy who printed up the shirts, who grew up in other countries—his dad worked at consulates and they were always traveling around—and this woman who's Haitian. I think she moved here when she was about fourteen, and she feels like she owes the United States this great debt for all that they did for her and her family. For a while I was dating a Latino guy, and that made things a little better, like, he wasn't black but at least he was a person of color. Other than that I've had pretty much consistently negative experiences with the black students at Boalt. And it makes me really sad.

If people refer to me as a black woman, usually I'll correct

negative experiences w/ blacks (handwritten)

- Identified => black
- correct them
check "other"

them. I say, "Actually, I'm half-black and half-Jewish." On forms, I usually check other. What bothers me is when they say you can only check one box. That's the only time I get mad. If I can check more than one box, I do. But when I've applied for financial aid, I'll check black.

I feel guilty about doing that because I feel like part of the reason that I got—not that I got in but that I got certain kinds of aid and stuff at Hampshire, and a little bit at Boalt—was because they thought that I was going to diversify their community in a way that I didn't. I think I did diversify their community, but not in the way that they were expecting, and so I feel like it's kind of using them. When I was applying to law schools, I checked black on the ones where I could only check one thing because I figured that I had a better chance of getting in. I liked schools the best that asked if there's anything about how you perceive yourself that we should consider. So then I could explain the whole thing. That was great!

I think black students I've been to school with have been so invested in having me choose because they feel rebuffed, like I think that I'm too good to identify with them. I don't think that's it. I don't think that identifying people on the basis of skin color really has a lot of validity. To me, a lot of being black-identified is cultural—like being Jewish is cultural or being Mexican-American is very cultural—and I didn't really grow up in that culture so I don't identify with that culture.

I don't think of my mother as being culturally terribly black; I don't really think of her as culturally being terribly identified with anything. She told me when she was at Talladega the Klan came riding through the town, and she went and sat on the fence to watch. I don't think you'd meet any other people of her age who would do something like that. That was just stupid. She had to have felt that she wasn't at risk, and I'm not sure where she would have come to that conclusion.

My mom doesn't seek out other black people; she doesn't feel like she owes them anything in particular, that they owe her anything. She doesn't have that kind of we-all-have-to-stick-togetherness that a lot of black people have that maybe comes out of a history of suffering together. I think it's really weird that my dad was going on marches in Washington in the sixties and my mother was at home watching soap operas. She just didn't go. You know, she cares about her family and she cares about her friends, and her work, but she doesn't care about a lot of issues.

My grandparents came from a very different generation and from the South, and so their understanding of what it is to be black is really, really different from what I perceive of as being culturally black. Their black friends would always compliment me on how well I spoke, that I didn't have a black accent.

When I was going to the meetings of Students of Interracial Descent at Berkeley, it was really nice to be with other people who'd experienced these same things, but the oppressed group I feel like my experiences are most like are gay men and I don't know why. I spend a lot of time with gay men. I'm really comfortable with them. A lot of my closest friends are gay men.

It seems like, for gay men, the community that they're in is one that was sort of thrown together by people's perceptions of who they were. They don't have anything in common except their sexuality, and because of the way people deal with them on the basis of their sexuality, they became a community. Maybe that's why: They created a community because of how they were perceived, not because of how they necessarily perceive themselves.

I was talking to one man about his being attracted to women and how that was something he's never been allowed to explore, because bisexuality in the gay community is such an issue that it's really putting his whole identity into jeopardy to do that. So he can be attracted to them, but that's something he can't express, really, even to himself. I could really relate to that—that for me to have any more of a black identity seems like an all-or-nothing kind of thing. If I wanted to explore what that would mean, I would have to sign the pledge or something. I can't sort of dabble in it and try to figure out how this would sort of fit, so I just don't do it.

Every once in a while something will happen that I wish I had more contact with, or that I'd had more of an understanding about. Most recently, it was the Rodney King stuff. I was really outraged, as a miscarriage of justice and as a person, but not as a black woman. That concept was very foreign to me.

There was a town meeting at Boalt, and people were talking about their reactions. I have a white friend who got beat up by a group of black men the night that the verdict came down. It may have just been a robbery, or it may have been that this was their way of expressing rage, and I brought this up at the town meeting. I said, "This is as wrong as what happened."

And this black man at school got really, really angry. He's like, "Well white people started racism," and you know, I couldn't relate to anything that he was saying. I'm watching all the black students in the audience, and even the ones who are a lot more moderate than this man are all nodding like they understand. And I just don't understand. I don't come out of whatever that cultural thing is that they all have in common.

Nya Patrinos
Age: 22
Residence: Philadelphia, Pennsylvania
Occupation: Theater wardrobe supervisor

Nya Patrinos grew up in an integrated section of Philadelphia called Mount Airy. Her parents—her father is white, half-Greek and half-Jewish; her mother is black, has a Cherokee great-grandfather, and is from South Carolina—met "around the Left in Philadelphia," Patrinos says. They married when they were thirty; both had been married before, she to a black man, he to a white woman.

Patrinos's mother, a psychiatric nurse, hoped for her daughter to identify as a multiracial person. In the last few years, Patrinos has started identifying as an African-American, and she says that makes her mother mad. "She said, 'You shouldn't let society define who you are,'" Patrinos remembers. "And I feel like, How can I not? I have to live in society. But she says, 'You're letting a racist world define you,' and she hates that and we fight over that issue if we ever talk about it, when we talk about it, but I don't know any other way to walk through the world. I identify as I do mainly because the outside world says I have no choice. And I think my mother's sort of upset by that. She doesn't think you need to identify like that, and that I should have gone through the whole world, my whole life, saying, 'No, I'm mixed, I'm mixed.' But I don't scream about it that much anymore, or bring it up before somebody else does.

"There was never a time when I would go into a room and say, 'I'm mixed,' but if there was any kind of discussion about it and people were saying what they were, I didn't want to deny anything. And I don't deny it now, but I don't know if I want to talk about it to everybody. I think I have more private zones than I did then."

Even as she settles into identifying more with African-American, Patrinos refuses to relinquish her personal connection to being mixed, based on her relationships with her father and his side of the family.

It's different when you have two very active parents who are claiming you, as opposed to maybe a woman who's been raped— like in slavery where a lot of women were raped by their masters— who has an interracial child that way. Or you have my father, who went to all the home and school association meetings. At certain points in elementary school I would have liked to have hid that I had a white father, but he was so active in everything! He would always be at this and that and everything. A lot of people always asked if I was adopted. I would never hide my father now, but I think: You're eleven, you're a shithead.

My elementary school was very white. It's a Quaker school, so you learn a lot and the teachers are pretty dedicated, and I remember feeling really odd there, just not really a part of what was going on. I remember sort of being an outcast until fourth grade. I remember people stepping on my coat and not having anybody to play with. I don't know if that has anything to do with being interracial or just maybe I was kind of a weird kid, but I do remember not really feeling very good there.

As I got older, I felt like I fit in a little bit more, but I remember when I left at the end of fourth grade, I didn't feel any kind of loss, like, "Oh, my goodness, I'm leaving all my friends." I was really fine about going somewhere else.

I really never found a community of people in college. I lived in a group house off-campus for a while, with eight people. I guess I knew all the fringe elements, the people who were writing, the

painters, the acting people, the people in the philosophy department—all the people sort of falling off the edge of the mainstream.
But I still don't know what frat house was which, which you're
supposed to know at Penn [University of Pennsylvania]. I failed. I
failed.

The African-American community at Penn is pretty militant,
and they don't want you to hang out with white people. There was
a W.E.B. Du Bois House where you lived if you were a "progressive" African-American. I could never find out when black student
union meetings there were because I lived in High Rise North and
they didn't want to put signs there because they were afraid that
white people were going to come. I know because I asked the guy
who was the president of the African-American student union, and
he said, "We can't get anything done with those people crashing
the meeting. You know how those people are."

I feel like I can never be a very militant African-American
person who hates white people because I'd hate fifty percent of
myself. So I couldn't really participate in that world at Penn because I'm not going to hate white people; it's just not what's going
to happen. I can't accept that, being mixed.

I think the black students just wrote me off. I'm sure people
knew who I was, because African-American men on the campus
kind of know who the African-American women are. I'm not
overweight, I'm okay-looking, so sometimes I would walk home
from the library and some guy would come and talk to me and
say, "Are you a graduate student?" And maybe I'm making this
up, but I think they saw me a lot of times with white people and
I got blacklisted. Maybe it wasn't as intentional as that, but nobody talked to me besides the one guy I asked about the meetings.

CHAPTER V

Self-Portrait

Michael Tyron Ackley
Age: 37
Residence: Oxford, Alabama
Occupation: Welder

Michael "Tony" Ackley did not respond to my advertisement in the Anniston Star, *a local paper. His wife, Gloria Ackley, did. She wrote that her husband had suffered because of his background, much of the abuse coming from his white mother's side of the family. For related reasons, he cannot read or write, which was why she was responding. All in all, she wrote, "I feel like he would be a very different person, if he had been raised in different circumstances (one race or the other) with a good family. My husband is really a good person—very good family man as long as everything seems to be going smoothly but cannot deal with any stress or change—Doesn't trust anybody—Always looks at the negative side of everyone & everything—Feels no self worth nor has any confidence."*

I interviewed Tony Ackley in the company of his wife at Quincy's, a popular family-style restaurant chain not far from their home. Up to this point, all of my interviews had been one-on-one, and I was uncertain of how a second person might influence the course of events. But because it was Gloria and not Tony who had contacted me, it seemed appropriate to include her. Also, I was concerned that without her the interview might never take place. Indeed, Ackley is a shy man. He defers to his wife frequently and refers to her constantly, although never by her name.

The Ackleys have been married seventeen years. They met under unusual circumstances: Tony and his mother needed a place to live—they were about to be evicted for nonpayment of rent—and his mother approached Gloria, a stranger who was twenty years old and married at the time. She felt badly for the then ten-year-old Tony and took them in. Gloria had four children from that first marriage (her husband died); she married Tony a decade after they met. After two years of marriage they had a son, who is now fifteen. Tony's mother now lives with them, which Tony says is purely out of Gloria's kind heart.

I don't know nothing about my mother and father gettin' together 'cause basically she lies about it. To this day she won't admit I'm black; she won't admit I have any black heritage in me at all. From the time I can remember, she told me my father was Mexican and Indian. She gives me a name, Donald Eugene Ackley, and says he lived in Arizona. That's all she tells me. My uncle—he lives out in California—he brought a man up here that was Mexican and Indian and tried to get him to admit that I was Mexican and Indian. The man said, "No way; the boy is half-black."

I've asked her, I said, "Give me some towns where I can go find him. I want to find him 'cause it means a lot to me. I'd like to see him one time, or if he's dead I'd like to know it." But she won't tell me anything about my father whatsoever. I've learned to live with it, but she can't.

Knowing my mom, she could have any kind of past, any kind. My mom was a drunken lush. I just tell you like it is. That's what she was. If she could find a man that would buy her something to drink and give her a good time, she'd go and whore a bit, 'cause she'd keep taking me to my aunts that lived in Oxford out here in the country, drop me off, and go off with her man and get drunk.

I'd be liable to stay out there two or three days, not see her, and if one of her boyfriends decided they want to beat me, they'd beat me. There wasn't nothing said about it. I had some uncles that'd do the same thing. If they'd walked by and take a look and said they want to beat me, they'd beat me. She's never said a word about it. I took a lot of beatings that I think I shouldn't a took, but she didn't care.

They beat me basically because they didn't like me and they was ashamed of what I was. I learned to live with it years ago, but nobody else could. I have one uncle and one aunt—it didn't bother them in the least. But the rest of my aunts and uncles, they would tolerate me, but I know they didn't like me. I have one right now, she's talking to me but she's lost her leg and she's got cancer and she thinks she's gonna die, so she trying to treat me better than what she used to. She wants to ease her conscience is what it is, because that's the same aunt who took her kids out of school because of me.

I was ten years old before I went to first day of school. The Blacks wouldn't let me to their school because they knowed I had a white mother and all my kinfolk was white. They said I was too white, I could not go to a black school; and the Whites said I was too black, I could not go to a white school. I was the first child, I think, in this county that integrated the white school, and the principal at the school just told 'em, "Look, the boy is ten years old. It's time for him to go to school." Said to my aunt, "He's gonna stay in school, so you might as well send 'em back." Soon as she seen I was gonna stay she sent 'em back, but she just had a little prejudice still. She was ashamed, that's what it was.

Because of that, I never learned to read from it. I went to a special class. I stayed in there one year. They learned me to count to a hundred; that was it. I skipped second grade and went to the third grade. I never had a teacher that took up time with me to learn me anything. I went all the way to the seventh grade. They just passed me from year to year.

I still haven't learned to read, and it bothers me 'cause I don't know what people are doing. It keeps me on the defensive.

I had white teachers when I went to school told me I wouldn't amount to nothing. Told me that I was dumb and I'd be lucky if I could get a job digging a ditch. And they never spent no time with me. I had one teacher when I was in the seventh grade that was a reading teacher. She tried to spend time with me. She had so many people in the reading class she couldn't, but she watched me come all the way up through grammar school, and she knew exactly how I felt. She said, "I know what kind of life you've had and I wish I had more time to help you with it, but I got so many students I just can't help you any more than I can help you now."

I quit in seventh grade. I had to go to work because when my mother would get a welfare check for me, she'd take it to the bootlegger or liquor store and spend it. My mother went to a boot-legger sometimes; it wasn't legal some of the times back. He'd buy back liquor bottles and give a nickel for a pint bottle and a dime for a half-pint bottle. I would take the bottles outside and save them, and that's how I'd get clothes to go to school. I'd take the bottles back during the summer, sell them to him, and go buy my school clothes, and then my mother would get mad because I wouldn't give her the money. I was about ten years old.

About that time, my grandmother died. When that happened, my mother took me and put me in my grandmother's house. I stayed in there for three weeks with quilts over the windows. Everything was dark, couldn't turn on the TV, no radio or nothing. I don't know her reason. I think she just went totally nuts. No food whatsoever. I ate nothing. I could've went to my aunt's; she wouldn't let me go to my aunt's. I had to go to people's house across the road and get food that they'd throwed out in the trash to the dogs. I ate biscuits, mustard, and onion for three weeks.

I was sitting out crying one day and one of my mother's boy-friends heard me and asked what was wrong, and I told him I was hungry. He went in and got talking to her and got her to go get something to drink. When she come out, he went and bought some groceries and I started eating. He throwed that up to me till the day he died. But I wasn't allowed to ask any of her boyfriends for anything. If I did, I'd get slapped, as simple as that. She took me to my uncle's house down in Oxford once because she was going off with one of her boyfriends. I'd say I was about seven, maybe eight years old. I wanted to go, I didn't want to stay there with [my uncle], so I run after her. My uncle went to check me. He slipped 'n' fell, he caught me, he slapped my face so many times and so hard my whole head was numb. I stood there with tears in my eyes; my face was completely numb, I could not hear nothing. She got in the car and left and went off with her boyfriend. I walked out into the pasture and sat out there until way after dark, waiting for them to go to bed before I went in 'cause I was scared he was going to kill me. But yet, she got in the car and said, "That's what you get." That's exactly what she said, and she got in the car with her boyfriend and left.

I know my mother resented the fact that I was black. She never said anything directly, but I could tell by the way she acted she was ashamed to be around me. She done anything she could to embarrass me or to put me down. When I was four and five and six years old, I had a hernia. She would make me take my pants down and show people the hernia, and it was embarrassing to me, 'cause I had a hernia the size of that coffee cup, literally the size of that coffee cup. It was up till I was about nine years old before I flat told her I'm not doing it anymore, but she would get a stick, a hickory, and whup me and make me show people.

People told me when I was first born a black couple in Jacksonville wanted to adopt me. But my grandmother told my mother, "No. You had the boy, you're gonna raise the boy." Sometimes I think I would have been better off with those people. They was pretty well-to-do for black people back in them days and since then their grandkids are growed up and some of 'em's lawyers and I think one of 'em's a doctor. But my grandmother said no, basically no. In a way I feel cheated because my grandmother done me that way, but I love my grandmother; I mean she loved me and I loved her and when she died I felt deserted, really I did.

She was my one strong family member. In her eyes I could do nothing wrong. My grandmother never whupped me, she never had to whup me, she could talk to me and I'd do anything she wanted. If she'd told me to crawl on top of the house and jump off, I would have jumped off because I know she loved me and she wasn't gonna let me do nothing that was gonna hurt me. When she died I was nine or ten, I can't really remember. I blocked a lot of that out. I never really grieved about my grandmother that much; people say I didn't love her, but at the time she died I felt deserted. She was the only one, she was the only one that was doing things to help me, because if it hadn't been for my grandmother, my mother would beat me with anything, anytime she wanted to.

I have black hair and white hair. Part of it's straight, but it's curly, it's aggravatin'. In this vicinity, it wasn't all that good. As long as I stayed in my hometown I was all right. Everyone knew me there.

I went out to the country once where I had a relative lived out there. There was a store about four miles away from their house, a little country store, so when we was kids, me and my cousin and three of his friends walked to the store to get a Coke and potato chips and cakes. They put their stuff on the counter and the man takes their money. I walked up and put mine on the counter and the man said, "I won't sell you a damn thing, nigger." That's what he said; that's words he said.

He loved my cousin, who was raised out there, so my cousin went in to get the stuff and the man told him, said, "You let him have it, I won't sell you nothing else." So he bought my stuff. I had to walk a mile to go around the curve where the man couldn't see me before I could get it.

I've had that to happen down here in different places. They sell it to me, but you could tell by the way they were doing it they really didn't want me to be in their store. But I've got to the point now it don't bother me, pretty much by basically just living my life like I've been living. I work around a lot of black people and white people; I have black and white friends.

There was a time, when we first got married, when I would not have come into a restaurant like this. I felt I wasn't welcome. The people would stare at me and I couldn't relax. Even when I was without her [Gloria]. There's still a lot of prejudice in this area; there's still a lot of prejudice. There's a place I will not go to out toward the country where my cousin lives. I got run out from there one time by two carloads of people that stopped me and told me to get my black ass out from there.

You can ask my wife. I will not go back out there. My cousin out there told me, "Now, they're not like that anymore. Come here." I says, "I ain't coming unless I bring a rifle, a pistol, and shotgun." I said, "That's the only way I'll come out here. I know how those people are." I refuse to go out there.

That incident was ten, maybe fifteen years ago, but still the same people live out there. My cousin says they've changed, but people like that just don't change, I don't think they do. Now there's one feller that lives out there, his granddaddy was into the Klan—that's real big out there—he come to work at the foundry where I work now. He had to change his ways 'cause there's more black working at our shop than there are white. I don't think he like the way his granddaddy was doin' 'cause you could talk to him, you know, he would try to treat everybody right, but when he went home he had to act a different way.

When I first went into the shop, there was as many black working in the shop as there was white. Really there was more black, and there was a black man help get me on out there, and my cousin was working, he went to the boss and said, "Look, my cousin needs a job," he said. "I'm gonna tell you he's a hard worker, but he's half-black, he's half-white. If it's gonna cause problems let me know." The man says, "As long as he works, I don't care." He brought me a application home, filled it out. I took it back, they put me to work two days later.

Before that I was working with the city of Jacksonville. I had a civil service job when I went down to the foundry. I'd been working with the city for two years, but I left because I don't know whether they were prejudiced or what but I worked two years and never had a day of vacation. I don't know what the rules really were, but in the city of Jacksonville nothing's illegal. They done what they wanted to back then; the chief of police run that town back then. I was making eighty-two dollars a week working with the city of Jacksonville, and I went to the foundry, worked three days, took home a hundred and thirteen. So I figured, well, I just died and gone to heaven.

I just take people the way they was raised and their background, you know. Most of the white people—it's not that way now but it used to be—most of the white people had nothing to do with Blacks. I can remember when I was a small child, if you had a toothache and you went to the dentist, you went in the dentist's back door—you didn't go in the front door—and if you went to a doctor's office you sit in a certain room by yourself. The doctor had certain instruments he used to examine you and other instruments he used on white people.

Like I told my wife the other day when we went to her nephew's wedding: I felt like a grain of pepper in a salt box. We stopped at a Quincy's on the way back; we walked in and everybody stopped eating and stared. We had our son and his wife and our daughter and her husband with us. There was a policeman sitting there, and he just stopped and looked for a long time. We find that we are more accepted closer to home. Everybody around here wasn't raised up prejudice. I work with a white man. He's a little bit older than I am. He says from the time he was a little boy he didn't know any difference, says he had black friends and white friends and they all went to one another's house, they sat down and ate. If he done something wrong their daddy whup him; they done something wrong his daddy whup them. He said he was a teenager before he realized there was any difference, but to him it didn't matter. We talk, we take our breaks and things, we talk a lot.

The hardest thing for me about having my background has been the prejudice, really, 'cause of not being able to do things that a lot of other people do. I've had cousins, they'd go in places and I knowed I couldn't go 'cause they just wouldn't allow me in the place. Around town I could go into the stores. Everybody up there knows me so it still wasn't that big a problem, but if I were to come to Anniston or go to Piedmont, I couldn't go into a store like my cousins did.

Most of the houses we've moved into we'd have to do repairs. I mean, I've fixed up a whole lot of houses. I always did it, I never called and said, "Send the plumber," you know. I work good with my hands. I never call an electrician or a plumber; I do it myself. I learned just by watching—reading's my only problem. I can watch something, I can do it.

Just like welding: I worked at the shop out there for about four or five years, and I just watched the welders and I run a machine that's basically like a welder but it cuts steel off. It got time to take the welding test, and the boss man told me he didn't want me to have the job. He said, "If you don't pass the test, you go back where you were."

I run the plate, passed X ray, they had to give me a welding job. I get ready to do something at the shop, they don't give me no training. They just put me on the job and say do it, and I find a way to do it, so everything they put me on I could do, it don't bother me. If it come to working with my hands I can do fine, but if I have to sit down with a piece of paper you can forget it.

Sometimes there are things I'm supposed to read, but basically my job's just welding. I don't have to read. You know, we have a safety meeting or something, they give us something to read or every once in a while we'll have a little form or something to fill out. Basically, I just sit beside somebody I know real good and write down what they write except for the name and the badge number. Numbers I do good with; I can remember numbers pretty good. But the writing itself, the words and the letters—I'm getting better. I can read a few more words when I get used to 'em. When we first got married, I couldn't spell her name. Now I can. I wrote it the other day and told her I loved her and it totally, totally blowed her mind. Usually I just write "I love you" and give her the note, and I wrote her name down and it kind of freaked her out a little bit.

My experience is definitely different from people who are all one thing. If they was all black or all white, they knew what they could do and what they couldn't do; they knowed their limitations of where they could go and everything. My limitations was on both sides really, because if I went into an area that was mostly black and they seen my mother, I couldn't do anything the black kids done, because they knowed if they played with me, people being prejudiced like they was, there was gonna be trouble for them. Basically I just had to stay at home or call trouble. So when I grew up, I had no one to talk to.

She'll [Gloria will] tell you I still don't talk much. I'm talking more now than I ever have, really. It's hard for me because I have emotions that run deep about the way I was born, the way I was raised, and about my father and not being able to read. Usually I get broke up about it. I mean, she'll pry it out of me. All these years she's talked to me, told me I'm as good as anybody else.

When I first approached her after her husband died, she didn't want to go with me because she's ten years older and thought I was too young. But I know more about the way things were going than she did. I'm what you call a street kid. I've seen things go on that she never could think of. Our daughter was going with a feller, and I told my wife he's no good, he ain't nothing but a con man. She wouldn't believe me. He finally showed her what he was, but I could talk to him and see 'cause some of my kinfolk was like that and some of the people I run around with was like that.

My mother never talks about those times and how she treated me. She didn't do none of that stuff, oh no—she denies it, she denies it. She's that type of person. She'd lie on a heartbeat. But my mother's hit me with bricks, she's hit me with broomsticks, belts. She threw a brick at me, broke my ankle, and then when she got to me, took a stick and beat me. See, my mother's basically just a mean person.

She's never worked. I had to take responsibility for myself; nobody else was gonna do it. I got tired of gettin' beat and said, this is it, time to stop. Last beating I had, my uncle beat me. I was about thirteen years old. He took a cow rope about an inch round, he whupped me with the rope. I said, "You'll never hit me again." I walked up the road to my other uncle's house, bought me a twenty-two pistol, loaded it up, and walked back there and showed it to 'im, told 'im, "Don't ever hit me again. I'll kill you."

He seen the pistol, called the chief of police. The chief searched me, never found the pistol, but the chief knowed I had it and my uncle knowed I had it, and he never touched me again because I was serious. I would have killed 'im, I would have went to prison for it because I was tired of being beat on. I'd been beat on for thirteen years of my life and it was time to stop.

I don't know how I stayed out of trouble all this time. I'll be honest with you, I don't know. Never been in prison. I've been in jail for drunk driving but never been to jail for nothing else. I used to run around with some people that's in prison now.

I would be in prison if it weren't for her 'cause I got to the point I won't take nothing off nobody no more, and I got a short fuse sometimes. I'll take a lot, but when I get to a boiling point my fuse goes off and I lose my senses and have no control. If it wasn't for her, I'd have been in prison a long time ago. She keeps me under control. It's not easy sometimes; I'll give you that. It's not easy. But she does keep me under control.

I don't know if there was an advantage I had either way in having this background. In this day and time, it's okay to have half-breed kids, but if you had asked me twenty years ago, I'd have said no. I think it's all right for the kid to be a half-breed as long as their parents is honest with 'em and tell 'em about both sides of their ancestry. That's basically my problem, 'cause I know nothing about my father whatsoever. I don't know whether he died young or whether he's still living. I don't know whether cancer killed him or he was a murderer or an alcoholic or what. All I know is about my mother's side. That's it. But I think as long as both parents let 'em know their heritage, I don't think there's anything wrong with it at all. I will say find a good place to raise 'em, though.

Interracial couples should tell their kids to be whatever they want to be. If they want to live their life as being black, live it as being black or live it as being white. Or if they want to live it, as I say, "sitting on a fence," both ways, black and white, that's fine, as long as they be the best they can be and they know what they are and they're happy with what they choose to be.

I've never known another half-breed like me, not to talk to. I seen some in town, but not like we would talk. I've gotten a lot out of the talk shows, like *Oprah*. She had a thing on there about interracial couples and marriages and things, and it helped me a lot listening to some of the thoughts they had. Some of the feelings they had, I had. Yesterday, Oprah was on about mothers that would not tell their children who their fathers were. The woman that was on there was just like my mother.

My mother told me one time when I was eleven, she said, "Your daddy come by to see you last night, but I wouldn't wake you up." I said, "Why didn't you wake me up?" "I didn't want him to wake you up." I said that wasn't fair to me. I don't think he come by. I think she just told me that playing a mind game with me. She used to try to control me a lot, 'cause as long as she had me under control she had somewhere to stay and a meal ticket, 'cause when I was little she used me to get a welfare check, but when I got bigger, she wanted me to work to support her. She would get mad. She'd say, "You don't buy any groceries." I said, "Because you won't cook 'em." She wouldn't cook for me.

I do most of our cooking now because my wife has a bad back. But I don't mind. She always says, "I feel bad about you doing it." I say until I complain don't worry about it. My wife, yes, that's the main one right there. Oh, she's learned me to open up and tell her my feelings more'n you know.

When we first got married, I kept all my emotions inside. I had no one to talk to when I was growing up. If I said anything, I got beaten for it so I kept my mouth shut. I could be riding in the car with my mother, and it'd be cold and I'd be sitting in the back seat. I'd ask her to roll up the window, I'd get slapped and told to shut up. I'd have to sit in the floorboard and curl up in a knot to try to stay warm. They'd be up in front drunk, and I'd be back there freezing to death. I wasn't allowed to get a Coke or nothing else, so I learned to keep my feelings inside.

One thing I would change, if I could, would be learning to read. That would make a lot of difference for me. Not learning to read was caused by the racial thing, because if I could have started school like everybody else at six years old, then I could have took my time like everybody else and I could learn to read. But once I got to school they just passed me from grade to grade to get rid of me 'cause basically no teacher wanted me in her class. They used the thing that I was too old and so they had to pass me, but I think a lot of them was prejudiced along the way. I had two teachers that treated me half-way decent. Two, all the time I went to school. I'd do anything I could for them, no hesitation. The rest of them I didn't care anything about 'cause they didn't care.

I told my wife that the only person that ever cared about me was my grandmother and her. That's the way I've always felt. I never felt like anybody ever cared, and I don't trust anybody. She's always getting on me: "You don't trust nobody," but that's the way I was raised.

My mother tried to kill me twice. She tried to feed me rat poisoning one time when I was about three or four. I can remember her trying to do it, but one of my cousins took it away from her.

Then she tried to put my head in a gas heater and burn me up.

She was cold sober and she was sticking my head in, and my other cousin that's older than me, he knocked her over the heater, hit her and knocked her over. I can remember her trying to do it. I can remember her telling me: "You little burr-headed son of a bitch, I'm gonna kill you." And I remember her trying to hold me down and feed me the rat poison, and I remember her trying to stick my head in the heater.

I didn't turn out like my mother because I had to learn to survive, that's basically what it is. The way I was raised, I was afraid to be destructive because I wouldn't survive. I had to learn to just deal with things and keep my mind off it or I wouldn't survive. The worst is over with. I do the physical work, my wife does the paperwork, it's a good combination. I do the physical work, she does the paperwork, can't beat that.

My license has white on it, but I consider myself a half-breed. It don't bother me a bit to say it or that people call me that, 'cause that's what I am. When I'm at work they call me half-breed. Even my boss man, the shop superintendent, calls me half-breed. They holler, *"Half-breed!"* I answer. I'm what I am and I can't change it. I might as well make the best of it. I've learned to live with— inside—myself, and basically I figure that's the only one I got to please about the way I am is myself. She [Gloria] knows what I am and she's happy with it. It doesn't bother her. As long as me and her is happy, damn with everybody else. That's strong language, but that's what I think.

CHAPTER VI

Friends and Strangers

I have a hard time with white girls, since most white girls—I don't know how to say it—they act like white girls. A lot of them seem to be real backstabbing. It was almost like it was ingrained in them from their mothers, this tendency to be backstabbing. It wasn't all of them by any means, but with a lot of white girls, you'd see them go over to their friends and turn around to talk about another girl as soon that girl left. My friend Shakela and I were like, "You could at least give her a minute to get away!" I did have some white girls who were friends, but most of them were considered outsiders, too, for whatever reasons.—Simone Brooks, p.313

My junior and senior years [of high school], I was popular, and I got along with everybody. At lunchtime I would always move around to different people, because I had a bunch of friends. The athletes sat together, people who live in the same neighborhood or kids who grew up together would hang out together. But me, I was at everybody's table trying to find out the latest on everybody else, so that was fun. And I've always been like that, even when I was younger.—Jacqueline Djanikian, p.309

To one friend, I was a quantity she couldn't process, and so she didn't understand me and she didn't understand my condition. When we would get into black and white discussions, the comment that would often come up was, "How would you know?" Because I had very strong opinions about the condition that we have and that our communities have. I developed them, I felt entitled to them, and if there was ever a disagreement between us, the delegitimizing factor was always, "How would you know?"

See, even my closest friends at some point burned me. Closest female friends. There were a couple of women that I knew for years, and we have since reconciled, but they burned me and they burned me as if I was a white girl.—Jeana Woolley, p.250

The comment I kept getting from kids was, "You're not white, you're black," or, "You're not black, you're white." People saw me the way they wanted to. If they liked me, then I was usually one of them; if they didn't, then I wasn't. You knew how people felt about you by whether they saw you as one of them or not.

When black kids said, "You're not really white," they were trying to be friendly, they were trying to give me a compliment. And I'm going, "No, I am." For me, it wasn't something to be embarrassed about; for them, they would have felt awkward being the opposite of what they were, so they projected that onto me.

Everybody was trying to change me for a while until they realized I didn't care. In the past I might have picked white one day and then black the next. But you just get to a point, at least I have, that it really doesn't matter. The people that are gonna dislike you because of your skin color really aren't people that you want to associate with in the first place.

Everybody keeps talking about the racism that white people have, the racism that black people have. I think everybody's basically a bigot, and they just don't realize it. I'm sure I'm a bigot. I probably think mulatto people are God's gift to this green earth way down in my psyche. It's not something I like, but if we're willing to admit that we may have prejudiced feelings, then we have a place to start from. We have that understanding of ourselves so that we can temper our judgment, we can temper our actions and find out what the truth is.—Mark Durrow, p.359

Around eighth grade I had a good friend, Julie, who was in orchestra with me. We both played the violin. I'd asked her to come over to my house a couple of times, and she couldn't. My mom—who knew her mother or knew about her mother from other mothers in the PTA—said, "Julie's mother's not going to let her come over here, and it's because we're black. If you can deal with being friends in school, that's fine, but you're not going to be friends with her outside of school." As my sister and I got older, that kind of conversation was common.—Bernette Ford, p.207

A lot of places I go, people assume I'm what they are. Whether it's Indians or Hispanics, whatever. Wherever I go, people start talking to me in their language.—Jeffrey Scales, p.181

To be honest, ninety-nine percent of my friends are black. There might be one or two white people I know, but not close friends. I was thinking about this a couple of months ago, just saying to myself, "I don't really have any white friends." I know Whites—I've never had a problem being around white people—I just don't have any white friends that I could say call up and say, "Let's go do this or let's go do that." I just don't.—Joseph Marable, p.176

I found that growing up, white people seemed to accept me more for who I was. I think black people are more pressured to be culture-identified in this society, and, therefore, if you don't fit into their mold, they have a hard time letting you in. Especially as teenagers and older children. I didn't have much exposure to Blacks as a young child, so it wasn't until fifth grade that I felt my first real outcasting from Blacks. By that time they were old enough to have learned how to do that. My experience with younger children, who were mostly white children, was that they didn't care what you looked like. If you were fun, you were fun.

I still have friends whose parents are racist and look at me funny, but can't tell their adult daughters or sons, "You can't be friends with that person."—Neisha Wright, p.87

I cooked one summer in a place in Connecticut, and a woman said, "How do you know how to make kugel?" My grandmother taught me how to make kugel, and I told her that my grandmother's Jewish. I've known this woman for years, and she could never remember that about me. That door opens and it just closes again; she could not process the information.—Nya Patrinos, p.134

Just after completing an interview for this book, I stood on a subway platform in Oakland, California, waiting for a train. When it pulled up, I reached the doors alongside two other people, one of them an African-American girl who couldn't have been more than eleven. Barely above a whisper, eyes downcast, she threatened, "You just better wait, peckerwood."

She spoke so softly that at first I didn't register what she'd said. When it sank in, twenty-two years dropped away and I was back on the Number 31, the public transit bus that took me from my suburban elementary school to my West Philadelphia neighborhood each day. I was about eleven years old then, too, and a black girl my age leaned close the entire, tortuous forty-five-minute ride, whispering in my ear as she tugged one of my braids. "You better tell me where you get off, cracker," she said, " 'cause I'm gonna get off with you and kick your butt." I stared hard at the pages of my book until the bully got off, one stop before mine.

A month ago, a strung-out man, probably homeless, probably high, perhaps mentally ill, came up to me on the street. "Give me a quarter," he demanded. "Sorry," I said, and kept walking. "Well then fuck you, white bitch!" he said. *That's mulatto bitch, buddy.*

Biracial people have no monopoly on confronting expectations or racial stereotypes based on their appearance. These expectations come from everywhere: from friends, strangers, coworkers, family, and often from both Blacks and Whites. Most typically, physical features—skin color, hair, nose and lip shape—are the basis of assumed racial allegiances or aversions.

Those automatic reactions often are influenced and even reversed when the less apparent side of the family is somehow revealed. What can be especially troubling is when the shift in
treatment is based solely on this revelation. The person whose
attitude is shifting—perhaps suddenly accepting the person they
once kept at a distance—often defends that shift as logical. "Now
I know I can relax with you," said one black woman when she
discovered that a white-looking acquaintance was biracial. "I know
that you're not going to say something ignorant all of a sudden."

Once a racial allegiance is established, the biracial person is
assumed to be part of one group, and so, by definition, not part of
any other. People who would never criticize another racial group
directly will often let slip a prejudice if they think they are surrounded by their own. These gems can shine at any moment, in
any conversation. Waiting for that comment, that disappointment,
hangs menacingly over new relationships. As a number of biracial
people said, "I am always waiting for the other shoe to drop."

White people often use color to describe a threat ("This big
black man tried to cut in front of me") or to explain failure ("She
was a young black crack whore") or to unwittingly point up the
insurmountable distance between worlds ("That cop hassled me
for no good reason—that's what the Blacks always complain about,
isn't it?").

Among African-Americans, the biracial person might be put to
the test. Blacks might talk about "white" behaviors they don't like.
Sometimes antiwhite statements will escalate in what seems to be
a test of where the biracial person's loyalties lie, of how much she
or he is willing to take.

Understandably, these frictions are troubling when they crop
up in friendships. But the passing comments of strangers, if they
happen often enough, can impress just as deeply.

Eliza Dammond
Age: 22
Residence: New York, New York
Occupation: Film production assistant

Eliza "Lalou" Dammond's mother is white, from Switzerland, and her father, who died when she was two, was black. They met in San Francisco while out to dinner with mutual friends. Dammond says she has asked her mother why she had children with a black man and that her mother thinks it was partly random, partly the times. "She wasn't like, 'I'm going to come to the United States and find a black man,' or, 'Black people are so exotic,'"

Dammond says. "Having grown up in Switzerland, I didn't come to this country with all the stereotypes and all the baggage about race that you have growing up American."

As well as Dammond can recall, both sides of the family seemed fairly free of racial baggage. She spent many summers on an aunt's farm in Switzerland, and she maintains strong connections to her paternal grandparents, having visited their Harlem home throughout her childhood. Her grandmother is a descendant of William and Ellen Craft, an American couple whose clever escape from slavery and subsequent community service have been documented in several books and films.

Dammond's strong connection to the two sides of her family has translated into a private identity that embraces both. But she still finds discord between what she knows about herself and how the world sees her. Indeed, she says, people are never sure of what she is: In New York people assume she's Puerto Rican, but she's also been asked if she's Indian, Moroccan, or Chinese. The only people who have ever guessed correctly, she says, are other biracial people.

As a kid I would say, "my father's black and my mother's white." Because my grandparents were such a large part of my life and still are, that counterbalanced the fact that my father wasn't alive. If my father wasn't alive *and* I didn't have any contact with his side of that family, that would have been pretty confusing. I still think it is confusing in a whole lot of ways. But I didn't have a grasp on what that meant in my life until I was older. As a young person, I didn't have people saying, "What? Your father's black and your mother's white?" or, "That's amazing!"

Because I didn't have a lot of being called a nigger or having my hair pulled, that's part of why I've grown into my identity without much trauma. People will say I could go either way, and I've had the experience that everybody wants to put a label on you. And a lot of people have trouble saying you're mixed; they want to say you're black or you're white. That's probably the most difficult thing I've had to deal with. I can't, I haven't—it's not even a matter of choosing. I even have trouble with that. It's not a choice. It's what I am, I feel. And black people have told me they have been insulted when I say that I'm half-black, half-white, because saying you're half-white is saying that being black is not good enough. And that's tricky because I certainly identify in many ways *more* with black culture.

I once got into this big argument with my close friend, who ended up saying, "You don't know what it's like to be black, because people don't look at you and think that you're black." I think that's partly true. I know there are reactions people have to you from your appearance. I know that because I know what it's like to have that as a woman, to have people react to you in a negative way, even if it's very subtle, because you're a woman. That's sexism. And even men who think they really understand what sexism is, don't—because they're not women. They don't see, not just the catcalling on the street, but the subtle rejections. So in that way, I don't know exactly what it means to identify as being black or even as being white.

Part of it is a matter of how people react. If I say I'm black, I've had people laugh at me in disbelief, tell me I'm not. I don't know altogether what it's like to have a black person's experience. But I do in some ways, and I really do feel that I am part black and I wish sometimes that people would really know that. I don't know how I'd do that, though. I can't say that I wouldn't want a white mother; that's disrespectful as far as I'm concerned. I mean, I love my mother very much—I don't wish she didn't exist and I don't want to exchange her for anybody.

But there is that feeling that you want people to believe you and to believe that you really do feel these things. And people have a hard time believing that, I think. Which is hard, because then you question yourself. You think, Am I really black? Do I act the right way? Maybe I don't act the right way. I don't have the right vocabulary, I don't have the right accent, I don't come from the right place, my skin isn't dark enough. All of those things, and that's tough sometimes.

Sometimes I'll say I'm black; usually I say I'm mixed. The most recent time I had a negative reaction was this past summer. I met a black student at Columbia, and we got on the topic of Howard University and he said, "So you have a cousin who went to Howard?"

And I said, "Yeah."

And he said, "Is she Hispanic?"

And I said, "No, she's black."

He said, "You're black!"

"Well, my father's black and my mother's white."

"What color skin was your father, so that you came out like that?"

So I proceeded to tell him the story of my ancestors. My great-great-great-grandfather and grandmother were slaves in Georgia, and my great-great-great-grandmother, Ellen Craft, was very light-skinned. They escaped from slavery by having her dress up as a man and pretend to be his slaveowner, and she took him on the train. He traveled in the slaves' quarters, and she traveled with other white passengers. She put a bandage around her head to make it look like she had an ear infection and pretended she was hard of hearing so she didn't have to do a lot of talking and conversing with people.

I grew up on that story. And my grandmother has really continued to keep that story alive. She narrated a short movie that was made about it in the early seventies, and she has done a lot of talk shows. It's pretty amazing to have a story like that, to have ancestors like that.

So that's how I responded to this person. My reaction was to explain why I am so light-skinned. I shouldn't have to do that. For me, that was my defense. I had to scramble to explain to him, and

I just felt so rejected by his reaction. I know I'm always going to run into people who are not going to be entirely satisfied by my appearance and by the way I act and whether I'm white enough or black enough.

It's funny, because I feel like I've had that all my life, even before race was so much of an issue, because of my name. It's the same reaction. People hear Lalou and they're like, *"What! La-who? Where did you get that name?"* Ever since I was a little kid I would let people call me whatever they wanted, just so I didn't have to go through the explanation. And I never felt like, "Why didn't my mother call me Mary?" because I like the name Lalou. I mean, it's my name. But it's that same sort of thing, that constant explaining of yourself. I'm never going to be able to please everybody, but when it comes to friends who still have trouble with your identity, that's painful in some ways.

Most questions pretty much come from black people. White people just don't understand at all. Not to be unfair to white people, but it's like what I was saying about being a woman before: It's not the same thing as *being*. It's just not the same issue for white people. Either they're not racists or they are. The level I was talking about before—not just the level of like, "What are you?" but more the personal level—it's more my experience with black friends than it is with white friends.

I didn't want to have any more to do with that person at Columbia, even though I thought he was nice and I liked him so far, but it made me uncomfortable and unhappy that he just thought it was so absurd. That's one of the main things that I've come to terms with: No one's ever going to be satisfied, and I'm the one who has to be satisfied. I have to go with what I feel because I can't let other people's opinions about this shape who I am because there's not going to be anybody out there—well, my friends, obviously, and my family—who acknowledge me to be what I am. If I let every negative thing affect me, then I'm going to be in the gutter, because nobody's ever going to be satisfied; they're going to want me to be what they see me as or what they want me to be or what their stereotypes want me to be. So this guy who scoffed at the idea that I was black, well, too bad for him. There's nothing I can do about it. He has his opinions, and his opinions are formed by things that have happened to him. When that happened, I was like, I can't go on letting people like that make me feel terrible.

Emma Baker
(See also page 32)

Emma Baker, whose father was rumored to be her mother's employer, says that although most older Blacks can tell she's black, her looks have set her apart her entire life. Her only true respite was a visit to Turkey in the early 1970s, when her husband was stationed in Istanbul for the U.S. Army.

"I went over during the Christmas holidays, and everybody there was the same," she says. "It was so peaceful. You didn't hear, 'She thinks she's something; she thinks she's better than anybody else.' You didn't see the looks on anybody's face like you would see back here. I didn't have to walk the line as such. There was no color mentioned, none whatsoever. Now it could have been because we were guests of theirs, but I got the feeling that they were like that all the time. That was the first time I had ever really felt like a free person, on the inside. I'm not sure if I'm using the right word or not, but that freedom to be me, to not be white and to not be black, but just to be a person."

There have been some people who mistook me for white, but I don't see why. When I left my hometown and moved to Columbia, South Carolina, that was when they first allowed Blacks to register to vote, sometime between '55 and '60.

I was in line down at the courthouse where you had to go to register, and this white woman looked around and started talking to me, and I started talking to her. She didn't ask me if I was white. She just started talking, and I just answered her intelligently. There was somebody else in front of her who was white, and the two of them had a time when the registrar got to me and asked my race. I said—at that time we were "Negroes"—and if those women had had false teeth they would have swallowed them. You should have seen the expressions on their faces. Needless to say, they had no more to say to me. I suddenly changed to them; I was somebody with horns and a tail and that sort of thing. So I was in line for about thirty-five more minutes, and they were just mum. They said nothing. Not even to each other.

I could see them looking, and one put her hand over her mouth and kind of whispered something. I think the whisper was, "I thought she was white," but I couldn't hear what it was. That kind of thing has happened on many occasions.

Back in '63 or '64, my husband was overseas, and this friend of mine invited me to dinner for my birthday and to a movie to see *Gone with the Wind,* and we went out for lunch. We got to this restaurant—at that time they had integrated the restaurants—and I saw this woman in there that my grandmother used to clean up for. Sometimes my grandmother would take me with her and she would have me clean the sinks, clean the bathroom—I would do whatever it was that I could. I wasn't tall enough to get over the sink, but she would put me on a little stool to stand on to wash the dishes in this woman's house. Back home they called me Emma Lou—I don't put the Lou on now—so when I saw her in this restaurant I spoke and she said, "Hello, Emma Lou."

She was sitting down, and she had somebody with her. Now she had come from our town to Columbia, and it's about fifty miles. She had this white friend with her, and my friend and I sat down at a table after we spoke. Maybe she was hoping I wouldn't sit down. She seemed friendly, and when she first saw me there was a waitress leaving their table, still writing as though they had given her their order. But they got up about five minutes later and left, and I don't know if they left because we were sitting down right across from them and my grandmama used to work for her and I was black, but they left. I thought that it was fun; by that time I had just decided that if somebody felt like that, then they had a problem, I didn't. We stayed there and had our meal; we were not inconvenienced, we were not sitting at the same table with her. We thought they had given their order and then decided that they weren't quite ready yet to sit down and eat with Blacks.

Saundra Robinson
Age: 47
Residence: East Point, Georgia
Occupation: Psychiatrist

Saundra Robinson specializes in teaching nonviolent conflict resolution as well as counseling adolescents. Like Emma Baker (page 32), she is often taken for white on appearance. Robinson's father passed for white throughout her life, and as a consequence, gave her little information about his side of the family. She says that a sixth-grade assignment to make a family tree prompted her to start asking questions. The answers eventually pointed her—decades later—toward owning the identity her father had rejected. "You're creating unnecessary pain for yourself," was one of the few things he said to her on the subject.

Being part of the black community is where she feels more comfortable, and "once I made the choice," she says, "I felt a whole lot better. I've been struggling with the results of it ever since, but for me, the personal choice was always there to be made." Her struggle stems from her appearance, which, taken alone, suggests to most people that she is white. She has felt a rootlessness through much of her life, and describes herself as a "tumbleweed."

An exception was when she traveled to South Africa as part of a delegation of African-Americans. Her group had an audience with the African National Congress leader, Nelson Mandela, then recently released from years of incarceration. She remembers him saying to her, "Welcome home, daughter. It doesn't matter how long you've been gone and how much transition and change has taken place, you're a daughter of the soil and you're a part of us."

"I have never felt that way in this country," she says.

Growing up in the fifties, everyone would always ask what I was. I had big old wild hair that was braided and things like that, but people never would ask if I were Negro; it was always if I were something else. And yet by about the midseventies, suddenly people would say, "Oh, you certainly don't look black and you don't do this black and . . ." It's like, man, all my life I got white people telling me what I am or what I look like. I had them telling me when I was little, "Well, you don't look white—I think you got something else going on in there." And then twenty years later: "Well, you don't really look black." That's the way it's always been; people trying to tell me who I am.

Let's say we're talking percentwise, then ninety-five percent of it's from white and five percent from black. Perfect example: The other day I had to call the police to my house for something, and it was a brother who showed up. And he's filling out the police report and this and that. They always ask for race and things, and he didn't, he just wrote in "black." And I had just come out casually and explained to him what was going on. Later on that same day, another policeman came back, white, to do a follow-up. He's filling out a report, and of course he puts down "W." I didn't tell either one of them anything.

I've always found that if you're in a crowd of Blacks and you're talking with them for more than five minutes, we're much more sensitive to things about people, and we pick it up. Whites hear nothing; they go simply by what they think they're looking at, and that's it. If you would just listen to what people have to say and how they feel and think, you're going to see beyond what you think you're looking at. People ask me if I'm Jewish, and I say, "No, I'm Episcopalian. Why? Are you looking for a Jewish temple or something?" And they look at me like that wasn't the answer they were looking for at all. Of course, it's just my hostility. I keep saying one of these days I'm going to get old enough to be at a point in my life where I'm not going to be bothered by that, and no one's going to ask me anymore.

Greg Wolley
Age: 37
Residence: Portland, Oregon
Occupation: Environmental education manager

From what Greg Wolley has pieced together —thanks to fractured bits of information from adoption records and surviving relatives—his Irish-American biological mother was married and had three kids when she became pregnant with him. His biological father was black, a neighbor with whom she had a brief relationship. Wolley assumes that the relationship and resultant pregnancy were "incredibly shameful and scandalous: This is the midfifties, and black men were still being lynched for just looking at somebody the wrong way. Needless to say, I was relinquished at five days old. My adoptive mother was told by the social worker that my birth mother's husband said if I was light-complected enough, if I looked enough like I could fit in, then I could stay with the family. I didn't make the cut on complexion, so I went out."

Wolley grew up in the San Francisco Bay area, raised by a black couple who adopted him as an infant. Based on appearance, he is generally assumed to be black. He grew up comfortable in a black identity and black family. But he has found that his profession, his interests, and his choice of where he lives have divided his world along racial lines.

In the eighth grade I had two friends that I hung around with: One was Portuguese and one was black. And in the ninth grade, I was kind of going through the black awareness, black power movement. That was a real important time, just learning about black history and growing my hair long. It was kind of scary to my parents because they had gone through all the phases they went through, from colored to Negro, and now we're talking about black, which was supposedly a derogatory term. James Brown had this song, *Say It Loud (I'm Black and I'm Proud)*, and that got on my father's nerves. He was like, "Why do you have to say I'm black and I'm proud, I'm black and I'm proud? Why can't you just be Greg? Why do you have to be black?"

I had Huey Newton posters in my bedroom with his gun belts and everything, and I was kind of semimilitant, but then at the same time my black friends and I all had white girlfriends. It was kind of a trend—it wasn't making a statement; it wasn't conscious at all. It was just a clique of kids that we fell into at school, and the way the Bay Area is set up, there's the flats and there's the hills. And most of those girls lived in the hills right next to Berkeley, very upper-middle-class. Our neighborhood was middle-class: young middle-class couples with growing kids and two cars and two TVs. It was a pretty average neighborhood, nothing really outstanding about it.

So we had this group, and my friends and I went to parties in the hills and the hill kids went to parties in the flats, and it was a great kind of cultural relations. I sometimes think back about the looks from some of the girls' mothers when we all walked in the house at nine o'clock at night, coming to a party. It was like, "Who's my daughter hanging around with?" But that was a good time, and I feel nostalgic about it because I look at all the tension and segregation on campuses now, even in integrated schools, and I just didn't feel that.

This was ninth and tenth grade. And I didn't know yet that I was actually biracial. I'm not sure when I found that out. I knew I was adopted, but I guess I just assumed both my biological parents were black because my adopted parents were black. And then at some point my mother told me my birth mother had a Swedish background. I thought, "Oh, that's interesting," and that's what I believed until I started searching years later and I got my nonidentifying information that said Irish.

At that point I identified as being black. I was comfortable with that, so I didn't feel that this information was an asset or a detriment. It was just who I was. It wasn't until I started going to college and keying into what my interests were and seeing that there weren't any black students in my classes, and when I started working and doing my career, which is environmental work, there were very few people of color doing things that I was doing. In the social and recreational spin-offs of that, which are backpacking and river rafting and a lot of other things I like to do, again, I wasn't seeing black people.

And now, living in Portland—which is a pretty white city—

and still working in natural resources, I have almost no contact with black people on a day-to-day basis, and I haven't made any new black friends since I've been up here. I meet people, but nothing's really come of it. If it wasn't for the black friends I formed when I was in junior high and high school—I have a handful I still feel close with—I maybe wouldn't have any, an uncomfortable thought.

Part of this not having new friends is that I felt like I didn't identify in a lot of ways with the average black guy on the street. In some way, yeah, because we're in this society together. I see the culture through the eyes of a black person or a person of color or a minority person, and that's every day and that's all the time. As far as things in common or conversations, it really varies, but I feel like some things are limited.

When I think about my black friends that I went to college with at UC Berkeley, most of them went into business, or their main focus was how much money they were gonna make when they got out of school. So they went into business school or dentistry or law or whatever, and they're doing well and they're successful and we still have links—we get together and we talk about some common things, we talk about relationships—but I've changed or expanded my values over time with spiritual exploration and doing a lot of environmental work, and that's very, very close to me, I'm very passionate about it. And I reach a dead end real fast if I start bringing those things up.

It's unfair to say that has anything to do with race—it doesn't—but it just so happens that the people I spend a lot of time with around these issues happen to not be black, for the most part. I'm excited and happy when I do find someone black that I click with like that. When that happens, it's bringing more parts of myself together in one place, under one roof. I often feel divided up or compartmentalized.

There are friends I have that never meet each other. Once when I was in the Bay Area in the mideighties, I tried to bring some old friends and new friends together. So I made up a flyer and I called it "East Meets West" because I was living in Marin County, in the west, but I grew up in the East Bay. I had Marin friends that were white and that I had worked with, and then I have East Bay friends, mostly black. It was just that strongly divided, and that's demographics, really. I did the flyer with the bridges and some Chinese symbols about people meeting together, and I sent those out.

I had this little potluck thing at my house, and people mostly hung out with people they knew. Part of it bombed 'cause the weather wasn't good. I had a table set out on a deck, and then it got cold and we ended up hip to hip on the floor of my little studio apartment, all sitting wedged around, forcing these social graces and passing things around. I didn't see any new friendships strike up because of that.

And then a couple times I tried to put kayak trips together because some friends I worked with had a kayak company. I was trying to get some of my black friends to come out on the water. I thought, "This is great! We can be outdoors and people can meet new people!" And that didn't happen, either. That didn't come off, either. They didn't go. They didn't want to do it. And I don't know how to mend that, so it's been a part of my life to have these friends I do these things with and those friends I do those things with. That's just the nature of friends in general; it's not necessarily racially motivated or intended. But often it seems to fall along those lines, and it makes you wonder, "Well, how much of that do I choose? How much of it am I just resigned to, saying, 'This is how it is'? Or how divided am I within myself and am I trying to, in some way, *keep* things separate?"

Going back and forth in different worlds, I realize how many social differences there are—communication differences, interests—and it helps me understand why there's so much division across the country. It's from isolation; there's so much isolation, and never the twain shall meet. So a lot of information is just not gonna make it into the black community about how to maneuver in certain kinds of circles.

As I got into my career, I was going through this kind of separation from so much black, black, black, and I wouldn't notice it until I'd get with my black friends, and they would be talking black this and black that and I'd go to their house and they'd have these statues from Kenya, and I'd go back to my house and I have stuff from China and India. And I go, "Is there something wrong with me? What's missing here? I don't have my *Ebony* magazine on the coffee table?"

When I get together with black friends, we talk from this black perspective—and sometimes I really identify with it, and some-

times I don't. I have friends who, even though they're educated
and doing fairly well financially, they still have this "The Man"
sort of attitude: "Oh, yeah, we know they're keeping us down, and
we can't do this and the glass ceiling and all that." And that's real,
but that's something I've never felt. I've always done whatever I
wanted to do: I've gone to schools and gotten into graduate schools
that I wanted to go to and I've turned down more jobs than I've
accepted. I've lived where I wanted to live. I haven't felt those
discriminatory things, so I think attitude has a lot to do with it.

I talk with black friends more about racial things. We talk
more ethnic problems and things that are supposedly peculiar to
black family, or relationships of black men and black women and
some things like that—which I tend to not talk with white friends
about—but then I have a lot of very liberal white friends that want
to talk about race more than I do.

There are a lot of white people that think if you're not white
you can talk for a whole race of people. My friends are more
intelligent than that, but I think that part of their attraction to me
is that I look different, and they feel that maybe I bring something
different to the table. But when I think about it, the things we talk
about and do are not ethnically induced. It's not like my friends
think, "The Dance Theater of Harlem is in town so let's call Greg
because that's something he can relate to." It's not like that. We
mostly do outdoor stuff; we hike and we have breakfast or we go to
a movie, just general things.

My sense of identity started to shift when I met some of my
birth mother's other children. That made a big difference, and
then so did realizing there is a multiracial movement under foot. I
felt like I wanted to integrate all myself and that I wasn't alone in
wanting to do that, and so when I realized there were people trying
to change legislature and change the census and everything, then
I felt more comfortable with it.

Initially I thought: My black friends might think this is
strange. "Here he is taking Irish-Celt dancing lessons or he's learning Gaelic language. Oh, God, he's gotten real weird on us here.
Who's he think he is? He's not black anymore." But they were
okay. I don't know all that they thought, but the reaction I got was,
"Hey, he knows more about himself."

Mostly, I feel divided, because when I'm with white friends I feel like I'm being myself, but at the same time, just visually, I know that I look somewhat different and probably am recognized as such. A part of me feels that's okay, that's special, that's unique, and there's nothing wrong with that, and I don't feel any barriers. And then when I'm with black, sometimes I feel more like an observer than a participant. I feel like I'm usually recognized as being black, and that's okay, but then I also feel like there's some of me that's being left out as far as how I'm perceived, or there's a whole part of me that isn't there. But then there's this comfort level being around black people or older black women, mother figures. It's very nurturing, and it's very comfortable. I found that older Blacks, seniors especially, they're always really proud of a younger Black that's successful or that they perceive as being professional or doing well or a role model for younger kids. There's this real pride thing that I like being around.

It distresses me that there's so much racial disharmony, and sometimes I wonder if Portland, or even the United States, will be the ultimate place that I live. I know there's ethnic and religious strife all over the world, and it's not something one can hide from, but this country is very peculiar to me, and I often feel like I'm not really of here or from here, so I feel like I need to really check out a lot of other places.

Looking at the big blowup that happened in Los Angeles with Rodney King and it's the same thing—people are living in the same conditions as they were in the sixties, but now it's their kids and their kids' kids. I don't feel that the government really represents me in many ways at all; not just racially but about environmental policies, social policies, all of which sort of accentuates my otherness, nationally as well as ethnically.

Despite all these internal quandaries and questions that I've had, I like myself and I'm happy with the way that I deal in the world and the way I deal with people. I've found that just sitting down with someone, the way I sit down with you, that's the best way that I link up with people. I just like making connections with people, and that's how I go through my life. I've had friends all across the spectrum, and that's how I always want to live.

CHAPTER VII

Work

I would say that my industry, advertising, is eighty-five to ninety percent Caucasian. There's only one black man working in the office, and he works in the mail room; there's one black woman working in finance and two black receptionists; and then me, an administrative assistant in the account department. So I am actually the highest level in the minority group. And then there's some Asian.—Jacqueline Djanikian, p.309

I wanted to be an actor, and I applied to NYU [New York University] Drama. I decided I was going to be honest with everybody about everything—about getting kicked out of the University of Michigan—so I had to write three long essays about the history of my life. I didn't get in, and I was really pissed off. Then I figured, well, it's all part of your past, and you gotta deal with it, you got to get it straight. So I thought, what would be the best way for me to get into NYU? The best way would be to go back to Michigan for a semester, demonstrate that I'm intelligent and capable, and then reapply to the school. So I did it. Reapplied to Michigan, they let me in. I did very well the semester that I was up there, took a full schedule, and I wasn't drinking so I did all my work.

169

I also got angry and frightened in terms of two things: One was the idea that I had to wait for somebody to cast me in something, and the other was that I was afraid that because I'm not stereotypically black—I don't have a natural and I'm not very brown-skinned—people wouldn't want to put me in black roles. And it wouldn't be cool for me to play Spanish roles because that would be taking work away from somebody else—if I was so fortunate as to get offered something. So to the whole thing, I said, "Fuck it. I'm just going to apply to film school. I'll learn how to make movies, and if I want to be in the fucking thing I'll put myself in." And that's what happened.—Michael Mayson, p.229

My office is the only state office in the country that is a liaison between the governor and the lesbian and gay community. So I am a resource person; I'm a therapist. And part of my job, as I see it, is to anticipate gaffes and to try to structure some way of making them visible within the state government. I'm working right now very hard on gay and lesbian youth. At least fifty percent of homeless youth are gay and lesbian. Probably between sixty and eighty percent of them are minority. All these things are the same to me; I really don't care what youth it is. I am in a pivotal place right now to do something about it; I am a pivotal person. The fact that I am black and Jewish, that I am a woman, that I'm a mother, that I'm fifty years old, that I am a lesbian—all of these things matter. They are a currency, and in the distorted state of things you can turn that into power.—Sandy Lowe, p.244

Say I'm in a room, right? And you got some Whites and you got some Blacks. I look at them talk to each other, and I see how they interact with each other and the little tensions or the little clashes of culture speaking to each other.

I'm sounding conceited, but the majority of this AT&T center is black, and I remember when my manager was a white guy, he would always talk to me. He felt more comfortable coming and talking to me than the other Blacks. Also, in the past, with the construction guys I worked with, it wouldn't seem like they would hold back. Maybe I'm psychotic or something, maybe I'm crazy, but I feel that they would be more open to me than they would to a black person, because they would say things about black people. If I was fully black and looked more black, then they wouldn't talk about black people. When a white person talks to me, I sense that they don't feel uncomfortable talking to me, and same thing with somebody black.—Valur Edvardsson, p.98

In the school where I taught PE last year, they had more than sixty faculty members, and even though we're teaching in San Francisco, it still looks like it's fucking Iowa or Montana. Last year's count was two Asians and myself. The rest were all white upper-class. What kind of messages get sent to those kids?

One person tried to invite me to her class: "Oh, come talk to us about your experiences in Africa, blah-blah-blah." They were reading Kaffir Boy. *And the day before I was going to go, I hear her telling her class, "Things are fine in South Africa and getting better every day." She literally told those little seventh graders that. At that point I opted not to be in the class because I could see I was going to set myself up to lose my job. I could see it. It was going to be me against sixty other people. You start talking about racial issues, especially with upper-class white folk, immediately they go into the denial stage of "Prove to me why this is true." Well, how many volumes am I going to sit here and beat my head against the wall to prove to you that our life experience may be just a little bit different from yours?—Brad Simpson, p.91*

It's just pitiful how few Blacks are in publishing. And as liberal as many of the people that I've worked with have been, they're still uncomfortable with the idea of working with black people. But people in the work force forget I'm black, and so it makes it easier for them. And then I can hire Blacks to work for me, and train them and try to encourage them to stay in the business. I've always tried to do that.—Bernette Ford, p.207

Much like school environments, every workplace is its own hermetic environment, its character defined by the employer, the employees, by the type of service performed or product created and the market served. Each one of these components influences the workplace's racial climate. Is the staff dominated by people from one racial group, or is it integrated? Do professional staff and administrative staff break down along similar racial lines? Is one type of customer consistently given special treatment? Who gets raises? Who gets promotions? Who socializes after work?

Reward and punishment at work are tangible, measured in paychecks and promotions, hiring and firing. What is not always so easily grasped is the motive for who advances and who is left behind. When are those decisions race-based, and when they are, how is the race of the biracial person evaluated?

Many workplaces and entire industries, even, have evolved to be or have always been segregated environments, intentionally or otherwise. Certainly, phenomena of glass ceilings, token hiring, head hunting through old boy networks, and affirmative action all have the potential to cast a racialized shadow over the workplace.

Like many people who find themselves the odd one out—the only Jew among Gentiles, the only man among women—biracial people often find themselves to be the anointed spokesperson for an entire group they are seen to represent. They may or may not be comfortable in this role of representative, but they are turned to for comment whenever issues of race arise. They may also be expected to deal with customers or employees or products about whom or which they are assumed to have a special understanding.

The book editor of one magazine I wrote for came to me repeatedly to review books that were either by or about African-Americans. The magazine had a circulation of 650,000, and was owned by a large multinational corporation. "I know that I always give the black books to you," the editor said, throwing up her hands and sounding a little apologetic, "but would you take a look at this?"

I wanted to review the books for her, to advance my career, but what was it she expected? I had, as happens to most African-Americans, become charged with the task of representing my race. That was an assumed expertise, the *only* assumed expertise.

At the same time, I was interested in most of the books she sent my way, and I was troubled by the possibility that if I didn't look at them, it was highly possible no one would. But I was also troubled by the other side of her recognition: What wasn't she giving me?

If not thrust into a role of spokesperson, then biracial people can find themselves looked to as mediators between black and white, either to explain behaviors and attitudes that one side finds inscrutable, or to communicate what one side is uncomfortable saying directly to the other.

❦

Robert Allen
Age: 23
Residence: Dorchester, Massachusetts
Occupation: Money manager trainee

Robert Allen describes himself as "sitting on the pickets of the fence. There's not a day that goes by that I don't think about race." His black father and white mother married, had Robert and his younger sister, and settled in the Boston area, where they lived in mixed and predominantly black neighborhoods. They divorced after twenty years.

Allen says he always checks "other" on forms. "If I'm not presented with an 'other' category, which is rare," he says, "I'll check off African-American. If people try to typecast me, I'll immediately correct them: biracial." Even though he says he identifies with both viewpoints, black and white, his identity at work, a financial brokerage firm, seems to revolve primarily around the black.

As a trainee, Allen often attends seminars. "Usually, I'm the only black guy, and so there are times when I definitely feel out of my element. Sometimes I sit there and I'm like, 'What the fuck am I doing here?' Especially in the most recent conference, I was looking around and all I would see is this sea of white faces, and I was like, 'What am I doing here?'"

The company I work for has about 130 employees. We only have five Blacks, and it's just something you have to think about,

especially where it's such a small company. There are really no
secrets there. When a black person is afforded an opportunity, I
think a lot of people tend to think, (A) is he really qualified for this
position? (B) is it deserved? and (C) is it a result of his skin color?

Some people have a problem with affirmative action; I honestly don't. I think it's a good idea. Blacks have been systematically
disenfranchised for hundreds of years, and I just think there needs
to be some type of remuneration or repatriation for what has happened in that past. And seriously, a lot of these companies, regardless of how much lip service they may give to affirmative action or
equal opportunity, they really aren't doing a whole hell of a lot to
bring any Blacks into their organizations. In fact, I think a lot of
these companies would prefer to have Blacks not join their organization, especially within the investment industry in Boston. It's
very, very WASP here, and if you don't fit that blond hair, blue-
eyed, Polo-suit-and-Brooks-Brothers-rep-tie, you're going to have
some problems; you really are going to have some problems. I hate
rep ties. I refuse to wear them. I wear bow ties. I like to wear them
just to piss a lot of people off.

Last summer, I was wearing a bow tie, and the vice president
of one of the departments I happened to be working in addressed
me as "Good morning, Mr. Farrakhan." And I was immediately
incensed by it, immediately.

I didn't say anything. I was so taken aback, because I really
didn't believe that he would have the nerve to just come up to me
and say something so overtly racist. I was stupefied by it. I had
never, ever confronted racism like that before, never.

What was so racist about his comment was that Louis Farrakhan has his own political ideology, and that's fine, and I tend to
think that a lot of his ideology is somewhat racist, somewhat discriminatory. That's my personal view. He's held as being extremely
dangerous in a lot of people's eyes, especially a lot of Whites', and
so for someone to make that reference between he and I just due
to the fact that he chooses to wear a bow tie and I chose on this one
day to wear a bow tie—I found the entire incident to be somewhat
racist.

I get fed up with Boston, but I really don't know where else
a black man could go and feel one hundred percent accepted, I
mean, *one hundred percent accepted*. At least Boston is appealing in

the sense that there are a lot of opportunities here for Blacks. If you're able to get your foot in the door and be a persistent bitch, I think you can definitely do it here. You can definitely do it here.

You have to be able to work the system and make it work, but the only other thing I notice is you have to bitch for everything. You have to stay in their faces, you have to hold them accountable for a lot of things; you really do.

We have a communications board at work, where people can put up any complaints or suggestions, ways to improve the company. And someone had put a suggestion up anonymously, saying, "You have no black wholesalers. You have no female wholesalers. What's going on here?" And it raised a good question.

Anytime something racial happens within the organization, I'm usually the first one people look to. Everyone comes to me and says, "What's your opinion?" I've developed a reputation for being somewhat of a corporate bitch, only in the sense that I'll put a suggestion up on the board—but I actually have the balls to attach my name to it.

So my managing director came, and he asked me about it. He said, "I really don't have a problem with hiring Blacks and minorities or women, but the only thing is I've been burned so many times dealing with Blacks that it's just not something that I do on a regular basis."

He was honest enough to say this to me, and I can kind of—I can't understand it, only, in a sense, I can. I can't say that's a practice that I would follow. I have no idea what his experiences were, to what extent he was burned or what bad feelings he walked away with—obviously he walked away with some bad feelings to make a statement like that. I think this is what happens a lot, especially within Boston's professional circles: One person may have a bad experience with, say, a Black or a woman, and they just seem to think that this entire gender or this entire race is imbued with this one bad experience.

Joseph Marable
Age: 31
Residence: Atlanta, Georgia
Occupation: Hair salon owner and operator

Joseph Marable is the younger brother of Sally Hobson (p.60). When he is not running his salon, he travels across the States and throughout the Caribbean, promoting a line of black hair-care products. He says he's never denied that his mother was Italian or that his father was black. "I don't feel that I've ever had a problem identifying with who I am. I've always identified myself or related to being black, I guess because that's more or less what I was raised around."

I'm very close with my mother and, not to choose sides or anything, but I guess I was always a little closer to my father; I favored my father a little bit more so.

At one point, when I was in the fifth grade—that was about 1970—I went through a phase where I didn't hate my mother, but in some ways I resented the fact that, for instance, if I had to go to school for a PTA meeting or something, my dad generally never went. My mother would go, and the other kids would see my mother and they would be like, "Well, you know, you look black, you got curly hair, but . . ." and then I would catch a lot of flak from that.

It wasn't an identity thing with me; it was just oftentimes kids, I think, can be cruel, and then a lot of times, too, I always felt like because of the way I looked people would assume that, "Oh, you think you're better than somebody else," or, "You have curly hair, you think you're cute." Oftentimes, even now as an adult, I'm faced with that.

People will look at me and assume things from the way I dress— you know, I'm a hairdresser, I'm selling beauty, I'm selling fashion, so I dress, not that I dress so flamboyantly, but I'm conscious of it. And I've met women that take one look at me and say, "I know he's probably got twenty women, twenty girlfriends that he's running around with." And that might not necessarily be the case, but people will assume that you're this way or that way. That's something we were talking about at the shop just today, how oftentimes people just look at what they see exteriorly and they don't even know you. They'll say five words to you and think they know you as a person and they don't. I think oftentimes I've had to prove myself because of the way I look, because of my hair, my light skin.

My attitude is, I don't like to judge people. I've found it to be true that you can meet a bum on the street and you'd never know, he can have a million dollars. But I try to be nice to all people. That's one thing I have had an advantage in from being biracial: I feel like I've had the best of both worlds, because, okay, on one hand, my mother was Italian or white and my father was black, so to a degree I feel like I've had an experience on both ends. Even though I wasn't really accepted by my mother's side of the family, I still had my mother. And in that respect I was always taught you shouldn't judge a person whether they're black or white or ugly or whatever.

From a hairdresser standpoint, one thing I hate is when people tell me, "Oh, you have good hair."

And I'm saying, "Define good hair."

"Oh you know, like yours, wavy, real nice."

And I'm saying, "My attitude is, if it's on your head, it's good." You're just talking about differences in textures and types. That's one thing that really upsets me, is when people say, "Oh, you have good hair." I think what it's about is oftentimes people identify with, let's say, a white woman with long, lustrous, beautiful flowing hair. A couple of months ago I was watching a show on PBS. They had a little black child, and they showed her a white doll and they showed her a black doll and they asked her, "Which one is prettier?" and she picked the white doll. And I think this goes back to slave days or whatever, that people were always kind of conditioned that white is supposed to be a symbol of beauty. I don't judge a person's hair texture by that. Again, I don't care if your hair is naturally coarse. If it's cut and it's shaped nicely, then it's nice.

When I started doing hair, my attitude was: I don't do black hair, I don't do white hair, I do green hair, okay? And money is green, and it's not whether you're black or white, it's texture and type. I was taught that you shouldn't limit yourself to doing any one texture. Most of my clients are black. I do have some clients that are white, very few, but I do have some because where my shop is now is kind of a liberal area: There's black and there's white that live and do business in the area.

Even though black hair is basically what I do, I do know how to do all types of textures, and I don't limit myself. I've had a situation not too long ago where a white businessman came in. He was referred to me by a friend and I don't think my friend told him that I was black or whatever. He just said, "This guy can cut your hair." I've had white people sit in my chair who were real hesitant, but then when they saw their hair come out, it was a whole different thing.

That's what basically happened with this guy. He walked in, and you could tell. I could sense the—not really tension, but he was a little, you know. Every time I get a new client I'll sit them down and I'll get a little history of their life-style, blah-blah-blah, what do you do for a living, this kind of thing.

And he said, "Well, whatever you want to do," and I could tell he was really kind of hesitant, but after I got finished with cutting his hair and he saw that I wasn't going to butcher him up, he felt a little better.

But from that perspective of hairdressing, not that a salon with Blacks and Whites can't work, but I was talking to somebody not so long ago, and I said to them, I said, "Do you think I'm too problack?"

She said to me, "White people live where they live and they don't necessarily want to deal with us unless they have to come in contact with us, so it's not wrong for you to feel like you live in a black community; you try to do business with black people."

And that's why sometimes I think, "Am I being too racist?" And I have to kind of stop and do a reality check myself and say, "Am I limiting my scope?" But from my own experiences with doing hair, I think that it's a very sensitive issue when you're trying to mingle Blacks and Whites in a salon. I'm not saying that it can't work or it hasn't, but from my own experiences in working or being around salons that tried to cater to both, it didn't work.

Emma Baker
(See also page 32)

*When Columbia, South Carolina, made a big push for school integration
in 1970, Emma Baker was transferred from her teaching position in an
all-black school to a previously all-white school. To ease the transition, the
school administration held racial sensitivity workshops for the teachers.
Exercises included Blacks and Whites holding hands and staring into each
other's eyes, and open forums where participants were encouraged to ask
the questions they'd always been afraid to ask.*

*"You were supposed to say anything that you felt about Whites or the
Blacks, it didn't have to be complimentary, just what you felt about them.
If it was something that one or the other said that would sting, we were
supposed to bring out our true feelings, whether it hurt or not. I did not
know until that year that Blacks were prejudiced against Whites. And I
had been black all my life but didn't know that Blacks felt the same way
about Whites as Whites do about Blacks."*

There are those who feel that I'm a snob and that I look
down on people who are darker than I am, so you pretty much have
to bend over backwards and go out of your way to be nice to those
people who are dark. This is what my life has been, always. At this
point, I don't do it as much: *I* know I'm not a snob.

I have relatives who are darker. I have some—they look pretty
much like they just got off the boat from Africa. They're my mother's sister's children and their father was big, he had the African
features and that sort of thing, and most of them came out looking
like their father. Very few of 'em, about four of them, came out
looking like their mother, which was pretty good.

Now there have been some advantages, like for getting jobs,
although it was not spoken. I'll start off from a low-paying, non-
skilled job, and I'll come up a little bit. When I was a teenager, I
went to apply for a job in a laundry, and in a small town in the South
during those times if you were black and you did not have any particular skills—you were not trained to do anything—it was hard to
find work. Most of the work that people my age got to do was work
for white people in their houses: cleaning up, looking out for the
children, that sort of thing. They had a cotton mill there, and be-

cause of segregation, no black females and very few black males worked there. The black males who did were those who cleaned up; they did the menial tasks for low pay. Even working in the mill, the weaving and some of the other work that the women did was hard, but it was not as hard as what the black males had to do.

So that was the only industry in and around there, and, of course, you dared not go to the stores: White teenagers worked in stores, five-and-dimes, grocery stores, and drug stores—you didn't do that. You didn't even bother to go to apply.

I went to the laundry to apply for a job. It was a combination laundry and dry cleaner, and it hired Blacks, but only to do the menial tasks. They handled the dirty clothes and that sort of thing; they didn't do anything where it took a little bit of brains. I went there, and when they found that I had finished high school, they took me on. I worked with a white woman who trained me to take in the clothes—and this was dirty work—to count the pieces, the number of pillowcases, the number of sheets, the number of everything that was in a laundry bag or a pillowcase. And that was good for me, being a Black, that was real good. You had to write that down on the ticket and then separate the clothes and put them in a bin. After you finished checking in clothes, you had to go up to what was called the front and check them out when the sheets would come out. There were Blacks who folded the sheets and pillowcases, there were those who did the shirts and whatever.

Well, I would have that ticket and I had to count them off; it was a kind of check and balance to see that all the things were there for the bundle. And this may sound small, but it was a big step for me, and I think, now, maybe they hired me thinking that I could do it, but I wonder, because there were Blacks in there who could count up to ten, who could count ten shirts, but they all were darker. They seemed to have been from a different cut of cloth, and the employers didn't like the way that they behaved, the way that they spoke—I think maybe they would not have gotten hired for this job. Because of that, these adults in the laundry, the Blacks, called me "white monkey," and there were always jeers and picks.

If there was something that was not quite right, I was supposed to take it back to the presser, the one who did it, and oh, boy, they were furious. Now if the white woman walked by the place where I would take the shirt back, they would mumble something or cut their eyes, but they wouldn't say anything. They did not treat this white woman I worked with the same way. They didn't say anything to her; they didn't call her names. Sometimes they would even use profanity if I would take something back to them; they would even use profanity. With her, they would have cut their eyes at her once she started to walk away, once she had her back turned to them, and sometimes they would say something under their breath—although I think she could hear it—but they would not talk to her like me, like they did to me.

Now that's one job where I think my color may or may not have helped me to get it. It could have been just me, the way that I carried myself.

Jeffrey Scales
Age: 37
Residence: New York, New York
Occupation: Photographer

Jeffrey Scales was raised in San Francisco and Berkeley. His parents—mother white, father black—met in Iowa, where they had both grown up. Scales started in his career as a cub photographer for The Black Panther Newspaper, *but was sidetracked more than once—as a geology student for a short time, as a film student, and for several years as the late singer Minnie Ripperton's road manager—before settling into photography full-time.*

His racial identity is pragmatic and political. "Theoretically, scientifically, I should have a certain amount of choice in the matter," he says. "That's not really the case. A lot of the choice is made by the world around me, and the world around me is not going to say I'm white; they don't treat me that way. I know that. I was raised to identify as black. I identify with being mixed as much as black, maybe even more so. It doesn't seem to mean that much in this country because they still treat you as a black person. It's a black and white world.

"Maybe I identify slightly more with being black than with being mixed, but it's hard to say. It's back and forth because most of my activity has been oriented to the black political sphere. In the workplace, I'm going to be treated like a black person, pretty much, so if I was to expect to be treated like something else, it could be very disappointing. So you sort of have to set up certain defensive measures, realistic expectations of how people are going to deal with you."

I have a lot of white-culture references in terms of work that I studied: a lot of European film for many, many years, and European art. I like having that, but a lot of black people don't know what I'm talking about or don't identify with that at all. As an artist, I've pretty much had to direct a lot of my work as black-identified because that's what people in the marketplace want to see from me. Society identifies me as a black person, so in terms of my work, it's very much supposed to be in that category.

In a commercial sense, in terms of the assignment work I get, it's very, very directed toward that because I'll only get assignments from magazines to shoot black people unless the art director specifically does something otherwise. And with record companies it's the same, because I don't ever get to shoot white artists or white subjects. Hardly ever. I don't like that. I went through a long period of time where I had to fight not being sent to go shoot crackheads in war-type assignments just because I do documentary work.

I've only had one magazine, the editor for *American Film*, call me and say, "We're not going to just assign you to photograph black people. We want to let you know that."

And they didn't. Although the fact that the art director there was a woman I lived with for five years has something to do with it. But the editor was fired when the magazine was sold, and the art director left and I never worked for them again, although they continued to use my covers in their TV ads.

In my personal art, I never got much headway in the work I had that was white subject matter, a lot of which was from before I came to New York. The first work the Museum of Modern Art bought from me was black subject matter; they never were too interested in white subject matter. And then with black curators, some were very supportive and their collections were primarily on black subject matter, so they would invest in me doing that.

I'm getting ready to start a series called "White People," now that I've established myself more as an artist. I think it will be interesting partially because white people have gone around the world describing other cultures within the photographic medium, and I haven't seen very much work of people of color visually defining them. So I just want to throw that out and see what comes back. That's going on concurrently with a "Young Black Men" series I'm working on, which is more important to me right now.

I'm still shooting things for ["White People"]. I was in Iowa recently for a family reunion, and I went to the state fair, where I did some nice work on that subject matter. And while I was in Europe, I shot a lot. In terms of Europe, I went to the motherland. Maybe "White People" will raise the question of what I can do beyond black subject matter; it will address those issues.

A black curator I know once told me that I get criticized in the photographic community by a lot of other black male photographers. And I said, "Well, they're just mad because I'm doing well."

She said, "No, they're mad because of the way you look."

And I said, "Well—"

She said, "Trust me."

I said, "All right." With people who've grown up in a small black community like various boroughs of New York, I think you get into the issue that I'm different. A lot of that has to do with coming from a different place, since I grew up in the Bay Area. It's a different vibe here, and I don't have the same vibe so I'm not brought in. You could say, yeah, maybe they don't like me because my hair is straight, but at the same time, it could also be on a linguistic level or some kind of other level—I'm not hitting the right buttons based on coming from a different, less cohesive place. It's like I speak with an accent or I was born in a different country.

I'm not in a lot of black artists' cliques, but part of that is my choice. I suppose it's because I don't get along with people. I don't know. I'm very demanding. My wife is always saying, "You're not a white boy. You're not going to get treated like you are." But I always expect to be treated as a very privileged artist.

I have high self-esteem in terms of my work, and I expect to be treated that way. I've noticed a lot of black photographers get used to accepting what I would call substandard treatment from both black clients and white clients. And I don't. I've gotten contracts from black clients that were so wrong I've had to pull out of situations.

Photography is such an exclusive profession. It was initially set up for privileged white men. When the feminist movement came into play, it got opened up to white women, substantially, through the actions of some specific art directors and women photo editors in the industry. But black people have never been part of that club. They wouldn't get assignments, or when affirmative action came into play they would get staff jobs where you would do a lot of creatively mundane work. But you were doing photography, you were making a living at it, so that was pretty good. A lot of creativity got stifled.

You don't see black photographers who are at the really prestigious high end of photography. You don't see any of that. You see a lot of black photographers that have staff jobs at *Newsweek* and *The New York Times;* black photographers doing photojournalism and documentaries.

But work is hard to get, and people can't just hold out for the primo assignments. My most prestigious assignments came from that art director I had a long-standing personal relationship with. And other than that, I've never been given a cover assignment by a white magazine. Ever.

The thing that was most frustrating to me was when black projects were treating black photographers like white institutions had treated black photographers because, I don't know why, is that all they were used to? I don't know what it was. But I had a lot of run-ins with the crowd of photographers because "I didn't get no respect." So I go my own way, but not totally alone. I've got my wife. She's with me, consulting all the way.

I like elements of white culture a lot: music and film—specifically, European movies, Italian movies in particular. And I listen to a lot of white music. I mean, I listen to a *lot* of white music. I'm the only person in my neighborhood with The Tubes blasting out of their car. My neighbor says, "I always know when you're coming because there's nobody else who's going to drive up in Harlem blasting heavy metal."

So I look at a real cross section of cultural things that interest me. I studied primarily white photographers up until I came to New York in 1984. A lot of that has to do with my mother being an artist—that a lot of my artistic training came from a white person and a white person who was a blood relative.

I think both cultures have a lot to offer; I like all my different influences. I don't know whether it's just my education, but it seems that I can grasp both cultures on many levels. As I said, how much I like European film—Wim Wenders—and at the same time how I can identify with new black film. I can identify with some of that ponderous European angst, but I don't see very many black people identifying with it in the slightest—that overanalysis of self. And at the same time I can identify with *Do the Right Thing*. In a lot of European films, it's the individual white guy wandering through the world, thinking about how it's affecting him, the individual. And it doesn't seem to be the same in black films. They seem to be more about how the world affects *us*, as opposed to just *me*.

I seem to have a broader base of influence in my art—a lot of European influence and white American influence—and it's applied to black subject matter more so than with a lot of photographers I've seen. I don't know whether that's just by my chosen course of study, but it has a lot to do with my ability to put myself in situations with white people where I can learn a lot. That has to do with linguistics, sort of like being bilingual.

Carol Calhoun
Age: 54
Residence: Stone Mountain, Georgia
Occupation: High school teacher

*Carol Calhoun was one of seven interview-
ees as Caucasian-appearing as I am. Most
of them, including Calhoun, identify themselves as black, clearly and firmly. Most of
them also explained, without prompting,
that they feel no choice in the matter, that
this is* necessarily *who they are. I suspect
this explanation is volunteered because the
question has been asked of them (as it has of
me) so many times: "You're so light,"
someone will say. "You could pass if you
wanted to. Why bother with all the trouble you're going to get?" This
question comes from both black and white.*

*"I've always been black," Calhoun says. People she meets will often
go to a mutual friend to ask if she's actually black. "See, and that's what
pisses me off," she says. "I mean, have you ever in your life met anybody
that wanted to pass for being black? I haven't, and if there is one, I'd like
to meet 'em 'cause I'd like to know why."*

*Part of Calhoun's explanation, too, is that although she was raised
by her white mother until she was eight, she was then adopted by a black
family. "This is the way I was brought up, and this is where I'm comfortable. Had I stayed with my biological mother I might not have, except
that in those times, a bastard child, or an illegitimate child of a mixed
union wouldn't have stood a snowball's chance in hell of being white. Not
at all."*

I'm going into my fourth year at the high school, and it has
taken the black children a long time to accept the fact that I'm
black. A lot of the reason is that they don't understand that Blacks
come in all shades, and I don't know why. I have the kind of
classroom where I can step out and chat for a moment, and the
second year I was there, every now and then a kid would knock on
my door and somebody would say, "Now Mrs. Calhoun, here's
Wilhelmina. You tell Wilhelmina that you're black, okay?"

It was usually the same kids doing this, and finally I had to say to them, "Look, I'm me and you're you, and I look like I look and you look like you look, and I'm not on display here any more than you are, so stop it."

And they got the message. But there's still this situation with one boy who's from mixed parentage, who's having so much trouble, and he had been in my room. I do alternative instruction, which means I have the children who commit infractions of the school rules, so I have children for a brief period of time and then they go back to the mainstream. This boy's name was Chris. Chris and I locked horns from the minute he walked in that classroom, and I wasn't real sure what he was, 'cause I also have to keep a racial count—which I know is supposed to be illegal, but I'm supposed to do it. So I was sitting there, looking at this boy, and I kept thinking, yeah, he is, no he isn't, well maybe . . . I went back and forth, and finally I asked one of his teachers, and that's when I got the background on him.

He went back to class and was complaining about, "That mean old Mrs. Calhoun, I just cannot stand her!"

And one of the other boys said, "Man, don't you know Mrs. Calhoun is black and she's on your side?" They had this little argument back and forth, and I was told about this by the teacher that all this took place in front of.

It was real interesting because after that, Chris would come to me at lunchtime and he'd say, "Mrs. Calhoun, will you keep my warm up jacket in your closet until I get through with lunch?"

We didn't discuss this thing in depth, but, you know, he kind of took to me.

Sandra Benton Shupe
Age: 31
Residence: Oakland, California
Occupation: Credit and collections manager

Sandra "Sandy" Shupe's parents met in a New Jersey nightclub. According to family legend, when her mother first saw her husband-to-be, she tapped a friend on the shoulder and said, "There's the father of my children." The two were married for thirty-five years, until her father died in 1989.

Shupe's father was the steadier of the pair, she says; her mother was "part gypsy." The family moved frequently— eighteen times one year. "My mother has a colorful past," she says. "She's a highly intelligent woman who did stupid things at times." One such thing, Shupe says, was to kite checks for a while. "She happened to get caught in Mississippi, where a judge looked at her and told her that for a twenty-five-dollar check in Mississippi back in 1960, any white woman who would come into his court with a black man deserved five years in the state penitentiary. Locked her up, gave me to my father, and we moved to Los Angeles."

Shupe was a baby when her mother went to prison, and over those five years, she became "daddy's little girl," she says. Except for a short stay in foster care, her father cared for her and her younger brother. "My mother wasn't really there for five years," she explains. "I would go see this woman at 'the hospital'; that's pretty much how I had it all put together."

In terms of how people treat me, from appearance I'm black, from actions I'm white. Does that make any sense? I bartend and cocktail part-time in a bar right here in Oakland. People will come into the bar, and they say, "It's good to see a sister behind the bar," so I find that black men accept me more quickly and as a black individual than black women do, and I've never been able to figure that one out.

With black women, it takes a little bit longer to make a friend-ship, because there's a little more standoffishness. One friend from my office, Jill—I think of her as one of the very beautiful people in life. She's got a wonderful, bubbly sense of humor, and she accepts everybody. Right after this stuff with Rodney King went on, Jill and I were standing by the photocopier, joking around, and I said, "How much longer are you going to be?"

She said, "What difference is it to you?"

I said, "Because I need to use the damn thing. How much longer are you going to be there?"

We're joking, we're just playing with each other, and she looked over and she goes, "Just remember there's one part of you I'm not really happy with right now." And I said, "You just remember there's one part of me that can still kick your ass."

So this is just part of Jill. But it took Jill a while to where she would talk to me. We would talk casually: "What did you do last night?" But now we talk about family, friends, things that happened early on in life. There's actual friendship, that's there, not just your casual "Gee, we're in the office today," say hello to each other and be cordial. She didn't quite know what to do with me at the beginning, but we've become really good friends.

Another woman from the office came to waitress at The Court, the bar where I work. She made the deadly mistake one day of saying that I didn't know where I fit. She told somebody that at the bar, and she got blown away by about six people. It's a small, funky little bar, and we have everything come in from your DA to your street scum. It's a big huge melting pot, everyone's accepted; it's just the way it is, and she really wasn't quite expecting what she got back.

People told her, "Where do you get off?" "What right do you have to judge Sandy in any way, shape, or form?" "She seems to fit in just fine here." She's getting this from every side. Somebody told me about it, and I just called her on it the next day, real plain and simple. She said, "I'm sorry, I'd been drinking, I wasn't thinking about what I said."

I said, "Why in the hell did you even say it? What was the point behind it? Is that really the way you feel, and if so, why don't you tell me about it? Let's see if we can't come to grips with it."

Everything's fine now. It just had to be pushed to the limit. I feel like a lot of times that's what happens to me. I have to be pushed, I have to be tested. *How strong are you? How much do you feel about the way you are or what you are? Where do you fit in?* And I just get to a point where I say, "Wait a minute now. I'm not going to play this game anymore." A lot of times, when I get angry I become black, when someone's stupid or when something's done that's unjustified. Then I get up on my soapbox and say I'm not going to take this.

But of course my mother would get angry, too. She's definitely not passive. If my mom has something to say, it's coming out. Period. End of story. And it doesn't really matter whether you like it or not. But the difference between us is if she sits back and she's white and she has an opinion about black, then it's okay, but if I have one, somebody's going to question it, whether they be white or black.

I don't know why that is, and that's what irritates me, that's what pisses me off. Like, gee, if I have an opinion about Martin Luther King, people ask, "Why do you have that opinion and how can you possibly feel that strongly about Blacks? How can you feel the repression of a black person when you grew up in lily-white suburbia?" Excuse me? Why can't I? I have to live it also, I have to go through it.

I have a tough time with Chinese people, not Japanese but Chinese. They're pushy. Partly that comes from working for a Chinese-owned bank. After four years I was fired, and everyone in the office, as a matter of fact, was fired, except for one Chinese employee. Left a real bad taste in my mouth. I'm not saying it's all Chinese; I'm saying that there's a rudeness that comes from it, and part of that probably stems from when I worked at the bank where the base of our customers were Chinese. They're pushy, they're arrogant, they come in, they want this, they want this now, they get angry with you because you don't understand what they're saying. And then there are some that come in and they're the most gracious people in the world.

But I tend to stereotype Chinese people. I'll be driving through Chinatown and I'll make some slur, and it's like, How can you do that? Why are you doing that? I catch myself doing it, and I have to think about it.

To realize that I have prejudices makes me very angry with myself. How can I expect anybody to accept me for me if I'm going to go out here and talk about Charlie Chan down the street? Just

because he happens to be Chinese doesn't make him a bad person.
So when I catch myself doing it, I think, "Well, you're making a
big mistake here. You're screwing up. You have no right to do this.
It's not fair to you, it's not fair to that other person who you don't
know." When I hear myself saying, "They make me mad," I
change it to: "*Someone* made me mad." And they're not *all* bad
drivers; *somebody* doesn't drive well. I'm guilty of stereotyping, and
I have to be careful of it.

Growing up, I couldn't be prejudiced about black or white. It
wasn't allowed in my family. So what do I do? I go find the Chinese. Why? They're different. When it comes to looking at races,
that's my greatest fault as far as I'm concerned. I don't feel that way
against Filipinos, so it's not just because their eyes are slanted. I
really think it probably has something to do with what happened
while I was at the bank, because I really enjoyed my job. Really
enjoyed it. I started off as a teller and worked my way up to an
assistant manager position and then, as terrible as it sounds, I think
part of the reason why I am no longer there is because I am black.
I couldn't have gone any further on their corporate ladder. That's
the way it was throughout the entire organization. There were no
black people, period, in any form of power.

We were all fired at once because somebody stole three hundred thousand dollars from the bank. All of us, except for that one
Chinese person. So we've filed a class-action suit against the bank.
Nothing's happened yet, and the bank's been sold three times, but
we'll see. I want somebody's hands to get slapped. I don't want a
big check; I'd like a formal apology, and I want to see somebody
hurt. I want to see somebody who's black in power at that bank.
It's that simple. So that probably is where my prejudice stems
from. And that doesn't give me a right to be prejudiced, but it does
help me to figure out what it is and to try and grow from it—but
that experience is still a bitter stone.

CHAPTER VIII

Love and Romance

I've never had any relationships with a white woman. They never are attracted to me. You know how you can be out at a club or somewhere and people flirt with you? I never had that from a white woman.—Jimmy Pierre, p.329

What's my dating history? White, white, white, white, black—of course, I was like ten years old—white, white, Filipino, white, white, white, white, white.—Mark Durrow, p.359

Who I date is a sensitive issue, because I have a sexual preference for white men, and I think that it could be perceived as being racially motivated in some way. I don't think sexual preference is a political thing. Well, it can be, it certainly can be and also, how can one ever absolutely say that on some unconscious level it isn't? But I really believe that it's not for me. It's not a matter of aesthetics; it's not that I think that white people are prettier or more attractive or more sexual or more desirable partners or any of that, it's just a certain kind of imprinting. Who knows where our sexual preferences come from? I think some people just prefer one race to another or certain types of coloring or one sex or the other.—Paul Whitaker, p.213

I've always just dated black women. I do notice that I'll go out with a white woman on a friendly level, but I'm more reluctant to get involved with them. In the back of my mind I guess I'm a chicken in that I don't want to go through what my father went through, unless it's worth it. And I'm wary. I always wonder, "Am I going out with her because this is forbidden fruit and I want to see what it's like?" If I feel like that might be there, I just stay away. But if I met one I really liked, say I met one in church who I really liked, I'd go out with her. And if we fell in love, well, my father would be a very happy man. I can see it now. We joke about that, me and my older brothers who are all black. I said to them, "I'm going to bring home a white woman." They said, "Yeah, Dad's going to throw a ticker-tape parade."

One time I went on a date with a white woman, and I called him and I said, "Dad, guess what?" He said, "What?" I said, "I went out with a white woman tonight." And he paused and said, "Good!" That's his thing, and it's not my thing.—John Blake, p.269

A lot of the closest male-female relationships I've had, particularly with black men, have not been positive because I was treated like a white girl, in the sense of the using, the disrespect that often goes on with black men who are dating women because they are white. It's almost like they're saying, "I'm going to prove that I can have this, but I really don't want it." It's almost a way to get revenge, and I became a target for a lot of that. It wasn't on a conscious level; it just seemed like some of the men I dated would not take me into environments where there were a lot of black people. They always wanted to take me the other way and put me on their arms, as long as they needed me to reinforce their legitimacy in terms of the majority population. But it would delegitimize them in the black community, and I was very conscious of that.—Jeana Woolley, p.250

I went out with white women for most of my life until the year before I met my wife. I'd grown up in a totally white neighborhood, and my mother's white, so there was a certain comfortability, as it were, around white women, being that I grew up with one. But I had a couple of painful experiences with people's families. Like I used to go out with a woman for many years whose family were total bigots. I was probably twenty-five, and we met through an old family friend of mine who's kind of like my cousin, who is black, who was lovers with this girl's sister, and their family was Armenian immigrants who would disown anyone who was involved in a relationship with a minority.

We lived together for a number of years, and it was always a secret relationship. Her family would have a big party and she would invite all her friends, but they couldn't invite me. So all these white people I knew could go to the party, but I couldn't go. There was a lot of hurt in that situation, and afterwards, I decided that I was going to look for a relationship with a black woman because I didn't want to go through that again.

When my wife and I first met, she goes, "Guys that go out with white women really like me." That's the way she described herself. It means that she is cross-cultural. A lot of things come from how you were raised, and she was raised in a culturally white and real academic environment in Portland, Oregon.—Jeffrey Scales, p.181

When I was younger I used to have these posters all over my walls, and all the guys on the posters were white: Andy Gibb, the Teenbeat type of thing, I can't even remember. And my parents were in my room talking about something, and my dad says, "Why don't you have any black guys up here?" And I was like, "That's a good question. Maybe because there aren't any magazines." And I kind of let that pass, but I still kept it subconsciously. That was a good question. Why didn't I?—Jacqueline Djanikian, p.309

I've been out with every type of man. I've been out with Asians, Indians from India, and I seem to prefer black men.

That's what really feels comfortable. But I never meet any black men. I'm always alone, and I'm a beautiful woman—if I must say so myself, since no one else is. I really think if I would open myself to white guys, I'd have a boyfriend. It's not that I don't want to do that, it's that I can't do it yet; I'm not at that space yet, so I can't force myself. I would like to evolve to that place and hopefully I will, but I see a black guy go by and it's like I have whiplash, my head moves so fast.—Deborah Gregory, p.302

I really am attracted to women that have some complexion, that have some pigment. The way I look at it, we're looking at the culture and the society we're in through similar eyes, and that's important in a companion.

The women I've been closest with have been women of color, but they've been women that sort of look like me. But I'm not real hopeful that I can end up with that, especially living in a place like Portland.—Greg Wolley, p.163

My friend Peggy was raised that you don't look at black men; you don't look at anybody but white men. Apparently her father was white and [American] Indian as well, but her mother was Indian.

And she'll say to me, "I know this really nice black man . . ." and then if the person is Japanese or whatever, she'll say, "This guy is single; I've got to find somebody for him."

She won't think of me, and I'll always be like, "Peggy, hello?"—Danette Fuller, p.364

The last couple people I've dated have been white. My friends and my family throw this in my face all the time. Let's just say if I brought home someone black, they would be thrilled.—Robert Allen, p.173

For some reason I have never been attracted to going out with or dating anyone white, but I've dated women that were very light and women that were very dark. It just so happened that the woman I ended up marrying was biracial—her father was white— and in some ways I felt there was a connection there with us because of some of our own experiences. I'm not married now. It just didn't work out. But she was very light, and that's why in some ways I felt we had a bond there because just like myself, she would experience, "Well, you're light-skinned, you have nice hair . . ." People would even look at both of us and say, "You probably think you're better than . . ." or this kind of thing.

And not to say that I wouldn't marry anybody white, but the chances are probably slim to none.—Joseph Marable, p.176

M. is the first woman of color I've ever been with. I was afraid of black women because growing up, what I got from black women was torture and terror, and I took that with me. I was heterosexual for a while, but even when I was heterosexual, my boyfriends were all white. Maybe I chose a Latin woman because the first time I didn't feel any discrimination was among Latins. And because she's cute. M. is the first woman I've ever been with who I will recount a story to and not only is she sympathetic, she understands because she's been there.—Neisha Wright, p.87

I dated one white guy, and when I brought him home, my father wouldn't even shake hands with him. My father professed to be so liberal, but he was afraid I was going to pass. My parents were of the generation of "What will people think?" And they were afraid that if some of their friends saw me with this white boy, they would think I was trying to pass, and I could frankly give a rat's ass what people think.—Carol Calhoun, p.186

In choosing a spouse, few people escape their parents' hopes for them. Often, in the area of love and marriage, typical parental aspirations are for good providers—loving, steady mates who will help build a strong new link in the family chain. In many families, parents will simply assume that their children's spouses will share the family's religion, ethnicity, and race. This last concern presents a twist for biracial children. Sometimes the parent will advise their child to avoid their missteps. "Don't make the mistake I did," one black mother said to her daughters (although she was still married to her white husband). "Marry a black man so I can have brown grandchildren," said another black mother to her white-skinned daughter. An Armenian father wants his biracial daughter to marry an Armenian man; his African-American wife wants her to avoid all European men. And, of course, there are those parents who don't care about race at all.

In a certain respect, biracial people can never re-create their family of origin, that intersection of two separate groups. They are a one-time-only generation, and so necessarily have to break new ground in their own relationships. And just as they cannot replicate their parents, they cannot look to public images—media, literature, films—for models, since there they remain virtually invisible.

A biracial person's choice of lover and spouse serves for many observers as yet another racial litmus test. The choice is seen as an affirmation of the biracial person's own racial affiliation.

Because color and other physical features are invested with such value in our country, some biracial people have found that they often attract people who consider them to be a sort of prize. A black lover might like the "high-yellow" biracial person; a white lover might like this tawny exotic flower, this person who is different—but not too different. As one very fair-skinned biracial woman says, "The men who would be attracted to me because of the way I look are men that I find disgusting. It's almost like I'm always in a trick bag."

Some biracial people choose a spouse who reflects their primary racial affiliation, just as most monoracial people have always done. But many have dated both black and white, and often other racial and ethnic mixes as well. What also crops up for some biracial people—in all life choices, actually—is an attraction to dualism, to people who also straddle bridges: biracially, biculturally, politically, religiously, or in some other fundamental experience.

Marpessa Dawn Outlaw
Age: 30
Residence: Brooklyn, New York
Occupation: Writer

Marpessa Outlaw's parents met as teen-
agers in their hometown of Philadelphia.
They married when Outlaw's mother be-
came pregnant with her, and at the time of
her birth, her mother was just nineteen. The
young family moved to New York, started
a bookkeeping and typing business, and
broke apart when Outlaw was about five
years old. Her father decided to go to Eu-
rope, she says.

"The way he tells it, he went over
there with an understanding with my mother that she and I would follow
shortly thereafter. Instead, what she did was take me home to her parents,
and she told him, 'Either come back now or you'll never see me and Dawn
again.' And he says he didn't believe her, she must have been joking, and
so he said, 'Yeah, go on back to Philadelphia.' I don't know why he said
that. I mean, why would she be joking? But she did, to make things simple,
and he didn't see us again, really, for many, many years."

Back in Philadelphia, Outlaw lived with her mother in a mostly Jew-
ish, virtually all-white section of town. When puberty hit, Outlaw was not
included in the flirtations that ran rampant among the neighborhood kids.

By and large, I was the outcast everywhere. When I was in
junior high, I remember once trying to be part of this clique of
Jewish girls in my neighborhood. Their idea of being racy was
going out with the boys from across the tracks who were *Catholic*
boys, sort of ruffians. And they would all meet in the schoolyard
and make out and stuff like that.

They sort of took me on as a kind of I don't know what, but
on a provisional basis, I suppose. I remember liking this one kid,
and he might have been mildly flattered, but he certainly wouldn't
consider me as a possible girlfriend or go steady with me or anything like that because I wasn't white. This one girl, Randy—she

was a bitch, as they all were, really—she said, "But you really consider yourself to be white, don't you? You know, your father's black and your mother's white, but you really consider yourself to be white, don't you?" I remember saying yes because I wanted them to like me. And she was like, "See? She really is."

I was uncomfortable saying that, but that was a brief phase. I don't think I said that sort of statement a lot. Rather quickly I went into a period where I was more likely to say I was everything, to embrace everything and be very sort of multicultural. I was trying to be very proud of that and how it put me apart, but instead of in a negative way I made it sort of a positive thing.

How did that work, actually? By the time I got to high school, people hated me even more; that's basically how it worked. But at the same time I was doing a lot of reading. The first person I ever remember reading was James Baldwin, and I felt like I identified with things he was saying—experiences I didn't really have, nec-essarily, but I *felt* like I did or I understood what he was talking about. So he made me curious and he sort of influenced my sense of self.

At about fifteen I got involved with this twenty-five-year-old guy. We didn't sleep together or anything, but he was sort of a boyfriend for a while. I met him at the deli up the street. He was Mennonite, a poet, too, which is why I fell for him. He had scrag-gly long blond hair, and he taught German at Temple [University]. He fed me my first taste of venison in his apartment. He was pretty sleazy, though. He also went for my girlfriend.

And then there was a guy named Bill who was this chubby guy, also white, who was a very good guitar player. And he was sort of a boyfriend for a while, too. That was pretty much it. I didn't have any dates, just liaisons, nothing ordinary. I didn't have a date for the prom or anything like that. And my mother basically in-sulted everybody out of the house if they dared come in.

Then I went off to college. I was meeting lots of men at that time, compared to high school—going out all the time. It was mostly white guys, because I had some illusion or some feeling that they were going to open doors for me. I was going out a lot with European guys, and that fascinated me.

I remember the last white guy I went out with. I was a senior in college, and he was about twelve years older than me. I liked

him a lot and he was a good influence, but one day I realized I
wasn't in love with him. At about the same time, he realized he
couldn't continue this relationship because he had things to work
out, so there was more sadness on his part than there was on mine.
He was always saying to me, "I see you with a black guy." That
was part his own insecurity, but I don't think I disagreed with him.
It just struck me one day that he was not going to be able to give
me what I thought I wanted or needed, as nice and as good a person
as he was. I started feeling more that I was a black woman, and I
felt that I needed to be with someone who shared more things in
common with me, including a similar background or similar issues.

That decision was a conscious one, although it wasn't, *"I'm
never dating a white man again."* It was just that the very next guy
that I met was Puerto Rican, a dark-skinned Puerto Rican guy,
short Puerto Rican guy, filmmaker. He had his own problems, but
that was like *Bam!* It was like that. And I hadn't gone out with a
black guy before then. I was relieved that there was less I had to
explain—or certain things that I wouldn't have to explain—like
myself. He just accepted me without being curious about me, not
wondering *what* I might be as much. Ignorant people can be any
color, but more and more I found people who weren't that way.

I feel pretty committed—at least in terms of what I would
really *like*—to the idea of marrying or having a long-term relationship with a black man. Even though I feel very international, in the
sense of what my interests are and where I would like to go and
things I would like to do, I feel pretty committed to that. More
certain is that I don't think I could have that kind of a relationship
with a white man. It's like almost anything but.

I know plenty of people with what they consider to be very
strong black identities—they're very vocal about what they believe
and blah-blah-blah—and they find themselves able to go out with
white people. Their personal sense of self allows them to articulate
in that way, and for them the two don't necessarily conflict.

I'm surprised at myself, too. This is something I still think
about a lot. I'm surprised at my disinclination for, say, having
children with somebody with whom I would feel that the black
blood would then be washed out or something like that. This just
doesn't appeal to me at all. And I feel that is a condition more so
vis-à-vis a white person than with any other race; in other words,

I'd much rather have children with an Indian, or someone mixed with *anything* than with someone who was white. Even though I wouldn't tell somebody else what to do and I also know that love is where you find it and blah-blah-blah.

I believe in all those things, and I may not end up this way. I may turn around and do something else. It's so tough. If I try to intellectualize if that makes sense, I wonder, *should* I be intellectualizing it? Should I think with my head or should I think with my heart? Is that ridiculous or does it make sense? I don't know. I can change my answer about that every day and still not know how I feel.

One theory I have is that people who feel less sure about who they are feel they have to shore that up with somebody else. Maybe so, but you can break everything down psychologically and it still comes down to the nuts and bolts, which is: This is where you're coming from, as opposed to where someone else is coming from.

I know what I want more than anything, and it's getting to be an idealized thing: someone who shares some of that stuff, not just from an intellectual standpoint, as a sympathizer, but someone who can empathize. They don't have to empathize in every single way, but they have to share *something*.

Kyria Ramey
Age: 22
Residence: Oakland, California
Occupation: Junior college student

Kyria Ramey grew up in Berkeley and recently moved to Oakland, the next town over. Her parents—father black, mother white—met in college. Ramey says she's not sure why her parents got together, that maybe her father was making a radical statement by marrying a white woman, and that her mother wanted a big family (there are five children) and thought he would make a good father.

Ramey, who is studying animal sci-

ence and hopes to become a veterinarian, says she likes animals more than people and is not very social. As a result, she doesn't confront many questions about her racial identity. "I don't really get into situations where someone has to figure out what I am," she says. "I don't have a lot of contact with new people so much. But I just say that I'm mixed, black and white."

Sometimes she feels lucky being in the middle. But at other times, she says, "I wonder if maybe there is something that I'm not addressing for some reason, like, do I have a problem with it? Is there an actual issue inside me that I'm just not bringing up? These are questions I ask myself."

As far as there being any prejudice in my immediate family, sometimes I think my mother. Sometimes. Against my father. I think that might be tied in with him being black. It's sometimes hard to believe why she would marry him. My first boyfriend was a black guy, and she just did not like him, and she would always kind of point out to me, "He's just like your father; he's going to be just like your father. He's no good and he's going to be just like your father." I was with him for three years, and afterwards I realized that he wasn't good for me, which I'm glad I realized.

It's interesting that the three older kids in my family now all have white boyfriends, and my oldest sister is married to this white guy. I don't know if that's come about from feelings we get from my mom—that's something I think about every once in a while, that we feel more drawn to white guys. My dad also has a lot of faults, and maybe it's something that we see in him that is kind of turning us off of black guys or something, I don't know.

I still feel like I'm making my own decision, whether it be influenced by how my mom feels or how my dad is. I'm not consciously saying I'm not going to get together with black guys; I'm looking for people who are just people and someone who gets along with me, whatever race they happen to be.

My boyfriend, who's Jewish—and I have lighter skin than he does—is actually more connected with the black culture than I am. He raps. Right now it's kind of a hobby, but he's eventually going to try and get a record or something like that. It's kind of funny to me that he's a Jewish white rapper. He raps about being Jewish, Jewish things, stuff in general.

Sometimes I have a feeling like he wishes that I were more black. He does these little jokes like, "I want you to cut your hair," because when my hair was really short, it was basically an Afro. When I was growing up it was an Afro. It was kind of weird seeing this white-skinned girl with a light brown Afro, you know? And it's weird to say, but that has been trouble for everyone in my family. My sister had the same kind of hair I did, and she straightened hers about ten years ago and has kept it straight since. And for the longest time, my brother had really wiry hair, and he'd have a really hard time because it would always be all crazy. Before we went to school, my dad would grab us and brush our hair back, so we have a couple school pictures where we look like Wolfman Jack. My mom would just let our hair be, and that was hard because we would get teased.

So my boyfriend makes jokes about, "Why don't you cut your hair short? I want you to have an Afro." And I wear comfortable clothes, but he would like me to wear tight clothes or more black-styled clothes. He says these things in a joking way, although I don't think that makes it any better. But I feel comfortable and confident in who I am, and so it doesn't bother me that much.

Nya Patrinos
(See also page 134)

Nya Patrinos says she has gone through different stages of reconciling her racial identity, wanting to be all one thing or another, wanting to fit in with different groups, only to find some sticking point that connected back to her feelings about being biracial. She has settled into an identity that is more or less publicly African-American, privately African-American, Jewish, and Greek. "I'm pretty content," she says. "I don't know really how I got to be at this point—I remember as a little kid trying to make my tongue into a bottom lip to try to make my lips thin, to pretend that my lips were smaller, but I haven't done that in a long time. I don't wish I could pass anymore, where for a long time I did. I'm not content with the world, but I think I'm accepting of myself."

As much as she has found a way to "walk through the world," questions still come up, especially when it comes to romantic relationships.

How I live as an African-American is about some basic things like: I would never pass as white. I remember all through

school, when people would see my father, they would think that I
was adopted. It would never occur to them that I could be mixed,
even though I look at myself and I feel like I'm exactly in between
my mother's and father's colors. But I feel like when I walk down
the streets or anything that I do in this world, people look at me as
a black person or an African-American woman, and so I felt like I
had to at some point accept that, or that is how I'm being defined
and I have to live with that, or negotiate that or whatever.

What that means is, when I'm in an all-white environment, I
know that I'm different. I live in a black neighborhood; I feel more
comfortable there than living in a white one. Of course, I'd mostly
like to live in a mixed neighborhood, but I really don't. It means
that my boyfriend now, who's white, won't take me home to meet
his parents, and it makes me feel terrible. He says when we go
there they're not going to talk to him anymore.

They've sort of written him off anyway. He hasn't lived with
them for ten years. He's an actor, they think he's gay, so there's
already a lot of rift in there.

He used to never see them until he started seeing me, because
he comes to Philadelphia all the time to see me and they live just
outside the city. He lived in New York for eight years, and I don't
think he even went back in Christmastime. But I'd still like to
meet them. I guess I could push it and make myself meet them,
but I wonder to what end it would be.

There are a lot of questions that exist when you are African-
American or whatever and are living in a mixed world. I date this
white guy; I go to my job, which is all white; half my family is white
and half is black; and my neighbors are black. So I'm living in both
those worlds, which I guess a lot of people do, even people who
aren't mixed, and there are a lot of questions that come up because
there's a lot of racism. For a while I thought, "Oh, I can't deal," and
I started dating this guy who was mixed earlier this year.

He was black and white, too, and he thought I was crazy
because I led these racism workshops sometimes with this women's
organization I belong to, and I have a lot of books on racism in my
house. He says, "No wonder you're so messed up, Nya, you've got
all these books around you. You know, it's 1992, there is no racism." He's a Philadelphia cop and he is mixed and he doesn't think
there's any racism!

I knew him in high school, but I always thought he was Puerto Rican. When we first went out I asked him if he was and he said, "With my Polish last name?" His mother is white, his father is black, and so there was some kind of comfort in that. And I was talking to him about my boyfriend and not being able to see his family, and this guy said to me, "I don't know how you can accept that. I would never accept that. I've gone out with a number of white women, and I've never had that happen." And he said, "If it's hard for him to deal with it, you should tell him how it's hard for you to be who you are every day."

So then that night I got home from being out with him, I was a little drunk, I called my boyfriend, two o'clock in the morning: "If it's hard for you to deal with . . ."

And my boyfriend said, "Nya, I know. I think about it every day. And we can go and see my parents, but what commitment are you making to me? Because once we go there, I don't see my family anymore. So are you making the commitment to stay with me? Because I'm not going to have any family."

I didn't know if I wanted to make that commitment. I just don't want those questions to exist, but they do. And then in the end, I saw this cop guy some more, but even though he's mixed and I'm mixed and you feel like maybe there are no racial questions—which I think there always are, because in this society you're blasted with this "White woman is the epitome of beauty," even if we're both mixed—but we really didn't have very much in common, and I don't see him anymore. Whereas my boyfriend—whose family I still don't see—I feel really comfortable with him.

I always look at interracial couples. I look at them and say, "When there's a black man and a white woman, is the white woman less attractive?" This is terrible, but I think about status: Can a white man get any kind of black woman but not the reverse? I think about that a lot. I don't know what my conclusion is. I always look at the interracial couples, and I seem to make them myself. I date a lot of white guys, and since people look at me not really as mixed but as African-American, I'm sort of making an interracial couple, even though I'm interracial.

I'm always looking, and I don't know why I ask myself that

question—maybe because of things I've read or things like that—but I do. I wish I didn't ask myself that question, but I wonder—because I know my mother is a lot more educated than my father. I think my mother is much more attractive than my father, and I love my father, but sometimes I wonder, now, if he was the exact same man and he was black, would my mother have been with him? And I'm not sure. I wonder a lot and because of reading that *Autobiography of Malcolm X*, I always think, is there some kind of status involved?

I wish the question wasn't there. I wish we were all nice people and we didn't have to worry about that and we were just dating people because we liked them. I wish it weren't so complicated. It seems to get ugly when you say, "Well, you know, she's with him because he's white or he's with her because she's white." It doesn't have anything to do with who she is, but it's some kind of prestige. I don't want that to exist in the world; I don't want it to exist in me. I know I date a lot of white men. Why do I do that?

First of all, I don't meet very many black men. In college there weren't any. And then people also talk about how when you have a certain education, you want to be with people that have the same kind of education. I live in a neighborhood where most, I can't say all, but most of the black men are on the street yelling things. It's a big crack neighborhood.

I used to live in West Philly, and people over there would yell at me. My boyfriend at the time was white. People used to yell from their cars, you know, "You traitor!" and stuff like that. Throw things at me. Just rocks or whatever.

When that happens, I get nervous. In some ways I feel bad; I feel like these people shouldn't be throwing things—I wish they wouldn't do that. In other ways they kind of trigger something in me. I say, "Why *am* I dating this guy?" Well, I like this person, that's why I'm doing it.

Then whenever I go back and I date a black guy—not because "Oh, I found a black guy," but because it just happens—in the beginning I always feel this kind of relief. I think, "Okay, now it's going to be easier. Nobody's going to throw things. Nobody's going to yell anything." And then there are the same normal relationship questions and it's not easier. Because relationships are hard. And then either he's a creep or we don't get along, which can happen with a white person, too. But that initial feeling of *it's going to be okay now* lasts about a week.

One problem that comes up with black men sometimes is that I wonder why they're dating me. I always wonder if it doesn't really have anything to do with who I am, but that I'm this light-skinned kind of attractive woman. That's a status thing, too, so I wonder about that. I want to be thought of as more. Sometimes I think the equivalent of being a light-skinned black woman is being a blue-eyed blonde in white society.

There are all these interracial couples now in Hollywood, and I always say to my boyfriend, "Did you see that?" And he always says, "No, I didn't see that." And I say, "Well, you're supposed to, you're in an interracial relationship. You gotta look at all this stuff."

He just doesn't notice. I don't think it's a bad thing, maybe; it's probably not really that important that Emilio Estevez and Paula Abdul are together. My boyfriend's probably thinking, "My girlfriend is a pretty intelligent woman, and she's giving me *People* magazine gossip." But somehow that's important to me.

Bernette Ford
Age: 42
Residence: Brooklyn, New York
Occupation: Editorial director, children's book publisher

Bernette Ford says she is usually taken for being Jewish—her father's background—by strangers and people who know her only casually. She has always identified as black, however; that's the identity her parents communicated to her and her younger sister as they grew up in a Long Island town, not far from New York City.

Ford is married to an African-American man, and they have a twelve-year-old daughter. She wonders about her daughter and dating. "There are no black boys in her class, and I'm really concerned about what's going to happen to her when she gets to an age where she's ready to start dating," Ford says. "I don't even think of white boys as an option for her. I'm sure she does. I probably wouldn't have serious objections if I liked the boy she brought home and he happened to be white, but I think it's very hard work to make a successful interracial marriage and to raise kids who are sane."

For Ford herself, white boys and men were never real contenders. "I never thought of having children with a white man. I never had a real serious relationship with a white guy after high school."

When I was a senior in high school, class of '68, I really liked a white boy, Steve, who was in several of my classes. I think he liked me, too, but he was in a very popular crowd. He would come over to the house and talk and play records or whatever, but we never dated. I think Steve was afraid to upset his parents or do something that wasn't conforming with the rest of his crowd. There was not much interracial dating in my town at that time.

In junior high it wasn't really dating because you would walk home with somebody and that was a date. Or you would call somebody, say, "I like you," and give a ring and that was your boyfriend for three weeks. But I really liked this guy [in high school], and I was really upset when he said that he couldn't go out with me. He never gave me a reason. It was really painful.

Years later I was walking down the street on the Upper West Side in Manhattan and I bumped into Steve. He was really surprised to see me. We had seen each other a couple of times during college because we both went to school in Connecticut, but I hadn't seen him for about eight years. He asked if he could come over, and I said sure. He came up and we were having a soda or a beer or something, and he told me that he was in love with me and that he was really sorry it didn't work out when we were in high school and he really wanted to see me. It was so weird. I was laughing 'cause this was the first guy that I ever really, really liked.

But I said, "No, it's too late. I'm going with someone else I really like." At that point, I thought he was immature and that he really didn't have strong convictions. I knew he had liked me, but he didn't have the courage to do anything about it. So I lost a little respect for him.

Sandy Shupe
(See also page 188)

When Sandy Shupe goes out on the town, the attention she gets from black men can alienate the black women she might be out with. "I love it when some man will refer to me as being yellow," she says, rolling her eyes. " 'Ooh, look at that fine-lookin' yellow woman over there!' Gee, thanks for that one. That really helps me fit right in."

I'm going to be conceited here and say I'm not a bad-looking woman. So to some black women, I'm a threat in certain cases. As soon as I go out with a black man it's, "She's white." I instantly become white to black women. They can't say it's because you're pretty, or because you're tall or because you have a good personality; the only thing that's wrong with you is you're white. So it's always been more difficult to date black men because of it, especially to go home with them to meet mom.

This guy I liked when I was in boarding school, when we had the Family Night, his parents came and they refused to sit at the same table with me. It was unacceptable. "I didn't send you to school to fraternize with white girls," his mother said.

Another problem for me with black men is I feel like I'm a little Kewpie doll, like I belong on a shelf. I'm seen more as a white woman than I am as a woman, and that's very frustrating, and it happens consistently. I wish I could have gone out and found a black man just like my dad. I wish I could go out and find a white man. Heck, give me a Chinese man just like my father—the boundary there is nothing. But every black man I've ever dated, I become a trophy, something to be seen.

One guy, Wayne, was a really good example. He liked to take me down to black clubs. "This is my girlfriend Sandy, and her mom's white." Why did he need to do that? Never got an answer.

Part of it, too, is that I haven't been treated properly by black men. I've never found the right black man who is going to treat me like a woman, I guess is what it really boils down to. I've never found my dad. I have very high expectations of any man, and I want the man I spend the rest of my life with to have the ideals my father had, and I don't find that in black men. My father never treated my mother as a trophy. God knows that's the truth, after what all she put him through. He just loved her, and I guess what it boils down to is that I've had relationships with black men but never really fallen in love.

Now my ex-husband, he was white. A month before we got married his father told him that he didn't want any little nigger babies coming up to his house and calling him grandpa. My ex-husband said, "Guess you won't have to worry about that because we just won't come to your house."

His father was a prejudiced bigot, but eventually I won him over. I'd poke fun at him, saying things like, "Why don't y'all come down, we'll have some ribs," or, "Got any watermelon up there at the house?" Things I knew would irritate him, but it was kind of like, "I'm not going to let you win on this one, you're not going to win. You're going to be around me and eventually you're going to wind up liking me. If you don't, too darn bad; I'm going to be there anyway. So you make the decision."

He made that statement a month before our wedding, and at one point we didn't even think he would come to the wedding. He did. He showed up with a big smile on his face. This is a man who didn't go to one of his sons' weddings, because he couldn't stand his daughter-in-law-to-be. And she was white.

I look at it this way: If anybody does have a problem that my father was black and I'm black, I'm hoping that it's my personality that changes the opinion, that takes away the stereotype. You know, maybe if I showed up with cornhusks in my hair and no shoes and dirty, then there might be a difference, but I like to think that I pick out a better class of people from the white side of society to be with, that are going to accept me for me. I do the same thing from the black side, because I can't spend my life fighting. It's not worth it.

CHAPTER IX

Other Forces

My mother's lupus permeated our life. For as long as I can remember, my mom was sick when I was young, and that's probably had a more profound effect on me psychologically than any of the racial questions. That's probably why I'm in therapy now.—Bernette Ford, p.207

My lesbianism is even more important than my race because it's something that I came to on my own, without any outside influences.—Neisha Wright, p.87

Actually, the fact that my mother was white didn't bother me as much as the fact that she was very heavy. She was always overweight. As a kid that bothered me more, although she thought it bothered me that she was white. She had a hard time, because my racial identity has always been black.—René Rambo, p.109

The two most important words in my life would be foster care: *That changed the course of my life forever. And then number*

211

two would be race. There's no comparison after those first two—
anything else would be a far run down the line. Those are the two
most important things that have shaped my life and have caused
me aggravation with a big A. If I could, would I change the fact
that I'm black and white? Absolutely not. What I would change is
that my mom wasn't there. I'd change that.—Deborah Gregory,
p.302

In a book such as this, where race is examined exhaustively (and exhaustingly, at times), it's all too easy to lose sight of the fact that race is never the sole influence in a biracial person's life. Depending on the day, the weather, or the concerns of the moment, the pieces that make up a sense of self come together differently. After all, *who* a person is can in part be defined by who they are called upon to be; one's identification with a political party may be stronger in an election year, one's sense of being American may be more acute while traveling abroad.

Fluctuations in identity, in which part of the self takes the spotlight at a given moment, can also be ordered by basic survival needs. Sometimes, the acute demands of one part of a person's identity can make it more present, require it to be more aggressively tended than any other. In this chapter, three people discuss essential elements and forces in their lives besides race—and explain how these often superseded race as an influence on their developing identities and concerns.

A gay man talks about his homosexuality in relationship to his racial identity: how the two have developed at different speeds, in different environments. A woman describes a childhood home life that was less remarkable in matters of race than it was in growing up surrounded by people who were aged and dying. A young man tells of two experiences—substance abuse and having been put up for adoption—that have had as much (or more) impact as race on his life choices and direction.

Although all of these people had been asked to tell only as much of their life stories as was necessary to understand their developing sense of race and identity, each one determined that these other parts of their lives needed to be told. And so here are tremendously important parts of life that stand alone, distinct from race. But, of course, they do not necessarily stand alone, and fair arguments could be made that they may not be distinct from race at all. Certainly, their stories serve as acute reminders that race in America does not exist or define itself in a vacuum.

Paul Whitaker
Age: 32
Residence: San Francisco, California
Occupation: Psychotherapist and psychological researcher

Paul Whitaker's parents met at Swarthmore College, outside of Philadelphia. His father was the first black student—and the only black student during his years there—to attend the school. He became a political scientist, with a specialty in Nigeria. Whitaker's mother was a French teacher at Swarthmore. For the first five years of her life, she had lived in Africa, where her parents were Protestant missionaries.

Whitaker's parents married when his father was twenty-one and his mother was thirty. They had two sons and separated when Whitaker was four, his brother, six. With his mother and brother, Whitaker moved to Norton, Massachusetts, a predominantly white town where he lived through high school. Although he was not close to his father, he regularly visited his paternal relatives in Pittsburgh, Pennsylvania, where they ran a funeral home. Whitaker says that through puberty, he was not very conscious of racial issues. "Apart from my mother saying, 'You're biracial,' which didn't have a lot of significance for me, I didn't quite understand racial tension. Obviously, as I entered adolescence I heard about it, but it really wasn't a reality to me because I had experienced being accepted by both races and feeling part of both races, so it was abstract."

When we talked about pop culture images of biracial people, Whitaker pointed out that another aspect of his identity, homosexuality, tends to be represented with similar melodrama. "So I'm tragic, times two, I guess," he says. "A gay tragic mulatto would have been great thematic material for a fifties movie."

Growing up, my identity was quite white. I physically am quite white. I'm whiter in terms of complexion and features than most biracial kids that I've met, more than my brother. I seem to have this mysterious look that can be identified as a lot of ethnicities. Most people think that I have some ethnic background, but have a hard time distinguishing what it is—Jewish, Italian, Arab. A number of things are more likely to be assumed than biracial.

Frankly, I wasn't identified by others in the white community where we lived as being black unless I chose to do so. So in a sense, since I was living with my mother in a white community and didn't appear to be black to the majority of people, my identity was very much white. Also, I wasn't close to my father, and I think the emotional distance meant that I didn't identify with him. I don't know how much that would have made a difference in my racial identity at that point, with all the other factors the same. If I had simply felt closer to my father, perhaps I would have had more of a black identity.

I used to catch flak for my hair. I frankly don't remember thinking that it was a racial slur, though, but rather as just isolating something about my hair. The only racial discomfort I remember feeling back then was when I heard kids say nigger, and it was clear to me they weren't thinking I was part of the group they were being derogatory toward at the time. So I felt conflicted. I remember that I did not identify my race at that time, at that age, so that there was a kind of hiding.

During that period, it seemed almost a technicality. If a form asked for my race, then I would check other and write biracial. Nowadays I often just write black. There's been a certain development in why I do that. Somewhat later on, I realized that to be part black is to be black in this society. But it's a strange position, I suppose, to be in some ways considered more black because I have black heritage, and also to have my particular lack of black identity or acculturation for as long as I did.

I started to become more aware and to have identity conflicts once I got to college. I was invited to a black student orientation, my roommate was black, and clearly I was being seen as a black student upon entering Wesleyan [University].

I started to become very aware of what I *didn't* have in terms of a racial identity, and was very uncomfortable about it. I didn't have any real knowledge of black culture, so I didn't feel I fit in, and that was painful, that was hard. I think that was the first time I struggled with my racial identity. I didn't know any black vernacular; I didn't have this sort of strong, not only language, but body language and knowledge. There was a lot I hadn't read. I had never thought about my musical taste being black or white, but simply that I liked what I liked. I did like a lot of R&B and black music, but I didn't consciously have a black collection of either literature or music. It wasn't something I had too much consciousness about.

At the same time, no one ever seemed to have expectations of me, not that they voiced. As far as I can remember, no one ever said to me, "You seem to have something lacking," so it was in large part that *I* had this sense that I would be judged for being too white, too middle-class. I try not to judge myself on that level, although perhaps I do. I guess I've struggled with that. But even to this day, I don't really adjust my personality or act any differently with Whites or Blacks. To do so would be false; it would be hypocrisy. If I had a comfortable exposure to both and it was really me to slip into [either one of] them, then the changing wouldn't be hypocrisy. But to affect this inner-city black persona I've never had, that my father doesn't have, is a bit false. I will play with it in the way I will play with any sort of identity, but I won't try to pass as being something different than I am. I still to this day, though, have some self-consciousness about feeling too white in black contexts.

I did very little about that when I was at Wesleyan because I didn't know what to do. I didn't actively become involved in black student organizations because I didn't have a black identity, so part of it was fear that I just was too white and wouldn't fit in, but also I didn't have any need to. That's one thing that makes me part of a very small minority amongst black people: I think it's quite rare to not have a need for black affinity. I didn't feel I needed that refuge or support or protection; I didn't feel I needed it to support who I was.

I started to be aware that the black part of my racial makeup had little significance to me. "Little significance" makes it sound as if I was totally unaware of racial issues, and that's not true; they certainly meant something to me, but on a personal level . . . ? In other words, probably my perspective was more akin to a white person who knew black people and liked them as opposed to a black person.

Still, no one ever said anything to me directly about not being black enough. It's something I've suspected and felt in people's behavior to me, but it's never been said to me. So I don't know where projection stops and reality begins along that dimension. Maybe it's partially not wanting to be aware, not wanting to take it into account, because I don't want to think along those lines. I just simply want to feel comfortable with who I am and how I've developed.

I felt alienated at Wesleyan, and I left after two and a half years. I felt culturally apart there, but it's not that I felt like the answer was black culture. Maybe I felt the class difference. I was educated, but I certainly didn't have the money that the majority of the students had—maybe that was part of it—although I wasn't too aware of money then. You see, I just felt alienated. The academics were very good, and I was used to that and I anticipated that, but what came as a surprise was that interpersonal dynamics were always competitive and intellectual, and I could never, so to speak, let my hair down. I could never really be myself, and that made me feel very uncomfortable.

From there I went to Hampshire College, but not directly. First I came to San Francisco for half a year because I was gay and I wanted to experience a gay community. It was really a very freeing experience. Entering the gay community had a lot more to do with my identity development and my needs for community.

For most black gay men a hierarchy of oppression does exist, where affiliation with the black community is considered more important politically, socially, identitywise, and yet, ironically, a lot of black gay men actually don't socialize much amongst themselves. That's changing and that's certainly not a rule, but there is a subset of black gay men who don't associate much because they associate gay oppression with the black community, the black church, and a particular type of strong homophobia that they'd experienced within the black community.

There's a feeling that homosexuals debase the race, and so there's a kind of shame some Blacks can feel about that subset of the race. I think that black gay men do experience that dual oppression in a very difficult way—*I* don't actually feel a lot of these things and a lot of this experience, again, for physical reasons and, I suppose, cultural reasons as well—but what happens often is that black men coming out into the gay community find and feel more acceptance from white males. And yet there's a fair amount of racism in white gay communities, [just] as there is in the white community at large, and so it's hard not to feel that there's danger or threats from all sides. It's pretty surprising and shocking that there is racism within the gay community. They should know better because of their own oppression for being gay. It's also unfortunate that Blacks can't see that gays are oppressed and that the similarities could bring us together.

Often I think it's very much the opposite, that Blacks want to have a group they can look down on, that there's some comfort in being able to take one's feelings of oppression and to become the oppressor. I think we see that in all walks of socialization. But that phenomenon is really saddening to me; it just really shows how blind people can be, that they can't make that empathetic leap that seems so obvious to me.

In terms of identity development, growing up I was much more conscious of the oppressive factors in society that would be a problem for me as gay than as black; that's not true of most black gay people. I think most black gay people feel that being black is more the case. But it hasn't been for me.

These two communities, gay and black, have an interesting, complex relationship to each other. Within the black gay community, you always say "black gay," you don't say "gay black"—that sort of thing—because it's generally felt that the black part of the identity is the more important affiliation, that in the hierarchies of oppression it's harder to be black than it is to be gay.

You put black first, much like in saying "lesbian and gay," you always say lesbian first. It's just the politically correct way to do it. The more oppressed is said first because if you say gay and lesbian,

it's an implicit preference, so you make up for it by always saying
the other, which seems a little extreme as well. I'm involved with
an organization called Lesbians and Gays of African Descent for
Democratic Action [LGADDA]. There's a great preponderance of
men in the group, and yet it's always going to be referred to as
"lesbian and gay."

Now for me, the issue of passing exists on both dimensions because
I have passed as straight and as white. I guess what makes them
similar is that awareness that oppression is out there, lurking at the
back door, and it's my decision to let it affect me or not. I have a
sense of the potential for discrimination or perspectives changing as
a result of factors or information I have control over.

I didn't need a black community to affirm my sense of identity at
Wesleyan because I didn't have much of a black identity at that
point. I'd say it's only in graduate school that I really started to
form a black identity, and only in the last few years, since I've
lived in San Francisco, that I've made active efforts to do so. I
joined the political group, LGADDA, and I've just been making
an effort to be more aware of black culture, in reading and making friends and activities, like in planning a party and thinking
about racial balance. These are the sorts of things that I didn't
use to think about.

  With something like a party, the motivation is to have balance
so that everybody feels comfortable, much like I seek sexual or
gender balance, or even sexual orientation balance. I suppose, for
example, I could have a party and invite only black people, but that
to me seems more artificial. I'm invited to all-black parties and I
don't think it's artificial that there aren't white people there, but it
would be for me because I would be actively excluding a lot of my
friends and I just don't do that. I know friends who have white and
black friends, and sometimes they want to have a party of all black
people, so I guess that may be reflective again of that thing about
needing the group. I feel like my needs from the black community
are more about my own growth as opposed to feeling a need for
protection.

I get a little uncertain of what it means to be black or white. In other words, sometimes I feel like I'm pretty white, and yet, I wonder then, well, what does that mean? What does it mean to be black or white, because it operates on so many dimensions.

When I feel more white, that's about something physical, about how other people react to me in terms of oppression or discrimination. It's also culture and class: middle-class, predominantly white neighborhoods, predominantly white schools. I don't see white people as different from me, and I think that's very different from most black people, maybe even very different from biracial people. I pass very easily as white, and so I have a sense that I do know what it's like to be fully part of white culture: being around Whites, being assumed to be white, being amongst white people for long periods of time. Also, the white culture is just more available for everyone on TV, in the media.

I don't know, however, what it feels like to be black in the sense of encountering the day-to-day assaults, the interactions that occur based on physical appearance. I'm not saying I'm not accepted by black people, but if I were darker-skinned and had more pronounced, African-descent features, I think some Blacks would trust me more. And to some degree I understand that, because I can be exposed, I can have an understanding, have sensitivities—but when you can pass, you can pass. It's a different experience, because it's the insidious stuff that really is the very painful part of prejudice.

Sometimes I think it's easier to deal with blatant prejudice. At least you know what you're dealing with. It's all the little subtle things: that you don't know if this person's being rude because you're black or are they just rude? Are they being patronizing, or is that the way they talk? Never quite knowing how one's race might be figuring into a job decision that's been made. I don't typically have to ask myself those questions; I assume that for the most part I'm usually evaluated as white.

In my own experience, I've seen dating relationships turn off as a result of prejudice once someone realized I was black. Usually it's an insidious type of situation where they don't let on, but you slowly realize it, and then some other pretext comes up. So, again, it's partly speculation, but I think there's definitely some truth to that; it's happened to me a few times.

In one relationship that comes to mind, I don't think there was a pretext, just a change in behavior. And I was aware of it. There was a distance that wasn't there before. The sex stopped. That's happened on two or three occasions. I don't know what people are thinking is going to be different, but they turn off. They like to think of themselves as people who don't sleep with black people. Nothing really has changed except that, the knowledge of the thought, so that's strange.

I do on a number of occasions declare that I'm black; I don't think I've ever declared I'm white. I think people just assume the white part; that's mostly why I would never say I'm white, because I don't have to tell anybody that. But I do say I'm black, because that's the informational part that's missing. I'm more apt to say I'm black than I'm biracial. Seven times out of ten I'll say I'm black, but the reason there is not that I identify more as black, but rather that I think it's more parsimonious if I say I'm black and I let them figure it out.

I don't tend to experience much racism directed at me. I see it more in terms of experiences that friends have and experiences that my race has. I think it affects my consciousness. I think that if I was gay and not black that I would also have an experience of oppression as well. It's hard to divide out what the developing factors were, but I have a very strong sense of oppression and of the artificial distinctions that are made between people based on stereotypical factors.

In terms of which is more present, issues of race or issues about being gay, I would say that up until moving to San Francisco, being gay was more present in my consciousness because I was more aware of what the problems were.

But being here in San Francisco, for the first time I really feel like I can, not *forget* my sexual orientation, but it becomes so normal, so omnipresent, so everyday, that I don't have to think about gay identity. I just think about being myself—whereas I'm more apt to think about black identity because I have to seek it out. It feels like more of a shift, more of something that I need to be conscious of. It was just the opposite, until moving here.

Pamela Austin
Age: 34
Residence: Philadelphia, Pennsylvania
Occupation: Graduate student in African-American studies

Pam Austin was born in New York. She lived in Harlem with her African-American father and grandmother for six years, and then was sent to live with her godmother's sister in Philadelphia, where she stayed until she was twelve. From there, she went to her godmother's sister's cousin, also in Philadelphia. Austin's mother and father never married. She speculates that her mother may have been married to someone else at the time of her birth, her evidence being that on her birth certificate, four other children were noted. Austin's mother regularly visited the Harlem apartment, but she disappeared from Austin's life soon after the relocation to Philadelphia. Austin last saw her mother on her seventh birthday, when her mother confided to a family friend that she was remarrying—a white man—and didn't see a need for him to know anything about all of this, so she wouldn't be coming back. Austin suspects that her parents may have continued to see each other despite that marriage.

Austin's childhood was defined not only by being an only child, but one surrounded by significantly older adults. Her father was two months shy of his forty-ninth birthday when she was born, and he was the youngest care provider she ever had.

My father was born in Norfolk, Virginia, in 1909. Yes, that makes him a lot older than me. My mother is white and Jewish and, from all that I know, lived in Westchester County in New York. I was born in New York City, and my mother's address on my birth certificate is the apartment I lived in until I was six, but I don't have any recollection of my mother ever living with us—with me, my father, my grandmother, and a great aunt. I remember my mother being around, minimally, once or twice a week, at least as far back as I can remember, and that's maybe two, two and a half.

She'd come down, she'd give me my bath, we'd play. Showed up, hung around, and spent the night with my father.

Now, obviously, if my father was almost forty-nine when I was born, we're talking about old people here. My great-aunt died when I was four; I remember that because I inherited her bedroom. My grandmother died of a stroke and whatever complications came from that when I was six. I'm the one who found the body. She was in a coma on the bathroom floor. All I knew was that Grandma wasn't answering me when I kept saying, "Wake up! Wake up!"

Her death meant, "Gee, wonder where Pam goes?" My father worked at the VA hospital in Montrose, which is in Westchester County. He was either an orderly or a nurse's assistant. Sometimes he'd work night shift, sometimes he'd work day shift. In any event, it would have been somewhat cumbersome for him to have a six-year-old.

For whatever reason, probably the obvious, my mother was not going to take me home with her. I remember being told later on that her family did know about me, but they didn't want a nigger in the family. I vaguely remember meeting them when I was about three or four, going someplace with her and then coming home and asking who those people were I'd met and being told, "Those were your grandparents." But that's all I remember.

My godmother Helen lived around the corner from us [in New York], and I spent weekends with her. She was my grandmother's best friend, so I ended up in Philadelphia with her family. Her sister Edith said, "I wonder what will happen to poor little Pam?" And the next thing she knew, poor little Pam was sitting in her living room, going, "Hi." And it wasn't as traumatic as a lot of people try to make it out to be. I moved into a house where I knew everybody. I even knew all the kids on the street because I had come down with my godmother to visit. So it was no great traumatic anything. I just moved. Missed my dad, but that was the only real trauma.

When I went to Philadelphia, it was just me and the adults, and they were older than my father. Can you say "spoiled"? It's great. I got to walk on water until I was twelve years old. It was wonderful. Somewhat indulged. To some extent, never really treated like a child. Treated like a short adult, which was fine. The only drawback was that kids got on my nerves. They made too much noise and ran around, and I much preferred sitting in the living room and hearing weird stories of relatives who worked in nightclubs in Harlem in the thirties. That was infinitely more entertaining.

There was nothing normal about my house. There was me. There was my godmother's sister, Edith. First off, virtually everybody on my street was southern, except for my family: all people born *in* Philadelphia, and we're talking about being born in 1901, 1903, and 1907. You got it: I'm living with people about at retirement age. Just them and me. And my godmother's mother lived with us. She was in her eighties and she was from Virginia, but everyone else was a born Philadelphian, and that's significant in this city, because there's a sort of class difference between the old Philadelphians who had been born here and the ones who came up from the South after the First World War. My family, the Lewises, had come up in the 1800s.

Here we sat, in a house we didn't own. We rented the first floor and the basement. And I'm living with people who owned— flat out—mink coats and Persian lambs and God only knows what else, *and did not run numbers*! It was legal money! Everybody else I knew who did that had something on the side.

My godmother, *whoooh!* My godmother was so strange. My godmother, when she was in Philadelphia, lived with an Italian bootlegger in South Philly during the Depression, eventually moved to New York, and got a job in the garment district.

My godmother's sister, Edith, worked at Sears until she decided to retire. Their brother Earl, by the time I was around, was working at Strawbridge's [a department store], but he had also worked in New York, during the twenties and thirties in the clubs in Harlem. So I spent a lot of my childhood listening to bizarre stories about gangsters in New York. Hey, it's different than your regular bedtime stories.

Their mother had come up from the South by then, and they all had jobs in service, they were all domestics. So I lived with them. There was always someone home at my house. I remember being baby-sat just twice because there was *always* someone home in my house. A lot of stability.

And I pretty much did anything I felt like until I really irritated the hell out of somebody. Yes, I was disciplined and hit when

I was supposed to be and all those other fun things, but for the most part, pretty much left alone. What was expected of me was whatever chores I had and not screwing up school. Had a question in a class once when I was in college: "How many people in this class had a problem going to college?" Meaning the money was an issue. And I always thought that was such a strange question, because as a kid it had never come up. It was just always assumed I was going. And I'm not even sure if anybody in the family had made it through high school.

So I was there until I was twelve. Now, here comes the fun part: See if you can keep this all straight. When I was eleven, my godmother, Helen, died. No, this was not a horrible shock. She had cancer. She had breast cancer that metastasized into something else. Actually, it was lung cancer that went to breast cancer. She was still smoking when she was in the hospital dying and had both breasts removed.

The first day of sixth grade, Helen died. I have to start this on a roll or I forget the order. Her mother died the beginning of June that same school year. So that's September of '69, June of '70. [Her mother] was old, she was ninety, she had been sick, but basically she was old. Helen dying was probably the worst thing to happen up to that point. More upsetting than my grandmother dying because I was only six when that happened.

My father died that November. That was fun. He had a heart attack. He had a massive heart attack and died. According to one of the guys who worked with him, he was walking up the hall, and he just slumped on the wall and fell and that was it.

They called from the hospital on a Saturday morning. Phone rings, Edith answered. They said they were looking for me, she gave me the phone, and there's this dumbfounded woman on the other end. She finally goes, "Is this Pamela Austin?"

I said yes. Obviously, I'd been listed as next of kin.

It's like, "Oh, you sound like a kid."

It's like, "Well, yeah, I'm twelve."

"Oh, can I get whoever answered the phone, could you put them back on, please? Please go get that adult." I gave Edith back the phone, and she's sitting there on the phone going, "Uh-huh, uh-huh," with this totally passive look on her face, and I'm standing there going, "Okay, fine, Daddy's dead. Wonderful."

And she finally just looked up and shook her head yes, like,
"It's not your imagination." I knew because why on earth would
anybody be calling me long-distance, person-to-person? So yeah. I
turned twelve that May. He died that November. That was not
fun, that was not fun at all. It was a miserable Christmas, because
by this time virtually everybody in the family was dead.

Just Earl and Edith and I were left. And did I mention there
was a slight alcoholism problem in the family? Helen drank J&B
scotch, Earl drank anything he could get his hands on, and Edith
drank beer. The first alcohol I ever had was Ballantine ale. Grew
up on it from the age of two. Here, take this, shut up, go sit in the
corner. Edith also drank Cutty Sark and Beefeater gin.

They were pretty mellow. They'd have parties periodically. It
was weird; it was like living in never-never land. There were all
these very old people, and there was me. And when all the friends
were over, as long as I wasn't real conspicuous I was just allowed to
be there. You know, everybody pretty much ignored the fact that
there was this kid roaming around. It's like out of a weird movie.
It really was. It never made any difference. They all smoked, they
all drank, none of them saw any reason to change those habits when
I moved in. No, I don't have an alcohol problem; I don't even
drink that much.

Earl was the only real loud pain when he was drunk. The only
two people I had a problem with within that family was Earl and
their mother, Mom Abby. They were really the only two that got
on me unnecessarily. Basically a jealousy problem. You know, here
Edith and Helen took me in when I didn't belong to anybody, and
Earl was always very jealous because as soon as he had too much to
drink, somebody bounced him out the front door. And his mother
felt as though by paying attention to me they weren't paying as
much to her as they should have been, because she was sick.

Any name-calling that went on, it was usually the two of them.
Within the family, the only time reference was made to me being
half-white or my mother being a Jew was from them. Okay, I'm
between six and twelve, they're seventy and ninety by the time
they died. Real adult behavior, but what can you expect? One day
Earl was on a really bad drunk, and I had to listen to long, lengthy
discourses on "half-white bitch" and "Jew bitch" and da-da-da.

Actually, the whole thing ended somewhat comically. I got

pissed, and being very rational, went and wrote this long involved letter to my father. Unfortunately, I didn't have stamps, so when it came time to mail it, I asked Edith if I could have a stamp to mail it, and she's like, "Well, give it to me and I'll mail it." She had not heard about any of this. Of course, she read the letter. And when Helen came down to visit at some point [from New York], she showed up, walked into the house, Earl was half-crocked, and it turned into a how-dare-you-say-the-things-you-said-to-Pam thing. She stood in the middle of the living-room floor and slapped this man silly, until she eventually grabbed him and tossed him out the front steps in the middle of December out into the snow. And left him sitting there until someone suggested that he might freeze to death. She opened the door, dragged him in, tossed him down the cellar steps, and locked the door until the next morning. So it wasn't that no one defended me. Unfortunately, they couldn't do much about their mother, outside of saying, "Leave the kid alone."

She said the same kind of stuff, but as I got older, it was very obviously just a matter of jealousy. When she felt better, she was fine. I was left in the house alone with her so that I could watch her and she could watch me. It was only when she was really, really sick or when she thought they weren't paying as much attention to her as they should have been, and there was nobody else to take it out on.

At the same time this was going on, I wasn't getting anything from people in the neighborhood. No one ever said anything. People would say things in school. I was in grade school in '68, when everyone got very black and proud, and there was this question of why I looked the way I looked. "Why is your hair the way it is?"

"I don't know. My mother's white?" Bad answer. Only one I had, but a bad answer anyway. That caused some problem but not enough to really make a difference. I got called things periodically—and my coloring made that a target—but other people got called other things for other reasons. Didn't get hassled by anybody older than my age until I was a teenager, and then the same shit everybody gets. If a guy says something to you and you don't answer him, obviously the reason you haven't answered is because you're a yellow bitch. I was like, "Oh, get a life!" No, this isn't the problem, it's your personality.

I was probably more hassled about being teacher's pet than

about anything else. Race started to be an issue in junior high and high school, but only with black kids, which was really strange because it had never been before. Maybe it was because I was now in these two schools, Masterman and Girls' High, that pulled from across the city, so people didn't know me. Race became an issue through a weird fluke. I started wearing glasses the beginning of sixth grade, and when you get your first pair, you don't know what you're supposed to be seeing. The guy sticks the glasses on you, that's it. And even with the glasses, I had to sit closer to the board or I was not going to see anything.

These were the first integrated schools I went to, and the black girls sat in the back row and the white ones sat up front, and I couldn't see so I ended up sitting up front, which didn't win me friends in the back. I think it had more to do with the age; girls, especially, tend to get real bitchy at about twelve or thirteen.

One friend I made then that I still have, Naomi, I guess we became friends because she was the other class reject. She was this nice middle-class Jewish kid with an Afro; her hair is infinitely kinkier than mine will ever be. A Jewfro or an Isfro, depending on whether you were political or not.

And the black kids gave her such a hard time because half these kids wanted to get Afros and their mothers wouldn't let them. They were still making them straighten their hair, and here's this little white girl with all this frizzy hair—and Naomi would get slammed into the wall periodically when she was going down the steps. It was miserable. We became friends. Lack of anything else. It's like, "Oh, yeah, okay, fine." See, I had better things to think about in seventh grade. Basically, everybody was dying. Call me anything you want, I don't care.

If you were to find the black kids that I went to junior high and high school with and told them that I was now a graduate student in African-American studies, they would probably die laughing. As far as they were concerned, I thought I was white. Which I thought was pretty funny, because I never did. But the fact that I didn't hang with them and didn't want to hang with them, that was the only thing they could decide I wanted to be. You know, "You hang with all those Jews."

It's like, "Well, they don't bother me and you do."

Every now and then I'll run into one of them and it's like,

"What are you doing?" I'm like, mumbling, "I'm in a master's program at Temple in African-American studies," and they're like, "Excuse me?"

"No, you're not imagining things." Now they're the ones who have gone horribly corporate and middle-class and live in the 'burbs. If I was trying so damn hard to be white in high school, why is it that I'm doing African-American studies and I'm still living in an inner-city, predominantly black neighborhood?

Basically, I have always been, in my mind, black, African-American, whatever the hell the word was at the time. I just happened to have a white mother. That's all. I don't have a problem with that. I read something somewhere where somebody didn't like picking because if they picked one over the other they felt like they were alienating one of their parents. It's like, "Uh, no. It has nothing to do with that." I was raised in an African-American community, I was raised by African-Americans, and that's what I've always been.

A lot of friends of mine were put in predominantly white private schools, got to about thirteen or fourteen and suddenly it was like, "I'm not like the kids at school. Where the hell do I fit?" That's a problem I didn't have, and I'm fairly happy about that. I had enough problems. It was one more I didn't need to have.

And even the problems weren't *problem* problems. It was just a piece of my life that wasn't like anybody else's. My problem with my life is that it gets so confusing to explain. Oh, yeah, see—there's a part we skipped in there. I went to Masterman; Edith died that January. It had been a really bad Christmas. Everybody was miserable, and she went on a bender for the week. I can't say I really blamed her. Had an aneurism and wheeee! Just like that. Yes, it was the day I was going back to school after Christmas break. I went to school, they took her to the hospital. She died January twentieth. She had a cousin, Aunt Roberta. I had to call her "Aunt" because I was too young to call her by her first name. I can remember being told, "That's *Aunt* Roberta, because she will be *real* upset if you call them by their first names." I went, "Oooh. Okay." Her brother, on the other hand, was James, because he didn't care.

But Roberta went to visit Edith in the hospital, and Edith said, "Would you take Pam home with you?"

So just Edith she got me when I was six, Roberta got me when I was twelve. And now, after living in the den of iniquity for six years, I ended up with a good churchgoing black Baptist. *Aaarrgghhh!* Now that gave me a bad case of the bends. It was really strange. I never *liked* Aunt Roberta when I was a kid. She gave me gifts on holidays like clothes—not someone to endear herself to a six-year-old.

I ended up at her house, which really was only about eight blocks from where I lived, but *totally* a world away. Up there was very middle-class: single houses, porches, small yards. Everybody had some sort of a job. She was widowed, she had no kids, and here this poor woman gets stuck with this twelve-and-a-half-year-old that has never been told that children are seen and not heard. Yes, we grated on each other's nerves for a while. But I lived through junior high and high school. It wasn't too terrible. Nobody else died.

How much of my identity was defined by the experience of having grown up with retirees? A whole lot of it. I've got eight hundred records, most of which are older than I am. I've got a 125-record Ella Fitzgerald collection.

Michael Mayson
Age: 28
Residence: New York, New York
Occupation: Screenwriter/director

Michael Mayson was born in Ohio and spent most of his childhood living in the integrated neighborhood of Lafayette Park, in Detroit, Michigan. He was adopted as an infant by a black couple who also had a biological daughter. His parents did not hide from him that one of his birth parents was white, nor did they suggest it was something that should affect his identity. Their lessons about race were more about what was expected of him as a black man in America.

Mayson remembers them saying that "as a black man, you start the hundred-yard dash on the starting line and the white man starts it on the ninety-five-yard line. You can't expect to win the race in that situation, so you have to try and work twice as hard, be twice as good—no time for slacking."

My biological mother was white. She lived in Youngstown, Ohio, a very blue-collar town, steel industry. She was unmarried, and she got pregnant by a black man. From what I know of the family history, she was upper-middle-class, and upper-middle-class white women did not get pregnant at eighteen years old by a black man in Youngstown, Ohio, in 1964. She wanted to keep me, and her mother said she could if—as some quote-unquote *mulatto* babies do—I turned out very fair.

If I turned out very fair and could therefore pass for white, then they could keep me in the family and there would be a scandal, but it wouldn't be as big as a racial scandal. When I was born, I was not fair at all. I was olive-complected and got darker in the next twenty-four hours, and as a result her mother told her that there was no way she could keep me, that she had to put me up for adoption. So she put me up for adoption, and it's my understanding that she came back to get me—once or twice, I'm not sure.

I guess it was a tough thing for any woman or person to agree to let their child just go. She did, and finally I was adopted by a black family in Ohio. And for all intents and purposes, my adoptive parents are my parents, in terms of my socialization.

After high school I wanted to be a doctor, for a lot of different reasons. One, because I wanted to help people, and I was always fascinated with the sciences. Two, because I knew I'd make a lot of money, and three, because it was very prestigious, and it was almost ingrained in me by this black bougie society I grew up in that you're a doctor or you're a lawyer, you're a very successful businessperson, or you're written out of the jet set. But my mind wasn't sophisticated enough to process all that, so I went to the University of Michigan and pursued my medical career, and I didn't make it very far.

I didn't make it very far for a lot of reasons. One was because

I didn't know it at the time, some people suspected it, but I was probably in the middle stages of what would soon be a very advanced dose of alcoholism, and two, because I wasn't ready. This was the world, University of Michigan was the world, and there were a whole lot of white people up there who didn't give a fuck about anything other than going to class and getting their grades. Not that there's anything wrong with that, but I was still into being a little social boy, and there's no time to be social when Chem 123 and Math 113 are knocking you on your fucking butt.

You got time to crack your book, eat some lunch, crack your book, eat some dinner, crack your book, and maybe go to sleep. So to make a long story even longer, my grades started really fucking up and I started fucking up and the worse my academic career got was inversely proportional to my drinking career.

By the first semester of my third year, I was kicked out. I just squeaked past my first year; I think I had a 1.99 first semester, and was put on academic probation. Shocked the shit out of me, because I'd always done B work, without working, so to work my ass off and get a 1.9—*Yo!*

In the middle of all that, I met my second girlfriend, Emma. She was from a place called Swampscott, Massachusetts, which is basically Grosse Pointe transplanted onto the north shore of Boston. Very white. Her family was from England, and she was haute preppy and was studying to go into investment banking.

But there was something that really fascinated me about her. I was attracted to her, first of all, and she was engaging. We talked about a lot of different things, but she was white. She was a prankster, and so when she called her mom and dad and said, "Guess who I'm seeing—I'm going out with a black guy," they said, "Oh, oh, yes, Emma, ha, ha, ha. Next month it'll be a Chinese guy."

Two years later she and I were still together. Her peers advised her that she would be ruining her career, that she just couldn't take me to Junior League, she couldn't go to all these social society functions she wanted to go to because I was black. How could she explain this guy, who by then was kicked out of the University of Michigan and had moved to New York and was floating around wondering what he wanted to do with his life? It just didn't fit.

But it wasn't really about me being a fuck-up. I think it all had to do with the fact that I was black. Because when I came to New

York, I cleaned up. This was the beginning of my sobriety, starting in 1985. At the end of my Michigan career, I was about to kill myself—not suicide, but my actions through my alcoholism and drug addiction had become so addictive that I was literally shooting my way to a liquid death, and it took a couple of people to tell me that. Finally, when they did, I ended up going into a drug and alcohol rehab. That worked. It was the spark that fucked up my drinking and drugging for the rest of my life. People who are in recovery will understand what I'm saying. It took me about a year before I could finally give it up totally. But when I did it was for good. A day at a time obviously, and that was almost seven years ago. It'll be seven years in December.

So Emma finally listened to the people around her. She said she couldn't deal with her friends on her shit all the time about the fact that she was going out with this black guy. And as a consequence, "Good-bye." Part of it had to do with the kind of person that she was in that she bought into her own *Town & Country* thing. I think she had an idea in her head of what her husband should look like, what he should be, and I really didn't fit it. And sometimes society's pressures are bigger than your courage to stick it out— obviously manifested through my entire birth.

How big does adoption figure into my life? It's colossal. Colossal in the sense that personally—and I don't know if this is the way I was raised or just the way I am—shit has to make sense for me. We go from A to B, to B to C to D, and when we go from A to F, I get all screwed up. For example, my notion of parenting is that no matter what, a mother does not give up her child. So I couldn't understand why it happened. It's still a question in my mind, not quite as dramatic as it was when I was growing up, when I personalized it, and said, "There must have been something that I did as a one-day-old baby to piss her off so much." You know, it's all negative, destructive energy, and I've been fighting with that, and I still continue to fight with it, although it's not as active as it used to be.

I've managed through recovery and therapy to deal with the issue of understanding that perhaps it was because she loved me so much and she felt the situation was not ideal for me that she would at least give me the opportunity to get into a situation that would be better. And, as fate would have it, I couldn't have asked for more. My parents did the best that they could to love me, and they provided for me one hundred percent. There was never a question, at all, of provision.

I first decided to look for my biological mother when I was about sixteen, after I had a big fight with my parents. I wrote this organization called ALMA [Adoptees Liberty Movement Association], and said I wanted to get a copy of my original birth certificate, to find who my biological parents were. I don't know why I'm driven more toward my biological mother than my father, but that's been the crux of the struggle, in terms of if I'm going to find somebody, that's who I'm going to find.

They wrote me back and told me there was no way I could do anything until I was eighteen. From eighteen to about twenty-two I was getting over being an active alcoholic and into becoming a recovering alcoholic, and so all the periphery shit went to the way-side, and over the last couple of years, I've asked or written a couple of organizations just to try and see if I can find some information, and I couldn't really come up with anything. Then, for some reason, something just clicked about six or eight months ago. And it was that I have to do what I can to complete this search, even if I don't find anything. I have to feel as though, when I go to bed or wake up in the morning I can say, "I did the best I could to try to find who this woman was, just to tell her that this is me and I'm okay, to say, 'How ya doin'?' "

It's as simple as that.

People look at you and they say, "What are you?" And you know what the fuck they're talking about, and sometimes you play with it and sometimes you answer the question. I have always identified as African-American. There was one brief period when I used to say mulatto, but I stopped because the word is really fucked up. Mule-otto, otto of the mule. Huh? I'm not otto of a mule. I just don't like the word. I think it's really a disgusting word. It should become hybrid, or what I told my friend Juliette: I said, "We're mutants, you understand that."

And she's like, "No, we're not."

I said, "Yes we are, because we cannot recreate ourselves. It took two different things for us to be. We're like nectarines."

I said, "It's not a bad word; it's a scientific word. We're a mutation."

"I'm not a mutant!"

Juliette grew up with one black parent and one white parent, and therefore she felt like a combination of both cultures. I didn't. Although biologically one of my parents was white and one was black, I grew up in a black home, socialized from day one. My grandma lived in Littleton, North Carolina, on a farm and all those things which I was and am very proud of, and it was always black, everything was black. From the time I can remember, "You gotta be careful about white people, 'cause sooner or later something fucked up is going to happen to you." That was the message, although Mom didn't say it quite like that.

In this argument I had with Juliette, I was just messing with her because she was trying to impose her views onto me. I said, "I'm sorry, I have no connection with your experience 'cause my black mama and black daddy are at home."

The truth is, I have problems with people who identify as both. Because I think—and see, now, this makes me sound like a jerk, but it's too idealistic in this society in which we live. It's just less practical to be idealistic. You can fight for that ideal, but I guarantee that when you walk into a building someplace that the white person who is going to be sweating you about something is not going to care what your mother or your father is. You don't look like that, you don't fit in.

All I say is, let's understand how society works. And after we understand that, then we can do whatever. If you want to go form your whole mulatto coalition, then go do it, more power to you, 'cause you in a sense have the best of both worlds, or at least have a multicultural experience. But that's not my fight.

And then people tell me, "Oh, well, you're just denying the white side of you." Well, maybe I am. But that's my bridge that I'll burn. I don't feel it. You know, I just don't feel it.

I may be searching for this white woman right now, but that's about who my biological *mother* is, and that's it.

It's sticky, the whole "Where do I fit in" question. I don't deny that it's valid that I am half African-American and half

European-American. But when I say that, I don't feel it; there's no connection whatsoever. What's sticky is that it's a valid point. That I'm just as much white as I am black in the United States of America. But I tell you one thing, when I walk through Harlem, and say, "Hello brothers and sisters, what's happening?" I get a much different response than if I walk on the Upper East Side and say, "Guess what, I belong here just as much as you do." "Get 9-1-1!! We got a crazy nigger out here!"

PART TWO

BELIEFS

CHAPTER X

Religion and Politics

When I was eighteen, I went to Israel for five months. That was different. First off, it was "confuse the Israelis" time. They didn't know what the hell I was. And there were certain things I couldn't deal with, especially with the Americans there. When they were home, they were the first to jump on the civil rights bus and so were their parents, nine out of ten, because they had raised good, liberal kids, and sent them off to Israel. Some of these kids made Aliyah [followed Jewish doctrine to return to and settle in the Holy Land] and stayed, but when they talked about the Arabs and they made jokes about the Arabs, well, they're the same nigger jokes I've heard all my life. They just changed the ethnicity. And when I told them that, they got real upset and said, "No, no, you don't understand."

"No, I do understand. You're the ones that are missing it."

And then some very well-meaning souls said to me, "You could make Aliyah and it wouldn't matter here that your father was black. At least he wasn't Arab." At that point, I was like, "Hmm. Time to get my return ticket."—Pam Austin, p.221

I was always the most ethnically, politically active member of the family. When I was fourteen, I became involved with the Black

239

Panthers and was doing a lot of the photography for The Black
Panther Newspaper. *And I was involved with them for several
years. I would go over to Eldridge's [Cleaver's] house and wake
him up every other day trying to get the paper out, being an
overzealous teenager. It used to drive him crazy.—Jeffrey
Scales, p.181*

*My father's side of the family is intensely religious. Jehovah's
Witnesses. Very intense black religion: Give up everything you have
here on earth because materialistic things are not what God set his
will out for you to have; there's a better life after the fact. Pretty
much that whole side of my family, sad to say, is flushing itself
down the toilet. When my parents got together, there was a lot of
fallout on both sides of the gamut. My father took a lot of abuse in
the Jehovah's Witness context of, "You're trying to climb the social
ladder by marrying this white woman." There are white Jehovah's
Witnesses, but in terms of a biracial kind of thing, it was,
"What's the matter? There's plenty of good-looking black women
here." So already, immediately, my parents were set up to
fail.—Brad Simpson, p.91*

*When I started college, once again I was an outsider, because
now it was the Black Power movement. Everybody's got these nat-
urals and black is in and I'm light and I've got this straight hair.
And I remember being stopped by a black guy who said, "What's
that shit on your head?"—René Rambo, p.109*

*Growing up, I really wasn't thinking about racial identity. If
anybody asked me what I was, I'd tell them I was Jewish.
My mom didn't convert; if you ask her, she'll tell you she's
Catholic, but I don't think she's been to church since college. My
parents actually got married in a Unitarian church because it was
the only one that would marry them in 1960. And I just had a lot
of Jewish friends, especially after I started going to school on the
West Side. It was like everybody was Jewish. My mom wouldn't
send me sandwiches on matzoh during Passover because she*

thought it was dumb, and I would be all embarrassed. I would throw my bread away so the other kids wouldn't see. I used to beg my father to take me to synagogue. He had grown up in an Orthodox home, and he didn't want anything to do with it.—Lisa Feldstein, p.123

In terms of the whole racial struggle, I don't care about white people in that sense, because my community is in some serious pain right now. So let's stop worrying about the white man this, the white man that. Let's take the white man out of the conversation for a minute, understand who we are, where we came from, what our accomplishments are, what our strengths are, what our liabilities are and chart a course of where we are and where we need to be. And then do it. You know, rather than sitting around blaming. But that's the whole nature of this capitalistic society we live in—blame and money.

In terms of priorities of what I need to do personally and then what I'd like to do for my community, the African-American community [is] first and foremost because if the Jews take care of themselves, and the Irish-Americans [take care of themselves]—and I don't mean to pejoratize anyone—then the whole melting pot can really work, you know, because everybody's fine. The Abramowitzes are fine and the Scamatallis are fine and the Johnsons is happenin' and the Gonzaleses are fine, and then we can all get together and share all the different things about us that make us unique, yet at the same time human. There's things that we all can learn about each other.

Some of the most exciting experiences for me, personally, have been being involved with relationships with people who weren't traditionally from the same group that I travel, because it's like, "Oh, wow, now we're here. How did you get here, and now how did I get here, and what can we learn and what can we share together, and now where are you going and where am I going and how can we get there together?" And most of the time it's, "I'll get there faster without you," but . . . —Michael Mayson, p.229

It is commonly said that the two subjects to avoid in social situations and among strangers are religion and politics. *Don't make waves* is the idea—don't assume that dinner partners or the next person in the bank line will share your perspective. These two subjects cut to the core of people's beliefs, and so can lead to virulent disagreement.

Race, for most Americans, is intimately and intricately connected to both. Just as school and the workplace present physical environments where the biracial person may face choices about racial identity, religion and politics present their own metaphysical testing grounds. In the religious arena, entire congregations, white and black, often live in passive, perpetual segregation. In some cases it is the particulars of the religion's evolution or doctrine that have influenced its membership. In others, geographical or social circumstances result in the segregation of the houses of worship.

Historically, the Bible has been used by some people to defend the separation of the races: White clergy used to cite passages as evidence that black and white should never mix. (As recently as 1991, a white Methodist minister in Pennsylvania refused to marry a white-black interracial couple, citing "personal and scriptural grounds.") Some other religions combine religious and secular concerns to justify racial separatism. Just after his conversion to Islam, for example, Malcolm X reviled the blood of "the white devil" that was in him. He later dismissed James Farmer, the head of CORE (Congress of Racial Equality) as an "almost . . . white man" because Farmer's wife was white. And when Jewish families sit shiva for the relative who has married a black non-Jew, the religious difference often seems to be a shaky alibi.

Other faiths, however, have turned the biblical ammunition around, as one man in this chapter illustrates, finding instruction for tolerance and equality in Scripture. The Religious Society of Friends (commonly called Quakers), long identified with community and political activism, were active in the movement to abolish slavery in this country. The Baha'i religion celebrates the spiritual unity of mankind and recognizes only one race—human.

For many leaders in the black community, there is no boundary between religion and the fight for racial justice. In New York City, the Reverend Adam Clayton Powell, Jr., held the pulpit of Harlem's influential Abyssinian Baptist Church from 1937 to 1971; he led a boycott against white Harlem store owners who would not hire black employees; and he was elected to fourteen terms in the U.S. House of Representatives. Abyssinian is now pastored by the Reverend Dr. Calvin O. Butts III, who has led brigades to paint over billboards advertising tobacco and alcohol that target Blacks in black neighborhoods, as well as to destroy the recordings of rap musicians he considers denigrating to black people.

Dr. Martin Luther King, Jr., a Baptist minister, led many people into civil rights battles from the pulpit. Groups such as the Southern Christian Leadership Conference (SCLC) and the Alabama Christian Movement for Human Rights (ACMHR) were cornerstones in that fight. At the same time, a parallel religion-based movement for the empowerment and equality of African-Americans developed in the Muslim Nation of Islam, led first by the honorable Elijah Muhammad, then by Malcolm X (before he formed the offshoot Muslim Mosque, Inc.), and now by Minister Louis Farrakhan.

In still other quarters, religion is casually assumed to be a constant in the black experience. Perhaps this is the legacy of the black church's long-held role as anchor for so many in the community it has served. Whatever the reason, several national, black-targeted magazines continue to refer unhaltingly to God in their editorial content—the universal applicability to readers a given.

Politics have been the forum for defining race and the hierarchy of racial privilege in this country since the first African slaves were brought here in 1619. Since then, individuals and groups have sought redress in matters of race through the powers of law, political office, and the interpretation of our government's underpinnings: the Constitution and the Bill of Rights. Measurements of progress and regress are marked by legislative acts (including *Dred Scott* v. *Sandford* [1857], the Emancipation Proclamation or Thirteenth Amendment to the Constitution [1865], *Brown* v. *Board of Education* [1954], the Voting Rights Act of 1964, and *Loving* v. *Virginia*).

Candidates for political office and appointment are increasingly viewed through prisms of race. Clarence Thomas's appointment to the U.S. Supreme Court was controversial for many more reasons than his former employee Anita Hill's testimony that he had sexually harassed her. Thomas was a black man nominated by a Republican president—an oil-and-water combination to many

Blacks and Whites alike. How much opinions of Thomas were further shaded by the fact that he has a white wife (who accompanied him to the nationally televised Senate confirmation hearings) can only be measured anecdotally (see p. 40).

Not surprisingly, the subjects of religion and politics came up frequently with the people I interviewed. As many grew up and experimented with religious and political beliefs, they found their beliefs about race were tested contiguously. They may have thought they were engaged in a purely political or religious exercise, but found instead that their race—often as it was determined by others—inhibited or accelerated their progress and acceptance.

As much as religion and politics have failed some biracial people, giving false promises of fairness and inclusion, others have found in those doctrines a way to make sense of race, to place it in perspective, to define it, to empty it of currency, or to divine in it a reassuring power.

~⦕⦖~

Sandy Lowe
Age: 50
Residence: New York, New York
Occupation: Director of the governor's office of
lesbian and gay concerns

Sandy Lowe's mother was the child of Jewish Ukrainian emigres who arrived in the U.S. in 1917 with their daughter in utero. Lowe's father was born in Tampa, Florida. He was black-identified, the son of a Cuban-Chinese father and a black mother. At age four, Lowe's father was orphaned when his father killed his wife and daughter and then himself. Lowe explains that her father was "an intellectual who rose to become the assistant coordinator of international labor and defense, which was the educational arm of the Communist party." He also fought in the Spanish Civil War. Lowe's mother, on the

other hand, was only a fellow traveler; she never joined the party. Still, the
entire family lived a political life: discussing issues of race and politics,
sending Lowe to progressive schools and camps, living in neighborhoods
where other children had names like Proletaria and Marx.

Lowe says the year Emmett Till was murdered was a turning point
for her. She was twelve years old and finally understood racism, she says,
"and that white people responded to me for something that was universal
and much uglier, much more deadly and dangerous than anything I had
ever imagined."

The civil rights movement, her father's political beliefs and activities,
being black and Jewish and a lesbian, have affected Lowe's outlook and
work. "All of this made me what I am today," she says. "I still work on
all these problems. I know that all these problems are connected, and
whatever part I work on is fine. I no longer think that the revolution's
gonna happen tomorrow afternoon, and therefore we all have time to work
on this."

I was born on Tenth Street in Greenwich Village between
Jane and Horatio, and I say I grew up a regular little Jewish colored
girl. I think of myself as being Jewish, not white. I don't think of
Jews as being white because they're Semites—they don't come from
Europe, even though they come from Europe—no more than you
would think of an Arab as being white. Most people don't think of
Arabs as being white. They're Semites, and so are Jews and that's
their origins. I know they spent several hundred years in Europe,
but Jews can self-identify. To me, Jewishness is not just a religion,
it's a culture, and I come from that part of the culture that was oppressed, that connected its oppression with the oppression of everyone else, that developed an ethos and a theory around what it
meant to be thrown out and dispossessed in the world. That's what
it means to me to be Jewish. I know that there are other ways that
other people have of being Jewish, but that's not my way.

I had a therapist that once called me counterphobic, which
means that instead of running away, I go towards what I fear. I hide
in the open. I bring my whole life wherever I go. So I will tell
people I'm black, I'm a lesbian, and Cuban, Chinese, and Jewish.
I will say that no matter where I am. To some extent that insulates
me. People shoot up: "What does this mean?"

What I want to say is, "I'm a complex human being like all of you," but most people don't think of themselves as that. When you're black and white you do, because it's really the yin and yang. People used to say to me, "You always want to be different," but we are all different and I could never conform. That was never a space that I fit in.

And I tried it when I was married, I tried to fit in that space—because then people didn't ask you questions, people didn't ask you what you did, 'cause they knew what you did: You were married. But it didn't work. I never fit into anything, and so I've learned how not to.

When I was younger, if there was a black boy anywhere in my vicinity, then obviously, by all our friends, we would be linked up. Ridiculous. Ridiculous. And for a while, I even went along with it to some extent. I was stupid.

And now I have stepped over the boundaries. I'm not sure I ever lived within those boundaries to begin with. I've always lived in another kind of world and always created a milieu for myself that was truly multiracial. Friends I've had for twenty or thirty years live in the same world I live in, although most of them are in relationships with other black people. It's just this place, this clearing that you make in your life, that who's ever around you loves you and whatever you do, it's okay. As you get older you make that space, you have some armor against the slings and arrows of people who don't know you—don't give a fuck about you, really—and who are going to make judgments about your life that they don't know shit about.

Bernette Ford
(See page 207)

As was the case for Sandy Lowe (see page 244), growing up amidst the civil rights movement and having parents who were active in it made politics—especially race-related politics—extremely personal for Bernette Ford.

I do remember that before my parents bought their house in Uniondale, on Long Island, they were looking for an apartment—because at that time my mom was sick with lupus and she couldn't do the stairs in the house in Queens anymore—and they ended up doing a lot of test cases for the NAACP because there was a lot of discrimination in housing then. My dad would go and look at an apartment, and then when my mom would come to sign the lease they would say it was no longer available. I guess that was in 1955 or so.

We always lived in black neighborhoods. My mother felt strongly, and my father probably went along with the idea that because she was black, we were black. She'd grown up in the South, where people were measured by the amount of black blood, and she felt strongly that was what our identity should be and she was very proud. She made that very clear, although I can't remember exactly what she would say. I can remember, though, as a small child wanting to be brown like my mother. I was very close to her, and I think that because my sister was brown and she was brown I felt like I was an outsider, even though my dad was white. I wanted to look like her.

I can't remember anything explicit that she said; it's just something that we grew up with. My parents were—I wouldn't say politically militant but politically aware, and they were pioneers and rebels in some ways. Having gotten married in 1949 was a big step. We had more contact with my mother's family. A lot of my dad's family lived on the West Coast. He was not real close to his sisters and brothers, though he was in contact with one of his brothers pretty regularly in Connecticut, so I did see that side of my family, but my mother comes from a large family that was very close, and we spent holidays together and weekends together and we just knew we were black people.

We were middle-class. When my dad was very young he was a Communist, and after my parents got married he probably calmed down a little bit because even though he had been a union organizer, now he was going to work in a factory and become a supervisor. So he was no longer on the workers' side; he was on the management side. But my parents had middle-class values, and every neighborhood we moved into was a step up. Uniondale was middle-class, lots of Levittown-type developments for middle-class communities, and the block we lived on was probably the nicest

block in Uniondale's black neighborhood—there was a black side
of town and a white side of town. So growing up, because I lived
in black neighborhoods, my friends were black, and although I had
white friends at school, they weren't people that I got together with
after school. You just didn't do it.

I was never really fully accepted by Blacks or Whites, so I was
always on the outside. I have vague memories of teachers being
shocked and surprised, if my mother came up to school, to find out
that my mother was black because I didn't look black, and I also
can remember that sometimes I felt left out of the group when we
were playing outside—not all the time, and I can't tell you now if
I wasn't fully accepted or if I put myself on the outside. I'm still not
sure. I tend to be a little shy and maybe aloof anyway, and I always
feel as if I'm an outsider observing what's going on. Anyway, I
don't know if they rejected me or if I just felt outside. I was part
of a neighborhood, I played at games, stayed out and caught light-
ning bugs, and when we got older we partied and played records
and went to each other's houses, but I never really felt fully a part
of the group.

When I was in high school it was during the sixties and the
civil rights movement, and I was kind of active in a youth group.
My parents were married by the Ethical Culture Society—they
were interreligious as well as interracial. My mom felt strongly that
we should have some kind of church community, but my parents
didn't want to have a dogmatic experience and my father wasn't
going to go to Christian church, so we went to Ethical Culture.
Most of the kids in the youth group there were white, but there
were lots of marches and sit-ins.

When I got to college, it was like it was the revolution. And
that was the first time I really felt sensitive, because I was identifying strongly with the black movement and there were times when
I was uncomfortable—not so much in my own college community
where people knew who I was, but if there were joint meetings of
Afro-American societies there would often be people who would
question my presence there.

I can remember some guys from Dartmouth coming down one
day to a meeting, and they said, "What is the devil doing in this
room?" They didn't say it to anybody directly. One of my friends
said, "She's not the devil; she's just light."

It was a very hard time for me because I didn't want to deny my father, and yet it was like being asked to sometimes. I didn't ever feel I had to, but it was painful, it was difficult.

The times were very different then than they are now. Even my sister's class, three years later, was much less militant than I was. But when I went to Connecticut College, there were twelve black women on campus—it was all women then—and out of eighteen hundred, we found each other and organized a black house we couldn't even fill up. We had to have a floor to start. We did a lot of work in recruiting and bringing black faculty to the school. When my sister got there, she took it for granted that there were more black faces on campus, and she was not into the black students' union or the Afro-American society as much maybe as I was.

Young people today don't even understand what was going on during the civil rights movement because they didn't live through it. To my daughter it's like, "Oh, Mom, that's the olden days." To her, Martin Luther King is like a dead president, along with George Washington and Abraham Lincoln. But he was very real to us.

There was one summer in particular when some southern kids who had been very much involved in school integration during the early sixties were brought to New York. I don't know if it was through Ethical Culture or some other organization, but about five or six of those kids came up to stay the summer, and one little girl, Debbie, came to stay with us to rest from the stress of what she had gone through. It was just very real; it was real serious.

Jeana Woolley
Age: 40
Residence: Portland, Oregon
Occupation: Business consultant

Jeana Woolley grew up in and around the
San Francisco Bay area. Her stepfather
was a tract-home builder whose work led
the family to move, both home and schools,
every year. Eventually her family moved to
Tigard—a suburb of Portland—for her
junior high and high school years. Two
weeks after she graduated from high school,
she moved out of her parents' house and
into northeast Portland, where most of the
city's African-Americans live. She's bought
a house and been there ever since.

Woolley looks white to most people. We spoke on the phone before we
met in person, and we debated which one of us would be more white-looking
than the other. I would call it a draw, although her permed hair gives me
a slight edge.

I was not aware of my true racial identity until I was twenty.
I was raised as a white child; my mother married my stepfather—
that's the only father I've ever known—before I was born.

It was my stepfather, not my mother, who told me. He saw me
struggling with my identity as a young adult, because I had moved
into northeast Portland, which was considered the black community, and many people there would ask me if I was black or white.
And I had been around enough to understand that most black
people do not mistake white people for being black—white people
have a whole different psychology about it. But it troubled me that
I was asked that question so frequently, so I started asking some
questions myself.

In a philosophical conversation, my stepfather revealed to me
that he was not my real father, that my real father had been black,
he had been mixed, and that it was sort of a one-night affair with
my mother that she was embarrassed about and ashamed of. I never
talked to my mother much about it because it was clear that no one

knew much about my real father. In fact, she could not even tell me his last name. See, my mother traveled a lot when she was a young woman. She sold magazines on the road with a traveling sales crew. They partied a lot. In each town they would meet people; they were young, and they would have a good time. And I'm under the impression that this was somebody she had met. I don't think he looked obviously black. I think he looked like he was ethnic, but I don't think she knew until she talked to him that he was black. So here I am.

My mother's family was very prejudiced. She was raised in South Dakota, born on the White River Indian reservation. I've always believed that my mother was part Native American. She sort of has a lot of the demeanor, the spirituality of the Native Americans. She's very gentle in a lot of ways. She was always sort of an enigma in her family, her and one of her younger sisters. The two of them were very close. They looked quite different from the rest of the family, and I always was under the impression that there was another secret that had not been told. But my grandmother died two years ago at the age of ninety-two, so no one will ever know. One time, in an almost playful fashion, I asked her about it, and she said, "Well, if it was true I would never tell you," which, to me, was almost like admission.

As I was growing up, my stepfather's relationship with me was different from with my two younger sisters. Ours was very stormy, and I never really understood it. It has probably affected a lot of my identity as a woman, and I'm really only in the last five to six years trying to sort through some of that in terms of how I relate to men, because he rejected me a lot.

He wasn't abusive physically, but he was very abusive to me emotionally. He challenged me a lot. He made negative comments to me a lot. And by the time I was a preteen, I was able to fight back verbally. I could defend myself. I could take him to task, and I did. We fought like cats and dogs when I was a teenager, and I was a very disruptive force in the household. Part of the stirring up I did was about race and social-justice issues. I talked about that a lot, but I was an unwanted force because I was very militant about it, and my mother has always had trouble when you deal with notions of disadvantagedness, because of her own poverty-stricken background.

When you start talking about people, particularly black people having problems because of their impoverished background, she can't reference that because she came out of an impoverished background. My grandfather could not find work, and they were very, very, very poor. They homesteaded on the reservation and lived in a one-room shack with a sod floor. My mother pulled herself up by her bootstraps. In her way of thinking, where she would always have trouble with the race question was that she figured other people could do what she did. I'd say, "But you don't have the stigmatization of color. People can't choose that as a way to segment you economically. So hard work works in your instance, where it may not work for people of color, black or otherwise."

As I've gotten older I really don't push these points with my mother anymore, because she comes out of a certain generation, I love her, and these are very sore points. I've been angry about this stuff for a long time, and there's this breach between us in that there was this secret withheld from me, and I've had to struggle to reconnect myself and to have a right to be who I am, both with black people and with white people. Identifying as black was a personal choice I made because it resolved something for me inside. I suddenly felt relieved; it explained all these things that didn't make sense to me. It was a revelation for me, and so inside it fixed a lot of things because I felt very disconnected from white people in general, as a body of people, not necessarily specific individuals. I've never related well, after a certain age, to most white people. They upset me, they turn me off. I was out of sync with the values—it was almost to a point of revulsion—and that's the sort of constant tension that was going on as I grew up. I don't think either one of my parents ever understood it very well, but they loved me.

I'm not sure I understand how anybody got through raising me. I was pretty incorrigible; I kept the house in a constant uproar. It was the sixties. I was infused with a sense of what was going on out there, and a lot in me responded to that. It was intuitive—I can't tell you anything more than that—and I was bringing this back all the time and processing it in the context of our household, challenging people and their belief systems.

When I say it was intuitive, I refer to some interesting things that happened to me, four or five incidents when I was very young:

identifications with blackness that didn't really relate to anything that came out of my environment.

One thing that was very important to my mother was education because she never got beyond high school herself. She really had the same kind of concept of education that many poor black people do in terms of feeling like it's *the* most important thing for children and the most critical element to their success. So when we moved around, she would do all the homework on making sure we got into neighborhoods with the best schools, and those were always white neighborhoods.

And so I didn't have anything that was stimulating me in terms of identifying with blackness. As would be true of most white people who don't have that connection, my concepts should have all been negative because of the exposures you get if you're not in connection directly with black people as a body of folks or in a communal context.

Now these are really small things that happened, but they're very important to me as I look back on them because they tell me something, like I was trying to make a connection and it was almost intuitive—and I believe in that kind of stuff. The first thing is that I had a little box of things that were important to me: trinkets, odds and ends. One of the things I acquired in about the fourth grade: a picture of an African woman with a baby on her back. I just thought that this was the most beautiful picture, and I was very attached to it. I cut it out of *National Geographic* and put it in my box of treasures, and there it sat for many years.

The second thing is when I was in the sixth grade, we had to do a report on a country—and I still have this—and I chose Africa. Most of the kids in the class chose European countries; I chose Africa. I chose the whole continent, furthermore. And this is quite a tome for sixth grade, a lot of cut and paste, a lot of stuff from reference books. Sometimes I think that I've lost brain cells instead of gained them. But there are places in there where I editorialize about the conditions of Africans, where I'm really reacting to people being treated unfairly in their own countries.

And then there were two dreams I had recurringly. I don't remember exactly when they started, but it must have been right around the age of eleven or twelve. I had the one dream for a few years, and then at around fifteen another dream supplanted the first, but both dealt with race issues in symbolic ways. I remember them vividly. The latter one I wrote down. I did a lot of writing when I was a teenager, and that dream is recorded.

The first dream was in sort of a Tarzan mode, like those fifties movies where white people go into the jungle and are captured by the Africans and the Africans kill them because they're white. In this dream my whole family was captured and put in a boiling pot—it's all these sort of stereotypical kinds of images—and then I am saved by the tribe. They killed all my family except for me and then made me a member of the tribe.

I didn't understand these dreams. I thought they were sort of weird, that maybe I had a strong survival sense. I didn't really go into analyzing them; I had no reason to question what they meant. But I had that dream for two or three years, off and on until I was fifteen. Over and over, almost like playing a tape.

The second dream was much more direct. It starts with hearing music, and it's in the rolling hills. It sort of looked like the California hills in places, so it was probably referenced off the environment I had grown up in. And there's a voice that's singing the blues, a moaning voice, just a guitar and a voice. All these children of different colors are running through these hills towards the sounds of the music. There's a sequence in the dream where they're deer. And then when they arrive, they become children and they're different complexions and we all sit down under a big weeping willow tree, where this old black woman is sitting. She is very dark, she's got a flowered dress on and it's tattered, she has this guitar sort of in between her legs. It's a bass guitar, a big guitar, and she's strumming the guitar and singing a song. And I am sitting in the front row. There's only this one part of this song that I remember from the dream, and the line goes, "Oh, yellow flower, my poor yellow flower."

When my stepfather finally revealed the big secret to me, I felt gifted. I felt like somebody had given me something back. And inside, I said, "I will never betray this." That was the notion, because it made me feel whole.

Since then, I have identified both privately and publicly as black. I've never gone and hid in the closet with any of this stuff.

I'm very involved, for example, in a lot of political things related to the black community, and I work through all of the gossip. I've got a twenty-year track record, and there are still people who basically say that I'm not black for one reason or another. They wanted proof of who I was, and I couldn't deliver it. It was sort of like, take it or leave it, but I couldn't deliver the *fact* of it with a picture or a name or a black side of the family. I didn't have any of those things to show, and I was very self-conscious about that, extremely self-conscious. I really had to sort through all of that confusion. Really, it was more self-consciousness than it was confusion, because I wasn't confused inside, but I was very *confusing* to people sociopolitically. As a result, people were always moving around me trying to find a crack in the armor, trying to find a way to entrap me.

To one of my closest friends, a black woman, it was just impossible to fathom unless there was some advantage to me. There had to be some reason why I was crossing over the lines— like that I could get standing and therefore get preference for jobs—because it couldn't *just* be because I was making that choice without some obvious benefit. I've been injured in a lot of my closest relationships by that sort of questioning, because once you're close to me, the worst thing you can do is question who I am. My friends don't question who I am.

But it's not the same kind of issue it was twenty years ago, when there were people in this town who knew me as white and then knew me as black. I've always thought that if people were thinking logically, if I was really trying to pass, I sure as hell wouldn't stay in the same town where people knew me as a white girl. There would be a much easier route if that was my objective.

But if there's a fight, I tend to walk into the fire. It's part of my personality. I say that the only way you get home is to walk through the fire. I really don't like the battle itself, but I want peace, I want to get through, and there's an integrity to it—I'm sort of hung up on the notion of being true to myself, regardless of whether people can deal with it, whether they want me to have it, whether they believe it. Because I know something now that makes sense to me, makes me comfortable, resolves things that were confusing to me as a teenager and a young adult. Nobody's taking that away from me, and I don't care if I have to go through hell and brimstone.

I'm beyond the point now where I really care what people

think about it. I do what I believe in. I participate in the things that are important to me as a person, and if other people can't deal with that, no matter what their disposition, color, that's their problem. It's not mine anymore.

Adebowale Patrick Akande Adegbile
Age: 25
Residence: New York, New York
Occupation: Law student and law firm summer associate

Adebowale "Debo" Adegbile's parents,
both the oldest of six, married after meeting
in a New York restaurant. His mother had
come from Dublin, Ireland, for an adven-
ture and better employment, and his father
came from Ire, Nigeria, to study. The fam-
ily first lived on Manhattan's Upper West
Side, in what were at the time racially and
ethnically mixed neighborhoods. Adegbile's
nursery and elementary schools were also
"pretty eclectic," he says.

When Adegbile was ten, the marriage broke up. His father returned to Nigeria, remarried a Nigerian women, and had more children. After his father left, Adegbile and his mother and brother moved to the Fordham section of the Bronx, a poorer and rougher neighborhood than he had known. He continued to attend private elementary and high schools on scholarship and was more often confronted with differences between himself and others on issues of economics rather than race.

From the outset my parents always instilled in both my brother and myself a very strong sense of where we came from and where they had come from and to be proud of our background. One line that followed me from as long as I can remember is, "I am an Irish-Nigerian who was born in New York." And that's something I've always been proud about. Before I even knew that it might attach some prejudice for some people, I always would boast that out; it was always the first thing that I said. Later, when I began to understand that people might react to this thing that I thought was so wonderful in a different way, I continued to say it because I decided whatever difficulty people had with it, *they* were going to have to deal with. I wasn't going to hide any part of myself or disavow any part of myself because I needed to conform to somebody else's idea about the way the world should be.

My parents taught me that. They were always very proud of both cultures, and their friends were African and African-American and Irish and German and everything else. The way they approached it was that they were going to make their kids real proud about who they were and trust that their kids would deal with situations as they were faced with them—certainly being there to help along the way, but almost not prejudicing us to what was out there. Some people might think that's naive or an improper way to go about things, but I thank them for it. They didn't deceive by explaining to us that the world was a beautiful place and that there was never going to be hardship; they just encouraged us to be vocal about where we were from, and I think that was a calculated decision.

I went to Connecticut College, this manicured New England campus, where I was the only African-American male to graduate in the class of '91. For most of my time there, I didn't feel isolated by that. Toward the end, though, I sort of got upset about it. I got upset because I was too comfortable. Everything was fine with me and I was doing very well. I didn't stop to think often enough about what was lacking there, in large part because I still had my friends at home. In high school my friends were almost 50 percent African-American and white Americans, whereas in college, I was ready to adapt and I did. The guys I played soccer with were the guys I became friends with

In my junior and senior years at college, I was very active in a number of activities, primarily with the office of volunteer services, being out in the community, tutoring at the public high schools, and doing things with people who didn't have the breaks that I had. That was an important part of my time there, [but] I realized that with all the volunteerism and stuff that I had done in college,

I hadn't taken time to take a leadership position—or any position, let alone a leadership position—in the African-American organization at the school.

Early on there was a mentor program, like a big brother/big sister program, and I had an African-American big sister. It was nice to have somebody around, but I didn't feel as if I needed anybody around. I was twenty years old when I arrived on campus, so it was a little bit of an artificial construct to have somebody younger than me telling me what life was about. Even though I hadn't had the college experience firsthand, my high school friends were preparing to graduate that year, and so I sort of didn't want that leg up. I think they had an early weekend for students of color and I didn't participate.

I was invited, and I chose not to participate. I knew Conn. College pretty well already, and I didn't feel as if I was going into an environment that was all that foreign, to tell you the truth. But my lack of activity in the minority community on campus caused me to be upset in my senior year because I thought to myself that there was more to what was going on there than me needing the organization, particularly as the only African-American male in my class: The organization needed me. That was not something that dawned on me, sadly, and I regret that now.

I changed that attitude in law school and I went to the early orientation for BALSA [Black Allied Law Students Association] students, and lots of my good friends are out of that group. BALSA's a national organization that was founded at NYU. We have meetings and all sorts of activities: academic preparation, rap sessions, different committees, community service, all sorts of things. It's a very powerful organization, probably the club that gets the largest chunk of the NYU budget.

Very, very early on, BALSA was fantastic. It was necessary. I didn't have soccer for the first time in my life, so it was now my foot in the door. I guess that's sort of unfortunate that it took feeling the need to do it, but I'm being honest, that's what it was. But also, for the first time I was in an environment where black testing, something I loathe, was rampant.

Black testing is the attitude some African-Americans have that you must do or be X, Y, and Z in order to be black. It's almost as if there is a self-imposed standard. We might not be talking about the three fifths that was in the Constitution, but it's imposed by members of the group. For example, who do you hang out with? You go to a BALSA meeting, but you hang out with that Italian kid or that Irish kid. Do you go to the BALSA activities? Do you go to the BALSA dances? Generally, I've been in schools where it was a wonderful thing to be an Irish-Nigerian. At NYU, I felt for the first time—although it could have happened before and I may have been unaware of it—that people were looking at me and saying to themselves, "Is he really black?"

Lots of the people are really bright—almost by definition— and people come from diverse educational and personal experiences, from all over the country, different colleges, different countries. And many of those people have different views about what it means to be a black person, particularly in relationship to the white majority at law school, and there's great discussion and great support.

But there are also factions, and some of the discussion that goes on there is antimajority, as distinguished from prominority. That was something that was unfamiliar to me, in large part because I am part of the majority in some respects, as I am part of the minority. Another way to read it is that I am the absolute minority. This was the first time I realized I was in a situation where somebody was going to try and force me to make a choice. And never will I make a choice to conform to somebody else's idea about what my ethnicity is. I've learned too much and been through too much to be pigeonholed into somebody's narrow idea about what blackness is, what Irishness is, what being a New Yorker is.

Certainly it's ironic that the time it came was at law school. These are supposed to be minds that believe in free speech and free expression. For example, at a BALSA meeting, there was a woman who appears to be Caucasian. And even being familiar with it as I am, it seemed a little strange to me that she was there, but I figured, hey, she's with the cause, whatever. But I specifically remember one woman saying to me that she didn't know what that woman was doing there. There's also another interracial person who has blond curly hair, who's African-American and Italian, and this same woman was saying that she's not black. I asked why, and the woman said, "Look at her."

Now this was a concrete manifestation of the testing. But it's

also a subtle, insidious thing that goes on all the time. Sometimes—they don't say it to your face—but I always felt that there
were eyes on me. I hung out with an Italian guy and an Irish guy,
and I felt as if some of the folks at BALSA were feeling I had in
some way compromised my position. Not everybody, but some
people. It's hard to articulate because nobody walked up and called
me Whitey or Uncle Tom, that's not what was going on, but you
sort of feel it from some people. Sometimes they say hi to you,
sometimes they don't—not so much a correlation with who I'm
with at a given time, but perhaps who they've seen me with.

I've shared this observation with other people in the group
who have similar ties to The Man, and they've had the same
experiences. Ironically, when I took this summer associate job at a
corporate law firm, some of my *white* friends joked that "Debo
Meets the Man," a spoof on the Homey the Clown thing [a character from Keenen Ivory Wayans's television comedy, *In Living
Color*]. That because I had taken this job—even though I am who
I am and believe in the things I believe in and am involved in the
things I'm involved in—the white majority paints me as a sellout.
It's interesting to see the hoops people expect you to jump through.
If a white kid takes this job, he's doing well; if a black kid takes
this job, he's doing well but he got it through an affirmative action
program and he's selling out.

Here's an even better example of black testing. Two third-
year students from BALSA sit on the admissions committee. Their
primary function is to read some of the African-American applications, to identify a couple they want to fight for: people that have
shown, perhaps not on the traditional standards, that they would
make a contribution to our community, our BALSA community,
our law school community.

We had a meeting to discuss what type of person we want to
advocate for. If the person has shown that they've been down with
their college black organization, their church organization, is that
the person we want? Or what if somebody just checks African-
American on the LSAT? Now, obviously, nothing could be more
subjective than that. I was of the view that we should advocate for
people we think would make a contribution, whoever they are.

There was vehement discussion. People said, "We don't want
somebody that only checks that box and doesn't put anything else

down about being black or indicating in any other way that they are black." But that's a subjective question. I may have a problem with how some people identify, but they're not *less* black to me. Certainly people identify in a variety of ways. Yet at this meeting, many people—the majority—were prepared to say that we need to see blackness, like, on the NYU application where there's an ethnicity statement and you can write about it.

I said that if that person who just checks the box has an application that as a whole indicates somebody we would like to have here, let's have them here. I said that I never held out as the criteria of blackness being able to recite "I Have a Dream," being able to quote *The Autobiography of Malcom X,* or Zora Neale Hurston or Alice Walker or Farrakhan or anybody else.

In the same way that this blew me away, I spoke to a friend from college the other day, I was telling a story and I mentioned the SS. She had no idea who the SS were. She was Jewish, and I thought she was teasing me. I was baffled. Perhaps it was just my educational realm, but I asked a lot of people, no affiliation with the religion, and they knew. She asked her brother and he didn't know either. But among the Jewish-Americans that I have known and have been very close with here in New York, it just wouldn't happen that they wouldn't know. Now my friend doesn't identify very heavily with being Jewish, but neither do I, and I knew. So that was interesting to me, but yet that wouldn't discount her in my view. It wouldn't discount anybody. If somebody never read or heard of Frederick Douglass, what does it mean? What are we evaluating and who are we to judge? And what are we doing to ourselves? If we set out criteria, aren't we limiting ourselves? If an African-American takes a job at a firm like the one I'm at, should the African-American community say, "He's a sellout," or "He's a leader?" Are these not the jobs that we fought to be able to get? And now all of a sudden we're saying, "He's not really down with the cause." "Look at him, he's making money."

You can't have it both ways, and trying to have it both ways is the thing I hate more than anything else. Down the road I suspect that many of these people [from the BALSA meeting] are going to take jobs like this one and at other firms like this one. That doesn't make them any less black, but they're going to be in situations where they have to be who they want to be and not allow somebody else's idea of who they should be govern their behavior and their conduct.

Certainly everybody has to make sacrifices along the way, and you have to decide what the bending point is and what the breaking point is, but to see so many intelligent people take that position . . . I don't know to what extent people were going with the flow—where people don't want to stand up and not be black—but that's how black testing works, because if you stop and put your foot down, you risk rejection. And in that discussion, even though I knew I was somebody that was already on the line—some of them were getting ready to push me on the Uncle Tom side—that was more than I could take. I stood up and said there's no specific criteria. For instance, I don't like Clarence Thomas. I don't agree with his views. But I'm not saying he's not a black man, and I think it's an insidious thing for people to say that, because then we are limiting ourselves.

But I have to say that while I refuse to adapt my conduct to whatever that magical set of qualities is that meets the criteria of blackness, I don't wish to alienate myself from that group by giving people any reason to think I'm trying to pass. If I choose to associate with white students I do, and throughout my life I've chosen friends on the basis of their character, of that I am certain, or their ability to kick a soccer ball. I'm prepared to choose on those factors, but the presumption that I don't want to give is that I'm trying to be anything that I'm not. And in BALSA there are some people, and this is sort of sad, who think anybody who is in a position to pass *will* pass. It's a sad remnant of "White is what you want to be," but I don't add fuel to that fire.

Natasha Wild
Age: 48
Residence: Berkeley, California
Occupation: Chinese teacher

Natasha Wild's parents—father, black; mother, white—met through their political activities in the San Francisco Bay area. Shared political convictions were not enough to hold her parents' marriage together, and they separated permanently when Wild was still young. Until she moved out on her own, she lived with her mother in Berkeley, except for a two-year period in her early teens when she and her younger sister lived with their father, several neighborhoods away.

Her father's insistence that she and her sister participate in his political activities pushed Wild away; in rejecting his path and the overall lack of community in her own family, she has created a very different life for herself.

My mother was born in New York and raised largely on Long Island but with some tours in private schools here and there, including the South. And my father was born in Oakland.

I guess my parents met in the late thirties. They were both involved in union organizing and were both leftists, and it was through political channels that they met. At the time, I think my mother was married to her first husband, who was Jewish, and my father was also probably married to his first wife.

My mother's family did the disowning trip because of the marriage, so when I was growing up I didn't have grandparents on that side. By the time they were making peace, I was in my mid-teens and I wasn't interested. I never called them my grandparents; they were always my mother's parents.

But my mother's and my father's personalities were very— there's a large lack of harmony, shall we say, between them. And so when I was six, they parted. I suppose it's amazing they lasted that long. They really were quite different. My father was a very pushy, strong character, and my mother was relatively self-effacing and shy and low sense of self-esteem and so forth. He had all these ideas about what everybody, including her, should do, like learning to build radios, all this electronic stuff, all this mathematical stuff. She had graduated from Sarah Lawrence in fine arts. She gave it a try, but it really wasn't a natural thing. I doubt he was very encouraging. A soft, sweet person he was not.

My parents' political involvement was not *so* unusual at that time, in Berkeley, but it wasn't real common. One friend in fourth grade, his parents knew my parents, they were political but it didn't come down to daily kid life, somehow. In 1952 I had a Hal and Ann Bass button and everybody else had Eisenhower and Stevenson, so I knew about that but it was not anything that put people off. No one said, "Who's that?"

When I was young, the way I saw myself was: I'm not *that*, and I'm not *that*, either. That's probably what I thought. I was both in a certain way, but in another way I was neither and I probably still largely think the same. In the white community there's no threat for me, maybe because I had a white mother and that's how I grew up, but no one has ever required me to be anything. But somehow, some of the time in my life when I've had to deal with black individuals here and there, they had expectations, and I always felt that I couldn't meet them and that I was passing. I don't know that it was ever stated, but I felt that there were expectations that I couldn't meet. But I *could* be quiet. I was pretty shy, and I could be quiet. If I didn't say anything, then no one might think anything.

I can't even say what I think people thought I should be, except probably that I should have more ties and experience being black than I felt I had. I wasn't growing up in a black community, and I didn't know many southerners close up. Later, my stepfather, who came along when I was around ten, was southern, but his family didn't come with him and we certainly were not close. He was from Arkansas, but my sister and I, we didn't like him. He didn't treat my mother well, and we didn't like that. They had these friends who were mixed couples and they had this kind of social group, and I remember looking at it and thinking, "Oh, yuck!" None of those people seemed like very good people to me.

And later, my father tried to kind of integrate us into black churches and stuff like that. He had made this decision that if there was any kind of community organization that that's where it was— that this business of being a Communist didn't get you to the heart of the Negro people—and so he was involving himself with churches. But we knew he was an atheist; we'd been raised atheist. And the contradiction was more than I could handle. I don't think my sister did too well with it, either, but there was no way I was going to buy that. I didn't know what he was doing. I didn't understand this business of the community and wanting to work with the community and finding your way into it or whatever. I just didn't have a clue. All I saw was that he was being really hypocritical, and I wasn't following.

This was when I lived with him. Also, he liked to volunteer our labor for various causes. I'll never forget running around some convention trying to sell Diner's Club cards. Oh, the resentments I have. I could not stand that. He was a person that used people as best he could, and he never saw that his daughters were anything to consider other than to help him with stuff.

He never figured out in his life that you didn't just make these assumptions—here, do this, here do that—the way he always did. From my point of view, that wasn't ever going to get me motivated to do anything. I was going to dig my heels in, if possible, right? In those teen years that I lived with him, I was probably quite rebellious and really didn't like a lot of styles he had. One thing my sister and I did like, though, was that he wrote an entertainment column for the black paper in San Francisco called *The Sun Reporter*. It started out as "The Mambo Roundup," but it became "The Entertainment Roundup," and he took us around to various clubs and we saw a lot of musicians and good music. This is one thing I'll be forever grateful for.

When I did have a choice about my own activities, I admired beatniks from afar. It was the age of sandals, skirts, and bare feet, and looking that kind of cool. It was also the age of social clubs; there was a discussion club and a folk song club that I joined in high school and liked very much.

They weren't full of much rabble-rousing, and, in fact, the political aspect for me was very different than for my sister, Leah.

I've never been an activist, whereas my sister is very much so and has been for all this time. Through our years growing up we both went to various picket lines and passed out leaflets and so forth and so on, probably related to employment, like against a bank in West Oakland that didn't hire black people. And there were peace marches I participated in, and this HUAC, this House Un-American Activities situation. But my political activities were tapering off by eighteen. Everybody else was starting, but I was winding up, and part of it was that my parents were both political, but there was so much else they didn't have together that it must not be the case that politics was the way to start out. Maybe you get there someday, but there's some other basic things to take care of first. I don't think I said that to myself in so many words; it seems like that was what I probably felt.

We had a little group when I was in high school that was some kids of other Communist parents. They were supposed to be study groups, but they were actually social—we had a *great* time together. We were supposed to be reading Marx; I don't know if I read the first page. I know that the books were on the shelves and so forth, but I don't personally think that I did anything. Some of my friends of that era did join the party, so there was not one way that everybody went.

In the tenth grade, I just wandered. I didn't do well, I wasn't very happy, and I didn't know any people. Toward the end of that year I started looking around to see what I would like, and I saw this group of people that were involved in this discussion club and this folk song club, and I decided I would see about pushing myself to get involved in that. I was very quiet, I didn't like to talk, and certainly if there were more than two or three people present I was not opening my mouth, so it was kind of ridiculous to join the discussion club, but the people I liked the looks of—who were kind of in the beat direction—were there.

The funny part is that ever since then, it seems that I often have liked something that none of the rest of my friends were going for. When I studied Chinese, nobody else was studying Chinese; I went to Taiwan, nobody else went to Taiwan; I came back, nobody had a clue about what that experience was like. My most recent one was a couple of years ago: I love salsa music and dance, but again, nobody wanted to do it with me, so I just do it by myself.

But I think back then, when I was not happy with the things that existed in my life and I saw something I might like, I pushed myself to do it. It's worked, each time.

I chose Chinese because I felt that there must be other things in the world beside what I knew about, and certainly the black-white situation was absolutely not something I was interested in. I didn't see any positive models, shall we say?

Anyway, some friends I had in junior high school went to Chinese and Japanese school after school, and I learned to write the numbers from them. And then in high school my favorite teacher taught an Asian history class and I developed a liking for Sung dynasty paintings. When I started college it was like the world was there, and all I had to do was tap and I could go somewhere. And I was thumbing through the catalog and *C* was early in the alphabet, and so I thought, "Wow! How about that?" The chance to understand those little old ladies on the bus. Turned out they spoke a different dialect. I think if they'd offered Arabic, that would have been my first choice, because I had a great fantasy life growing up. I used to read a lot, things like *Arabian Nights*. These other places really intrigued me, and my present place didn't intrigue me in the slightest.

By the time I'd gotten to high school, the only thing I probably thought about in terms of race was that I didn't fit and I wasn't even going to bother to try. Through a lot of my life, I felt very alienated from any kind of mainstream: white mainstream, black mainstream, whatever, because of the politics and the lack of religion— all these things everybody else seemed to have we definitely didn't have. So therefore there was no group to belong to, and after a while, I must have figured out that I had to go and find what I liked, but there was not any kind of community to belong to. That wasn't happening.

I don't even know that I thought of it as an uncomfortable state to be in. When we're older, we form our own communities, and of course I do like having friends and family. I'm not particularly a loner sort of person, although in those years I thought being a hermit sounded pretty good sometimes. But it was a romantic notion more than anything else.

But I might have felt some resentment at people expecting me to be something. I remember my Chinese teacher telling me that one of the main reasons I was chosen to go to Taiwan as part of this overseas program—I didn't have a high grade point average—was my being black. I was stunned because I went through the world without thinking anybody was thinking anything about me. And I wasn't thinking; I was just out there doing and being interested, and I was just shocked. Shocked. I wasn't going to refuse to go, but I felt it was a little bit false pretenses somehow. Again, I was cheating. Someone was going to think I was black, and that's why they thought I should go.

When I was in Asia, people never believed I was American. I had a hard time convincing them, and I couldn't understand why that was. Then I realized I never saw anybody that looked like me in the American movies. You were one extreme or another, but there were no cuts in between. People thought I must be some Chinese somewhere, but mostly, "How about Ceylon?" "How about India?"

"No, no, no. *Mei Guo! Mei Guo!*" ("United States! United States!")

And then I came back and thought I was going to just fit right back in, and the first day I was back, someone asked me what I was. I was horrified, because here I was supposed to be American, back on my own soil, but someone asked me what I was.

In these last years, people rarely ask me. If it comes up I always say both or neither. But you know, after thinking about it more, I'd probably go more in the direction of neither. If I were to be both, I would feel that I would have more of a sense of each community inside myself. And my mother wasn't part of a community that I could ever see. She's just pretty much by herself and has been for a long time. And on the black side, if I had ever felt part of the community, then I could say that I was. I feel that I'm not a good representative, and if anybody hires me because I'm black it's a joke, because I'm not bringing anything that is in *their* minds with me, except some history and some color. There's certainly history. My parents and grandparents and great-grandparents all existed, right? But as far as *my* bringing some headsets or experience, I don't have those things, and I could never speak on them. I could never represent it particularly, and I could never represent the other side either.

So what kind of identity is neither? Well, one thing that I have thought was that it makes me less parochial or something like that; the business of being a citizen of the world is a very easy concept for me. It's hard for me to be an American, just straight-out American, and hard also to be black or to be white.

Somehow, in the end, I think it's positive. In some of the things I've said it probably hasn't sounded particularly positive, but I think having a more worldly view than a regional view is a much better thing. As far as this community business that I didn't feel part of, I have found that community doesn't have to mean people that have been in the same place for generations. And that really has opened me to things a lot of other people don't seem very open to. Part of what I like to do for people is open them to other things. In teaching Chinese, that's certainly an avenue for showing how things can be other than what you know already, and that seems really valuable to me, to see what else is in the world besides what you've grown up with.

John Blake
Age: 27
Residence: Decatur, Georgia
Occupation: Newspaper reporter

John Blake grew up in west Baltimore, Maryland. He has half-brothers and -sisters who had two black parents, but he and his younger brother have a white mother. As a child, he was ashamed of this fact, wanting only to belong in his black west Baltimore neighborhood. Blake was targeted by others because of his skin color, garnering attention that was alternately good and bad. "When I was younger," Blake says, "I got in fights because I was light-skinned. But then when I reached adolescence, I was getting women because I was light-skinned. It's like, 'Come on you all, make up your minds.'"

I found Blake through Larene LaSonde (see page 334), an Atlanta woman who is trying to launch a multiracial research institute and has

*already started a support network for multiracial people. LaSonde found
Blake through an article he wrote for the* Atlanta Journal-Constitution,
*where he discussed his racial background. When I met him, he was in the
midst of figuring out how to excuse himself graciously from LaSonde's
group. "It's not what I base my identity on," he explained. "Some of them
are so gung ho about being biracial: 'I'm biracial and we should really get
together, we should do this, we should do that,' and it's not a big deal to
me. When I think of John Blake and what's important to me, I base my
identity on my values and my faith, not on who my mother and father
happened to be. I can't help who they are. I can help what I become."*

My mother and father met each other in Baltimore. That's
where I grew up. My mother came from a very working-class, poor
Irish neighborhood there where no Blacks went. My father was a
merchant seaman, and he was kind of the black sheep in the family. If there was something a black man shouldn't do, he would do
it. He was what you would call back in those days a "crazy nigger."
I don't like using the word, but in his day, the most forbidden thing
a black man could do was to be with a white woman. And that's his
big thing; my father's really into white women.

He met my mother in the hospital where they both worked.
She was a nurse's assistant, and in between sailor trips, he would
work in the morgue. He saw her in the cafeteria, went over and
started talking to her, and before you know it this little romance
developed. He would go visit her at her house. He told me stories
about how he would get in a cab to go over there, and it'd be a
black guy driving who would say, "Okay, where to?" And he'd say,
"Oh, so-and-so avenue."

The guy would look back at him and say, "You sure you want
to go there, partner?" He'd get there and the cab driver would say,
"I can't wait for you, I gotta go."

Her father didn't like it. Her father was this handyman who
had a drinking problem, and he would call the police on my father,
call him a nigger and all this kind of stuff. But my father's very
persistent. They kept on seeing each other, and she became pregnant with me. When that happened, he went up to New York. He
thought New York was a little more liberal, that they would accept
him, and they had me there in '64. Even up in New York, they still
had problems. For instance, he went into a bar in a white part of

town. My mother and my father sat at the bar, they drank, and after he put the drink down, the bartender would take the drink and right in front of him he would smash the glass.

They were living in Brooklyn; that's where I was born. He told me there was a lot of racial tension at the time, and sometimes they would walk out into the street and black people would say something to him and sometimes white people would say something to him.

By '66 my brother was born. About '67 my father grew tired of the arrangement—he never married my mother—and they split apart. I was sent to the black side of my father's family and raised among them in a black neighborhood. Really, they were like foster homes. My father was away most of the time, so he sent us over to these so-called baby-sitters' homes, and we would just sit over there for about six months out of the year when he was away, and when he would come home we would live with him. We called the people who took care of us names like Aunt Fanny, Mama Katie, but they weren't our relatives. We never met our mother. They just told us that she was white, that she was Irish, and she was sick and we couldn't be with her.

I don't want to get too specific because this is on the record, but I can say she was already in fragile health when she had my brother. Combined with the pressure that comes with having two mixed kids in those days, she wasn't physically or mentally equipped to take care of us. That was why we weren't sent to stay with her and we never saw her. We heard stories that she was alive, but I just took it as no big deal.

What was kind of tough was growing up in an all-black neighborhood in the early seventies. Because of my complexion, I used to get in fights all the time. I didn't start them; it was other people who wanted to fight me. They would call me white boy, and that was when you had black pride. Kind of like now with the Afro-centric movement, people very much into being black and I wasn't, I guess, black enough, so I had to get in fights.

When somebody would call me a white boy, I would get so mad, I would get so tense. And I never told anybody what my mother was. We'd get to parts of school where they would ask you to identify the race of your mother and I would never put white. It was too embarrassing. I just lied.

Matter of fact, I grew up with this hatred of white people. It's a funny thing. We used to go to movies like *Superfly*, my father used to take us, and you'd see these black heroes just beating up the white man. In my neighborhood white people were symbols of evil. They were rich, they didn't care, they looked down on us, they thought we were ignorant. I remember thinking when I was maybe ten or eleven, What would I do if a white person walked into my neighborhood? I remember thinking it was my duty to hurt them; that's how I thought, that was the mentality. I guess it's weird, 'cause all the while I knew I had a white mother.

So that's the environment I grew up in, being ashamed of my own mother. I felt like a secret agent and didn't want anybody to discover my identity. What made matters worse was that my father went down to South America and married a Spanish woman who looked white. When he brought her up to live with us, I wouldn't walk out in public with her because I was ashamed for my friends to see me walking with a woman who appeared to be white.

Then I'm seventeen years old, and my father comes up to me one day and says, "Do you want to see your mother?"

I'm like, "What?"

"Yeah, you want to see your mother?"

We went to see my mother. My brother was with me and we went out to this hospital in suburban Maryland, and we were very quiet in the back of the car. It was our half-sister who took us out—she's not mixed. My father didn't come along. We're in the car, and I have all these thoughts racing through my mind, not anger, but like, "What's the use now? She's not my mother. What am I supposed to do? Run to her in slow motion while the music plays and say, *Mama! Mama!*'" It was that mixed with curiosity; I wanted to see who she was.

My brother and I walked into the hospital. It was pretty sad because people there are very sick. We walked into the room and saw this very skinny, old-looking white woman who came up to us smiling. That was our mother. We had to hug her and sit on the couch with her, and we didn't know what to say.

Our sister tried to break the ice. She said, "Well, John, tell her what you want to be when you grow up. Tell her about your schoolwork." And I told her and she listened. She didn't seem nervous at all, she just seemed very gratified to hear us. My brother was into photography at the time, and to mark the occasion he decided to take a picture. I still have it. He takes this picture: She's sitting next to me and I have my arm around her. I'm leaning back, I have this nervous smile on my face, and you can just see I didn't feel comfortable. I left and said good-bye and she said, "Keep in contact." I said "Okay," and we went on home.

But when I met my mother, that was the beginning of the psychological transformation of myself. It changed my attitude toward white people. Before, white people were distant. They were what I saw on television, they were people who mistreated Blacks, who kept us in slavery. I loved history. I would read all the time and get mad. I would read about slavery and I'd start to think. The white people I saw on TV were rich and well-to-do—we used to look at *The Brady Bunch*, and my brother and I were like, "Wow, we can't live like that!"

But when I met my mother, I saw how she looked—she looked terrible, she was in awful health—and I started learning more about her history because I started asking my father about her side of the family. He told me how poor they were. He took me to their side of town. They lived in these little row houses that were worse than where I lived, and what I began to realize through my mother is that black people aren't the only people who suffer. White people suffer, too, and I can't say all white people are evil, because when I looked at my mother, she didn't hate me, she wasn't mad at me, she was very comfortable. And I started to change. But that occurred over a period of time, because I started going back and seeing her. I still do.

Because of her health, we can't have in-depth conversations. It's pretty much that she's talking to me almost like she's a child. "Hi John." She says the same thing, she says, "Can you bring me coffee? Can you bring me cigarettes? I'm scared. I don't want to be here." She'll say stuff like, "Oh, you look so handsome," and that's it. We have the same conversation again and again, and we never talk about race. She's just a woman who needs attention and needs help. She's not this symbol of white oppression, she's a woman who needs help and I can't see white people's evil when I'm around her.

In my office, when I'm around my black colleagues and they talk about, "Look what the white man has done to us, look how the

white man's evil," I can't accept that deal anymore because I see
my mother standing before me, saying, "I need coffee and cigarettes," and that's all she wants.

We never talk about race, she and I, but for my father it's a big
deal. He calls us his little half-breed sons. He doesn't perceive that
as being negative; he thinks it's funny. But to me it's just symp-
tomatic of his lack of sensitivity. His big thing was to have pretty
babies. He used to take us when we were kids, "Come here, come
here," and take this pomade grease and smack it in our hair, put
the part on, and whip it over and stand back and admire us and go
out in public and brag to people that he produced these two pretty
babies with the light complexion and the good hair. He's very dark.
He doesn't like himself and that's his thing, so I can't talk to him
about this. I won't even try to.

But my brother and I, we're pretty close in age, nine months
apart, and we have the same views in that we both grew up hating
white people. Living in our neighborhood it was like the weather—
you couldn't escape it. That attitude soaked into you because it
was prevalent, but when we met our mother it changed us. Also,
our faith helps us. My brother's a very committed Christian and I
am, too, and I became that way in college. To me, being Christian
and perceiving certain ethnic groups as inherently evil is incom-
patible; it just doesn't make any sense.

I was raised a Baptist but I'm not into that now—my church is
nondenominational. My faith was something I gradually slid into.
It was something that engulfed me. A lot of incredible things
started happening in my life—nothing bad like I was about to die
and I saw Jesus before me saying, "Come on, boy!" It wasn't
anything like that. I found out that a lot of my best friends, who I
really admired, were Christians. I started reading, and I thought I
liked the way this guy Jesus carried himself and he became like a
hero. It was really a lot more remarkable than that, but that's the
condensed version.

When I found out my mother was Irish and I met her, she was
all into Catholicism, like, "Get me this medal, get me Saint Jude,"
I'm like, "Who is that? I'm a black Baptist. I don't know anything
about that." But I read about Irish people and about their history,
how much they suffered: the potato famines they had in the nine-
teenth century when all these people died; how they have a history

of other countries coming in and taking them over, conquering them, so much so that a lot of them don't even know their native language, which is Gaelic. I saw parallels in their history with black history, and that went back to the same point: Black people don't have a monopoly on suffering. Everybody suffers. I've heard that Europeans call the Irish "white niggers," so to me, being Irish and black, it's no longer a contradiction.

This is where I've seen how my biracial identity has kind of influenced my work. I've written stuff that's gotten a lot of attention here in Atlanta, and those pieces tend to revolve around race. When the *Jungle Fever* article I wrote about my life was in the paper, it just exploded. They put me on radio shows; people were calling me up. It felt good, like a kind of release, because here's something I was ashamed about for so many years and all of a sudden I'm talking to people about it. But after a while it became a drag. I got tired of it. I felt like pausing while talking to a room and saying, "Yeah, I'm biracial, but *big* deal." But they probably would have thrown me out. I guess they wanted to hear some tragic mulatto stories.

People say, "You really write well about race." White people at my job come up to me and say, "You can make it understandable to us." It seems like when white people want to talk about race and want to ask, "Why do black people do that? Why do black people do this?" they gravitate around my desk. I guess I'm safe. I'm not going to go, "It's because you enslaved us!"

I'll answer their questions, but I tell them, "I can't speak for all black people. I can tell you from my experience." I try to give them some insight of what I have, but I don't claim to know too much. What I've noticed is that I've written a lot about what Blacks do to one another. For instance, I wrote an article called "Soul Patrol," and it's a term I coined for Blacks who try to tell other Blacks, "You're not black enough." If you live in the suburbs, you're not really black; if you like classical music, you're not really black; or if you're light-skinned, you're not really black. There's one way to be black and if you don't fit in, you're excluded, you're banished.

I think that's so stupid, and I wrote about that, about how some of my black colleagues got on my case and said, "You're an Uncle Tom." Why? "Because you fraternize with too many white people." You're not supposed to be around white people, you're not supposed to interact with them. As one person told me, "I work with them five days a week; I don't want to see them after that." I don't feel that way, and I don't feel like there's one way to be black. I don't feel that just because one guy stands on the corner in the inner city and he grabs himself and he raps, that makes him more black than somebody who lives in the suburbs. What is being black? What is it being white? What is it being a woman or a man? I think a lot of it, for me, has to do with the fact that growing up, Blacks could be just as cruel, just as mean as white people when it came to racism.

At my job, black reporters will say, "What have you written now? Why are you in trouble now?" because they know I'm not afraid to take an unpopular stand. They know I'm not afraid, for example, to go to lunch with a white woman, and I don't care if the black women are saying, "Oh, you're just into that." I'm not afraid of that. I'm not afraid to have a white friend; I'm not afraid because I'm used to being on the outside, I'm used to being made fun of—being biracial has prepared me for this.

When I hear a lot of Blacks talk about race now, a lot of it's in real simplistic terms. When I was sent to LA after Rodney King, I spent a lot of time covering gangs—Bloods and Crips—and we would get in these conversations. I'm about the same age as them and I'd say, "Come on, man, why you killing some other guy because he's wearing blue?" And they'd say, "Oh, the white man making us do it, the white man bringing in the drugs, the white man . . ." And I would say, "Did the white man come to your house, wake you up, drag you out of your bed, put the gun in your hand and make you pull the trigger?"

See, being biracial has kind of demystified white people. They're complicated like us, they got problems like us, and they're not one type. Like us.

In the end, what *does* black mean? I think we're unique, the way we were brought here, slavery, families split apart, cultures taken apart. I think of our contributions to this country, what we've done with jazz music. I think of our creative energy, how we've added some spice to this country. But I'm not going to say only black people are like that, only black people have soul, only black people have gone through that type of suffering. So if I come down to it, I can't think of what it means to be black. I can think of what it means to be John who's a Christian, whose mother's white, father's black, but what does it mean to be black? What does it mean to be white? White people never have anybody come up to them and say, "You're not being white enough." But we have to contend with that.

Sure, white people have their JCPenney's, they have their Hush Puppies. . . . Seriously, though, those questions are so hard. I get knots in my brain trying to think about them. But when I go to church, for instance, and I see black people and white people together, relating to each other in a real loving way, I—how can I put it? There's a scripture I really like, from the Galatians. Paul says, "There is neither Jew nor Greek, slave nor free, male nor female, for you are all one in Christ Jesus."

To me, when you get down to a real basic level, I believe in a brotherhood of all people. We all share pretty much the same experiences. People want to grow up, they want to love somebody, they want to have a family, they want to work, they want to produce something to be proud of. I think anybody can relate to that. It's like when you go to a ball game and you see guys who are black and white talking about baseball. Color doesn't matter.

I'll give you another example. My father was over there in Vietnam. He spent a real long time over there, and I was always attracted to reading about men in combat. One of the things was that if you talk to any veteran, they'll tell you that in a life or death situation, when you're depending on this man next to you to live, you don't even give a damn about his color. You all bleed red. That's where I find my refuge, those kind of moments, those kind of life and death situations where you realize that we're all human, all those situations—I guess you would call religious—where it doesn't matter. You don't ask anyone, "What does it mean to be black and white?" We just say we're human, we're brothers and we're sisters, and we've got differences, but we're still part of the same family. That's the way I think.

CHAPTER XI

Self-Portrait

Zenobia Kujichagulia
Age: 43
Residence: Oakland, California
Occupation: Executive director of emergency services center for poor
and homeless people

Zenobia Kujichagulia was not born with
this name, but has used it for years in ar-
ticles she's written for publication. Gener-
ally, everyone except for her mother calls
her Zenobia, and the last name she uses at
work is a compound of her husband's name
and her family name. Although she allowed
me to photograph her, Kujichagulia wanted
to protect her mother's feelings by not using
the family name.

"Kujichagulia" is one of the seven
principles of Kwanzaa, a celebration created by Ron Karenga in 1965 for
Americans of African descent. This particular principle, as Zenobia Ku-
jichagulia describes it, means "the right to define ourselves, create our-
selves, think for ourselves, instead of other people doing it for us." Her

choice of "Zenobia" applies that principle. It is one of the few African names, she says, that survived the assimilative years of American slavery.

When I first called her, following a lead from an Oakland Tribune reporter who often interviews her on homelessness and other poverty-related issues, it was clear she was not leaping to talk to me. Not only was she busy with her work, but also she said she thought it was dumb for people to identify as biracial or triracial, and I sensed she was reluctant to be included alongside them. Whether I wore her down with my pleading or she felt charitable, I'm not sure, but we met two days later. Immediately, she shared her anxiety about the interview.

This is a subject I don't discuss a lot from a real personal perspective. Now and then I'll do workshops for somebody, or I'll do technical assistance, or a consultation, especially as it applies to people who are providing services to folks, but this is one of my little issues that I not so cleverly cope with by turning objective and dealing with from a removed place. I just thought I would say that up front. There are parts of my family that seem to have fixated on this whole thing, and they wear it into the ground and I get sick of it.

There's a certain component that *never* talks about it: That's my father and his siblings. They basically just pass for white, and it's a they-don't-know-what's-wrong-with-the-rest-of-us kind of thing. And then there are the ones who don't try to pass, but they do the stereotypic tragic mulatto crap, or quadroon or whichever configuration they fit in. I think *they* even consider *themselves* tragic. I've got some high-drama people in my family, which I admit to being affiliated with at times.

I have these cousins over in Daly City who didn't know they were black until their father died. They were at the funeral and when some black folks came, the rest of them were like, "Ooh, Who are these coons?" And so it was a real trauma for the oldest boys to find out they were black. So they would talk about it all the time, and it would just really, really get on my nerves and other people's nerves in the family.

If I take my personal issues out of it and look at it from more of a clinical place, I think for those particular individuals the discovery process was so traumatic that they've never finished processing it. And they keep trying to resolve it by talking about it, but they don't go to the next step. Ever.

For others who go to the next step or didn't have the same discovery process and therefore can't quite relate to it in the same way, then it's a distasteful thing to keep doing over and over. Clinically, though, I really do understand it.

But it just gets on my nerves. I was going with a guy who had none of these problems, and one of my cousins was over—this was years ago when we drank quite a bit and smoked weed. We were sitting there, and we'd been smoking and talking and drinking, and my cousin starts this whole damn story, and my other cousins were sitting there going, "Oh, God." So he's telling my boyfriend about this, and he got to the part where he says, "I didn't even know I was black until my father died!!"

And my boyfriend did this great thing. He just said, "Oh man, I know you were really glad to find out you were black." And we were just cracking up, and my cousin was like, "Oh. Oh. Oh, yeah, yeah." It had never occurred to him to look at it that way.

What I did was place things in my own mind a certain way a long time ago and then just leave them there and go forward. That placement was not only just an acceptance, but a celebration of being a person of color, and going from there. And then of course, I tried to make it simple, to just say, "I am black. There's nothing else involved in it; there's no other discussion." I can provide information and assist people who view it differently and go through their traumas, but it has nothing to do with me personally.

My mother's father is a Swiss-German, and my mother's mother was British, Irish, Scot. Both were born in Kansas, in the country. They were farm people, and I doubt that my mother saw more than one or two black people before she ever graduated from high school, out in the middle of the Flint Hills.

And in my father's family, my grandfather was black and white and my grandmother's father was black and Cherokee and her mother was white. Must have been real interesting.

So my mother went into the small town nearby to go to nursing school. It was a college town, a place called Emporia, Kansas. And it was where my father was from. When they met, she did not know he was black. She did not know that until after they were married.

I don't think it ever occurred to her at all. She just thought he was incredibly handsome with his black curly hair, and his blue-gray eyes, and tall—and tan, right? So it was some time before her family knew, and her family and my father's family never got along real well, although they did get together sometimes and they were courteous to each other.

The two were really different. The cultural stuff was one thing. My mother's people were farm people. Kansas is a divided state, then and now. It's got pockets of serious Klan-type activity, and then very liberal areas. Where my mother grew up—I think there was one black family in that entire area—had been a part of the Underground Railroad, and people generally had a very progressive outlook. My seriously white relatives were very open and loving and kind to myself and my siblings, and never in any way did anything to make us feel less than. They did not really like my father's people because they drank. None of them drank. Most of them never smoked. They were straight and narrow types, religious but not fanatical. They were hardworking, they went to church, if they told you it was going to be X it was X.

And my father's people, although his parents were not heavy drinkers, my father and all his siblings are alcoholics. And they didn't associate themselves with being from the South, but there was a lot of rural South culture in there that was real different from midwestern farmers who were Lutheran Presbyterians. There was that kind of cultural difference.

My father completely, totally identifies as being white. It didn't ever really come up that he had to say it; he just behaved as though he was and that was that. He was in the navy as a white person. He and his siblings all just behaved as though they were white. It was their children who rebelled—not all of them, I might say, but most of us rebelled and said, "This is crazy. What's wrong with you people?"

My father has not talked to me since 1971, and the last time we had a conversation it was real unpleasant. I had gone to Boston, where he is, mainly to see if we could have any kind of relationship, and I did that against my better judgment. Of course, my mother was like, "You should get along with your father somehow." They've been split since I was a senior in high school.

And I went to try and talk with him, and well, see that picture over my desk? With the giant Afro? That's what I looked like. That was me. Permanent rods and rinsing with vinegar. I didn't actually perm it: I first rinsed it in vinegar, then rolled it in the rods, and then combed it out. The vinegar will make your hair curl more. If you can get any curl in it, the vinegar will do that. So anyway, that's how I went to see him. He threw a fit and said, "We can't go anywhere, people might think I'm colored."

And I said, "Well, Dad, you are." I thought he was going to have a stroke, he was just spluttering, and he said to me, literally, "There is no reason for you to act this way. The taint in our blood is far enough removed that there is no reason for you to act this way."

But that was the most overt conversation we were ever able to have about it. And all the rest of it, from being a child and going through adolescence, I had to get from my mother. Aside from all this, he was really a lousy parent. His thing was that he was a ladies' man, and he would disappear for weeks upon end. So we were in the navy and we would be stuck off in God knows where with no friends or relatives around, and he would just disappear.

My mother had a discussion with me when I was about five. As I have looked back, I think what really prompted it was that we were in Virginia and my father was gone a lot. We were having a very hard time financially, she was incredibly depressed, totally isolated, and I became somewhat of a parentified child. She talked to me about problems, and I think she had all kinds of anxieties and concerns about racial things. So she told me this wonderful thing about being a bouquet of flowers of the universe, how wonderful it was to be all these things, how very lucky we were.

The way she was brought up, in her heart, that is how she looked at it. And so she started me out with this really wonderful glowing feeling about who I was, and she was pretty specific and very progressive for the times. Then it sort of all went downhill after that, because she didn't have any mental or experiential ammunition to give me for what was going to unfold. Also, I don't think she thought it out, because the end of her talk was: *"But we don't tell anyone."* Which immediately didn't equate, especially in the mind of a five-year-old. If it's so terribly wonderful, why can't you tell anyone?

Not much later, two experiences really caused the shit to hit the fan. First, because my father was passing for white and my mother was white and the schools were segregated, my sister and I started out in white schools. But in second grade, I was moved to the navy base school, which was integrated.

My best little friend in class was the only other black girl there. And one day all the kids were picking on her. They started pushing her, and I thought she must have done something wrong. I asked what was wrong and they said, "She's a nigger."

I said, "What's that?"

"A Negro. She's Negro. Look at her. She's colored."

I said, "Yeah. I know, but so am I."

It was like time stood still. To make a long story short, we both got our asses kicked. I had two broken ribs and a black eye. And the teachers watched. I never saw her again. My parents took me out of that school, and my father was furious at me because I had told. So he told them I was suffering from delusions and I got transferred. That's when it all sort of went *crash*! Less than six months later, when we were close to getting transferred out of Virginia, the second thing happened. And that really, really did shape my outlook and was why I became so militant in life. It must have been the summer I turned seven or eight. I always get it mixed up, and I think it will be obvious why. It was a very traumatic experience.

I saw a man burned to death. It was a black man. And I was the only other black person in the crowd. I had gone into a neighborhood next to the base to get my father a pack of cigarettes and kind of walked into the situation. This brother had stole a loaf of bread—it's a classic story—and a crowd encompassed him. They had brooms and things and they were beating him back in the circle. They threw gas on him and tossed a match, and I came just before they did that part. And I was a little kid, so I worked my way into the circle to see what was going on.

Terrible, terrible experience. The thing that impressed me most at that moment was this: It was about anger. To me this was the epitome of what anger was, because I looked around the circle and I saw the faces of men and women and children, distorted with hatred, screaming "Burn the nigger! Get the nigger!" and laughing, but a hideous kind of laugh. The rage was so clear. So for me, this is what anger is. And I spent the rest of my life, until I was about thirty-five, having real issues of ever demonstrating anger.

Because if you have real anger, that's what happens, you get totally out of control. It also set in my mind that by and large, this is what white people are about.

And I guess in a way there's this bizarre choice: You become the victim or the victimizer, or something in between, which is, in a sense, where I stood. Literally. I knew I was a part of that mob, and I knew I was a part of that man. Also, I've thought and thought about this for years—and I do not believe that I have exaggerated this in time and in memory—but I felt that man looked me directly in the eyes. And also, it wasn't anyone I knew, but I felt like he knew that I was a black child and he knew I couldn't save him.

So I ended up really dealing with a lot of survival guilt, like, "Why couldn't I, this eight-year-old child, save this man?" And "Why did I have to stand there and do nothing?" Like I could have done something.

Was I guilty for not saying, "Excuse me everyone. I want you to know that I'm black, too?" Oh, yeah, right. And just a few months before, I'd had this experience at school. Truthfully, I don't remember going home, I don't remember anything for months after. And I generally have very clear memories from that time. Eventually my mother said something to me like, "People can be very cruel, people can be wrong." She was trying to give some kind of apology for people, but it left me wounded and not knowing how to process what I'd not just witnessed but been a part of.

From Virginia we moved to England, and we did not ever again live on a navy anything or go to a navy school. In England we lived in a regular British community, we went to regular British schools, and we were the laughingstock, my sister and I. We had these southern accents and we were these weird Americans. And people were always asking me if I was jaundiced. When I was younger, I actually had much more of an olivey tone. I told them I didn't know if I was jaundiced, go ask my mother. And once someone asked me that and I said, "What do you mean?"

And they said, "Well, your skin is so yellow."

I said, "That's because . . ."—I was still trying to hold on to this—". . . I'm a very lucky girl. I'm a bouquet!" I laid it all out as my mother had told it to me—and, of course, it was white first and then Indian and then there was Negro.

They were so appalled! God only knows what my mother and father told them to clean that one up. But my mother set me down then and told me that it caused problems for daddy to tell these things. I remember asking, "Why, if it's so wonderful?"

And she gave me this thing about how life isn't fair and people are prejudiced and remember Virginia, and that's what it means. So I was supposed to keep this secret, and I hated it, absolutely hated it.

We stayed there about two and a half years, then we left and went back to Kansas to stay with my grandparents on the farm, which I loved. By then we had these proper British accents, so we were these hilarious city slickers to all the kids in the country. Those were actually the best years of my childhood, with my grandparents out there. It never came up. Everyone was white and that's the "but." I often couldn't figure out why I felt so miserable during those years, because they were the best years of my childhood, but clearly the trauma of Virginia didn't go away. It was there; I was traumatized. And a secret like that makes you sick. So that was going on even though now I was in this environment that was much more pleasant. Also there was just the isolation of never seeing anyone or talking to anyone who seemed to have any similar experience. And the people in that immediate area of the Flint Hills of Kansas are really, really good people. They're seriously white people and they're seriously great, but I was isolated. In a way it was even worse because I didn't know what the problem was.

The only thing my grandparents ever said, and I did not realize why until many years later, was that my grandmother called me her little Egyptian princess. I always felt incredibly ugly as a child and never thought I wasn't *ugly* till I was about twenty-five. My grandparents used to do quite a bit to try and convince me that I wasn't ugly—that's why she used to call me her little Egyptian princess. Also, she was trying to give me something there. But they didn't know how, either, they really didn't.

After we became good country kids with a midwestern twang, we went to Boston and we were real hicks. We lived near Medford Square in a primarily Italian area, and while I was there I got to know a lot about Italians. Actually, I was mistaken for being Sicilian a lot. I liked Italian everything. I thought it was interesting and fascinating and a nice culture.

And I was getting into my adolescence pretty full-blown, so I had become pretty defiant toward my father. My parents were very strict, but I absolutely detested him. He was still taking off for weeks at a time, and he was very disruptive and punitive when he did come into our lives. So those years were not happy ones.

We lived in Medford until I was through the tenth grade, and then we moved to Emporia, where my father was from. Everyone in this small town knew who my father's people were, so all the white kids knew I was black, and all the black kids knew that my family persisted in passing for white, so they all hated me. I went into the eleventh grade with no one speaking to me, but by the twelfth grade the other black kids in the school realized I was not my father's people and so I had friends.

Towards the end of high school, I was this very, very serious teen. I wrote poetry; if my mother had let me, I probably would have worn all black. High drama, high-strung. Melancholy as well. I wrote a poem once about being on a raft in the middle of the ocean, and sometimes the raft would almost wash up on the shore, almost, and just when you thought that's where you were going to be, the tide went out and you'd be back in the middle. You'd go this way and then that way. I felt like that sometimes, like no one was ever going to let me be on the shore anywhere.

I thought that out very thoroughly, and I could just visualize it sometimes. I knew who I was, but my biggest problem seemed to be everyone around me. People would say, "Well, what other people think can't hurt you." What utter crock! I mean, that's just real shit. I can't even believe you tell people stuff like that.

I finished high school in Emporia. My best girlfriend got married about two weeks after we graduated—I was the maid of honor in her wedding—and then I got on a Greyhound bus. I had twenty dollars in my pocket and I left. First, I went back to Boston, because I had made a few friends there, and I was there for a summer. Then I decided to go to college, and the only place I could go was in Emporia. It was a college town and if you graduated from high school there, it was guaranteed you could go.

I tried to go to college there, but I just couldn't deal with Emporia anymore. I had come to the end. It was 1966, and things were getting militant. When we did a demonstration in downtown Emporia to have the right to change clothes in the department store, my mother totally freaked out. I would tell you that was why I left, but that's not completely what happened.

I had my very first boyfriend and I loved him madly. It was the summer of '67, boys were getting taken out of college and sent to Vietnam, and we thought he was going to go. So we were supposed to go to New York and get married. The summer of the Newark riots, I went to New York, and he was supposed to meet me there. I got there, I got a job, and as I was working and waiting for him, the riots and all that stuff was unfolding. During the riots, me and another girl got chased by a mob out of a white neighborhood and into this black neighborhood and then we were chased out of there. We were both light and we got chased out of both places. That was the epitome of what was happening for me at that time.

Then my boyfriend didn't come. He never came. I cried so hard all summer long, and among other things, I kept wishing I was ignorant, that I didn't care and that I didn't know about anything, I didn't understand anybody's perception or different perspective. But I lived through it. It was a terrible, terrible time, and I lived through it.

Eventually I made my way out here. I came to San Francisco, summer of 1968. I went to Haight Street to see what the hell was going on. I was ready to drop out of anything. I knew I had family in San Francisco. I had never met them, but I knew they were the black side of my family. So I met them and they completely took me in. These were not relatives who passed—finally, the real deal. It was excellent, excellent. People from my complexion on, all features, all colors, eyes, hair, everything.

I did go through a couple of rough years, though, and the cousin I hooked up with there was also going through some things. We did drugs for a couple years, and we really got out there. But we also started getting involved with the Black Panther party, and ultimately my strong sense of politics overcame everything else and we left San Francisco and moved on this side of the bay [to Oakland] and got really involved, although I never joined the party. I'm considered an oddity in that because I was *very* close to the inner cadre, but did my best not to know the things it was dangerous to know, although sometimes I knew them. So I was able to really establish myself fully in the party with my beliefs and my experiences and channel that rage and all of that hurt into constructive action and to be accepted. That was very good.

But as I was coming into that, before we came on this side, there were some harder experiences in San Francisco. Folks were getting real militant in San Francisco, '67, '68, and sometimes the militancy meant they were not exactly patient with those of us who have less melanin. There were a couple times where people weren't just rude, the "You don't look black enough" kind of thing. My cousin, who is obviously a black person, and I were on Haight Street once, and a guy came up and slapped me. He just slapped me; he came up and slapped me! And said, "You white-lookin' bitch, you think you're better than everybody, don't you?"

He slapped me hard. He knocked me down. My cousin jumped on him and was trying to kill him, but this was a pretty big guy and we really couldn't have a dialogue with him. At first I was ill-equipped to deal with it, and at a certain point, in a sense, I accepted that it was my fault. I had some guilt about it, and that particular time and place made it very hard. I was very militant—I am very militant—and reading Malcolm's autobiography, the thing that struck me the hardest was where he talked about the anger and the disgust of having the white rapist's blood in your veins. God, I related to that so strongly. At the same time, felt very guilty for thinking that, because my mother and her people were good to me. In some ways it would have been a lot easier if they had been racist. My cousin who didn't know she was black until her father died, her mother did screwy things with their heads, telling them, "The reason your hair is like that is because you have a vitamin deficiency," and, "Your father was the whitest man I ever knew." Stupid shit like that. My mother didn't do any of those things to me. She tried her best and her family did, too. If I could have just written them off, it would have been simpler. It wouldn't have been right, but it would have been simpler.

Another cousin and I dabbled in the Nation of Islam and went to the mosque, put long skirts on, and tied our hair up. When we went in they wanted me to take mine off so they could look at my hair, and they looked at my fingers to see if I had dark enough rings around my nails. They deemed I was black enough to come in, thank you very much. We tried so hard to believe the theories, and then they would do the teachings about how Doctor Yacub had created white people like devils in test tubes. We tried, and I couldn't do it. *What? My mother and her people are a freak of nature?* I don't know, maybe they are.

You have to figure out what you're going to do with all the messages you get, and when I do give presentations, one thing I get people to think about is that for people who look like us, it's like a double negative. We know that no matter how much self-esteem you're given, a black child in this country will still, even if it's unconscious, get the message that there's something wrong with them, that they're less than. At the very least, they'll know a lot of other people think that. But when you look like we look, then not only is *that* happening, but you can't even look the way you're supposed to look. *Supposed* to look. So it's like you're wrong twice. There's something intrinsically wrong with you twice.

You know you're never going to be white, which is real fine with me. It has been harder for me to not be considered black enough. That's always been harder. And that was very, very painful for me in the sixties and part of the seventies.

As I got into my mid- and late twenties, though—from focusing on the issues I wanted to work on, establishing credibility and a reputation for my work, i.e., who I am, over and over and over—it became easier. I found I got less of the shit from people in general. When I was younger, especially in my early twenties here, people would just stop and stare at you, white people, black people, whoever. You were this weird oddity. In the setting I was in, which was more and more totally a militant black environment, it was even there.

Some light-skinned folks were militant to prove they were black enough, but I wouldn't say that they in any way dominated that scene. There used to be a joke in my family that the lighter you were, the more country you would probably talk in public. And the same thing applies in politics: Because that part would be questioned, you had to jump the baddest and be the blackest. Those of us who never bought into "light is better" ended up trying to make up for it. What I may have ended up doing was to buy into the same prejudices in a backwards way. I knew all the options represented the exact same dynamic, but I didn't feel I had a lot of choices.

I've had people say to me, very angrily, "But you can choose!" I'm always astounded. I understand that white people think that, and what they will never really get is that I don't ever remember having a choice. Who I am inside has been there since I have memory. I suppose there's this choice where I would clearly be choosing to pretend to be something else. But there really aren't choices from my perspective. And that's what I meant when I said I know what all the choices are. In my mind, I could not make · them. I felt like I needed to be very militant because that's how I thought and believed, and still do. That was my salvation.

We have to remember, too, that I read and I read and I read, and so I know history inside and out, the good and bad and the ugly. I know black people's history, in Africa, but here as well. And I know about the color lines and all of that. I knew clearly what I would never ever repeat, what I would never fall into as a light person—and some of that has got to be connected with my experience with the mob. Even beginning to think that I would choose a side that had any remote connection to that kind of hateful destructive behavior, to adopt that somehow, has never been a choice for me. And it's been hard for me that other people always thought I had some kind of choice.

And I never felt that biracial was a choice. I worked at Upward Bound [an academic support program for educationally and economically disadvantaged youth] when I was in my midthirties and one kid in the program, an adolescent, came to talk to me. His mother was white, father was black, and he asked me, "Why am I not black *and* white? Why am I just black?" He was asking me for some justice around it, and all I could give him, based on where I was at that point, was not especially helpful, I think. I gave him the historical why, talked about how it got laid out in slavery and the way it is today. And I tried to present it to him that you can feel good about being black, that it's a good thing. Later, after my daughter was born, though, I felt like I had failed that kid.

I felt like what I did to him was tell him that half of him just wasn't valid. And that's the same old shit, you know. How could I turn around and do that to somebody? I was *astounded* I did that to him. I know why I did it, I know all the rationale I used, I even understand the logic of it, but I ended up realizing that it still was unfulfilling for him, and ultimately, for me.

Years later, I went back to him and told him that our conversation had haunted me. And we just talked about it a little more, and I tried to say that societies do not seem able to validate, much less recognize, that human beings are sometimes two things. But that it's still valid if you are made up of those things to embrace those things. Even though that's not personally the way I deal with it, if that's where another person is, then that's their right. I do feel strongly about that. And as I have come to that, I am less angry with my siblings, who consider themselves to be universal human beings.

When people are two things, that's what they are. It's not even what they want to be. But the thing is, society insists that you're one, and I think it becomes most intense when it's about black and white. It's also very true sometimes in other cultures. I have a friend who's a Navajo married to a Hopi, and they try to figure out how their son is going to cope with everybody trying to make him choose. You're either going to be Hopi, or you're going to be Navajo, and he's both. It's always easier for me to understand those examples than to look at it in myself.

I know *intellectually* that it's accurate, that people are biracial and triracial. It's probably more because it has created so much conflict and pain for people that I just shut down around it and don't want to deal with it. And because my own struggle has been so hard. I've *never* been confused about who I was. I *never* wasn't sure or felt lost. What I have felt through my life is under attack for it and angry at the attack, and that's probably why I hate dealing with the whole thing.

The Native American part of me is unfolding, and in the past six years, I have been on a quest to be accepting and lay to rest the issues about the white part of me. But clearly, that will always be the white part, as opposed to who I am as a black person. Truly, from the bottom of my essence, that's just the way I am. I suppose I could sit here and pick apart and figure out step by step why, but the way I experience it is: That's just the way I have always felt.

I would say my personal life, my truly personal life, is primarily black, but it is integrated with all kinds of friends. Native American, white, Asian, Latino. My work life is totally integrated.

There have been times when I have purposefully worked in predominantly black environments; in fact, most times I have set it up that way.

[When I was dating] I absolutely steered away from light-skinned men. Although I thought I was really getting more accepting of myself when I was in my midtwenties, and I dated a guy who was as light as I was for a while. My family teased me because I would always date men who were much browner and with nice fine velvety skin. I definitely by and large have done that. And when I married my husband, everyone said, "Uh-uh! We knew you would do that." I hate when they do that, although they're right.

I remember when our daughter was little, when she was trying to figure out what people were and why they were these things. Really small kids, when you tell them, "You're black," that's a real puzzling thing. You just taught them their colors, right, and now you're telling them they're black? Once, a little kid said, "You're white."

And I said, "No."

This little girl got a puzzled look, and she said, "Pink?" She was really trying. So I explained it to her, and kids always have the same, okay-but-I'm-puzzled look on their face because in terms of a color, it doesn't compute.

My daughter made me have to deal with some of this on yet another level. I feel like I've been growing a lot about all of it over the last few years. She made me stretch yet again, though. And it was real simple. I purposely set out not to set her up in the same way [I had been], and to try to get her specific information and ammunition to go with it and everything else. I was unprepared for her wonderful developing self-esteem, having lacked one so entirely.

People, of course, are so ignorant, and her hair is very straight and fine, although it's wavy, and so people would ask me stupid things when she was a baby, like, "What is she?" or "What's her dad?" or "Whose baby is that?" Then when she was getting bigger they would pet her hair and ask her what she was mixed with. She would say, "Why, I'm black." And she would say that first, because I always stressed that first, right? And told her how wonderful that was and what that meant and we studied African history and black history and all that stuff, and she would say—because she knows and loves her grandmother, and I'm sure she thinks of her aunt and uncle this way because they're such universal human beings—so she'd say, "I'm black and I'm Cherokee and I'm white!" And I just freaked out. Because, although I'm sure it's very obvious to most people, you'll probably never hear me saying, "I'm black and I'm Cherokee and *I'm white.*" I just don't add the last part. I never do. And right away I found myself getting ready to say, "Lynn, don't say that." And I said [to myself], "Ahh! Cut your tongue! Oh, my God, this is how it happens! This is how you become your parents, this is how you repeat the cycle." So, of course, I did not say that, and I had to really struggle with myself around it. And she's beaming and I was like, "Aaarrgh."

She wanted to know more about the Indian stuff. That made me actively seek out Native American connections and explore that. And actually, in doing that, I realized that is something that I always felt a loss of, and when I was in my early adolescence, I had such an interest in that and I couldn't get anywhere. I tried to get information from my grandmother, and just got shut down so greatly that, I realized later, I pulled back from it. Well, in connecting in with the Native American community, it sounds hokey, but I literally have discovered a part of myself, and/or recognized a part of myself, as I've learned about many things that are quote, Native American: cultural traits, just certain ways of viewing things. Ways that you think about the earth and all of the environment. It's different. It's not even like Greenpeace. There's a type of spiritualness, there's a kind of nonjudgmentalness, a way of listening and processing information and looking at things that, in being in Native American environments, I find myself being so in tune that it scared me, because there's that part that somehow didn't belong in other places. It's been a very remarkable experience, and I feel like my daughter gave me that gift because she, I would say, enabled it, she forced me to seek out that part. And true to the kind of person I've become, I didn't do it for myself, right? See, I did it for her.

I have a theory that as I have become more self-confident and more assured of myself I have projected differently. People ask me less, they seem to mistake me less. When they do make mistakes, the correction, by and large, is much smoother and creates less of a disbelief. The last time it happened, it hadn't happened in years, but I was somewhere with people that knew me real well and they introduced me to someone. This was an all-black environment, and as they introduced me to this woman, one friend says to me, "Zenobia, tell her what you are." So I knew what was coming, although I didn't expect this woman to go all the way off.

I said, "I'm black and Cherokee." Like I told you, I always leave the last part off.

The woman looked at me and said, "Like hell you are."

I said, "Yes. Like hell I am."

And she said, "No, I mean"— like I didn't know what she meant—"I mean you are *not* black. You might be Cherokee but you are *not* black."

And I said, "I'll be sure to tell my daddy you said so." And she just started cussing, ranting and raving, and I looked at her and I looked at the friend and said, "I think I'll go now," and just went across the room.

CHAPTER XII

Prejudice: The Monster Within and Without

All people have prejudices of some sort, really, which might sound like a cop-out, like I'm trying to excuse my own, but there's something about human nature that pulls towards fears of difference or creates stereotypes about groups. I see myself doing that and I don't like it, but I see that the mind and the intellect do a lot of things that aren't particularly rational. But there's an ethical, important distinction to make between behavior and thought. I'm more conscious of the thought level of prejudice, and then I would hope my behavior ultimately doesn't reflect that. I feel I am ultimately mostly accountable for how I act and not necessarily what I think.—Paul Whitaker, p.213

I'm very prejudiced against people with southern accents, white people with southern accents. But one of the best editors just came to work for me a few months ago, and when she came to me, applying for the position of editorial assistant, I was really desperate to hire somebody, and I couldn't tell the personnel director that I didn't want to hire this woman because she was a white woman with a southern accent. So I hired her and she turned out to be great—and a great person, too—but I am prejudiced against white folks with southern accents.

I expect them to be racists. I spent a lot of summers in New Orleans when I was young, and it was during the civil rights bill and we got chased by crackers, my sister and I. It was an ugly experience. There were a lot of times when we drove down there with my mother and her brothers and we couldn't stop to eat or to go to the bathroom. I have angry, bitter memories about that. My parents didn't go to Louisiana together until late in the seventies. They couldn't have; they wouldn't have felt comfortable. They weren't trying to be pioneers or to attract trouble. They weren't crazy.—Bernette Ford, p.207

The [adoptive] family I grew up in was actually quite preju-diced about Blacks. It's not unusual with Creole people; they gen-erally believe Creole is a different cultural group and ultimately, I guess, superior. They tend to distance themselves in some ways, or try to keep the Creole culture alive. Growing up I would hear black *as a negative term, even thought my [adoptive] mother is fairly brown-skinned.*

In the family, sometimes the term black, *or even this really negative term,* black and ugly, *would come out to describe large facial features. Broad noses, big lips—things like that were not okay. At that same time, it's not as if my parents didn't have any friends that looked that way, but my father would say this thing: "Oh, you don't want any women with hair so short you could smell her brains, okay?" Or he'd talk about attitudes of black women, all black women: "They get evil, they get mad for no rea-son. You don't need that."*

I think I learned some prejudice from those kinds of com-ments. It's sometimes more on a gut level than an intellectual level because I know it's ridiculous—but then I'm also very tuned in to stereotypes. As far as having a blanket prejudice or stereotype, I don't say, "White people this, white people that," but then I'll fall into a mode of typecasting in my mind when I see black people dressed a certain way, who are loud and talk a certain way; I seem to be more aware of that and feel some embarrassment by it. When I feel that, I examine it. I think, "Why does this bother me?" These are people I don't know and I may never see again, but I think maybe I'm being associated with them, and that they're not helping to move things forward, just perpetuating the polarity.

Since I've been in Portland, I've felt more initial discomfort with a black male walking at night in my direction. I think that's because young black men have been typecast as criminals and violent. I go high and then I go low again; I feel it and then I go, "Oh, this is another person." But I don't feel that if I'm in Oakland or San Francisco or Los Angeles. Portland's a peculiar place, and these images are constant. I was down in southeast Portland, and some man had assaulted someone. They had this mug shot of him, and he could have been any one of thousands of black men because it was a poor quality picture. They put it on storefronts, and it's very fear-inducing. I'm not immune to it until I realize it's wrong and it's not realistic and it's not true. But I've partly become a product of my environment here, even though I'm a person of color.—Greg Wolley, p.103

Can we skip this question? I think to a degree we all have some prejudice. . . . It's probably not fair to say this, and it's prejudiced to say, "I don't like white people," but, in a large part, I don't. That's probably my biggest thing.

I just don't trust them; I just don't. And that's probably my biggest hang-up; I just don't trust most white people. And I guess that's probably not fair, again, for me to say. It's just like judging a person by just looking at them, before you get a feel for who they are, their character and what they believe in. It's kind of a sensitive issue with me.—Joseph Marable, p.176

I don't look at a black person, a white person, a Korean, or whatever and immediately think I know exactly how they're gonna be, what they're gonna say. I don't think that I do that. I do have a reserve of negative feeling towards Jews, even though I have since met and continue to meet plenty of Jews I don't feel that way about or who I like very much. But that comes from how I grew up, the people I grew up with. I don't really meet those kind of people anymore, who were unwavering in their support of Israel to the detriment of everybody else around them.—Marpessa Outlaw, p.198

My prejudice is passive in the sense that it's there but I choose not to allow it to interfere with the communication or the relationship, but when it comes up I become very sensitive about it. It tends to come up with almost every white person I meet. In my mind I say: "Sooner or later they're going to say something really stupid that's going to make me really angry, but I'm going to be cool and I'm not going to let it interfere with the friendship or whatever it is that's going on here." And as soon as it comes up, then we get into a fight about it or whatever.

It doesn't actually happen that often because I have very few personal relationships in general; I have maybe four or five really close friends. One is white, if I need to make that distinction, but he's not my white friend, he's Pete.

I think I have a lot of prejudices; it would take a long time to try to explain all of them. But for the most part my policy is, let's deal with the human being first and see what happens, because I may be wrong. Or, let's give this person a big wide street to walk right down and fuck up.—Michael Mayson, p.229

I kind of have a little prejudice of my own thinking that I'm ahead of everybody else in the race against time because I'm already mixed. I have this hidden theory that eventually everybody in the world is going to be mixed with something or another, so I got a jump on it.—Danette Fuller, p.364

There seems to be a culture of silence about prejudice in this country—not applied to identifying prejudice in others, but in terms of admitting to one's own prejudices, *especially* racial ones. Even though discussions of race have become trendy, the talk is generally kept theoretical, or, if at all personal, will center on how the race-based prejudgments of others have affected the person speaking out.

In an informal and completely unscientific survey, I have asked white, black, and biracial people if they have prejudices. My findings are that most Whites say they do not; many Blacks say they do not (though some say that black people *cannot* be prejudiced, that at most they only reflect the prejudice of Whites); and most of the biracial people say yes, they do have prejudices.

Everyone knows that prejudice is unfair and insensitive and very, very unpopular. To hold sweeping, irrational attitudes about an entire group of people goes against basic ideas of justice— against the idea that we are all individuals. Still, when asked if they had any prejudices, some biracial people came back with a swift *"Oh, yes!"* followed by their specific targets. The most common statement was: "I'm prejudiced against people who are prejudiced." Others got down to the nitty-gritty: They talked about distrust of white men in suits; disdain for American white girls but not women; gut dislike of Chinese drivers or male Nigerian musicians or loud Blacks or backstabbing Whites or people who are unattractive. A few were reluctant to talk about their own propensity to stereotype, embarrassed that they could have such feelings, having been victims of the same and feeling that they should know better. Almost none said they had no prejudices at all.

This casual survey suggests an interesting possibility: that biracial people tend to be more honest about the prejudices that *everyone* has but most people are ashamed to admit. Why would this be? One possibility is that biracial people often have more exposure to *varieties* of prejudice than others do.

More than one biracial person have described themselves as "a racial spy." Because so many have the still-unusual experience of close relationships among *both* Blacks and Whites, the opportunity to hear prejudices voiced by both sides is more likely to present itself. Fears and prejudices tend to seep out from even the most politically correct mouths when the speakers think they're among their own racial group—or at least with someone who has partial membership, verifiable through one of their parents or their skin color or features. Perhaps witnessing prejudice flow in the two directions exposes its universality, and, in showing its commonness, disarms it. In fact, my wildly unscientific survey supports this theory further in that the biracial people who said they had no prejudices tended to be those who essentially lived in only one of the two worlds.

Now having admitted it, what does it do to a biracial person's sense of self to hold a prejudice knowingly? Can it sit dormant in the mind, or does it metastasize, a poison eating away at a person through its acknowledged presence? Are people obliged to try to rid themselves of the prejudices they feel, or should they simply accept them? Is it healthier to keep quiet, to ignore the prejudice, not even giving it validation by giving it voice?

When people talk about their prejudices, they define how they see themselves as much as they define the distance they feel from other people. Similarly, when they talk about the prejudices of others, especially those directed at them, they are often defining themselves in describing their reaction.

—————·∞·—————

John Blake
(See also page 269)

Even as John Blake works diligently to rid himself of the stereotypes and prejudices he developed as a child, he acknowledges that there are some he just can't seem to shake off.

I still have prejudices against white people. I still do. Sometimes I feel it's unfair that numericallywise, white people have the easier way in this country. A white man doesn't have a one in twenty-one chance of getting killed like I do as a young black man. And I feel like they don't know what we've gone through. They're probably all spoiled and go home and make fun of us. Sometimes it's real ugly. Particularly when I was in LA, and I would go out on these gang shootings and I would see all these young men die. I just knew that if young white boys who lived out in the suburbs were dying at that rate nobody would tolerate it. And that made me mad as hell.

But then I would think about my mother, or this guy named Kevin I met in Chicago, at the Church of Christ I went to there. This guy was Farmer Boy, but we became best of friends because we shared the same faith, we shared a passion for art. I think about people like that and it puts that prejudice in perspective.

All I know is that by the next century, this country is not going to be *Leave It to Beaver*. I saw the future in LA. I saw Asians, I saw Hispanic, I saw all different types of people. The white people were the minority. W.E.B. Du Bois talks about how, being black, you learn how to live in two worlds, you learn how to be around people differently, you learn how to adjust. If you're white, you never really had to do that before. In a sense I feel sympathy for them because they're going to have to learn how to do that pretty soon, and I'm already doing it.

Now, I don't know if this is also prejudice, but I get really angry when I hear black people try to blame all their problems on other people, *all* their problems, and we have a lot of problems, because of our unique situation. To me, when people start talking about *what the white man did to us*, that just takes away our dignity. We're not puppets, we have free will, we have dignity, we have strength. Is that a prejudice?

Ever heard of Shelby Steele [author of *The Content of Our Character: A New Vision of Race in America*]? Some of his stuff I don't quite agree with. Some of it I really like—when he says that Blacks should stop thinking of themselves as victims all the time. But I listen to people talk about him in the newsroom, and they say, "Oh, he's got a white mother and he's married to a white woman, he don't know what he's talking about." Takes away all his authority. And I told my friend who sat next to me at work, I said, "I tell you, if it ever got known my mother's white . . ." because so many people would think it disqualifies me from being black. And the funny thing about it is that most of the Blacks on my job— people getting on my case who say I don't know what it means to be black—they grew up in suburbs, they never grew up in the environment I did, an inner-city black neighborhood—west Baltimore, North Avenue—you don't get much worse. But *they're* going to tell *me* what it means to be black. That's what I go through a lot, and I make a joke out of it. I say, "Yeah, I'm the sellout. Yeah, everyone got to have a sellout like me."

Deborah Gregory
Age: 37
Residence: New York, New York
Occupation: Magazine writer and editor

Most of the information Deborah Gregory has about her family history comes from her half-sister, Janet, who is eight years older. Apparently, their mother (they also have a younger sister, and each has a different father) came from a large sharecropping family—thirteen children—in North Carolina. Their mother left her hometown and came to New York, where it seems she worked as a prostitute. Gregory's father, who may have been Irish-American, was much older.  *He started out as their mother's client, and became her boyfriend, eventually setting her and her daughters up in an apartment that may have been in a building he owned.*

I didn't know I was interracial till a few years ago. My older sister Janet says that apparently my mother and my father fought a lot and he kicked us out. We went and lived in a hotel and my mother didn't have any money, so she went down to welfare to get help and they told her she was sick and she needed to go to a hospital, and so she signed over rights to her three children, and we were separated at that point.

I was two, my younger sister was six months, and Janet was ten. Janet didn't live with me after that point, and while she came to visit me in my foster home, nobody talked about my family there. Actually, my foster mother didn't know a lot because Janet concealed it from her; she didn't want her to know.

I would look in the mirror because I was pretty light and I would wonder what I was, but I never thought that I was half-white, because I asked my older sister, who distorts reality, quite frankly, and she told me we all had one father, our father was Puerto Rican, and his name was Joseph Novez. She says now she did that because she didn't want the foster family to know the truth. She thought it was a stigma, and she didn't want us to be hurt by that or for them to know.

My foster parents lived in the northeast Bronx, in a neighborhood called The Valley. I stayed with them until I was sixteen, and my foster mother died. They were black and very dark. My foster mother was very dark and very mean, and Janet didn't tell her. Janet said that my foster mother would ask her questions, [but] Janet didn't want her to know we were half-white because they would pick on us. My foster mother hated white people, but Spanish people didn't come into her consciousness. She was a racist, just obsessed with how horrible white people were. I don't remember her ever saying anything about Spanish people; the world was black and white.

So I thought I was half–Puerto Rican, and because of that, I learned Spanish very diligently and that became part of my identity. When I was sixteen I got a job in the supermarket because they needed Spanish-speaking cashiers, and I told them that I was Spanish. I had to wear a button that said, *"Habla Español,"* and I was very proud of that.

I wore a Puerto Rican flag on one side of my jeans pocket and a black flag on the other, and I remember one day leaving school, and some of the black kids said, "Hey, *mira! Mira!*" ["Hey, look! Look!"] They were making fun of me 'cause they obviously tuned into that I was having an identity crisis, and they were right. I was. I wasn't even half–Puerto Rican. I didn't know that, but they picked up something unconsciously.

School was hard because I had a lot of emotional difficulties, so even though I was a bright student, it was very difficult. I felt that the black kids always picked on me, and then there were things like the fact that I was in the IGC class. That was for intellectually gifted children, and it was really embarrassing, because then they *really* picked on me. Where I came from, it was not something to be proud of, and my foster mother couldn't read or write, so you know it was a sore point between us. I tried to conceal it and tried to play it down, but there was a lot of tension about that.

I was kind of disappointed when I found out I wasn't half–Puerto Rican because I had a lot of racial issues. I didn't like white people, because of my foster mother, and I always picked on them and said nasty things, so it hurt me a lot when I found out, and I was really furious at my sister.

The reason my older sister finally told me the truth about my father was that as I became an adult, I had gotten the feeling that she was lying to me about things. One day, when me and my younger sister were having a fight, she screamed out, "You're just half my sister!" She intuitively knew, and she was right. I wouldn't pay her any attention because she was very hateful towards me—we would take out the anger at each other because we were unhappy—but she was right, we are only half-sisters.

By the time I turned thirty, I had been in psychotherapy for a while, and, more than anything, that was probably why I was probing into who I am and what I am. So something prompted me one day to write my sister the nastiest letter you've ever seen, this scathing letter about how horrible she was to us when we were growing up, that she was in another foster home and she didn't take proper care of us, visit us, make sure everything was okay, and that I know she's lying through her teeth about something. And that was really it: "I know you're lying about something."

And so my younger sister called me and said, "Janet's really upset." Janet can't see because she had a stroke, and my younger sister told me, "She couldn't read the letter, and she had someone in her church read it. She was really embarrassed at what it said, and she said that she's ready to talk to you." So I called her and she said, "I didn't want to tell you that our fathers were white, and we have different fathers, that our mother was a prostitute."

It was all really things that I knew anyway; I just knew them to be true and I was furious. I don't even think I could continue the conversation with her, I was so angry. To be honest with you, for whatever reasons, the circumstances I've grown up in, I have denied that I'm half-white. That's the orientation I come from, the way I was raised. Whatever need I had to do it for, it's just something I could not face or deal with in any way.

People used to say it all the time. In school, they would make jokes. One day I was sitting at a table: "You ain't black. Your father was the mailman." There were enough questions asked that I could have figured it out, but it was very suppressed, it wasn't something I felt allowed to feel or talk about.

Not just from my foster mother, but from society, too. If

you're black, you're black. If you're an ounce black you're black
and it's so absorbed in you that you don't question. "You're light-
skinned? You're black! Everybody's black!"

When I found out for sure, it was a trip. I had to face all the
racism I had against white people—which was tremendous. I had
white friends, but any opportunity I would get to put someone
down, I had no problem saying, "That white bitch," or, "Look at
that Milquetoast!"

When Janet called me and told me this horrifying thing, I was
ready to kill her. She said, "I did it to protect all of us because I
didn't want your foster mother to use it against you."

In a way, she's right about that. But I said, "You know, you've
waited an awfully long time to tell us." It was unforgivable as far as
I was concerned, completely unforgivable, and I hung up the phone
on her and didn't speak to her for years.

I went to my therapist immediately and said, "Look, this is
what Janet said." And it was funny, she wasn't surprised at all, as
I remember now. I think she even said, "You knew that." And
then we did a lot of work around this. It's been really hard; it still
is. And there's so much still to be done about it in so many ways.

All those jokes I made, all those comments, all this putting
down of people all the time and my father was white? That's
incredible. I especially relished attacking white men, I noticed.
I've always had white girlfriends, but white men: yuck!

Besides the question of me being half-white, my father was
white, and I felt such rage towards him. He wasn't any great shakes,
obviously, so this news from my sister was first manifested in a lot
of rage towards whoever he was, that he victimized my mother. I
had a lot of rage towards white men, and to a degree I still do.

Even now, years later, I'm afraid of them. I basically still don't
trust them and am trying very hard to work through that, because
I really don't believe in segregation. I think I used to, but I can't
now because it really would be denying who I really am. Now that
I *really* know, I can't pretend I want to live in a world that's one or
the other. I really don't. It doesn't feel right. But I still don't feel that
secure around white men. I notice that. I still need to work out all
that stuff about feeling inferior, all that stuff that you somehow ab-
sorb from the culture, and I basically am afraid of them. I find I'm
mistrustful towards them. I just don't know what their agenda is.

Up until that phone call, I was black. And then if you asked, I was half. But basically, I was black. Now, it's really painful, but what I've realized is I can't comfortably say that I'm black anymore. I'm really biracial, and that means something different. And I'm scared about that, partly because I am a writer for a black women's magazine, and while I don't think they would reject me, I'm afraid of what black people will say, I really am.

There is a faction in the black culture that thinks we shouldn't differentiate because it takes away from the power of blackness. And in a way, by shifting more towards biracial, I think I might be taking away from that. But it's something I have to do for myself, and also because I don't agree at all with this idea society has that if you are half-black that you should just be viewed as a black person. I think that's outdated and that we need to have more awareness about mixed-race people.

Having an awareness of mixed-race people would be more positive, more enlightened, more real, like the reality of the world. Things are not just black and white. And in a way I almost see it as a little way to bridge the gap which is so far apart from one side to the other.

Without a doubt the race stuff has been the most horrifying to face, to own up to the feelings I have. Now what I'm going through is the black part, which is horrifying, absolutely horrifying: facing the hatred, the self-hatred, the rage that I have towards the way I was treated by the black kids who called me Casper when I was growing up, by my foster mother who was always saying, "Don't think you're better than me because you're light." That was her favorite line. I must've heard that only ten thousand times. It's so odd that we were all light, her foster children. She asked for light-skinned children so she could pick on us, I think, because my foster brother was not related to me and he's light, too.

Facing the black part is hard because no one talks about this stuff—we all hide it. My therapist said, "You should write an anonymous essay: 'I Hate Being Black.'" There was all that about being white, but the much deeper part was about being black and the way black people treated me; having to face up to how we're taught that white people are superior and having grown up with people who could actually prove that to be true, because they were so dysfunctional. How horrifying that was to face and to own and to heal through!

For example, there are the black girls who wear the gold earrings and the ones who always beat me up, the ones that are always mean and give me the dirty looks—really looking at me like they want to kill me—and who I run from. I had a lot of rage towards them, and I've always suppressed it. It came out recently and forced me to face a lot of things that are just so painful to face, like, how do I feel about girls like that? Do I think I'm better? It's more of a classism than a racism thing, but do I think I'm better than black people like that? No, but from working through my rage at them has come this incredible thing where I actually feel compassion, which is something I *never* felt when I looked at black people like that. I always felt rage, and my therapist says it's because I never separated myself from them because of this thing society has: I always saw myself mirrored in that and never even accepted who I am and that maybe I do have talents, that I don't exactly hold that despair I see in their faces, that feeling of not having anywhere to go, not amounting to anything. That was always instilled in me, and it wasn't true. It was my foster mother's projection from where she was, not being able to read and write, and not being attractive or having a personality or anything.

I had been carrying that inside of me, and when I looked at them, I saw me and how painful it is, the guilt that I feel, having to separate myself, having to own that I was given more. It doesn't look like it on the surface, because I grew up in foster care, but I am smart and I do have things that can get me out of the ghetto, so to speak, and some people don't, they really don't. It's an illusion to think that black people can be completely united. No race can be. Asian people will clearly tell you the Chinese don't socialize with the Japanese, the Koreans and so on. And we're supposed to think that all black people love me? Please.

I'm over it now, thank God I'm in therapy and I see wow, I can really look at black people and say, "There's nothing wrong with being black." I could never have said that before.

On some level, my rage towards those women was really from that place of thinking what white people say is true. And part of that is grouping all black people together. That's ridiculous! It's

ridiculous to say I love all black people. It's just not reality. I finally
came down to what life really comes down to, which is that some
black people are okay and some are not, but this notion white
people passed down is that all black people are stupid, ugly, this,
that, and you really have to start differentiating. Obviously, I
bought into it, like probably ninety-nine percent of black people
do, and they'll never admit it.

I'm at the point of saying, "What do I do with all this information I've got?" And in order for me to be who I am and to live
in this body, I'm going to really have to define my own identity,
which is a pain in the fucking ass. It was easier when I just thought
I was black and I was like, "Power to the People!" This is really a
whole new ball game, and I'm scared in a lot of ways, but also
committed to being whoever I am. But I am scared, to be honest;
I'm scared of the flak I may get.

I'm definitely a woman of color, but to say that I'm all black,
no way. I can't say it with a clear conscience. It's not true. I'm
half-black. If both my parents were black, cool. I can see exactly
the person I'd be: I'd be the epitome of The Black Bougie Woman.
I'd open my own black magazine. I can't do it now; I've got to go
somewhere on a road in between, and I have no idea where that is.
But I feel like the biracial thing is a big part of maybe who I'll be
in this world, with what I do and where I'm going.

Jacqueline Djanikian
Age: 26
Residence: San Francisco, California
Occupation: Administrative assistant, advertising

Jacqueline Djanikian's father is Armenian, born in Valence, in the south of France. When he was twenty-one, he came to San Francisco, not speaking any English. He met Djanikian's mother through friends, and she taught him the language. They traveled the world together before they married in 1965. They had Jackie, and then three years later, her brother.

Djanikian's mother was born in San Antonio, Texas. She came to San Francisco, where half her family lived, for college, and then decided to stay. When Djanikian was between the ages of seven and fourteen, her family lived in Paris. When they returned to San Francisco, she went to French and bilingual private schools. There, just as was true in France, she was about the only person of any color in her classes. Transferring to an all-girl Catholic high school that was more racially mixed was a culture shock for her, she says, but also a turning point.

When I went to high school, a lot of the black students weren't middle-class, they weren't in the same class that I was, and I never had really interacted with any other black women or guys except for my mom and my mom's family. And so to fit in and to really understand what my background was as far as being black, and to understand other people's backgrounds and why sometimes there were fights between Latin and Asian and what the gruff was—because I've never witnessed this at all and I was very curious—I had to really adjust myself and learn how to interact with all these different cultures. It wasn't very difficult for me because I'm always very social and want to learn everything about everybody.

I'm black because my mother is black, and, technically, you are whatever your mother is. This is according to documents, paper, the hospital, everybody. Somebody was telling me about this. It's actually the law. You are whatever your mother is, so if your father's Jewish and your mother's Catholic, you're Catholic. You can't be half-Jewish or whatever. My brother could pass for white, but he is black because that's what his mother is. The mother dominates. So I consider myself black. I am closer to my mom, also, and to her family because they're here, and my dad actually lives half the year here and half the year in France. And he's over there now, and I don't see his family except when they visit.

And it's not only the law; it's just my choice, actually. That's the way I want to live my life—as a black African-American, not as a Caucasian. I could never pass for Caucasian if I wanted to. And regardless of whether it was legal or not, it's sort of like my mom and I have a very close bond, and because she happens to be black, that's who I feel I am. I'm a black woman.

When you grow up you just make that choice. You either decide you want to be African-American, or you want to be Caucasian. And it might have to do with your skin color, it might have to do with how people perceive you. I'm obviously African-American. You could never look at me and say, "Oh, she's white."

I don't think it's possible for people to identify as both. Take my brother, for instance. If someone were to come up to him and say, "What's your race?" he would say black. It's just a choice you've made yourself. You can identify with both races, but you *are* one or the other. You are not both. I identify with both, but I am one.

Between black people, when we see each other on the street, there is acknowledgment that takes place. We don't have to say anything, it's just eye contact that no other race really does. I notice that. My friend and I actually talked about it. There's an acknowledgment and it's really interesting. You don't even have to know the person; you can just look at them and there's something between you, like a togetherness, I guess.

It's a good kind of unity thing because life's rough out there. And compared to other black people and black women, I think I've been very lucky. I've been sheltered from the things that a lot of other black families and black children and adults have to deal with. I've got a really great job; I went to a great school; I've been all over the world; I've gone to French schools and speak the language fluently. Not too many black people actually can say they've done a lot of that stuff.

When I was in high school, I was sitting in my chair, and there was this—she's really fat—this black student, and she asked me why I talked the way I did, because I didn't talk like I was black. I looked at her and I was like, "Probably because I went to a completely different school than you did." I didn't know how to give her an explanation. What kind of question is that? It's just the way you are brought up, the way you're born, what kind of community you live in.

I feel part of the black community when I'm with my black friends because we usually go out to things like the jazz festival, where there are more black people around. More so than if I'm with my white friends, since there might not be that many black people simply because of the places we're at, North Beach or cafés or whatever. A lot of my black friends are in black sororities or black fraternities, and they're always having social gatherings, having raffles, doing things for the black community.

I didn't join any sorority. I saw what they had to go through—there was no way in hell I was going to be put through that humiliation. I wasn't really interested. If you could see what my friends looked like going through their pledge thing: They couldn't wear any makeup, their hair was all whacked out of shape, they looked like they were dying. I couldn't. No. And another reason I didn't do it is because it wasn't me. I'm never one to be in the club thing. Even with the black student union at college, I was never really in it. I would never go to the meetings, but all my friendships were there.

I started identifying as black when I was a junior in high school. I just did because of the black women who were in the school, my friends there. Even though we came from totally different backgrounds, you sort of come together. It's a melding thing, and it doesn't matter where you are; you just feel comfortable and at home, kind of. I started to feel that way then, because all my life I'd been with white kids, and even though I didn't feel like I was inferior, it was a completely different feeling being with white kids than being with black kids. You just feel closer, I don't know what it is; it's just something.

I can identify with the white race because my father was white and I've lived that life-style and I know what it's like to live in an all-white neighborhood or to associate with everybody who isn't black, except myself or my mom. I understand the culture, and I understand their way of thinking. I understand how they can be bigoted. I see people from Blackhawk, which is a really rich, hoity-toity area in the East Bay, and I see how they can think that the Fillmore neighborhood in San Francisco is totally like, "Oh, my God, these black people! I don't want to get on the bus because they're going to try to rip me off. They're a bunch of thieves and thugs." I can associate with that, because when I get on the bus and I go in that neighborhood, I think the exact same thing, even though I'm black.

Some black people with two black parents might think that way, too, but my friend, who's black—because of her background and the people in her past and where she's lived, growing up in that kind of neighborhood—she understands where they're coming from more than I could. So where she would think it's no big deal and could say, "Hey what's up?" I couldn't because of the way I was born, the way I lived, and the way I was bred. And so I go, "Ugh."

She would know how to relate better than I would. You have to actually get into that kind of a life-style, you have to learn it, to get to know it. You can't be comfortable with everything.

Simone Brooks
Age: 17
Residence: Portland, Oregon
Occupation: College student

Simone Brooks's mother is white, from Canada; her father is black, from Tennessee. Brooks was raised almost as an only child. She has a sister, older by nine years and also biracial, from a relationship her mother had years before meeting Simone's father. Brooks is precocious, academically and socially. When we talked, she had just finished her first year at Hampton University, a traditionally black institution in Virginia.

Most of the time, I was more separated out from people because I was smart, and I was put in the little group that sat aside and did the higher-up courses. So that made me stand out a little more, especially because I was a year younger than everybody. I noticed that difference before I noticed any color difference.

I don't remember hearing any questions from other kids until third or fourth grade, and then they were really comments. At first it was because I was smarter, and people would say, "Oh, you're trying to be uppity." And those would be black kids, usually. White kids really didn't say anything to me, except for the kids I was in the little study group with. I was one of those kids that everybody was friends with, but I wasn't friends with that many people. A lot of people liked me, but I liked very few people. It seems like I know everybody, but I'm not close to most of them. I try to keep my distance because you can't trust most people, and most people, if you get to thinking you can be close to somebody, then they won't be there when you expect them to be. The friends I have are people I know will always be there for me. It's usually a very small number; you only have a few friends in life. I have a lot of acquaintances, though, and I know what they're good for, I know what I can go to them for.

My parents always taught me to be polite—you treat everybody the same no matter what. And until they do something that detracts from that, you have no reason to treat them as any less than your equal. I did that wholeheartedly, especially when I was really young, and I used to get hurt, because people wouldn't be there for me. I'd be like, "Well, why didn't you do it?" And they'd almost just walk away. And I'd feel real hurt and left out, almost. So I learned my lesson.

My third-grade teacher had us playing a game where you would run to the board to do math problems. He had distributed the group that was really good in math evenly in the lines, so we wouldn't win. And I guess I went up there, and it was a really hard problem and I did it and everybody was all happy on our team, and this black kid was in the line that was losing, and he was like, "Well, you think you're all this because you're smart, but remember you're still black."

I was like, "What does me being black have to do with anything? What's the connection?"

I told my parents about it later, and they were like, "Well, what he was trying to insinuate is that because you're black you shouldn't be good in math. But being black is not going to detract from you in any way. All it is is a skin color and a culture; it doesn't have to do with intelligence." And I remember I was satisfied with their answer and went about my daily business.

In sixth grade, I was considered *really* smart and was in the little accelerated classes, so my friends were usually people in my class. I was almost always the only Black that was in those classes, so I was hanging out with a lot of white kids. I started to feel cut off, and I said to my parents, "This seems like it's getting to be a problem. I don't have any black friends."

I was looking around and I'd go, "I'm the only black person here." I knew I was black and I knew that in the group I hung around I would hear racist comments. Even from friends. One girl was looking at a whole bunch of guys standing over to one side of the school yard, and they were pushing each other around and stuff, like kids do at recess. And she said, "Look at those people over there. They're always fighting." And they were all black. And I knew, even though she probably wasn't thinking about this, that if she said "those people," she was including me. And I don't fight like that. I said, "Excuse me? No. *Those people* don't always do that, because I don't always do that, number one. Number two, it's obvious not every black person at this school was doing it. I don't think you should make generalized comments like that."

And she was like, "Well, I didn't mean you."

And I was like, "Well, you did mean me, because you're talking about black people. So you did mean me."

And she was like, "Well, yeah, but you're not like that."

And I said, "Well, no, but I am. If you got to know them you would realize that." It's kind of weird that I made that statement, considering I didn't know most of the kids that well, but it was something that was ingrained in me by both my mother and my father: "You're black *and* you're white. You have to accept everything about yourself, otherwise you're not going to like yourself. But claim your black first, because that's the part of you that needs sticking up for most."

I've had to defend my white side, too. And that didn't happen until high school. People would say, "Oh, you're a sellout, you're white." I'd say, "You're right. I am. You're absolutely right. I'm not going to be ashamed of the fact that I'm white. There's no reason for me to be ashamed of that." But I've had it from both sides, and I've dealt with it the way my parents taught me to. And they're right, the black side's the one that almost always needs protecting, so I claim it first.

I knew that I was black because my parents told me I was black, but after my freshman year in high school, I went away to Clark-Atlanta University, a black institution. I went there for a six-week program in science, engineering, and math. And that was all Blacks and they were all the same level I was. And I was impressed. I was like, "Wow. These are Blacks who are just as smart as I am." This is the first time I had seen it, because even the other black kid who was in my classes at home, wasn't—boy, do I have an ego—at the same level I was. I knew that I could write better, and I knew that I was better at math. It's just one of those things; you know when you're good in class. And when I went to Clark-Atlanta, I found people who were at my level, and older kids who were doing the things I wanted to do, and all of a sudden I was like, "Wow." I got my first taste of what black culture is. I saw black men and black women interacting, I saw black professors. I saw the way they spoke proper English.

I went to that program because for about four years, my parents were in charge of something here called the Black Colleges Conference. My dad was chairman of the committee, and ever since I was really little, I used to go to help out. I'd carry boxes and all those type things. So all the recruiters who would come knew me since I was little. They knew my grades, they knew everything about me, and one man from Clark-Atlanta University just loved me. He thought I was great; he thought I was fantastic. And he said, "All you have to do is pay for your plane ticket. We'll pay for everything else; you'll have a stipend."

Of course, my parents were like, "Okay. Go ahead." So I went. Going there was the biggest change in my life. But when I came back, I realized I didn't want to be here anymore. At this point I went to high school at Wilson High School, which is across the river in southwest Portland. White people all over the place. Ooh! I was like, "This is oppressive." I didn't like it freshman year, because the environment of Wilson is very cliquish, I mean *very* cliquish. I remember telling my mother of incidents where I would see a black guy walk up to a group of white guys and they would be talking as if they were friends, and he would turn his back, and, immediately, their expressions would change. I could see it, and I was like, "Why isn't anybody else seeing this?"

It would be like, "Ha-ha-ha, laugh-laugh-laugh," then he would walk away and you could see hatred on their faces. To me it was just right there. And I was like, "Mom! You won't believe these people!"

It was funny to feel so distanced from white people and be surrounded on all sides by them. It's really an amazing feeling, the most oppressive feeling I've ever felt in my whole life. You start feeling like you're not safe. First of all, you're in a school with a lot of white kids, which wouldn't necessarily be so bad if you knew that if something started to happen—like they started killing all the black people—there would be black people who lived nearby that you could at least go to and know they'd help you. When you go to school in a neighborhood that's completely white, all of a sudden you realize you're really completely cut off, and if somebody started doing something to you because of your color, you wouldn't have any help. You realize just how scary that is. You would have *no* help. None. Zip.

There might be a few white people in Portland who would help, but they're not known for that here. There wouldn't be enough. There are too many racist people, and at school, the popular white guys were all racist. I mean, obviously, verbally racist.

One time I had on some shirt that had various statements on it about being black; "I'm black and I'm proud. It's a black thing, you wouldn't understand . . ." And they were all positive comments. I guess "you wouldn't understand" wouldn't necessarily be positive, but it was on there, nevertheless. I think my hair covered that one. But this guy started yelling something like, "I'm white and I'm proud of it," and he said, "And I'm so white and I'm so proud that I could kick your da-da-da," some abusive statement about how he could prove something to me with violence—which he couldn't have anyway. But some white power thing. I guess he finally calmed down and had gotten all that out and was feeling better, and he said, "You know, if I wore a white power T-shirt in this school, they'd probably make me take it off." And I said, "You're probably right. And that's not fair. So you could wear one and you could dispute it if you like, but I don't care. I could care less." And I left. I wasn't impressed so I just left. But I remember thinking, if you had seen the look in his eyes when he first started, I was like, "I'm glad I'm not around you alone." After that point, if he was in the hall and the hall was empty, I would turn the other way.

My senior year of high school we had a homecoming assembly. The basketball team was on stage: There were five basketball players, and they were all black. And the football team—which happened to be all white because we didn't have any black people who could play football that year—they were sitting in the audience and they started yelling, "Why don't you niggers go back to Jefferson?" Jefferson is my neighborhood high school. At that point, things began to be a little stressful.

On the East Coast, people are prejudiced and they're not afraid to say it, so you can accept it easier. You go, "Okay, I can respect you for that view. I realize you're racist and I don't think it's right, but at least since you said it I can respect it." Here people try to act like they're your friends and they don't care, but they do and they are racist. They're lying and you can't respect liars. I don't. And so that's what ends up making it harder for me to make friends here because I realized, especially as I went through high school, that I couldn't trust white kids. I found it hard to trust them anymore. The way my parents had taught me to trust everybody at first, I couldn't do that anymore. From so many of the kids that I thought were friends, eventually I started hearing those racist comments, and I was like, "No." As soon as I heard them, I'd be like, "No, don't speak to me again. I don't want to be near you."

They'd be like, "Simone, you're overreacting. We're not talking about you." And when they say that, I'd say, "Well, you are. You're making a generalization, so you're including me. If you don't want to include me, don't include everybody."

So when it comes to people, I don't like this city. I love the look of it. I have a Portland book that shows what it looks like and I took it to college with me. I show it to everybody. I think the Northwest is gorgeous, but the people are ugly inside.

CHAPTER XIII

Are We a Family?

For me, the same way black people have a sisterhood or a brotherhood, that's something that I felt towards this mixed guy who worked at the same restaurant I did—that we had this connection just because of who we were.—Kyria Ramey, p.201

I don't really feel a particular connection to mixed people. I understand what they've gone through, but I don't necessarily say we are closer because we're both mixed. Sometimes you feel further apart. There's this one girl I know, and she associates with black men and she's really into being black. And we're friends, we're acquaintances, but I don't really get along with her. I think it's probably because she's so into black athletes and black men and that's all. She doesn't even go to the same types of places I go to. She would never think about going to a bar unless there were thousands of black men around, and for me, pshhhhhh, I don't need that. So sometimes it's good, and sometimes, you know, it's just okay.—Jacqueline Djanikian, p.309

I've been getting this INTERRACE magazine for the past couple years, and it makes me feel good that the whole topic of in-

terracial relationships and families has gotten big enough or con-temporary enough that there's a publication about it.

Before I moved up to Oregon, I started to form a group of biracial adoptees. And then I got here and found out about the Inter-Racial Family Network, so I called them. I was looking for biracial adults, and there are a lot of kids running around but not many people in their thirties, and so they gave me a list of people in Portland and I called a few of them. Nothing really happened out of that. And then I started meeting a few biracial adults, and I got interested in what the people from the network were doing. I helped give a workshop a couple years ago where I told my whole story. People are always real interested, especially parents. I found that a lot of them, since I'm one of the very few biracial adults they know, want their kids to have some adults to identify with. They want me to talk about how I feel about myself so their kids can hear. I find myself really drawn to biracial kids, black and white mixed kids, especially boys who don't have a father.—Greg Wolley, p.163

I go to the meeting, and everybody's looking at me trying to see where's the white in me and I feel uncomfortable. I don't want to have friends based on their mother and father; I want to have friends based on who they are now. And to me, the former is what this group is kind of about. I may be wrong, but I don't want to get into it.—John Blake, p.269

Somebody said "mixed" once, as in a race separate from Blacks and Whites. I was just like, "Excuse me? We have enough races as it is. Don't try to put me in one category on its own, thank you very much. I have no desire to be put on a little pedestal."

I think Blacks wanted to make it "better than" and I think even Whites wanted to make it "better"—not better than them, of course, but better than Blacks.

So I was just like, "Don't even try it. I have no desire to be separated." I'm separated enough as it is. I'm separated as a woman; I'm separated from Whites because I'm black; I'm sepa-

rated from Blacks because I'm part white. I don't need any more separation in my life.—Simone Brooks, p.313

I didn't really have a choice, you understand. Because I was adopted, I grew up in a black family. Now I can't speak for you or anybody else who grew up in a biracial home, but I found, for me, in my black environment that it was not healthy to sit on the fence.—Carol Calhoun, p.186

Start a little club? No, I don't think so. What do they do? Does everybody just sit around? I always wondered about that. Within the last five or six years, I've noticed that there's more the trend to want to come up with a third race. "We're neither." "We're something else altogether." "Let's come up with some sort of word, and we'll be that."

Considering who has been running this government lately, I look at that sometimes and I think, "You know, it's real possible for them to look down at this group and say, most of you are educated, most of you come from middle-class homes, okay, we could use those people, and you're not like those poor black folks over there, those folks down on the ground. You're different." I.e., better. And it's like creating that whole mulatto class that existed after the Civil War with everyone saying, "Well, you're a little bit better, a little bit different. Why don't you come over here with us?" Co-opting that whole group of people, using it as a buffer zone.

The problem is, when the shit hits the fan you get dumped right back down with everybody else, because the vast majority of white America is not going to deal with you as being white. That's the bottom line. That's just the reality of this country. The country was founded on racism, and it's been working on it very well ever since.—Pam Austin, p.221

Biracial people may find it pleasant to talk to each other, to share the common experience of negotiating color lines, but should they unite to carve out a separate territory on the racial map? The very idea draws criticism from myriad corners: from Blacks who either don't want their ranks diminished or who perceive the delineation as a way for biracial people to distance themselves from blackness; from Whites who can't see the biracial person as anything other than black or who, as parents of biracial children, feel that their own white status should be either counted equally with the child's other half or somehow even prevail; and from biracial people who simply want to exist in one camp or the other without fanfare, or who have decided, because of their experience, that all ideas of race are fallacious.

For centuries, though, people have built communities in this country based on having mixed-race heritages in common. Usually black and white, but sometimes mixed with Hispanic or Native American, the groups have identified themselves by their mix. Entire cities, like New Orleans, Louisiana, and Charleston, South Carolina, have generations of families that were self-proclaimed octaroons, quadroons, Creoles, and blue veins. According to historian Paul R. Spickard, in his book *Mixed Blood*, a social group for interracial couples and biracial people called the Manasseh Society existed in Chicago, Illinois, from 1892 to 1932, its name drawn from the biblical half-Egyptian son of Joseph.

Currently, there are more than forty multiracial networks around the country. Unlike the communities in Charleston and New Orleans, they tend to attract families and individuals where the mixing is close at hand and not embedded in distant, much earlier generations. Network membership typically splits three ways: families made multiracial through adoption; interracial couples and their children; and, to a significantly lesser extent, mixed-race adults (who generally identify the point of mixture as being no further back than their grandparents). The particular mixtures vary with the location of the group—for example, there are more part-Asian people on the West Coast, more part-Latino people in the West and South.

The groups are typically hybrids of support and socializing. They often evolve out of academic and religious institutions, and out of shared needs, like exposing younger children to adult role models or to other children with similar family compositions. Some groups take on a more political agenda. Often, this is an effort to change the racial classification on forms. Project RACE (Reclassify All Children Equally) in Roswell, Georgia, has been lobbying to have public-school-system forms changed to add a "multiracial" category, followed by blanks for mother's race and father's race. RACE and other groups—like the Association of Multi-Ethnic Americans (AMEA), the national base for dozens of affiliated chapters—have made various attempts to convince the U.S. Bureau of the Census that it should accommodate and tabulate people who identify multiracially.

There are newsletters and magazines as well, two of the most highly produced being *New People*, out of Michigan, and *INTERRACE*, out of Los Angeles. The publishers of *INTERRACE* are planning a new publication: *Biracial Child*. Multiracial publications feed the hunger to see oneself as part of the public landscape, present and past, and to look at race without restraint. Sometimes they veer in the direction of gossip and fanfare, not always well researched in their claims of who is multiracial and who is not. Some of the publications call for open dialogue but also promote specific perspectives, for example, that "multiracial" is the only appropriate and healthy identification for children of interracial couples. Other times, they bravely take on controversial subjects— transracial adoption or interracial dating—clearly trying to go beyond rhetoric to get to the heart of each issue.

Some networks sponsor large conferences and events. In the spring of 1992, the Washington, D.C.–based Interracial Family Circle sponsored a conference on the occasion of the twenty-fifth anniversary of the Supreme Court's decision to overrule existing antimiscegenation laws (*Loving* v. *Virginia*). More than two hundred people attended the Loving Conference, including Mildred Jeter Loving, the surviving appellant from that historic case.

During the day-long conference, attendees participated in such workshops as Interracial Images in the Media; What About the Parents: An Honest Dialogue; and Biracial/Multiracial Category/Progress to Date. At another conference, in Detroit, organizers decided to tackle one of the biggest practical issues faced by white parents and their biracial (or transracially adopted African-American) children. They called the workshop Bring a Kid and a Comb.

Joy Zarembka
Age: 19
Residence: Haverford, Pennsylvania
Occupation: College student

Joy Zarembka's mother is from Kenya, and her father grew up in St. Louis, Missouri. Zarembka's parents met in Kenya, where her father started a high school (after a tour in Tanzania for the Peace Corps and finishing college in America) that her mother attended. "It's not as bad as it sounds," Zarembka says. Her mother was about twenty-six at the time, her schooling interrupted repeatedly by the needs of the family farm. Both sides of the family accepted the relationship with open arms. Zarembka and her younger brother grew up in Pittsburgh, Pennsylvania, except for a year they spent in New York before their parents separated.

A few months before we spoke, Joy had gone with her best friend and her mother to Kenya, her first trip there since she was two years old. The trip was shocking for her, in that she was viewed in ways she'd never experienced. She and her friend, who look very different but both have light brown skin, were asked frequently if they were twins. At one point, someone asked that while Zarembka's cousin was present. "Don't worry about it," her cousin told her, "We just think all white people look alike."

I consider myself a black person within this society, and that's interesting because my mother is from Kenya, and so she doesn't have a lot of the black culture of America. I think she disagrees with it; she doesn't like a lot the black culture of America. So the black culture that I know, that I've been socialized into, hasn't come from the home. It hasn't come from my father, of course, and it hasn't come from my mother. So it's basically from school and peers and TV.

Some of that culture is about a certain mentality within the black community that is necessary to survive within this society. Personally, I feel there's a lot of racism and discrimination, and unfortunately it's really hurt the black community in many different ways. And so there are a lot of survival tactics that need to be used to get ahead within the society. I'm not talking about devious acts, but there are certain things that are considered to be part of the black culture: Being late for wherever you need to be is acceptable; expressing your opinion about something, expressing our laughter at certain times is acceptable. Often, American society is really stifling, kind of smothering, but the black community is more expressive, whether it be in music or art or dance. There's a lot more freedom within it.

From my mother, I don't think I've learned the hardships that black people historically have gone through. She has more of the immigrant mentality, which is like, "You're here in this wonderful country, make the most of it." Get yours, or whatever. My mother, being an American-African—as opposed to an African-American—her mentality is totally different because she feels that there's no need for welfare, [that] people need to get off their lazy butts and do what they need to do. I totally disagree with her about that because I think there's a lot that holds people back in the educational system, in the way resources are handed out, in the old boy network. There's a lot more to it. But I don't know if that's just the difference between our political views or whether that's a difference because my mother's from another country.

I feel that I'm a biracial person, but I identify with the black community. I identify with the culture of the black community of America. I'm both things, rather than one or the other, because there's not a substantial biracial category at this point. It's not a unified front. If someone asks me, I'm biracial, but I gravitate towards black activities, black organizations. For biracial people, there isn't anything like that. I also think there's a problem if you start splitting up—"Well, I'm biracial"—when to some extent, most black people in the country are multiracial, most have white blood anyway. The one-drop rule was just one drop of Negro blood way back when made you black. There's a lot more people who identify as black who are a lot whiter than I am.

I have this one friend who's like, "How can you split up the biracial and the black? You're just making us more divided. You're making the black community more divided." So in that sense I do identify with the black community. I want to work for the struggle of the black community, but I also can't ignore the white side of me, because it's an integral part of me. A lot of my ideologies, a lot of my feelings about education and just life in general have come from my father. And I know a lot of my privilege has come from my white father. A *lot* of my privilege. Like the fact that I can be sitting here, at Haverford College, twenty-three thousand dollars a year, is from my white privilege. I can't ignore it because I have had so many benefits from that. And I'm talking institutionally.

All black people must learn about white society and white ways and white values; growing up with a white father, I have even more of that. Going to Grandma's house for every Christmas and different holidays and things. And also having a very intellectual family. My aunt went to Radcliffe, another went to Swarthmore, one went to Purdue. We'd get nothing but books for Christmas. That makes me very different from a lot of other black people who don't have this crazy intellectual background. They don't have this network, because people have been denied even the right to education for so long that the network is not there to help you. And I have that; I have a lot of connections. Not that I've used these to get where I am, but having that support has really helped me to extend, to be academically oriented.

My mother never really pushes me to do work. I don't think she could even tell you what classes I'm taking right now. My father calls every week and asks, "How's this class? How's that class?" And again, that may not be race-related, that may be just the personalities of my mother and father.

That's another thing. It's very hard to distinguish whether it's just me as an individual and this is how my family is, or me as an individual and this is how race has affected my family. It's very hard for me to tell the difference because this is the only thing I know. And I'm sure that can be said of a lot of different things within one's life, but that happens to me a lot. I don't know if it was reversed and my father was black, would he still be so interested academically? I don't know if it's my father's personality or if it's my father's race. You can't separate them, so it's really hard to know which is the driving force.

*   *   *

I really became clear about my identity last year when I first arrived at Haverford. We had what we call Tri-College, which brings in freshmen of color and upperclassmen from Bryn Mawr, Swarthmore, and Haverford. You talk about some of the things you're going to face at a predominantly white institution. We did a lot of sociology, a lot of journal entries, and a lot of reflection. That's when I really began to understand where I fit into society. That's when I started doing the most critical analysis of my identity. It was two weeks long at the end of the summer, right before you get here. And they want to make it so you have a network, because there's not a lot of people of color on each campus.

At Tri-College, you're split up into groups: Asian-American, African-American, and Latino. My freshman year, there were only three biracial women, and we all just went into the black category. I mentioned it to someone, and they just blew me off and threw me in the black category. This year, when I worked as one of the student resource people at Tri-College, there were so many more biracial people, people were like, "Hey, can we have a biracial group for just a second?"

There were about fifteen of us, and we sat down. Each group was supposed to present themselves to the rest of the Tri-College. And we were like, "What are we going to do? We could split ourselves in half. . . ." We sat there thinking and thinking. And then we were like, "Let's think about what it means to be biracial." We started getting into this conversation about all the terrible things: You're torn between this and that, you don't know what to do, you don't know where you fit in, you're marginalized, going on and on.

Then the conversation switched—this was the most amazing day of my life—the conversation totally switched over. People were like, "*But*, with two cultures you have your way into this and you have your way into that, you get to have all these great experiences because you get introduced to so many different things." Everyone picked up on it and was like, "Yeah, I never thought about this and that." We weren't concentrating on our presentation at all.

This was a mixture of all kinds of people, and none of us

looked alike; it didn't seem like we'd have any kind of common bond—and it was really uplifting for everyone.

Then everyone's like, "So what are we going to do?" I looked around, and there's this one guy who's going to be a freshman at Swarthmore, and I said, "It looks like someone in our group does feel as happy as we do."

This kid was basically bawling because he was saying he never really identified with his side of ethnicity and he basically can pass. He's half-Asian and half–European-American and he really had never considered it. He didn't have any Asian friends, and it really hit home, I guess. He was really going through a lot of emotion, and it was really a lot for him to grasp. He looked like he was going through an identity criris right then and there.

But it was also a good thing because he really came out learning a lot. And I'm happy if Tri-College made one person understand themselves a little bit better. And when it came time for our presentation, we went and stood in line, all kind of hugging, and we each said about one sentence. This one girl said something like, "When people ask what race you are, you're part of the human race." That's the same cheesy thing my parents used to tell me when I was little. They wouldn't choose for me. I'd go to my parents and say, "What race am I?" And they'd say, "The human race." Basically, it was, "Figure it out for yourself, Joy, and get back to us later."

The multiracial group on this campus started last year with four other people, two women who are half-Asian and half-European and a biracial boy who is half-black and half-white; his father is from Kenya. We tried to get it started up, and it's been kind of mixed. Sometimes we get a lot of people, sometimes we don't get that many. Sometimes we're talking about emotions, sometimes we're talking about organization. We're kind of in the formation period right now; it's going to be interesting to see where it goes.

One thing we're trying to do is get the [race] question changed on our admissions application, because right now it has five or six categories and it says choose one, then it has a dash and says other. We've been trying to figure out what we want to do. If you write biracial, then you'd have "I'm Jewish and I'm dah-dah-dah-dah." Some people might have more than just two. Maybe just take off the "check one," so if you wanted, you could check black *and* check white. That's what I've been doing all my life. I've had to recode tests because it messed up the computer. That was me being an obnoxious little kid, too. There are certain times I'll choose, and I'll choose black if need be. For my college application I might have checked black. The pressure to not mess up my application was more than my identity at that time. But all of my essays were written about being biracial, so it was obvious that my point was coming across.

But my participation in the group is not so much about things like forms. At first it was interesting to hear other people's stories. They were really intriguing to me. It seems like almost all biracial people have them. I realize that I've been fortunate because my parents' families get along and are accepting of us. But I know that other families are not, and for them it's still very much a faux pas. I really want to know what we can do so other people don't have to go through it.

Jimmy Pierre

Age: 35

Residence: Oakland, California

Occupation: Construction worker

Jimmy Pierre's parents met in Los Angeles when his father came to work as a presser for his mother's dry-cleaning business. Both were married to others at the time, but eventually divorced and married each other, driving to Mexico for the ceremony because they couldn't marry in California. His mother is white, from Wichita, Kansas, and his father, who died in 1988, was black and from Louisiana. After they married, his parents relocated to Oakland, where Pierre grew up.

After he was born, his mother's sister told her to leave him behind "with his people" and come home. "To this day I have never, ever seen one of my mother's relatives, not one," he says.

Pierre says that when he was five his parents both went to jail. His mother has told him it was for stealing food. They were gone six months, during which time a neighbor took Pierre in and cared for him. At the age of seven, he started to get flak from neighborhood kids about being so light-skinned, having light green eyes, and curly hair. They called him "white boy," often in the context of saying, "Let's go get the white boy." When he could get away with it, he would tell people that his mother, who is ethnically Welsh, was Mexican. His father was distant; both parents drank. "My dad I didn't care about, but my mother, she would always make sure that I had whatever I needed: money, clothes, so on and so forth. But the drinking really sent me off the wild end. I couldn't stand my mother when she was drinking because she was intolerable, she just was uncontrollable."

Pierre found that he was best accepted by older boys, and then by older men. At fourteen he tagged along with a thirty-year-old man who was a pimp and a drug dealer, who would take Pierre with him to watch while he had sex with women. The man introduced Pierre to drugs, shooting him up with heroin. By the time Pierre turned fifteen, he was addicted. In 1986, when Pierre was serving time in the county jail, he became devoutly religious. He has since been trying to stay clean—sometimes lapsing—and he has completed a manuscript, "Why Say No to Drugs: Because Jimmy Didn't," which he hopes will educate school-age readers to the dangers of substance abuse.

Coming up, I had been ashamed for a long time that I was interracial. I used to do drugs so that I wouldn't have to think about it. When I do drugs, I don't think about nothing but just being high. But then I got stuck on the drugs to the point where they weren't just there to hide the shame I felt for who I was, but because I liked them.

I was a heroin addict for eight years, and I got off heroin through cocaine. I got sick one time and did some coke, and I haven't done heroin since. But coke was more a monster than heroin was. That used to be my whole thing, just all I think about. Now I don't even think about it, and I'm growing out of it a little bit. Sometimes, if I get some money in my pocket, I get restless and I'll do it, but, God willing, I'll continue to recover.

                              *   *   *

For years, I would not identify with myself as being an interracial child. Of course I was raised in a black community, all my upbringings were black, but television pretty much raised me. I was always keyed in on the TV, so that I can say television pretty much educated me about the world, current events, and so on and so forth. Even though I was in a black culture, I was still a media child.

The media was black, white, Chinese, Latin, and everything, so I feel as though as a person I became well-rounded. No one is different. We are all human beings, even though we're black, white, Chinese, Japanese, or whatever. We are all human beings and are able to communicate with each other in terms of being reasonable. A lot of people will say, "Oh, no, I can't talk with him, he's a black guy." "Oh, no, I can't talk with him, he's a white guy." "I don't fool with niggers." "I don't fool with Mexicans," so on and so forth. That's a fallacy. We are all human beings, and I would hate to think that God made us all the same, made you the same, me the same. Then we wouldn't even have to look in the mirror. I'd just look at you and say, "Oh, there I am." What God did in terms of making all different nationalities is a beautiful thing because it's what makes the world go around today.

My mother—sometimes I have to get away from her because she says things that really insult me, even to this day—she never identified with me as being an interracial child. She always identified me as being her child and her being a white woman, then that's the way it was for her: I was a white child. She was married to a black man, but yet she was still prejudiced. And even though she got along well with black people, she would say things to me like, "Why don't you be like my people and not like your father's?" She would be grinding on me about nothing in particular, just about the way she wanted me to dress and the way she wanted me to wear my hair, things she wanted me to do. I wouldn't really hear it until she became drunk, and then she would use that nigger word. It would be *"nigger this"* and *"nigger that,"* and *"those niggers this"* and *"those niggers that."*

I had a lot of hardship in my life because of being an interracial child, because of my mother's interracial marriage to my dad. They

were always going through problems, and my father never wanted
to be seen out with us; he kind of had a problem with it, too,
because he never would take us nowhere. I've never had family. I
never had no cousins, no uncles, none of that. All the people that
I have had are people that have adopted me or I have adopted into
my life, so I never knew family. And that was hard. I always
wanted to know, "How come Mama don't ever take me and introduce me to my uncles and my aunties? How come my daddy
don't never take me to introduce me to my aunts, my uncles,
cousins, something?" That shit was hard. I mean, that shit was
difficult. So when people would bring me into their family stuff, I
loved it, but there would still always be that little part of me that
felt like, "Hmm, you're an outsider."

But I always identified with black people because I've always
gotten along with anybody and anybody. I don't make a difference
with nobody. You know, we all have come up in cultures, we have
different ways of being and carrying ourselves, but I recognize that
in all people, and it's never made a difference. You treat me right,
I'm going to treat you right.

I had a few white friends, but to this day I can't say that I have
one white friend I could pick up the phone and call right now and
say, "Hey, how's it going, guy? I haven't seen you in a long time,"
or something like that, because primarily all my life I've been
raised in the black culture, and all my friends have been black. And
on a professional level, I worked in black families and in black
businesses, primarily.

I have an ex-girlfriend, she was telling me, "You're not mulatto, you're black."

I said, "No, I'm not." I said, "I'm a mulatto," which means
a mixture of colors in Spanish. She really had a hard time dealing
with that. She had a hard time dealing with my mother, too, because every time we'd get in an argument, she'd talk about my
mother being an old white this or that, which brought a lot of
resentment to me, because I don't make no difference to nobody.
We're all people, we're all human beings, we come from the
same creator. But to my ex-girlfriend, how I identified was important because she didn't want to be involved with someone
who had white in him. I think she's prejudiced. I'm not involved
with her anymore. But I think that was primarily what it was.

And it caused a lot of problems because of my mother being a white woman. It doesn't make no difference to me if she's purple—she's my mother.

I didn't start identifying with who I was until I was nineteen, where I had gotten to the point where people would ask me what I am, and I would tell them, "I'm a mulatto; I'm a mixed child."

It basically came from seeing all the hell my parents had lived through for thirty-four years and how they had stuck together. And I said, "Well, this isn't something I should be ashamed of, this is something I should be proud of because of my parents, even though they had a lot of problems, and they went through a lot of changes." I said, "This is something I should be proud of. I am a mulatto person. This is what I am. And this is how I identify myself." It even got to the point where if I'd go apply for a job and they had down race characterizations, I would draw a square, check it, and write mulatto.

I even had considered starting a mulatto organization, where people of interracial heritage come together and we have different functions and this, that, and the other, because I think it's important. It's just as important as it is to have black functions or white functions or Latin functions. To me it is, as an interracial person.

I answered the ad for this book because I wanted some involvement. Because I'm proud to be mulatto. And I said, "Here's somebody doing something on interracial people, and this is what I want." Because there's not a lot of that going on around the Bay Area, and I just haven't tried to find out about any organizations that are down with mulatto stuff. There's a lot of interracial people, and to me it's just not enough functions involved.

It's not like you just have to make a stand, you know, like it used to be with Black Power? *Black Power! Black Power!*

Mulatto Power! Mulatto Power! There's not a lot of that going on, but I do want to actively be involved with things that have to do with being interracial. I think it's great.

Larene LaSonde
Age: 46
Residence: Decatur, Georgia
Occupation: Law firm administrator

Larene LaSonde grew up in Mount Vernon, New York. She says that for many years she was not clear on her father's racial identity—a combination of Russian Jew, Scot-Irish, and Cherokee. "I was eighteen before I really understood that my father was white," she says. "All the relatives on the Indian side of his family had married black women, so it was easy for them to pass off that my father had some black blood. But he didn't."

Both her parents grew up and met in Mount Vernon, which LaSonde says was too small a community—only four miles square—to create any meaningful segregation between Blacks and Whites. Two of her father's siblings also married black people, and both sides of the family accepted her parents' marriage.

LaSonde's schools varied, from predominantly white to fairly well mixed. Because she is fair-skinned and has wavy hair, she says she got her share of teasing, was called "half-breed" and "pinto" and had her hair pulled and shoes stepped on regularly. To prove herself to the black girls who began to accuse her of stealing their boyfriends, LaSonde became politically active. She started a NAACP youth council and led a three-day school boycott to protest inadequate transportation facilities for black students. "I was so black, I was the blackest person in Mount Vernon," she says. For several years after high school, LaSonde continued to organize sit-ins, more boycotts, and helped develop a welfare-rights organization, sitting on the local Urban League board.

"My politics had to be better than anybody else's," LaSonde explains, "[and] my ethics had to be in place because I was never trusted. I had to be surer of my facts than anybody else. I probably started out trying to prove that I had value to that community. Now I do it just because it's right, it's the appropriate thing to do. I don't have to prove it anymore, I don't have to prove anything to anybody anymore."

The expertise she developed has helped her in her current efforts to

organize on multiracial issues. "I believe we are the special people," she
says. "We're where everybody's trying to get."

She has formed a social-support network in the Atlanta area, circu-
lated a questionnaire on racial identity for biracial people, and had col-
lected forty-six responses by the time we met. When asked if they would
change their race, she reports that 90 percent of the respondents wrote that
they would, choosing one side or the other, but all declined to say which they
would choose. Most also noted that they experienced emotional stress as a
consequence of being biracial.

LaSonde is active in efforts to get racial classification forms changed,
and hopes to establish a research institute that will investigate health issues
for biracial people.

I choose to call myself mulatto. Why? There's passion in
it, and you know what my politics are immediately. And if I say
it in public, people know that I am prepared to defend the
position.

The first time I heard the term used in something other than
a negative way was when I got married to my second husband. He
called me mulatto, and it wasn't patronizing. He found a poster of
a woman, and it said "Octaroon" over the top. He had it beautifully
framed and gave it to me.

I had accumulated hundreds of black history books over the
years, and so I started to review them and find the mulatto, find out
where she came from. I spent the next five years doing that self-
imposed study, and as I discovered her—and him, but particularly
her, for me—I realized that the term *mulatto* had been given a bad
rap, that there were places in society where a mulatto actually had
a structured presence, a relationship to the community, a relationship to government.

Leon Higginbotham [a senior circuit judge on the U.S. Court
of Appeals, Third Circuit, and a law professor] writes about the
laws regarding interracial marriages and the first interracial child,
how the tone and tenor changed so that there was a time when
white fathers actually identified with their children. Then it became impractical, since you're in the business of selling bodies.
You can't afford to give any preference to any one body, even if it's
your own flesh. A mulatto has a right to their white parentage, and
I can see there's been a bad rap given mulatto children who actually

wanted to know their fathers and the benefits of training under
their fathers. They come into the world with whatever DNA that
comes from their father. Why should they not have a right to it? But
when you see the writings, it was presumed that they were striving
for something beyond themselves.

As I started to read that, I got mad, and my study became
more intense and I took it further. I started writing about what I
was feeling, and I got some pieces included in small publications.
I wanted to start developing a body of research towards a book,
because there's not the research that would give us any statistics
that are really usable. Then I hit on this issue of us really being
invisible people. We *are* Ralph Ellison's invisible man.

There's no information about us; those statistics you see are
pulled out of hats. They don't know how many interracial marriages there are because people still don't declare themselves,
and if my questionnaire responses are correct, there are biracial
people who have not even considered themselves biracial. And
how many people have already crossed the color line? Ashley
Montagu [an anthropologist who wrote *Man's Most Dangerous
Myth: The Fallacy of Race* (1964) and *Race and IQ* (1975)] said he
believed that from the early 1940s forward there were about five
thousand to ten thousand crossing the color line every year. How
many people are over on the other side of the fence? Is it possible that if we gave them an option of being what they really
are, they would actually come forward? I don't know, but that is
a goal.

Forgive me, but I don't think you're going to get that in
the interviewing of individuals. See, I have always been so aggressive; I want to get to as many as possible as quickly as possible. If we start giving them support that there is somebody
actually interested in statistical gathering and disease factors and
longevity, maybe then they'll say, "Well now, rather than more
tragic mulattos, there are millions more like me," and "I got that
problem, too," and, "Yeah, we're pretty much generally like
that." If they can start seeing themselves, if presented with a
mirror that fits, we'll get a lot more people coming forward. Two
and three people are showing up every month inquiring about our
group.

It has also been a very interesting process to me to see who came forward and why, and taking the time to talk with them individually has been really, really important to me. They call me all the time: "When's our next meeting? Are we going to have a picnic *and* a meeting in August?"

"Oh, come on, give me a break, do we have to do both?"

"Yes, we need both."

I'm interested in health issues because nobody's ever asked, and because very specifically, I think that a race of people that are identified by their health issues have an identity.

I'm asking, I think, reasonable questions. I want to know how long we live? If a psychiatrist like Alvin Poussaint [who collected identity data from thirty-four biracial Harvard University students and staff in 1984] has so much information that he can describe for me my psyche, and he's a doctor, why wouldn't he take it to the next level and say, "Okay, these people are different, maybe negative, but different, and if they're different there, where else are they different?" I would be satisfied. I wouldn't be satisfied, but you could say to me, "Okay, I have checked all this out and there's no difference. Except for the stress factor, except for the possibility that they have some better opportunities and it's easier for them to get through certain doors, there's no real difference." I'd probably say, "Bullshit, that shouldn't be." But I need to be satisfied. Prove it to me.

I watch a lot of PBS and a lot of *Discovery,* and the most inane studies you have ever heard of are actually funded. Yet you've got millions of people in this country for whom there is not a piece of information that's of any relevance in 1992.

If I can get funding for a health study, my first priority is biracial black and white. If I've got any control over the money, that's who's going to get studied first. That is also the group I believe this country is quote-unquote beholden to, because there have been so many negative studies done about them. In the period when we were forming our opinion of race identity—and I'm talking about the turn of the century—it was not the relationship between white and Indian that was paramount, it was a concerted effort to reduce the black-white interracial relationships. And in that process, studies were conducted in order to prove that we were less than even our parent group. I mean, if they didn't think black folks were human, they certainly didn't believe we were.

This society has a responsibility to put some money behind refuting some of that. It's never been refuted, the reduced fecundity, the body's misshapedness, and the short lifespan. If they can determine I've got a short lifespan, how come they can't tell me how short that lifespan is? But, all right, I'll say it, I'm going to Prudential Insurance, because they're the ones that funded some of those studies, which are still out there.

But I wonder if we can get new studies funded when the U.S. Census Bureau tells me that the reason there's no information on biracial people is because if they actually broke up those numbers, the impact on Head Start and apportionment would be skewed so badly that the black community would lose, and you don't want to do that to your community, do you?

When I called the U.S. Census Bureau, I got a black woman on the phone who was very, very honest with me. She said, "I'll tell you exactly why it hasn't been done. Because it would skew the statistics and could really impact on the funding the black community depends on for Head Start and on apportionment regarding voting and block-grant monies."

I was very disheartened with that notion; it raised this cloud of guilt. Should I pursue this issue? Could I wind up being the reason some poor little black kids aren't going to get Head Start monies? Is that realistic? And I haven't gotten an answer to that, but I decided to press on anyway.

I have a friend in Guyana, who said that in Guyana they saw the problem as so acute, they wiped out race completely. Everybody was Guyanese, no race at all. That is not a reality here, I don't think, in my lifetime. Maybe in my grandchildren's time, but it's not a reality in this lifetime, and I gotta deal in realities.

It's my belief that all groups ought to have some kind of identification links, but this society particularly owes something to biracial black and white. Number one, because it made their parents' relationships illegal. And it drew black people into the conspiracy by talking about race pride, and race pride did not include sleeping with white men or white women. So if all we're suffering is emotional distress at this point, it is linked back to that time. It wasn't something we brought upon ourselves; it was society's racism. It is the last vestige of slave racism. The one-drop theory, if you think about it, clearly is the last vestige of the slave codes; it's the only law left that is still enforceable, if not by statute, by pattern and practice. I have black professors at Atlanta University who took that position. "You've got a drop of black blood, you're black."

I said, "You're quoting a slave code!" *Code noir* is what it was originally called—the black code. Quoting a slave code to me! I'm not denying that drop of black blood, but I am not going to be dictated to by it. Absolutely not.

My brother made this statement twenty years ago: "I am just going to sit on the fence until you all join me." And he's right. I have finally joined him, and it's not a rejection of either one; it's a different fence.

Setting up controls for the studies I want to do will be a little tricky, since the black parent, at least, is likely to have some Native American or white ancestry. But in fact, De Kalb County issues a status on health every year, and in that pamphlet, you can look down a list of those diseases that kill white people, and on another page you can look down a list of those diseases that kill black people. Now when they did those studies, they did not say to the black community, "You've got all these race groups, and so we're going to have to skew this study in order to include all your race groups." They listed them as black. There's got to be some way that I can at least look at people who are majority black parent/majority white parent.

I was wondering: On the average, are biracial men tall? Are they short? How many children do biracial women generally have? These are questions for the regular community, but nobody associates them with us, and yet there are millions of us who don't fit in either category. I cannot look with any integrity at a list of diseases that kill white folks and a list of diseases that kill black folks and know where I fit.

At least we could begin with that information. Eventually, you can expand into greater complexities. My grandfather's father, the Indian, lived to be a hundred and four. Am I going to live that long? My black grandmother is going to be eighty-six, and everybody says she's going to put us all in the grave. I'd like to know if I've got any of that. My white grandmother, my Russian-Jewish grandmother, died of multiple myelomas. What do those factors mean to me? What do I draw from either one of these parent groups? Do I have a lesser propensity to sickle-cell anemia because of the Russian Jew or because of the Native American? What percentage caps it? What crosses the line? I don't want to get into that whole hybrid issue of superior versus inferior. That's not the goal. I just want to know how much of the white, how much of the black creates someone who has immune factors.

One reason we are at this problem in 1992—and there has been so little to address this problem thus far—is because the job of protecting these children should have rested with the parents. But given the precariousness of their own circumstances, the parents were loathe to bring attention to their relationship. They knew what they were going to hear: "Hey, you made that bed, you had that choice." Yes, they had choices, but we don't have any choice. We are born what we are, and we had no protector because parents didn't have any way to protect their children. There wasn't an institution. Even within their own families they could not protect the biracial child. Look at the parents who don't tell the truth to members of their family regarding these children. You can hide your husband, you can hide your wife, but you can't hide that kid. At some point in time the kid is going to surface. Maybe as this is developing, my approach and my focal point should be the parents, should be the stress that they're under, their history, and how they can best help their children. Maybe that's the way I ought to go, except I've got this tribe that I can't lose and don't want to lose.

One woman I've talked to keeps coming to the group, but I'm not sure we've gotten to the stage where all her questions have been answered. She's always seen herself as a black woman, and I said, "But you're multiracial," and she said, "Yeah, I'm beginning to understand that." And that is what getting this information out is about, and that is why I don't have a choice but to do this, because if nothing else, it's making it easier for the next generation to self-identify, and make choices based on the comfortability with that self-identification.

Marpessa Outlaw
(See also page 198)

Although her mixed racial heritage has caused her problems over time, setting her apart from neighborhood kids and classmates as she was growing up, Marpessa Outlaw has come to see it as having certain advantages as well. "In a way, now I'm kind of glad for what my upbringing was because I feel like it exposed me to a lot of things. I feel like I've done a lot of things firsthand, not just from reading a book or something. Most of the black people I know, for instance, can't say that they have a white person in their immediate family, so they have just a different way of looking at some things."

I think sometimes those networks are a way of not dealing with issues. I hate the idea of it being like a cheerleading organization. For some reason it just feels a little embarrassing. I don't even know that I would get along with those people. I don't feel the compulsion to join one, even though I like finding people with whom I share that background—nor do I want to go back to Africa. The networks strike me as a bunch of people who are whining a little bit. It's hard to say those things, because I don't know if it's an excuse to be an exception to a rule—that's what it strikes me as. But I also don't think other people can blindly say, "Don't talk about it because it's not important." It's a very hard line to travel. It's probably a way of being accepted and finding people who are like you, and that's a supportive thing, but I think it can be a cause for some people to avoid more painful issues. The problems do not go away, the problems of how you are perceived or how you perceive yourself do not go away because you joined a club, I guess. I don't know. Like I said, I just don't think there's any rules about anything.

When people say, "Oh, you think you're different, blah-blah-blah," well, you *are* different, but so what? It goes back to that "you think you're better than us" kind of thing and it doesn't necessarily have to be that way.

I still get that, in certain ways. And then I can do it myself. It all depends on how someone else talks about it. I can be equally annoyed if I hear someone say, before you even ask them, "My mother's Scotch, English, Russian, blah-blah-blah, and my father's black and Indian, da-da-da."

It's just too precious; it's like the person is trying to show how unique they are. It irks me. Laying that all out on the table first thing is just kind of naive. And it doesn't necessarily tell me what kind of person you are, either.

However, when I hear other people talk about people who do that, who come across to them that way, I feel defensive for the [biracial] person, like, "You don't really understand, you're just getting annoyed because you're from black folks and they're from black folks and you're seeing this [biracial] person and you just think that she's too cute. You don't really know what any of that means except what you think you know." So I can go back and forth, but I'm equally alerted by people who will either pretend that none of that matters or who make it matter too much.

Bernette Ford
(See also page 207)

Bernette Ford has never thought of identifying as other than black. "My mother took me to see Imitation of Life, *and I was probably quite young," she says. The movie, made first in 1934 and then remade in 1959, is a wrenching tearjerker that follows two women, one white and one black, and their daughters. The black mother, devoted to her child, is terrifically betrayed when the daughter chooses to pass for white. "I cried," Ford says. "I cry at everything. I cry at a commercial if it's very sentimental. I couldn't see how that girl could have tried to pass; I couldn't understand how she could have."*

I asked Ford—who is very fair-skinned and often assumed to be Jewish—why she didn't think of herself as passing for black.

"No one has ever asked me that question. I've often teased my father and told him that he's trying to pass for black, but he doesn't have black blood. Because . . . because in my family there are people as light as me who are not the result of mixed marriages."

What I'm hearing and what I've read in a couple of articles recently is that young people now in college almost want to define themselves as mixed-race people; they want to have a race that's different from black and that's different from white or that's different from Asian, and it's not my experience. My experience is an identification with the black race.

This movement makes me uncomfortable because I think the races are so mixed anyway, especially the black race. I don't think you can have a spin-off race. It seems a way of protecting yourself, perhaps, from some of the pain without really having a reason politically or personally to do it. It's like in the seventies when people were always T-grouping [therapy-grouping].

Maybe that's good. I don't really know. But it doesn't work for me. The race situation in this country is so complicated, so serious, that it diverts attention from the serious heart of the problems of black people in this country. It's yet another splinter group that doesn't need to splinter off. Although from what I've read, these kids really feel that they are multiracial, that they're not one or the other. And when I grew up I don't think it was possible to feel that way. There was no other choice for us during my generation, but I think [younger] generations have different choices.

In terms of the individual that I am, I think I'm a product of my family and my society. I can't picture myself in a vacuum without all those influences. And I can't picture this country having no race problem, so I can't picture the ideal, or the utopia for me or for my kid.

My nuclear family was really circumscribed by what society dictated. I can't tell you whether my parents would have preferred to have lived in a white neighborhood, because they couldn't have lived in a white neighborhood at that time, at least not comfortably and without worrying all the time. They chose to live in a black neighborhood. They really chose to raise us as black children because they thought that's the way society would perceive us. I think my parents were very much aware of what they were doing. Most people who go into interracial marriages have personal issues they're working through, maybe rebellion against a family. I don't believe it happens by accident; I think people find each other, [that] there are connections and symbiotic things that happen between people who fall in love. In particular there are probably issues of identity for people who get together in an interracial relationship, because at least when my parents got married it wasn't acceptable.

I've had a very great, tight-knit, close group of black friends who I've known since college, and so I was protected from ever having to experience much rejection or attention for being so light-skinned. When I was in junior high school, I can remember a black girl saying to me, "You're so light you think you're good." I heard that maybe once or twice when I was growing up.

My daughter has been told by black kids in our neighborhood, which is a fairly mixed section of Brooklyn, that she thinks she's white because she's light. It's very painful to her, but I think that's always been around; it's kind of a given. My mother told me that might happen [to me], so I was prepared. I think she probably armed me, saying, "That's gonna hurt you but you'll be okay."

To my daughter, I say, "They're ignorant. They don't know anything. Don't pay any attention to them." But it doesn't help. Nothing you think will be helpful is helpful when you're raising your own child, 'cause everything you think to say that sounds good to you doesn't help. You have to live it yourself. They have to live it themselves. You can't protect them from pain.

What my mother told me probably didn't protect me from pain at the time, but it armed me for getting through the pain and feeling okay about myself.

On a certain level I have a feeling of ease in situations where other people might not, but I also have a feeling of dis-ease too. I've often been in cabs where the cab driver assumed I was white and was taking me home to Brooklyn where I live in a black neighborhood, and he's said, "How could you live here?" and things like that.

I say, "This is my neighborhood and this is where I live." If they get me into conversation, I usually have fun with it. Sometimes I tell them that I'm black and sometimes I don't. It depends on the person.

When white people say something really racist in front of me and I can tell they think I'm white, sometimes I say something and sometimes I don't. It depends on how strong I feel, because it is so powerful a feeling that I'm afraid I'll cry or not say something people will listen to.

I wouldn't want to change my background. It's made me what I am, and I'm happy with the way I am. I'm not happy with everything, but I feel as if I'm lucky, as if I had a lucky family. I feel as if I had two really good parents.

CHAPTER XIV

The Next Generation

Just like I had no sexual preference for my kids, I have no racial preference for them, because I wanted my children to find their own milieu. I know that sounds incredible, but the fact is they have to come to terms with the world like I came to terms with the world.—Sandy Lowe, p.244

My best friend is biracial, and we both feel the same way, this fear of having white kids. We don't want white kids, and I'm not talking about skin color, I'm talking about kids who don't have a good sense of being part black, and I think that's really important to both of us. It would make me really, really sad if my kids didn't grow up with being black as part of their identity.—Eliza Dammond, p.155

As you get older, you begin to think about marriage in a little bit more serious way, and I wonder what it's going to be like for the kids, and how my decision of who I marry may impact them and their identity. I still don't know what to make of it, and when all is said and done, it's going to happen with the person I want to marry, but it's going to be something I'm going to have to think about. I suppose the best possible scenario would be to marry an Irish-Nigerian, so that I could cast a little monster in my image. I joke sometimes that I'm going to marry a South American–Asian, so that my child can check every box on every application. Ethnicity! Yes!

I view my life as, not a struggle so much, but certainly some type of quest to balance. Anything I would do to tip that balance and to upset the balance and to put children in a position where they could not balance would be something that I would have to think about. I'm told kids choose to do what they want to do anyway, and I'm sure that's exactly what will happen, but I would want to do everything I could to impart what my life has been like and why it's a good thing, and why it's a strength and something that has been good for me.—Adebowale Adegbile, p.256

My sister is married to a white man who's Swiss. She's very fair, and he's very fair, so the kid is almost devoid of hue. But there's a little bit in there. That's all we need! She can be in the revolution! The next of the leaders!—Michael Mayson, p.229

There was never any question for me. I've never been attracted to white men. I don't like them as far as dating. People have encouraged me, since the number of black men available is so small—I just have no attraction. There's nothing I can do to relate to them. I have a new co-worker who I would say is a cool white boy. But since I'm still in child-bearing age, I would never marry anybody other than someone black because I would never have a mixed child. It's too hard. The society is too racist, the parents don't know how to deal with it. It was very hard for my mom to come to grips with, that her parents never accepted my brother and I, nor the marriage.

Personally, I think kids who are from a mixed black-white union, and the mom's black, are better adjusted. Because the mother knows they're black, the mother knows how they're going to be dealt with in society and can prepare them. My mother, she couldn't view me as a black kid, and so that was really hard. I

think my brother and I are crazier than other kids. I really do. I
don't know a lot where there's a black mother and a white father.
*   If mixed kids are raised white, they have a hard time when*
they find out they're niggers. Society is just too racist. I would
never do it to a kid. I am not against interracial marriages, I'm
just against them having children. Some of those little kids don't
want to be black. And I think it's hard, because they're going to be
black when they get out into society.—René Rambo, p.109

At no point in people's lives are their feelings about race and being biracial in America likely to emerge in greater clarity than when they contemplate having children. As they prepare to become parents themselves, biracial people think about their own parents—what they did right and what they did wrong. All the concerns captured throughout this book converge on the biracial parents-to-be as they plan on how to protect their children from the pressures, risks, and assaults of the world. As parents themselves, what will they teach their children about race? How supportive and welcoming will the extended family be? Where should the new family live? What schools will be good for their child? All parents face these quandaries; for biracial people, who may have come to find even the most innocuous situations transformed into racial testing grounds, those same questions are even more portentous.

The people in this chapter can be split up into two groups: those who are thinking ahead to when (or whether) they will have children and those who have children now. In both cases, people are vastly influenced by their own upbringing and their experiences with race. These factors help determine who they will have children with and how much of their own experience will be helpful as their children inevitably face the puzzles of race.

After all the work biracial people may have done to sort through the crossed wires and mixed signals given out about race, how much of their findings and solutions can they hand down to their children? Does all that work have to be done over again? Or, as it was for many biracial people and their parents, is the child's experience always going to be fundamentally different from the parents'? Does the unrelenting march of time—the inevitable shifts in social and political concerns from generation to generation—

necessarily dictate a constant reinvention of racial identity? If that is, in fact, the natural order, then what do biracial parents have to offer their children?

Some biracial people see their own identity as an object lesson on the possibilities of integration and racial harmony. They are a living model of a barrier-free world. Others, having found their way with no one's help, expect their children will have to do the same. Still others have found, from their own lives, reason to uphold convention, repeated demonstrations of why it is easier, better, or more correct to keep a line between the two racial groups—a clear, hard, fast line.

To some extent, as the number of biracial people increases in this country, the choices they make about how to raise their children and how to influence their children's attitudes toward race will help determine not just how future generations of biracial children will be welcomed or shunned by society at large but also how all Americans will view and value race into the next century.

Nya Patrinos
(See also page 134)

Nya Patrinos says she doesn't remember her parents talking about race when she was growing up. "I read a book a few years ago about mixed-race children," Patrinos says, "and it talked about parents who try to pretend like there's no racism, and that's sort of my parents. Now, I'm doing revisionist history of my childhood, but there were really no racial problems. We lived in a mixed neighborhood, I went to mixed schools, all their friends were mixed couples—not all but a lot of them—and it was so normal. Everything was thought out; the world was like that. And then I started finding out when I got older that this wasn't the world, and I was really mad, because I wish my family had said, "Okay, this is a really racist society."

Patrinos says parents shouldn't tell this to a child who's too young to understand, but that parents should prepare children for a world that "isn't always nice." At the very least, parents should tell their children that

racist neighborhoods exist. "It doesn't mean you have to take 'em there,"
she says.

It's really important that I grew up in a mixed neighborhood.
It would have been *horrible* if I had grown up in an all-white neighborhood, like when I went to an all-white school for a while. But
you need that perspective. You need to know there's something
else out there. Knowing about racism would have made me less
vulnerable to some of the things I had to face, because I had
rose-colored glasses. When things happened that were very racist,
I was shocked and crushed because I just didn't think the world
was like that. I thought the world was just very mixed and very
happy to be that way. Which maybe a part of the world is, but not
much of it.

I don't think I'll be ready to have kids for a while. Maybe by
the time my boyfriend's ready I'll be ready. Also, racially, I would
worry. I don't want my kids to—this is so terrible—I don't want my
kids to be white, and he's white, and I'm so light. . . . I think if we
have kids I might want to adopt them. I'd probably like to adopt
interracial kids because I don't want to have white children. Not
that I don't like white people or whatever, but first of all, there's so
many black children or interracial children who need to be adopted.
People don't want them because people want white babies, so I
would hope to do something like that, because they never knew
where to put interracial children. There were big things in the
seventies that they didn't want to give them to white families. I
have friends who were adopted by white families, and I think it
would be good as an interracial person to adopt interracial kids.
After my brother and I got older, our parents were thinking about
adopting interracial kids, because they felt like they had the experience of doing that.

If I did have kids with my boyfriend, it wouldn't mean that I
wouldn't love them or I wouldn't be able to be a good parent for
them, but I think it would be hard for them to understand what it
means to be African-American. In some ways when I was little I
didn't want to be African-American. I would have wished so much
that I could have passed for white and I could have been white and
that I wouldn't have to deal with any of those things. But I'm glad

of being African-American and the fact that I'm dark—or not that I'm dark but I couldn't pass—means that I had a lot of experiences just because of the way I looked. I had to live my life a certain way, and I'm glad of that. I'm glad that I have to live as an African-American woman. It's made me much more of a thinking person. So many things I could take for granted, I don't take for granted. Even my father, who's white, he says to me, "I don't really live as a white person anymore."

I laughed when he said that, but then I started thinking about it, and it's like, how could he, really? Because he has three African-American children: two mixed children and my sister is African-American. He's raised us all and his wife is African-American. He has to deal with and has seen so many things, and I'm sure he has gotten a lot of shit at times for his life. I don't think he looks at the world the way somebody would who hadn't gone through that. He has a real insider perspective of an African-American person. How could he not?

If I had children who could pass for white, I would be afraid that they would want to put me away in the closet and not want me to come to school or something like that. I have to really think that out some more, because the more I talk about it in talking to you, it just, I have to think about it, looking at your white face and knowing that, you know, you're a good person and you can have some connection.

Heidi Durrow
Age: 22
Residence: New York, New York
Occupation: Journalism graduate student

Perhaps because of her familiarity with journalism, Heidi Durrow was much more concerned than other people I spoke to about what was on or off the record and how her comments would be used. "I just want to say that whatever I say, yes, that is what I believe," she said. "But that's also what I believe today, February 28, 1992. I know it's not what I believed ten years ago; I don't know if it's what I'll believe ten weeks from now or ten years from to-day. Hopefully I'll grow and change and maybe my ideas won't change, but maybe they will."

Durrow's mother is Danish and her father is African-American, from Portland, Oregon. They met on a German military base, where he was stationed and she worked as a nanny. Durrow says they planned to marry in South Carolina, his next assignment, but state laws still prohibited interracial marriages there, and so they were married in Denmark instead, in 1965.

As a young child, Durrow lived in Europe and Turkey. The day she turned eleven, she moved to Portland with her mother and two brothers, one older and one younger. Her father's plan was to serve two more years in the South, visit Portland often, and then retire from the service and join the family.

When we moved to Portland, the marriage broke up. My mother took care of all three of us. She was a woman who'd never had a job in her life, not as an adult and definitely not as someone who was going to support three kids. She went to Portland Community College and worked part-time, and we were on welfare and we lived in a poor black neighborhood in northeast Portland. And that's when we became colored, I think.

Before that, I had no idea that I was black, that there was such a thing. I remember going into the elementary school, and people thought I was so strange. I had lived in all these different places when they had always lived in Portland. They may have moved a couple blocks away or something like that, but they'd always been in northeast Portland.

They thought I looked very different and they thought I talked very different because I talked white and that was very strange. I had no idea people talked the way these black kids talked. I had long hair like I have now. I had these big green-blue eyes, and so it was sort of a fascination. I don't remember having a sense of being biracial before that.

I spoke Danish at home, and at school I listened to kids who used black English, which I just thought was the most ignorant thing I'd ever heard. I didn't have the awareness at that time that it was a dialect and it has rules and a system—things I only actually learned in college.

And I wanted to be just me. I'm sure you've heard that a lot. Everybody who's biracial: "I just want to be me. I don't want to be black or white." But you have that pull, you have that tug. And you have to be something because people look at you and they know you're brown-skinned. And although you don't have nappy hair and you do have light eyes, you're still black to them. You don't look white. So that's when things got strange.

I remember in high school my mom was working at the bookstore a block away from school. I had a very good friend who's white, and she knew my mother and she'd seen her in the store and at plays because we did theater together. One day I said something about my mother being Danish and she said, "Your mother is Danish?" I said "Yes," and she said, "Oh, my gosh, all this time I thought she was black."

It's just amazing how people get into this mind-set of thinking what you are when you're not really. My mother does go to tanning salons—she's going to have skin cancer—and she has a permed hairdo, but she doesn't look black. She looks like a white woman who goes to tanning salons and perms her hair.

But I thought that was a very telling moment—that people don't always see all there is to see. I think that's what happened to me through all those years: The white people saw that she speaks well, she's smart, she's the only one that's in our advanced-placement classes—white enough. The black people saw that she's brown, she lives in the ghetto like we do—she's black. It's that easy for them. People see what they want to see, and then they'll claim you. Not claim you, but label you. Because it's not really about claiming you. The white people don't want you around. You're not really white. I'm not saying it's a maliciousness involved at all. It's just there's an awareness that you are different. And for Blacks—and it's not for all Blacks—there's sort of this feeling that yeah, she is black and yes, we'll call her black, but she's not black like we are. Everybody knows you're having a different experience. You're just trying to say, "Yes, I am just me. I am having this different experience, but God, I want to belong somewhere. And if I'm in this limbo, then where am I?"

I didn't belong. I was an outsider. I was in these advanced-placement classes and I talked to the white students who were in the class, but they weren't friends, they weren't good friends. I was recognized by the black community as an outstanding black student, of course. That used to upset me, that they would claim me because I did well academically, but I wasn't a part of their world. I don't know how much of that had to do with the type of black people around. I wasn't around middle-class black folks; I was around urban, lower-middle-class, poor black kids who, at least when I was at the school, didn't have an eye for the academics. And I did. And so I don't know how much that was to blame for me being an outsider as me not exactly being black like they were was to blame. I can't tell anymore.

Being academically oriented was just something I did. No one ever said, "You will do well." I knew how to get A's, and so I did. It was just something that came naturally to me. There are also a lot of other issues that probably should go into this, but then it becomes too big. In my family, we have an issue of alcoholism, and so some of these things that I do as far as achievements go—in recovery books I'm called "the super child," the one who tries to make up for the difficulties in the family by achieving academically. Also, I knew that if I did well in school, I would be able to leave that place and go to a really good school. I was excited by that prospect—I ended up going to Stanford—because I said, "God, if I go to these places, maybe then I'll fit in. Because maybe what's separating me is that I'm intellectual, I'm a scholar. And maybe I can hang with the black people in these universities because obviously they're smart, too. So there won't be a difference and they will accept me."

That didn't happen. To a good extent, it was my own fault. I didn't know how to dance, so I didn't want to go to the parties. I didn't live in Ujamma, the black theme house, and I didn't visit there. I didn't pledge a black sorority. I didn't believe in that, I didn't want to subject myself to that whole pledging thing in the name of sisterhood.

I lived at Ujamma my senior year because I wanted to be around the black people and I thought that would be the best way. That didn't work either, but I gave up on it very early. I don't think it was a matter of people not liking me because I was a biracial person, but because I was simply an outsider to these predetermined circles that they had already formed in three years there. I had a single room, and that worked against me also, because only people I invited in came in.

There is another incident I can tell you about. I was a columnist in my senior year for the *Stanford Daily*. And every Thursday—it was a black day, *Cosby* comes on that day also—that was when my column came out. I wrote about black issues and I got flak for it. Not that I heard, but people would tell me things like, "I heard so-and-so say you didn't have a right to talk about these things because you didn't identify the right way."

I wrote one column that started off something like, "I woulda, coulda, shoulda been a black power activist if it weren't for my hair." It was about looking the part that you play and talking about how I could never be a black power activist because I didn't have dreads and that I should probably be corporate America woman instead, because of the way I look.

The white people I know laughed. They thought it was funny, because it's tongue in cheek, but I didn't get a response from Blacks who read it. I don't think it was positive. And I think it was that week that a friend of mine said, "I overheard so-and-so talking to a group of her friends, and they thought it was inappropriate for you to discuss that."

As far as relationships go, I have always dated black guys, no white guys. People ask me that all the time. I have no sense that a white man would ever be attracted to me. And people don't understand. They're like, "Oh Heidi, you're so beautiful. How could you even think that?"

Because. I don't feel sexual around them. How could I possibly feel sexual around white men? I just don't. I use this example: If I were to walk into a room of black men, for a job interview, ten black men sitting around on chairs, definitely, definitely, someone would pay attention to me. I would feel attractive and sexy. But if I walked into that same room with a bunch of white men, I wouldn't feel that way. I wouldn't even notice if someone was paying attention to me that way.

It wasn't a conscious choice to only date black guys. I found them very attractive, especially the tall black ones. I hate to say this, but I know it was true for guys I went out with in high school, that I was black enough for their parents, for their mothers in particular, but I was white enough for them. I have straight hair, when I blow dry it, and I'm light-skinned.

Sometimes that works against me. I think black women hate me. This is the biggest battle in my life. For the most part, I don't have black women friends. And I don't know for sure why that is. Maybe we just don't have anything in common, although I'm sure we do. I have a feeling that they see me and they have ideas about who I am because of the way I look. I'm also quiet, often, and they might take that as a snobbery, as "I think I'm so pretty because I have all these European features about me and I talk the way I do. I have this long hair that I play with." And it really hurts because—depending on what day you talk to me nowadays—I have, for the most part, identified as a black woman.

That's been the hardest thing of all, of looking the way I do. God, maybe it would have been better if I had been—do I sound conceited if I say that I know I'm an attractive person? I know I'm not ugly. But had I been unattractive and still had the features I have, maybe I would have been more accepted. Maybe not. But that's been the hardest thing. Because I'm down with Anita Hill, she's a fellow sister black woman. Go ahead, girl, you know?

But people don't see that, I think. Black women don't see that I want to be part of that community. And it's naive of me to think that because I say I'm a black woman they will embrace me. Or even this idea that all black women *should* be unified may be naive.

But I think to some extent it's true. There's a common history, a common oppression—this way that we're treated in the world, that should be able to link us and it doesn't.

This week I was rereading an essay by Audre Lorde, a black feminist lesbian writer—I think she's the poet laureate of New York. She wrote an essay called "Eye to Eye," and in it she talks about this rage at black womanness that black women have, that we cannot catch each other's eye when we walk down the street, that we avert the eyes when we see each other, that we judge each other so critically when we don't measure up.

Maybe things will be different for biracial people being born today, but it just doesn't seem fair—I don't think interracial couples are being completely honest with themselves when they say either, "I don't notice this racial difference," or, "It doesn't matter," or, "It's something we can overcome." Race is such a subtle but powerful force in people's lives that they can't even know the ways it affects them and the way they treat each other.

It's upsetting to me that these two people come together—whether they love each other or whatever it is—in ignorance, an ignorance they can't overcome when they have children. And kids grow up like me and we are confused and we are conflicted. And we don't belong. And that is so unfair. I guess I'm bitter. Not toward my parents, but they should have known better, I think. They should have known better. And this is what these racist white fathers say to their white daughters who want to marry black men, but God, there is an amount of truth to it: "What about these kids? How do the kids turn out?"

I'm not like David Duke. I'm not ready to pass laws that say people shouldn't do it, but if I had any power over any human being, if a white friend said to me, "Heidi, I'm dating this black guy, what do you think?" I would say, "I don't think you can do that. And I definitely don't think it would be fair if it ever became serious and you had children."

I know how this sounds, and that's why I had to preface this by saying I don't know that I'll think this way in ten years, but I do right now. It's kind of sick. I think it is sort of a strange perversion. What does it mean? What do I think about myself? I really don't know. I'm not a bad person because of it, but I certainly am a confused person. I don't think it's bad, but it causes so many troubles for me because my parents had this idea they could live in this world and their children could live in this world and everything would be okay.

But we haven't been okay. And we have had problems. Sure, not everyone is as confused about things as I am, but how many other people in the world have to decide who they're going to be? We have to create ourselves. Once we become conscious of being in this world we have to either decide to be what people see us as or we have to decide not to be that—there's a moment of creation. We have to accept the fact that if you look white, then certainly you have to be white in some ways. Because I have this belief that you can only be what people see in you, to some extent.

So yes, I guess I am upset. My parents should have known better. I think it's idealistic to think that everything will be okay. And, of course, everything wasn't okay. They ended up divorcing, and that had to do with a lot of things. Maybe they shouldn't have been together in the first place, but I think race had something to do with that. It's a very strange thing. And I'm thinking about it all the time. My mother is living with a black man again, and I wonder, what is this about? I can't understand it. My fiancé's parents, his mother is black and she's remarried to a white man. I see that relationship and it seems like a very strong and healthy relationship, and that's why I say I'm conflicted, because that seems to work. But, of course, I know they're not having children.

In a way, being biracial has made me special and different, and I revel in that sometimes. I just really do. And I will play it up and let it be theatrical and I will accentuate these things that make me different, like my eyes.

Last night I felt like I was on stage. I was at a really nice restaurant and it was a closing dinner—my fiancé's an investment banker. It happened to be all men on this deal, and they were there with their wives. There were three other black people there, and there was my fiancé, who's black, and myself. And I knew I was on stage because I knew I didn't look like these other three black people who were there. I knew I didn't look like these white women, and I looked so exotic. I put on mascara to accentuate my long lashes and my eyes and made sure I didn't put any curl into my hair with a curling iron so it would be straight. And people were fascinated by me, you know? I played it up because being biracial makes you special, in a way. And people like special sometimes, and they like different. And then you're treated better.

Sometimes I'll make a point to say my mother's not just white. Get that: My mother is white, but she's Danish and guess what, I speak Danish. And people lean forward in their chairs and are so excited to know this special, different person. And I say, "Yes, I eat *frikadeller* and *aebleskiver*." You get to be different.

But on the other hand, that's what makes it so terrible. Because no one else is like you, and you are so alone in this. You have no place. Sure, like I said, you have to decide to be black or be white, just to stay sane, but you don't always feel that way. At one point, I decided I would be black. But I'm not always comfortable because I still want to be special, and I'm still not really black. But it's sort of like, if I don't accept what people see in me, then I'll go crazy. There's too much dissonance. It's really hard. It's really hard that this specialness, by virtue of being biracial, is celebrated, sometimes, and the other times it isolates you and makes you realize how alone you are in your being, in your very identity. And it's scary.

I believe you shouldn't be defined by what people see in you. If someone treats you like a slave, that shouldn't stop you. But we live in a world where you deal with people every day who define you by what they see in you, and oftentimes you cannot get around that. So what do you do? If you don't accept their view and they have that view, there's dissonance. I cannot stay sane in that world. I cannot. There's just no way I can say, "I am this one thing and these people are seeing this other thing in me," and not feel turmoil. In a politically correct world, no one would define you by how you look, and, sure, you shouldn't have to accept that. But you do have to accept that, and, yes, it does create you in a way, how people treat you.

Let's talk about attractiveness. When I was little, I wore an Afro and had big buck teeth with a big gap. I looked like a little boy. And people treated me like a little boy. So I got earrings. They didn't treat me like a little boy anymore. But people never looked at me like I was an attractive person. And I never felt attractive. Then at some point, people started telling me that I was pretty, that I was attractive, that I even looked like Vanessa

Williams. And I started to feel pretty and think of myself as pretty. And that has become part of who I am.

This reaction they have to the way I look, that's what I'm talking about with this idea of race. That if people see me as black, they tell me I'm black, they experience me and deal with me and talk to me as if I'm black, then in some ways, I am.

I'm just as Danish as I am black. And I was raised more Danish than I was black, for sure. But beyond telling people that, I can't do much else, except wear this sign on the front of me that says, "Excuse me, I'm a white Dane." There isn't too much practical to do. But it's sort of funny. I told my fiancé that I was going to do this a few weeks ago, and he laughed at me. And I said, "No, I'm really serious, I'm going to be white for a while."

And he said, "Well, Heidi, that's going to cause some troubles for you, because then you'll be in an interracial relationship."

I said, "Oh, shit." I said, "It doesn't matter, we're not having kids. I don't want to have kids."

Mark Durrow

Age: 20

Residence: McMinnville, Oregon

Occupation: College student

Mark is Heidi Durrow's younger brother (see page 351). A drama major at Linfield College in McMinnville, Oregon, Durrow plans to transfer out of the school, even though he has only one year left. The drama department has been a disappointment, he says, especially when his professor tells Durrow he won't cast him in a part because he is black.

Although Durrow has undertaken a self-directed course of study to learn more about black culture, he adamantly refuses to identify racially. He will identify culturally however, as in, "I'm Mark Durrow. My culture is European–African-American."

At the college, which has a total enrollment of fifteen hundred, there

are eight black students. In that count, Durrow includes himself and his
best friend, also a European–African-American.

Most of my growing-up time was spent as an air force brat,
and I wasn't really focusing on race because I didn't know that I
was a color, one way or another, and I never consciously thought,
Oh, this is an Asian person; oh, this is a white person. It may sound
crazy, but I never noticed that my mother and father were different
colors. Maybe I thought I was white, maybe I thought I was beige.

Then I came to Portland, and I might have still thought I was
just like everybody else—and up to that point pretty much everybody else was white. But then I saw black people, a lot of black
people, and I went, "Whoa, there are a lot of black people. Cool."
That was the only thought that went to my mind, and then I just
went on. I never realized I was gonna be clumped with these
people; I never thought I was gonna be clumped with anybody
because I was just a kid. I didn't understand that since you look
this way, you belong with these people over here. I'd never seen
these people before, I'd never talked to them. My childhood was
basically racism-free.

Then, during high school I was with a touring acting ensem-
ble, and at some of the locations we traveled to we got hate stuff
written on the walls, like "Niggers go home," and all this really
intelligent stuff. I thought, "Okay, that scared me." Then I come
to Linfield my freshman year, I'm going through complete culture
shock. There are all these people who grew up in the country as
quote-unquote rednecks, who've never talked to a black person in
their life. They keep coming up and asking me stupid questions
like: "Do you tan? Do you like watermelon? Are all your lips big?
Do you like black women or white women better? Is there a difference?" There's no real way to answer these things except for
frankly and just say no, no, no, no, no. It's sad.

I knew when I came here I was gonna face a ton of racist stuff,
and I actually went through withdrawal symptoms from African-
American culture, so I just started going around asking professors,
going to libraries, anywhere, to try and get as many books by black
authors that I could, and I just sat down and started reading *Man-*
child in the Promised Land, Soul on Ice, anything I could get my hands
on. Then I started putting quotes up on my dorm-room door. One

day I put up a quote by Elijah Muhammad, and I prefaced it with
an entire page of explaining who Elijah Muhammad is, what the
situation was, and what the meaning is behind it. I wrote all that to
make sure if anybody looked on my door and saw this, they'd see
this huge preface in the beginning to explain this statement, which
was like eight lines long. I'd always put things up on my door;
every day I'd put up a poem, I'd put up a quote from a book,
something that touched me that day in my readings. Later on that
day, I had swastikas on my door and people drawing burning
flags and "KKK," and it enraged me. I mean, someone was threat-
ening me.

I can't even remember what this quote was, but I decided to
put up the preface to it because earlier that day I was told that
people were starting to call me "The Militant" because they knew
what books I was reading. I'd sit in the lounge and read books like
The Autobiography of Malcolm X. People who didn't even know me
started calling me the Militant Negro on Campus. I'm all, "Why
am I militant?"

"Well, you're reading these books."

I'm like, "Yeah? I'm just reading them; that doesn't mean I'm
militant." So I decided to preface the quote with an explanation of
what the book was saying, because obviously people were making
judgments about these books without even looking at them. It
wasn't that there was something inflammatory in the comment.
Being able to look at it from a white perspective, a Euro-American
perspective, I can say that it was nothing inflammatory, but I prefaced it with an explanation of what was being said because people
were obviously starting to read things into the stuff on my door and
the books I had that wasn't there. I was trying to avoid that type of
situation, and after all the Nazi stuff went up on my door, I went
to the president of the college. After a little while he dealt with it,
although nobody was caught, nobody fessed up to it.

We still have people walking around campus who have Confederate flags hung outside their door every time prospective students come by, to try to scare away black students. For whatever
purpose, there are a ton of Confederate flags around this campus—
it's wonderful. And we have an intramural football team called the
Klan, K-L-A-N, and you just sit here and wonder about it.

So why did I come to this school? Truthfully, I couldn't afford

New York University. So I saw this school and I liked the campus and the atmosphere here, and I knew there'd be racial stuff, but I wasn't gonna let that scare me away. I think that also prompted me to go here, because there might have been more hurdles for me to overcome. I figure if I run into racism, I'll deal with it one way or another. I don't think I'm going to come to any real bodily injury or anybody else will, so if I come here maybe I'll learn something about the people who are afraid of me and who I guess I'm afraid of, and maybe learn a little more about me. I think I've influenced at least one person since I've been here in the way that she views African-Americans, so if that's the limit of people I've touched, then I think I've done a good job. There's a reason for me to be here. I'm not sure what it is, but if I can change the way one person looks at African-Americans, then I did a good job. Because I can make that crossover, it's kind of my responsibility to see if I can do that. Maybe I have this messiah complex—I guess I'm sacrificing myself for the people.

I've talked to black people who hate white people, and I'm able to talk to them and they'll open up to me, but I can turn around and talk to white people who don't normally associate with African-Americans, and they'll talk to me even though they won't talk to African-Americans.

On a really simplistic base like that, I think there's some channels that are open to me that may not be open to someone who thinks they're a little more pure in blood, maybe only because I don't think I've clicked onto any one culture completely, one hundred percent. Until I was nine I was European-American, and then after that I tried to assimilate the African-American culture, and now I have this weird mix where it's one or the other depending on the situation.

The mix is really comfortable because it allows me to fit into the situation based on what's appropriate at the time. It works for me because it's not like I'm putting a mask on; I'm not changing who I am. I'm just revealing a different side of myself, opening up another aspect of the way I feel to a situation, and I'll just change the way I talk. Everybody can talk in different ways: When they're at home they're a little looser, when they're at work they're a little more formal, when they're out with their buddies they talk differently still, and so all I do is just change the inflections in my voice and the pronunciation of certain words to fit in with the situation that's at hand. It's not like there are two personality differences going head-to-head. I really don't think that the cultures go head-to-head at all; I think they fit very well together.

Culturally, it's probably a great thing for people to be mixed, because it gives them more insight. If you're talking *racially*—and I don't think we should judge people on that basis—if I say, "It's better for people to be mixed," that's got as much validity as when people say, "It's better for people to be pure-blood," I feel very neutral about the idea of people being mixed *racially*, except for politically and socially, 'cause the more people that are mixed, the harder it is for other people to be racist. The more families that have interracial blood in them, the harder it is for those families to be nucleuses of racism. If every white family can have at least one black branch, and every black family can have at least one white branch, then it's a little harder for them to just arbitrarily hate. "Cousin Hubert, he's a Negro isn't he, and oh, he's kinda cool, I can't hate him." And maybe they'll think about it in the future. In that sense, heck, everybody should be mixed then, if it's gonna stop the hatred. Wonderful! More power to it! Other than that, I don't really think it makes a difference.

My mother asked me once what race I was. I was about seventeen, and at that point I said, "I'm African-American."

And she's all, "What about the European side of your culture?"

And I said, "When people out there react to me, they react to an African-American; that's all they see. Actually, what they see is black. They don't see culture, they just see color."

So at that point I said, "I am black and let's leave it at that because that's how most people out there wanna respond." And then I realized it was insane to let other people run my life, so I said, "Okay, I'm European–African-American." It's not a thing about skin color, it's not a thing about eye color, it's a thing about culture. European culture, because that's where I was born, that's the way I was raised; African-American because that's my adoptive culture and that's the culture I'm trying to assimilate right now.

I came from such a Eurocentric background, it's hard for me to tell how well I've assimilated African-American culture. My best friend here is also Euro–African-American, but culturally he's just

African-American, and I'm able to get along with him and culturally share things with him, but it's hard for me to say how well I'm doing because I'm still learning it.

I don't think I can say I'm done with that assimilation process yet, because for me to arrive at that point I'd have to be able to get married, have children, and then try to raise them up with an understanding of both cultures. When I've successfully done that, when I've been able to pass on to another generation an understanding of some of the things I've tried to learn, then I would have done a good job. Till then, I'm still working on it. I'm still a novice at this whole thing.

Danette Fuller

Age: 24

Residence: Portland, Oregon

Occupation: Receptionist

Danette Fuller grew up shuttling between Portland, Oregon, and a rural town in southern California. Her mother is white and her father, now deceased, was black. She is raising her two-and-a-half-year-old son, Devaldo, on her own, although his father has recently begun to visit Devaldo on a fairly regular basis.

People don't ask me what I am as much as they used to, but these days, when anyone does, I say "American." That's my new one. But I still go with "mulatto" or "black and white." I just don't choose. There's no reason for it.

Even when I fill out employment applications, I still do "Other," or I choose not to respond or I put "American" and see how they like that. Especially when those census things came around, I think I picked all of them, or something funny, just to be obnoxious.

It's an irritating question for me. I'd rather they demolish it altogether. Why not? Why is it absolutely necessary for anybody to know what anybody is? Of course, it's interesting in conversation, and it's nice if you're learning about your own heritages.

Eventually I plan to do that when my son gets older. I think we're going to try to trace roots. I actually invited my grandpa over this past weekend for dinner. He's never been over here. I've lived here two years now, and he's never been. My father and he were never close; I don't know exactly why, but I just decided it was time for me to get to know my grandpa. It just came across me, I said, "Hey! This is an idea."

He came over last weekend, and I was really amazed. When my father would have him over, he'd always come about fifteen minutes early, and he'd eat and he'd stay maybe forty-five minutes and then he'd leave. He was here for four hours, I couldn't believe it.

There was golf on the TV. I was thankful for that because I didn't really know what I was going to say to my grandpa: It's like, "Um . . . where are you from?" I know that he was a chef on Union Pacific for a long time. He retired from there. And he played golf. So he's a real golfer, he loves golf, and he's like, ninety-something or another. He lives to play golf. I keep telling him when he's feeling better, he's going to have to teach me how to play golf. He's been a little tired lately. He says he had to cut down to eighteen holes, but someone told me it was like a real long time to play eighteen holes. I just said, "Gee, what did he do? Spend the whole day out there?" I think he's repairing TVs and VCRs just because he gets bored, and I've heard rumors that he's going out with forty-year-old women.

He lives over in north Portland. I don't go over there very often. I used to go quite a bit to let my son visit with my dad, but now that he's gone I don't have any ties over there other than my grandpa. I have everything that I need shoppingwise over here, and there's nothing over there that I like to go and visit or anything. No parks that I feel safe at or anything.

I have problems with Devaldo's father, Troy, because he was raised in a black family and just has different ways. He'll say things sometimes, like, "That's too white." Excuse me?

We get into little tiffs about how Devaldo's being raised, and I don't want him raised with any prejudices whatsoever. I just tell Troy, "Well, that's the way you were raised. I don't want to raise Devaldo that way. Whether you choose to change it or not, that's your business, but just don't teach our son that hatred."

On Saint Patty's Day I made a big deal about doing green things and having Irish stew and everything, and on Martin Luther King Day we rented a video from the library. We rented a video on the Martin Luther King marches, and I just got so upset because those people were being treated like dogs just because of their color, and it was ridiculous. I just get real uptight about that. Why are people so ignorant about color? It's just a color. It's just skin, you know? People of different colors should be more aware of how other people are raised, of their culture, just not to insult them or to make fun of them. It's insulting if people think, just by seeing a black person in a white neighborhood, "Oh, are they going to steal something?"

There was this great program on, I don't know who it was— Ted Koppel or somebody, Dan Rather. I taped it because I thought it was great. It was a bunch of kids talking to this guy about prejudice, and it was just really good for the kids. They made the blue-eyed kids wear these collars and treated them similar to what Blacks were treated like in the sixties and early fifties and everything, and those kids learned what it was like. And it was really bad for them to see a hard way, but it was good for them to learn that people have feelings, and you can't help your physical appearance and people are people and it doesn't really matter.

Devaldo and I, we haven't really done race things yet. I just teach him when we look at shows. I don't even think he knows the difference. He visits with his dad's family every now and then. They're real dysfunctional; alcoholism runs through his family. After I was pregnant, I started asking all these questions and found out that three generations of Troy's family are alcoholics and drug addicts, and two generations of my family are alcoholics and drug addicts. And I am so terrified. I said, "God, it would just break my heart," but what I've been doing, I've already even gotten drug information and little storybooks from Partnership for a Drug-Free America.

I've gotten that pamphlet and started reading it to Devaldo

like a regular story, and I've gotten him "Say No" little coloring books. I try to get family-oriented movies, nothing rated R, but I mean, I can't be completely keeping him away from that because I feel like he needs to know what's there, so when I watch things like that I explain to him. I say, "This is what's going on, and that shouldn't be happening, but it is, and people do that all the time, and that's just the way it is and we're working to try to fix it." When we watched that Martin Luther King thing he was like, "They're bad, Mommy, bad."

I said, "I know."

I said, "A long time ago they used to think that people weren't right just because they had brown skin, and [that's] not right and they were really bad to do that." And I try to teach him that it doesn't make any difference. I said, "Just like you have curly hair and Mommy has straight hair *and* curly hair sometimes and Daddy's got different hair, we're all different, but that's what's so special about us, and that's what's nice." I try to teach him things like that.

I thought my parents should have talked to me about it or tried to figure it out, but I don't think they knew themselves, so they just didn't try at all. They didn't know what I would be going up against because they never had to deal with it themselves—of course, my father had to deal with it because he was black.

I think I probably will, for a long time, continue to have a lot of prejudices against me because I am mixed. I don't know why people have a problem with it, but I do get a lot of dirty looks. There's a strong sense that if you're a full race then you're better. I think that's with every nationality. And because I'm half of one and half of another, it's always that, "You're not full-blooded. You're this, that, and the other, so you're not as good as we are." So that's one of the downfalls of it.

I'm going to tell my son every race that he is. He's American, which I'll probably have to argue with his dad about, but in my point of view, he's going to be, because how can you tell somebody that [they're black] when their grandma obviously is white and Irish. If she didn't dye her hair, she'd have stark red hair.

I'm actually the only mixed child in my parents' generation of kids, but I have cousins that have mixed kids; even my sister has a mixed child. So I don't know what they're going to do with their kids, but I know what I'm going to do with mine. I'm gonna just try to inform him that he's this, that, and the other, and he has every right to go wherever he wants to go and do whatever he wants do. Whenever he follows the rules, he's fine.

If he says he wants to be black, I'll tell him: "Look, you have black in you, is that good enough? You can explore every aspect of your heritage if you choose to. If you don't then that's your decision." It's not mine to make for him; it's his life. I may hyperventilate and bite my nails off—just as long as he does everything legal and right, we'll be okay.

I had nightmares when I was pregnant that he was going to have real red hair like my mom really has naturally or he was going to be bald. The whole time I was in labor I was like, "Can you see the head yet? Does it have hair?" It was really funny.

And I kept dreaming that I was having a boy. I wanted a girl, and I ended up having a boy, but I was happy. I was like, Cool. It's good I got a boy. He's healthy, he's got ten fingers, ten toes. And he's precious.

I don't have anything other to tell him than that we're mixed with this, that, and the other, and you have every right as an American to be an American. That's what America is for: the big melting pot, supposedly. Somewhere along the line some people got lost, but I think that was the original idea.

Carol Calhoun
(See also page 186)

Carol Calhoun and her husband have two children: a daughter, Leslie, twenty, and a son, Brian, twenty-two.

I am the bastard child of a white woman and a black man who, as I understand it, was married, had a family, and was a respected person in the community. Now I never met him; I knew absolutely nothing about him except what I have just told you. I have been told that when I decided to go to Los Angeles to college for a year that my mother—and I refer to my mother and father who adopted me as my parents, and I refer to my other mother and father as my biological parents simply because I have no real ties with them—but anyway, I understand that there were some biological siblings living in Los Angeles. Apparently through the years they had made some waves to try to *reclaim* me, I guess is the word—as if I was a piece of chattel of something—but anyway, none of that ever came to pass, and so I know nothing about them.

My biological mother met my parents when she was pregnant with me. She was, as I understand it, poorly educated, from the country, and had moved to the city, the city being Omaha, Nebraska, and she roomed with my mother's uncle there as a boarder. That's how they came to know about me and even encouraged her at the time of her pregnancy to consider adoption, and she didn't want to do it. She felt that somehow or other she would work things out, certainly no different from the way women feel now.

At any rate, I don't remember a lot. She was a kind person, she worked hard, in my child's mind's eye, and that's all I could relate to even at this stage in my life. She was an older woman—she may not have been, she may have just had a hard life, who's to say? At any rate, I remember moving a lot, and we'd always end up going back to this Uncle Joe's.

My birthday is in December. About the time I turned eight, my biological mother started talking to me about the fact that I was gonna go live with this other family. I never questioned anything; I mean, she said that they were gonna take me and everything was gonna be all right and hopefully we would be able to be together again, and I went off fat, dumb, and happy about a month later. It was really one of those intrigue type things: She took me in a taxi and we met on a corner and I got out of that car and into this other car, and that's the last time I ever saw her.

The next day they took me home on the train to Chicago, and I've never seen or heard from her again. Now my mother tells me that [my biological mother] asked her to have some pictures made, and I do remember the pictures that were made when I was nine years old. By this time I had long hair; she had always had my hair cut in a shorter Buster Brown haircut.

I could remember children saying they couldn't play with me because I was colored. It was one of those things that one day they were my friends and the next day I was colored and they couldn't play with me. I certainly didn't understand, and I think that my going back and telling that to my biological mother may have been one of the things that might have triggered her decision.

Both of my adopted parents are black. Now my adopted mother is every bit as fair as the pure driven snow. However, she has very Negroid features, and she doesn't have straight hair. But her grandmother was pure-blood Mexican, and she's got a whole lot of mixture there in her background, too. My father has brown skin, and the only thing that I can relate to in terms of another ethnic group is the Native American Indian, and Cherokee in particular, in his family. He's deceased now, but he had sisters and one brother still alive, and I've never heard any of them talk about any white people in their background but have heard them talk about the Indians, so, at any rate, there I was at age eight, off to another life.

In Chicago I lived in a completely black neighborhood and of course became immersed in this new black family. My mother had a sister who had a couple children, and my father had a number of sisters and one brother, all of whom had children, so now I had a family. I don't remember a family in Omaha.

I ran into so much prejudice. Chicago's South Side is black, and here I am with long hair. Oh, it was awful. I tell you who was one of my classmates—and he suffered every bit as much as I did—was Donald Stewart who was the last president before Johnetta Cole of Spelman [College]. Oh, it was unmerciful. I got beat up continually, and I tried to learn to fight but it was a losing battle. I was just not a fighter in the sense of physical fighting. My parents didn't know what to do to help me, so they took me out of the local public school and put me in the University of Chicago lab school. 'Course there were practically no Blacks there at that time, but I stayed in the same Girl Scout troop I had been in, and that was all black, so here I was still involved with these same girls who hated my guts just because I was the complexion I am.

I do remember one white girl at the University of Chicago saw me talking to a girl who happened to have been a cousin and [the white girl] said to me, "What are you talking to that black girl for?" or "colored" or whatever she called her. And I said, "Well, she's my cousin," and boy, I tell you, her nose turned up. She said, "Your cousin? Are you that, too?"

I said, "Well, yes." She never spoke to me again.

I try not to let it worry me, and I've tried to help my daughter benefit from some of these experiences I had, but you know we all have different experiences and hers was quite different from mine and the environment and the people we were surrounded by when she was growing up, so her whole situation was different from mine.

When we were in Rome, New York, she didn't have a tough time. Brian was the one who began to have a tough time as he got older and got interested in girls. You know, those Italian boys didn't want this black boy looking at their women—the macho thing—but Leslie was fine. Then, when we moved to Atlanta, when she was twelve and he was fourteen, Brian moved here. It was heaven for him. I remember he told his dad one day, "Pa, I've died and gone to heaven."

In the meantime, Leslie just remained all white. In my talking to her and trying to coach her and get her to understand some things and to accept some things, one day she said to me, "Look," she said, "I'm going to be affiliated with the people I'm comfortable with, and I'm comfortable with white kids." She said, "The black kids make me feel like crap." Well, I could relate to that, too. And then the other thing about it is the way you're raised and the way you interact and react. She said she's comfortable being white so of course her mannerisms and the way she carries herself are more the way a white girl does as opposed to the way a black girl does, you know what I mean? It has a lot to do with that, too.

My son Brian is brown-skinned. In fact, Brian looks Mexican, Hispanic almost. He has a very rich pretty brown skin, and has a full head of beautiful black hair that's curly, and Leslie has gorgeous long curly hair. Now, see, Leslie would look very fair if she were just sitting here with us, but when you see her in a picture with her buddies who are all white, she looks dark.

Leslie has this friend up at school [University of Tennessee at Knoxville], and they were friends, but they were kind of attracted to each other. His name is Michael. And when my husband John and I were up there in the spring, I had said to her, "Well, are we gonna get to meet Michael?"

"Oh yes, you're gonna get to meet Michael, and we're gonna take Michael to dinner," and so forth and so on. Well we got there and we went straight to her house before we checked in [to our lodgings], and Leslie said, "You're gonna have to leave. Michael's on his way over here, and I don't want you to meet him."

Well, this was a complete turnabout, and John was not real happy about this, but we left. She didn't give us an explanation. She said, "You are not going to meet Michael. Leave."

So we left, and as we drove out of the alley we saw this black Blazer turn the corner—and I knew he drove a black Blazer—and I said there goes Michael now. On the front of his Blazer was this big flag, the Rebel flag. And I said, "Oh, my God."

She didn't say much about it while we were there that time, and finally I got her to talk about it and I said, "Leslie, what's going on with Michael?"

She said, "Michael is a really nice person, and Michael and I could have a real thing going, but his parents don't like me because I'm black." And that's the first time I've ever heard her say she was black.

And she told me just last night on the phone that Michael has the same birthday as her, which was July eighth, and that Michael would not let his parents take him out to dinner because [he and Leslie] were gonna do something. They are going to do something this weekend; they didn't get to do [anything] on their birthday. They're still really good friends, and she said Michael really wanted her to come out and have dinner. She said, "But I am not going out to Michael's house because I know how his parents feel about me." And so I'm saying all that to kind of work through some things myself, and maybe Leslie is beginning to get some identification.

Like I say, this is interesting with this Michael business 'cause I'm just kind of beginning to get a feel for what's going on there. If his parents didn't feel the way they felt, then she wouldn't have had a problem, but I think she found out his parents felt this way and she wasn't going to give him the opportunity to meet us. Even though Leslie and I and Leslie and her dad have differences of opinion, that really showed me that at least she does have some family feeling and she's not going to do anything that's going to alienate us. And I'll tell you, if she couldn't let her brother meet him—even though she and Brian fight like cats and dogs and have a lot of differences of opinion—if she couldn't take him home to meet her brother, I don't think that would have worked a bit.

My son had some interesting experiences at the University of Georgia in Athens. Some of his white friends invited him to some fraternity parties and [the other fraternity brothers] hung out the Rebel flag and they vacated the room and they said, "Why are these niggers here?" He doesn't fight. I mean, there's no reason to fight. He just told his friends later, he said, "You know, man, your fraternity brothers didn't appreciate your inviting us," and so that meant that his friends, if they wanted to be friends with him, had to be friends with him someplace else, not in their fraternity house.

You can't sit on the fence. It's that old thing of not being accepted either way, within your mind you have to make a decision what you're gonna be, and then you can move forward. When you don't know what you are, whether you're a dog or a cat, or a man or a woman, or black or white, then I think you cause problems for yourself; that's my personal opinion.

I didn't really have a choice, you understand. Now I can't speak for anybody who grew up in a biracial home, but I found, for me, in my black environment, that it was not healthy to sit on the fence. I had to make a choice, right, and when it came time to get married, well, I knew a lot of white kids, but I never dated any white guys.

But I'll tell you what I didn't do: I didn't choose a real dark husband. That wasn't so much what I didn't choose as it was that dark guys wouldn't date me because they didn't want to be seen in an interracial situation. And if some really dark guy wanted to date me, he had an ulterior motive. The only really dark guy I dated and had a really fulfilling relationship with—and I would have married this guy—he was part black and part Filipino, see, so he was already a mixture, and he was a gorgeous black man. We would have had some beautiful babies. But I mean anybody else, there was always an ulterior motive there.

People thought my adoptive parents were my biological parents. I fit in. I looked a little like my father and I had the complexion of my mother. My husband is as brown as my father was, and I'm probably almost as fair as my mother, with keener features and straighter hair. And I certainly thought that by marrying a man the complexion I married, my children would never have to worry about this. And guess what. I got one as light as me and one brown-skinned. I just really did not want to put any child through the hell I had gone through. So many people saying, "You think you're white," or, "You think you're better than we are." That's the main thing I can remember from my school days, and I think that carries through now with a lot of people who seem to have a problem with race. You know: "light, bright, damn near white."

Omatteé Carrasco
(See also page 82)

Omatteé Carrasco wanted to be interviewed for this book in part because she recognizes how quickly things change. She believes that biracial people born before and after her will have experiences different from her own, but that what she has to say about what she's experienced is one link in a much greater chain. "I feel like I'm a part of history," she says.

I was doing research for a class I was taking called Afro-American Sexuality. There just aren't a lot of books or materials on the topic of people like us, and if there are, they all fall primarily into one category: the tragic mulatto syndrome. For my class paper I got into the concept of where the term *mulatto* came from and the thought that these people would be sterile like mules, that type of hybridization. I chose that topic because I wanted to research it and because I wanted to contribute something—a little term paper. It'll go in the collection of all the other ones out in my garage, but I was so pleased to hear that you were doing scholarly research. The topic needs to be addressed.

It's important because I'm raising multiethnic children—their father is Mexican-American—and their experience is already so totally different than mine. I identified black from childhood, and I never feel that I got any benefit from my mother's culture, her white heritage. I felt that I was denied something, denied a part of myself, because I never really quite fit in. My children, on the other hand, they are free; they have more of an opportunity to express themselves as Hispanic, or to express themselves and accept themselves as being black. When I was growing up, it just wasn't like that, particularly the black/white. I was a product of the sixties, and my sister was a product of the fifties, so my parents' relationship was during a really difficult time. There was a lot of racial tension and turmoil. We're beyond that now, and my children don't have to worry about being harassed on the basis of their cultural upbringing, not with the same intensity I did. It still exists, but not with the day-to-day where you can't walk out your door without someone gawking and gaping and asking you what you are. People aren't as shocked; they're coming to accept this new breed of people, or whatever, a lot more. I still get questioned a lot, but not anything like when I was growing up.

I feel more free now to be left alone, to grow and make my choices and decisions, raise my children the way I want to. I like that. I think that for their children, maybe this won't even be an issue. People are already talking about giving us a heritage, giving us a nationality, making us a census box. We don't want to just check "Other," do we? I've checked "Other" many times, but have you ever even imagined that day when we can go and check that box that says we're not any one of anything? I stopped wanting that to happen because, well, what are you going to do? You gonna have a box to check for the black and white, and then a box to check for the Hispanic and black, and then a box to check for the . . . You know what I'm saying? I want to see the day when there are no boxes, that's what I want to see. I would rather see them just eliminate the box, stop trying to shove people into boxes. They don't *even* fit. They don't belong.

I still don't just volunteer to people my ethnic identity—I think whether I was multiethnic or not, I would still prefer to feel that people enjoyed me as the *person* I am, and not *what* I am.

I feel the same about people that want to know, "What's your astrological sign?" I'm like, "Well, how many more boxes do you want to cut me up and shove me off into? I'm just one whole person. I'm me. Can we enjoy each other from that perspective? Let's look at the bigger picture."

I don't want to let cultures die. I used to do Ballet Folklorico when I was a little girl. I learned to speak Spanish in elementary school. My grandmother sent us to bilingual summer school. I want my children to experience that. Especially because they're Hispanic, but that's not the only reason. It's beautiful, the dresses, the music, the dancing—but also because I want to say, "Baby, this is yours, this belongs to you. This is your birthright, this is your heritage." And no, I don't feel that anybody handed me one on a silver platter; didn't hand it over with a sack of shit, either. I have nothing. And I don't even know if I've ever dealt with my children from the aspect of being anything other than Hispanic and black. They know my mother. She comes here. They know she's white. But I want them to have all of their cultures, and I have no white culture to give them.

I wanted to talk to you because I want to make a contribution, any contribution I can make. I'm not scholarly. I don't think I'll ever write that great American novel. I've had that fantasy in my heart and in my mind, but God will have to show me if there's a time for me to do that in my life or not. But this is an issue that I definitely—I got started on it, I wanted to do it, for myself and for every other interracial person out there. I'm glad you're here, and I'm glad you're interracial. I'm so glad you're interracial I don't know what to do. I don't know if I could have sat here and spoken to a black person or a white person. You know you have that advantage, right?

I want my kids to be able to go and pick up a book about themselves. I've tried to educate my children to their culture, not just their own, but all different kinds of culture. They can go to a bookshelf and pull down a book on the solar system or they can read about Egypt but not about themselves.

Afterword

Just as each of the forty-six people in the preceding pages had a unique story to tell, so will each reader come to different conclusions about the lessons of this book. Whatever conclusions we draw, there is tremendous value in trying to unpack the emotional and intellectual baggage of race. After all, what does *race* mean to each of us? What distinguishes *race* from *culture* and *ethnicity*? How much of what we believe belongs to us and how much is what others would have us believe? And how do these beliefs contribute to our personal growth or the growth of our communities?

After listening to so many people talk at such length about race and racial identity, I came to understand that no single factor that influences identity can be examined in isolation from any other. I also became convinced that the pressures in our country to separate black and white—and to make biracial people choose one over the other—are epidemic. And it was remarkable to have confirmed and reconfirmed the power that race wields on a personal level, even while it has no single, universal meaning.

Given the force of social conventions and taboos, I took heart in the courage of the people who spoke to me. They knew their names and pictures would hold them accountable to their words, and still they agreed to offer up some of their most personal and private beliefs. To talk about such a difficult and complicated topic had its bleak moments, where I was overwhelmed by hearing the same struggles and pains repeated again and again. What encouraged me each time were the recurring examples of individuals taking on the challenges of race and identity with determination and humor.

Did I find the "tragic mulatto"? I did find some people who seem vanquished by this racial legacy, but also some who have little relationship to it, many who have made peace with it, and some who celebrate it. Most of all, I found myself, a little sliver of me, in each person. But I wonder if I also would have found as much in common had I talked to sixty-five people at random. I think so. In fact, it's very hard at points to separate the commonalities that have to do with similar racial backgrounds from those that are part of the basic human condition.

Race is the focus of this book, and the frequent opposition of *white* and *black* has a peculiar resonance in this country. But conflicts of experience and group identity are profound for other people as well. Biracial people from other racial backgrounds may well identify with many of the stories in the book. Also, people who were born in the United States to immigrant parents constantly face similar clashes of belief and culture. And children of couples that have merged religions, class backgrounds, and even geographical origins within the United States contend with having to resolve differences.

I had a professor some years ago—a black woman—who said matter-of-factly that to be born black in this country is to be born with a hundred-pound weight on your back. "The question is," she said, "how will you carry it?" To be biracial, it seems to me, is to be born with a weight that is anywhere from fifty to a hundred and fifty pounds. The question remains: How will each person carry it?

Racism is a burden for all Americans. It continues to stigmatize, oppress, and isolate. To transcend it requires that we recognize true cultural and individual strengths, values, and experiences. The path is a difficult one; it demands the courage to speak unpopular truths and wrestle with unpopular feelings. But if we are, as Jeana Woolley said, "willing to walk through the fire to get home," then we will all get home.

Acknowledgments

I have been the fortunate recipient of many kindnesses and much luck in the making of this book. First, thanks to family and friends who helped me find interviewees across the country. I thank them also—especially my sisters, Diane and Margaret—for their encouragement.

Thanks to Amy Cohn, for suggesting I turn a smaller project into this book, and for leading me to Will Schwalbe and Bill Adler, who made the excellent decision to support that idea. Thanks also to Will for his excitement about the project and his tremendous help along the way. And also to Michael Goodman for his sensitive copyediting.

Thanks to Robert Friedman, Mindy Thompson Fullilove, Iris Marcus, and Alice Siempelkamp, for reading excerpts of the book at early stages and providing essential direction.

For providing essential direction at even earlier stages, thanks to William T. Lankford III and Joan Kron.

Stacy Morrison, with significant help from Alix Browne, transcribed boxes and boxes of interview tapes with skill and enthusiasm. They were truly my first readers, and helped me recognize what a treasure I was amassing.

I could not have developed such a wonderful network of book

participants or passed through the months of travel and research so smoothly without a mother lode of help. Assistance came in many forms: jotted-down telephone numbers on scraps of paper, dogged efforts to track down subjects, warm meals, lodging, good cheer. I appreciate every kindness, and especially want to thank a few: John Brown, Keith Brown, Lois B. Bye, Edward Cooper, Joe Cunningham, Kevin Fagan, Juliette Fairley, the Atlanta Funderburgs, Richard Gehr, Joyce George, Nila Grutman, Elizabeth Kadetsky, Steve Koch, Jim Hough, the Huebner-Venezias, the MacKay-Angeleses, Brett Mahoney, the Marcuses, Nancy and the late Robert Maynard for their generous loan of office space at the *Oakland Tribune*, Robin Miller, the Oshanas, and the Weisbords.

I had the pleasure of interviewing many more people than I could ever fit into one book. But each conversation added to my conviction that this was a book to be written, and each helped define and refine the book's structure. For that assistance, I thank: Vanessa Algotsson, Beth Blumklotz, Melissa Bray, Helen Broady, Jennifer Brody, Muriel Harvey, Ed Holten, Juanita Martinez, Gabriel Owen, Jonathan Ramey, Mary Sigmann, Christian Vigneaux, and Randall Wright.

No one has offered more support, assistance, patience and food preparation than my husband, Jamie Newman. I am eternally grateful for each.

The interviews in this book are testimonials to the human spirit. I was awed by the people who allowed me to enter their lives and I thank them all.

Index